# 2011

# The up-to-date guide to organisations

@nd online

**Key Organisations: also online**
The whole directory in searchable form with live links to thousands of websites plus our helpful, new searchable database. Simple to use.
See www.carelpress.com /KO

# Introduction

Welcome to Key Organisations – the essential, annually updated, contact list.

## Always updated

More than 3,000 addresses have been carefully checked and more than 1,000 important changes have been made.

More organisations have been added. In particular, we've included many new websites and 'dead' sites have been removed. Where we know that an organisation is likely to change in the near future that too has been noted.

## Organised with you in mind

We list organisations by the key word in their name eg Adoption and Fostering (British Association for), but we make an exception when reorganising the name would make the details less easy to find or would make a well-known name unfamiliar.

When an organisation changes its name, we include a cross-reference from the previous name. When the name of an organisation does not describe what it does, we include a brief description.

## The Thematic Guide

When you are interested in a particular area or subject, but do not know any specific names, you can look under the appropriate theme. So the Children's Orchestra appears under both Music and Children/Young People. The themes are listed opposite.

## New and improved

With Key Organisations you also get free online access (single user) to the pdf pages with live website links. And you can access our fantastically helpful, new searchable database. Enter a key word here and generate a list of useful, current, relevant organisations - live and ready to go. **See www.carelpress.com /KO**

You can make this available to everyone with an inexpensive site licence – unlimited access including home use for just £9.95 + vat.

Key Organisations is also available as part of our Complete Issues Package with Essential Articles and Fact File – giving you statistics, articles about issues and relevant addresses all together - including site licences!

Find out more here:
**www.carelpress.co.uk/EAandFFoffer**

Publication information
© 2011 Carel Press Ltd, 4 Hewson Street, Carlisle, CA2 5AU, UK
Tel 01228 538928  Fax: 591816
info@carelpress.com
www.carelpress.com
Editorial team: Anne Louise Kershaw, Debbie Maxwell, Christine A Shepherd, Chas White
Database: Sadie Baker, Debbie Maxwell
Subscription manager: Ann Batey

Cover design: Anne Louise Kershaw
Logos: Craig Mitchell
Printed by: Finemark, Poland
British Library Cataloguing in Publication Data
Is available for this publication
ISBN-13: 9781905600250

# Themes

# Thematic Guide to Organisations

**NB This is a broad thematic guide – inevitably a number of the categories overlap.**

**Within each theme the organisations are listed alphabetically by key word as in the main listing.**

## Activity Holidays & placements

Activity Holiday Association (British)

Africa and Asia Venture

Archaeology Abroad

ATD Fourth World

Backpackers Club

Brathay Exploration Group

BSES Expeditions

BTCV

Calvert Trust

Camp Mohawk

Commonwealth Youth Exchange Council

Country Holidays for Inner City Children

Environment & Nature Conservation (Young People's Trust for the)

Exchange of Commonwealth Teachers (League for the)

Farms for City Children

Forest School Camps

IVS

Jubilee Sailing Trust

Lattitude Global Volunteering

National Trust Working Holidays

Outward Bound Trust

Pax Christi

Project Trust

Quaker Voluntary Action

Raleigh International

Scientific Exploration Society

Volunteer Action for Peace

Waterway Recovery Group

Wind Sand & Stars

World Challenge Expeditions

WWOOF Association (International)

## Addiction

Addaction

Addiction (Action on)

ADFAM

Al-Anon Alateen

Alcohol Concern

Alcoholics Anonymous

Blenheim CDP

Children of Alcoholics (National Association for)

Cocaine Anonymous

Drink Helpline (National)

Families Anonymous

Frank

Freshfield Service

Gamblers Anonymous & Gam-Anon

GAMCARE

Help – For a life without tobacco

London Drug & Alcohol Network

Narcotics Anonymous UK

Tranquillisers, Antidepressants and Painkillers (Council for Information on)

## Adoption/Fostering

Adopted Children's Register

Adoption and Fostering (British Association for)

Adoption and Fostering Information Line

Adoption UK

Childlink Adoption Society

EveryChild

Fostering Network

Intercountry Adoption Helpline

NORCAP - Supporting Adults Affected by Adoption

Norwood

OASIS

Post-Adoption Centre

Register Office for Northern Ireland (General)

Register Office for Scotland (General)

TACT

Talk Adoption

## Alcohol

Addaction

Addiction (Action on)

ADFAM

Al-Anon Alateen

Alcohol & Health Research Unit

Alcohol Concern

Alcohol Education and Research Council

Alcohol Focus Scotland

Alcohol Studies (Institute of)

Alcoholics Anonymous

BNTL-Freeway

CADD

CAMRA

Children of Alcoholics (National Association for)

Drink Helpline (National)

drinkaware.co.uk

London Drug & Alcohol Network

Portman Group

Roofie Foundation

Science in the Public Interest (Center for)

Tacade

Turning Point

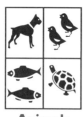

# Animals

African Conservation Experience
Animal Aid
Animal Aid Youth
Animal Defenders
Animal Health (National Office of)
Animal Health Trust
Animal Rescue (International)
Animal Rescuers (UK)
Animal Welfare Trust (National)
Anti-Snaring Campaign (National)
Anti-Vivisection Society (National)
Ape Alliance
ARKive
Avicultural Society
Bat Conservation Trust
Battersea Dogs Home
Bird Council (British)
Blue Cross
Born Free Foundation
Brooke Hospital for Animals
Budgerigar Society
Butterfly Conservation
Canine Partners
Captive Animals' Protection Society
Care for the Wild International
Cat Fancy (Governing Council of the)
Cats Protection
Cinnamon Trust
City Farms & Community Gardens
  (Federation of)
Companion Animal Studies (Society for)
Compassion in World Farming Trust
Cruel Sports Ltd (League Against)

Crufts Dog Show
David Sheldrick Wildlife Trust
Deer Society (British)
Divers Marine Life Rescue (British)
Dogs for the Disabled
Dogs Trust
Donkey Breed Society
Donkey Sanctuary
Dragonfly Society (British)
Entomologists' Society (Amateur)
Environmental Investigation Agency
Eurogroup for Animals
Farm Animal Welfare Council
Farms for City Children
Fauna & Flora International
Feline Advisory Bureau
Fishing Hurts
FRAME
Froglife
Fund for Animal Welfare (International)
Gambia Horse and Donkey Trust
Gorilla Organisation
Guide Dogs for the Blind Association
Hamster Council (National)
HAPPA
Hawk & Owl Trust
Hearing Dogs for Deaf People
Hedgehog Preservation Society (British)
Horse Society (British)
Humane Slaughter Association
Hunt Saboteurs Association
Kennel Club
London Zoo
Lord Dowding Fund for Humane Research
Lost Doggies UK
Marine Conservation Society
Marine Life Study Society (British)
Naturewatch
Ocean Mammal Institute
Onekind
Orangutan Foundation

Ornithology (British Trust for)

PDSA

People's Trust for Endangered Species

Pet Advisory Committee

Pet Behaviour Counsellors (Association of)

Pet Care Trust

Pet Health Council

Pet Month (National)

PETA EUROPE Ltd

PetLog Database (National)

Pets as Therapy

Pony Club

Prevention of Cruelty to Animals (Scottish Society for the)

Primate Protection League (International)

Rabbit Council (British)

Rare Breeds Survival Trust

Red List of Endangered Species

Redwings Horse Sanctuary

Respect for Animals

Royal College of Veterinary Surgeons

RSPB

RSPCA

Shark Alliance

Small Animal Veterinary Association (British)

Support Dogs

Uncaged Campaigns

Understanding Animal Research

Viva!

Vivisection (British Union for the Abolition of)

Whale & Dolphin Conservation Society

Wildlife Aid

Wildlife Trusts (Royal Society of)

Wood Green Animal Shelters

World Horse Welfare

WSPA

WWF-UK

# Architecture

Archéire

Architects (Royal Institute of British)

Architectural Heritage Fund

Architecture and the Built Environment (Commission for)

Architecture Foundation

CABE

Friends of Friendless Churches

Georgian Group

Great buildings

Landscape Institute

Open-City

Royal Scottish Academy

SALVO

Twentieth Century Society

Victorian Society

# Arts

Access Art

Access to London Theatres

Action Transport

Age Exchange

Apples & Snakes

Arc Theatre for Change

Architects (Royal Institute of British)

Architecture Foundation

Art and Design (National Society for Education in)

Art Fund
Art Library (National)
Art Therapists (British Association of)
Artists Against Racism
Arts (National Campaign for the)
Arts and Business
Arts Council (N. Ireland)
Arts Council (Scottish)
Arts Council England
Arts Council of Wales
Arts Disability Wales
Arts Education Network
Arts in Therapy & Education (Institute for)
Arts Marketing Association
Artsline
Artswork
ArtWatch UK
Ashmolean Museum
Authors' Licensing and Collecting Society
Ballet Organization (British)
BBC Studio Audiences
Benesh Institute of Choreology
Birmingham Royal Ballet
Bolshoi Ballet
Book Trust (Scottish)
Books Council (Welsh)
BOOKTRUST
BRIT School for Performing Arts and
    Technology
British Film Institute
British Library Sound Archive
Brontë Society
Cambridge Past, Present & Future
Cello Society
Channel Arts Association
Children's Literature (National Centre for
    Research in)
Chinese Arts Centre
Cinema & Popular Culture (The Bill Douglas
    Centre for the History of)
Circus Sensible/Circus School

Circus Space
Classical Association
Contemporary Art Society
Crafts Council
Creative Partnerships
Dance UK
Danceconsortium
Design and Artists Copyright Society
Design and Technology Association
Drama (National)
Drama Association of Wales
Drama Schools (The Conference of)
Drama Training (National Council for)
Dramatic Need
Drawing (The Campaign for)
Edinburgh International Book Festival
Edinburgh International Festival Society
Edward Lear Foundation
Engage
English National Ballet
English National Opera
English PEN
English Touring Theatre
European Youth Music Week
Festivals (British & International Federation of )
France: culture and communications website
Frankfurt Book Fair
Georgian Group
Headlong Theatre
Hull Truck Theatre
ICON
Imaginate
Italian Cultural Institute
IXIA
Live Theatre Company
London Charity Orchestra
London Schools Arts Service
London theatres: online
Lowry
Mousetrap Theatre Projects

Movie Review Query Engine

Museums (International Council of)

Music Council (National)

National Opera Studio

National Theatre

National Youth Ballet

NODA

Northern Ballet

Northern Broadsides

Northern Stage

Open College of the Arts

Open-City

Out of Joint

Performing Arts Medicine (British Association for)

Performing Rights Society

Poetry Library

Poetry Society

Polka Theatre

Project Gutenberg

Public Monuments & Sculpture Association

RADA

Rambert Dance Company

Redundant Technology Initiative

Roundhouse

Royal Academy of Arts

Royal Academy of Dance

Royal Ballet

Royal Opera

Royal Scottish Academy

RSA

RSC

Saving Faces

Science, Technology & the Arts (National Endowment for)

Scottish Ballet

Scottish Opera

Scottish Youth Theatre

SCRAN

Shakespeare Association (British)

Shakespeare at the Tobacco Factory

Shakespeare Birthplace Trust

Shakespeare Schools Festival

Shakespeare's Globe Theatre

Shared Experience Theatre

Skylight Circus Arts

Sound Sense

SPIT

Storytelling (Society for)

Student Drama Festival (National)

Studies in British Art (Paul Mellon Centre for)

Teaching of Drama (National Association for)

Theatre Council (Independent)

Théâtre de Complicité

Theatre for Children and Young People (International Association of)

Theatre Network (The Amateur)

Theatrenet

Theatres Trust

Twentieth Century Society

UK Film Council

UK Theatre Web

Unicorn Theatre for Children

Venice in Peril Fund

Visual Arts & Galleries Association

Voluntary Arts Network

Welsh National Opera

Women in Publishing

Writers' Guild of Great Britain

Writers in Education (National Association of)

Youth Arts Wales (National)

Youth Music Theatre (National)

Youth Opera (British)

Youth Orchestra (National of GB)

Youth Theatre of GB (National)

Youth Theatres (National Association of)

## Care/Carers

4Children

Alzheimer Scotland

Anchor Trust

Anxiety Care

Arthritis Care

Attend

Baby Lifeline

Breast Cancer Care

CACHE

Care Council for Wales

Care Quality Commission

Carers (The Princess Royal Trust For)

Carers UK

Chance UK

Childcare Link

Christian Lewis Trust

CLICSargent

Contact a Family

Counsel and Care

CROSSROADS Care

Cruse Bereavement Care

Daycare Trust

Disability Law Service

Disabled Living Foundation

Early Years

Epilepsy (National Society for)

First Steps to Freedom

Help the Hospices

Home-Start

Human Rights Society

Hyperactive Children's Support Group

Learning Through Action Centre

Marie Curie Cancer Care

Medical Foundation for the Care of Victims of Torture

Muslim Welfare House

Palliative Care (National Council for)

Pastoral Care in Education (National Association for)

Pituitary Foundation

Pre-School Learning Alliance

Pre-School Play Association (Scottish)

Pre-School Playgroups Association (Wales)

Prison Advice & Care Trust (PACT)

Sickle Cell Society

Skills for Care

Social Care Association

Solicitors for the Elderly

The White Ribbon Alliance

Treloar Trust

Twins & Multiple Births Association

Voice

Who Cares? Trust

## Censorship

ARTICLE 19, The Global Campaign for Free Expression

Film Classification (British Board of)

Freedom of Information (Campaign for)

Index on Censorship

Information Commissioner's Office

Internet Watch Foundation

Press and Broadcasting Freedom (Campaign for)

Video Standards Council

# Charities (general)

Big Lottery Fund
CF Appointments Ltd.
Charities Aid Foundation
CharitiesDirect.com
Charity Choice
Charity Commission for England & Wales
Children in Need Appeal
Comic Relief
Computers 4 Africa
Disasters Emergency Committee
Do it
G-Nation
Jane Tomlinson Appeal
Justgiving
Medical Research Charities (Association of)
ShareGift

# Children/Young People

1 Voice
100 Black Men of London
4Children
Action for Children
Additives (Action on)
Adopted Children's Register
Adoption and Fostering (British Association for)
Adventure Activities Licensing Authority
Afasic
Africans Unite Against Child Abuse
Al-Anon Alateen

Alone in London
Anti-Bullying Network
Army Cadet Force
Artswork
Aspect
Baby Greenhouse
Baby Milk Action
Babyworld
Barnardo's
BASPCAN
Big Read (The)
Boarding Concern
Boys Brigade
Brainwave
Brandon Centre
Brazil's Children Trust (Action for)
Bully Free Zone
Bullying Online
CACHE
Cafcass
Camp Mohawk
Cardiac Risk in the Young
Careers Research & Advisory Centre
Catch22
Chain of Hope
Chance UK
Channel Arts Association
Chernobyl Children's Life Line
Child Accident Prevention Trust
Child and Adolescent Mental Health
    (Association for)
Child Bereavement Trust
Child Brain Injury Trust
Child Contact Centres (National Association of)
Child Growth Foundation
Child Poverty Action Group
Child Protection in Sport Unit
Childcare Link
Childhood (Alliance for)
Childhood Bereavement Network

ChildHope UK

ChildLine

Childlink Adoption Society

CHILDREN 1ST

Children and War

Children are unbeatable

Children in Need Appeal

Children in Scotland

Children of Alcoholics (National Association for)

Children with Leukaemia

Children's Book Groups (Federation of)

Children's Heart Federation

Children's Rights

Children's Scrapstore

Children's Workforce Development Council

Children's Bureau (National)

Children's Commissioner for England

Children's Hope Foundation

Children's Legal Centre

Children's Literature (National Centre for Research in)

Children's Orchestra (National)

Children's Rights Alliance for England

Children's Service

Children's Society

Christian Lewis Trust

Church Lads' and Church Girls' Brigade

Church of England Education Division

Cirdan Sailing Trust

CLICSargent

Clubs for Young People (National Association of)

Commonwealth Youth Exchange Council

Connexions

Council of Europe Youth

Country Holidays for Inner City Children

CRIN

Cyber Mentors

Dad

Dad Talk

Dad's House

Daneford Trust

Daycare Trust

Deaf Children's Society (National)

Depaul International

Depaul Nightstop UK

Disabled Children (Council for)

Down's Syndrome Educational Trust

Dramatic Need

Duke of Edinburgh's Award

Early Childhood Education (British Association for)

Early Years

Education & Culture (European Commission Directorate General)

Education (Department for)

Ellen MacArthur Trust

Endeavour Training Limited

Environment & Nature Conservation (Young People's Trust for the)

Epilepsy (National Centre for Young People with)

ERIC – Education and Resources for Improving Childhood Continence

European Youth Card Association

European Youth Forum

European Youth Information and Counselling Agency

Every Child a Chance Trust

Every Child Matters

EveryChild

Fair Play for Children Association

Fairbridge

Families Need Fathers

Find a Parent or Child

First Light

Fostering Network

Foundation For Peace

Foyer Federation

Free the Children

Get connected

Gifted Children (National Association for)

Gifted Children's Information Centre

Girlguiding UK

Girls' Brigade

Girls' Venture Corps Air Cadets

Give Us Back Our Game

G-Nation

Grandparents Plus

Handsel Trust

Headliners

Hideout

HIFY-UK

Hope UK

Hyperactive Children's Support Group

Imaginate

Include

Jeans for Genes

Jewish Lads' & Girls' Brigade (JLGB)

Just for Kids

Kids Company

Kids for Kids

Kidscape

Lavender Trust

Leap Confronting Conflict

Learning Outside the Classroom

Lesbian Information Service

Lifetracks

likeitis.org

Live Music Now!

London Children's Ballet

London Youth

Marine Society and Sea Cadets

MATCH

Maternal & Childhealth Advocacy International MCAI

MAYC

Mermaids

Midi Music Company

Missing Children website

Montessori Centre International

Motorvations Project

Mumsnet

Music for Youth

NABSS

National Youth Ballet

NBCS

need2know

Norwood

NSPCC

NSPCC Asian Child Protection

Ocean Youth Trust

Parenting UK

Parents & Abducted Children Together

Pastoral Care in Education (National Association for)

Philip Lawrence Awards Network

Plan International UK

Play England

Play Wales

Playbus Association (National)

PLAYLINK

Pod Charitable Trust

Pre-School Learning Alliance

Pre-School Play Association (Scottish)

Pre-School Playgroups Association (Wales)

Prince's Trust (Head Office)

Pyramid

Quality in Study Support and Extended Services

Railway Children

Raw Material Music and Media

REACT

Restless Development

reunite

Rona Sailing Project

Roundhouse

Runaway Helpline (under 18)

SADS

Save the Children (UK)

School Food Trust

Scottish Youth Theatre

Scout Association

Sea Ranger Association

SEBDA

Seven Stories

Shared Parenting Information Group

Sick Children (Action for)

Siobhan Dowd Trust

Smallpeice Trust

SmartParent

SOS Children

Sparks

Tall Ships Youth Trust

Teenage Cancer Trust

The White Ribbon Alliance

Theatre for Children and Young People
(International Association of)

Thesite

Trackoff

UK Parents Lounge

UK Youth

UNICEF UK

United Reformed Church

University of the First Age

Urban Saints

Values Education for Life (The Collegiate
Centre for)

Voice

Voluntary Arts Network

Voluntary Youth Services (National Council for)

WATCh?

Whizz-Kidz

Who Cares? Trust

Willow Foundation

Winston's Wish

Wired Safety

Woodcraft Folk

Worldwide Volunteering

Year Out Group

YMCA (National Council of)

YOMAG

Young Christian Workers

Young Concert Artists Trust

Young Father's Initiative

Young People in Focus

Young People with ME (Association of)

Young Scot

YoungMinds

Youth Access

Youth Advocacy Service (National)

Youth Agency (National)

Youth Arts Wales (National)

Youth at Risk

Youth Choir of Great Britain (National)

Youth Council (British)

Youth for Christ

Youth in Action

Youth Information

Youth Justice Board for England and Wales

Youth Music

Youth Music Theatre (National)

Youth Opera (British)

Youth Orchestra (National of GB)

Youth Sport Trust

Youth Theatre of GB (National)

Youth Theatres (National Association of)

Youthhealthtalk

YouthNet UK

## Citizenship & Community Issues

Arthur Rank Centre

ARX Advocacy Resource Exchange

Better Transport (Campaign for)

Bevan Foundation

Blenheim CDP

Breathing places

British Legion (Royal)

Business in the Community

Changemakers

Citizenship (Institute for)

Citizenship and the Law (National Centre for)

Citizenship Foundation

Citizenship Teaching (Association for)

City Farms & Community Gardens (Federation of)

Common Ground

Common Purpose

Communities and Local Government (Department for)

Communities in Rural England (Action with)

Community Composting Network

Community Dance (Foundation for)

Community Foundation Network

Community Legal Advice

Community Matters

Community Media Association

Community Pubs Foundation

Community Rail Partnerships (Association of)

Community Self Build Agency

Court Service

Crimestoppers

Criminal Defence Service

Criminal Justice System

Crown Prosecution Service

CSV Education for Citizenship

Do it

Education of Travelling Communities (European Federation for the)

Every Child Matters

Forgiveness Project

Foundation For Peace

Friends, Families and Travellers

General Register Office

Get Global!

GFS Platform for Young Women

Global Ethics UK Trust (Institute for)

Groundwork UK

Gun Control Network

Gypsy Association

Habitat for Humanity

Hedgeline

Homeless Link

Immigrants (Joint Council for the Welfare of)

Immigration Aid Unit (Greater Manchester)

Integrated Education (N. Ireland Council for)

Intermix

Leap Confronting Conflict

Learning Through Action Centre

Letslink UK

Local Government Ombudsman (England)

London Citizens

Missing Persons Helpline (National)

Pensioners Convention (National)

Pet Advisory Committee

Philip Lawrence Awards Network

Placement Survival Guide

PlanningAlerts.com

Public Services Ombudsman (Scottish)

Runaway Helpline (under 18)

Science in the Public Interest (Center for)

Show Racism the Red Card

Skills for Justice

Social Care Association

Social Issues Research Centre

Social Workers (British Association of)

Squatters (Advisory Service for)

Surname Profiler

Transforming Conflict

UK New Citizen

Undercurrents

Voluntary and Community Action (National Association for)

Volunteers For Rural India

Working with men

World Civil Society Forum

# Complementary Medicine

Acupuncture Council (British)

Acupuncture Society (British Medical)

Alexander Teachers (Professional Association of)

Alexander Technique (Society of Teachers of the)

Chiropractic (Anglo-European College of)

Chiropractic Association (British)

Chiropractic Patients' Association

Complementary and Natural Medicine (Institute for)

Dr Edward Bach Centre

Healing Organisations (Confederation of)

Herb Society

Holistic Therapists (Federation of)

Homeopathic Association (British)

Homeopaths (Society of)

Hypnotherapists (Online National Register of)

Medical Herbalists (National Institute of)

Osteopathic Council (General)

Reflexology Association (British)

Shiatsu Society (UK)

Tisserand Aromatherapy Institute

# Consumers, Commerce and Business

Adbusters

Advertising Association

Advertising Standards Authority

Africa Now

Anglo-German Foundation for the Study of Industrial Society

Arts and Business

Banana Link

Bankruptcy Advisory Service

Blind in Business

British Standards Institute

Building Societies Members Association

Bus Users UK

Business & Professional Women UK Ltd

Business in Sport & Leisure

Business Link

Business Shop Network (Scottish)

Buy nothing day

CAMRA

Cash Machines (World Wide Locator of)

Chambers of Commerce (British)

Chartered Management Institute

Chartered Surveyors (Royal Institute of)

Chartered Surveyors Training Trust

Chartered Surveyors Voluntary Service

Citizens Advice

Community Pubs Foundation

Competition Commission

Consumer Credit Counselling Service

Consumer Direct

Consumer Focus

Consumers International

Corporate Watch

Credit Unions (Association of British)

Crown Estates

Dairy Council (The)

Direct Marketing Association

Directors (Institute of)

Economics & Business Education Association

Education Business Excellence (Institute for)

Effective Dispute Resolution (Centre for)

Egg Information Service (British)

EIRIS

Ethical Consumer Research Association & ECRA Publishing Ltd.

European Central Bank

European Information Centres

European Investment Bank

Facsimile Preference Service

Fair Trade Shops (British Association for)

Fair Trading (Office of)

Fairtrade Foundation

Farmers' Markets (Scottish Association of)

Farmers' Retail & Markets Association (National)

Financial Ombudsman Service

Financial Services Authority

Fiscal Studies (Institute for)

Food & Drink Federation

Food Commission

Fredericks Foundation

Freecycle

Freegle

Gas & Electricity Markets (Office of)

Home Business Alliance

Homeworking

Howtocomplain.com

Information Management (Association for)

Intellectual Property Office

Legal Services Ombudsman

Lorna Young Foundation

Mailing Preference Service

Marine Stewardship Council

Mentoring and Befriending Foundation

Moneysavingexpert.com

My Supermarket

National Debtline

Naturewatch

Office of Government Commerce

Patent Office (European)

Payplan

Personnel & Development (Chartered Institute of)

Phonebrain

Phonepay Plus

Pipedown

Post Office

Postcodes

Postcomm (Postal Services Commission)

Rail Regulation (Office of)

Road Haulage Association

Save our Building Societies

Shared Interest Society Ltd

Simple Free Law Advisor

Sleep Council

Small Businesses (Federation of)

Social Entrepreneurs (School for)

Stock Exchange (London)

SustainAbility

TaxAid

Technology Means Business

Telephone Preference Service

Tour Operators (Association of Independent)

Trading Standards Institute

Traidcraft

Trainline

Unite

Water Services (Office of)

Which?

Women Entrepreneurs (British Association of)

World Trade Organisation

YOMAG

# Contraception, Pregnancy & Birth

Abortion Rights

Action Postpartum Psychosis

Active Birth Centre

AIMS

ARC

Baby Greenhouse

Baby Lifeline

Babyworld

Birth Trauma Association

BirthChoice UK

Bliss – the premature baby charity

Bounty Healthcare Fund

BPAS

Brandon Centre

Brook

Conception & birth

COTS

Dad

Donor Conception Network

Education for Choice

Family Planning Association

Fertility Friends

Fertility UK

Gamete Donation Trust (National)

Human Fertilisation & Embryology Authority

Infertility Counselling Association (British)

Infertility Network UK

Interact Worldwide

La Leche League

Life

likeitis.org

Margaret Pyke Family Planning Centre

Marie Stopes International

Meet A Mum Association

Midwives Association (Independent)

Miscarriage Association

Multiple Births Foundation

Mumsnet

National Childbirth Trust

Newlife Foundation for Disabled Children

Nursing & Midwifery Council

Planned Parenthood Federation (International)

Post Natal Illness

Post-natal illness (Association for)

Sex Education Forum

Stillbirth & Neonatal Death Society

Tommy's, the baby charity

Twins & Multiple Births Association

UK Parents Lounge

Unborn Children (Society for the Protection of)

Voice for Choice

Your Life

## Counselling

Advice UK

Ahimsa

Albany Trust

Anxiety Care

Arbitrators (Chartered Institute of)

ARX Advocacy Resource Exchange

BEAT (Beat Eating Disorders)

Befrienders International

Bereavement Network (London)

Birmingham Settlement

BPAS

Brandon Centre

Broken Rainbow

Brook

CALM

Carers (The Princess Royal Trust For)

Changing Faces

ChildLine

Citizens Advice

Communities Empowerment Network

Concord Media

Connexions

Counsel and Care

Counselling & Psychotherapy (British Association for)

Crisis Counselling for Alleged Shoplifters

Cruse Bereavement Care

Cry-sis

Dial UK

Donor Conception Network

Down's Heart Group

Eating problems service

ENABLE

Everyman Project

Family Rights Group

Frank

Freshfield Service

Gamete Donation Trust (National)

Handsel Trust

Hereditary Breast Cancer Helpline

Hideout

Honour Network (The)

Infertility Counselling Association (British)

Kids Company

Lesbian and Gay Switchboard (London)

MALE

Marie Stopes International

Medical Advisory Service

Miracles

Mosac

Muslim Women's Helpline

NHS Direct

No Panic

NORCAP - Supporting Adults Affected by Adoption

NSPCC

NSPCC Asian Child Protection

PACE

Parentline Plus

Paul D'Auria Cancer Support Centre

Post-Adoption Centre

Prisoners' Advice Service

Public Concern at Work

Rape Crisis

Relate

Relationships Scotland

RESPECT

RoadPeace

Roofie Foundation

Samaritans

SAMM

SANE

Seasonal Affective Disorder Association

SEBDA

Survivors of Bereavement by Suicide

Talk Adoption

Teacher Support Network

Triumph over Phobia (TOP UK)

Victim Support

Wessex Cancer Trust

Who Cares? Trust

Youth Access

Youth Advocacy Service (National)

# Dance

*refer also to the section on Dance Drama, Music & Performing Arts Schools*

Ballet Organization (British)

Benesh Institute of Choreology

Birmingham Royal Ballet

Bolshoi Ballet

Ceroc

Community Dance (Foundation for)

Dance Council (British)

Dance Education & Training (Council for)

Dance Teachers Alliance (UKA)

Dance UK

Danceconsortium

Dancesport UK

English National Ballet

Festivals (British & International Federation of )

IDTA

ISTD

London Children's Ballet

Men's Morris & Sword Dance Clubs (National Association of)

Morris Federation

National Youth Ballet

Northern Ballet

Rambert Dance Company

Royal Academy of Dance

Royal Ballet

Scottish Ballet

# Death and Bereavement

Advocacy After Fatal Domestic Abuse
Bereavement Network (London)
Cardiac Risk in the Young
Care Not Killing
Child Bereavement Trust
Child Death Helpline
Childhood Bereavement Network
Compassionate Friends
Cremation Society of Great Britain
Cruse Bereavement Care
Dignity in Dying
Friends at the end
Help the Hospices
Human Rights Society
Infant Deaths (Foundation for the Study of)
INQUEST
Lone Twin Network
Natural Death Centre
Palliative Care (National Council for)
REACT
SAMM
Survivors of Bereavement by Suicide
Winston's Wish

# Developing World

Action Aid
Afghanaid
Africa and Asia Venture
Africa Centre
Africa Now
African Initiatives
Africans Unite Against Child Abuse

Anti-Slavery International
Baby Milk Action
Banana Link
BOND
Book Aid International
Brazil's Children Trust (Action for)
Broadcasting Trust (International)
Brooke Hospital for Animals
Burma Campaign UK
CAFOD
CAMFED International
Canon Collins Educational Trust for Southern Africa
CARE International UK
Chain of Hope
Christian Aid
Chronic Poverty Research Centre
Comic Relief
Commonwealth Education Trust
Commonwealth Scolarships
Commonwealth Society (Royal)
Computer Aid International
Computers 4 Africa
Concern Worldwide
Cross Cultural Solutions
Development Education Association (DEA)
Development Education Project
Developments
Disability & Development (Action on)
Dramatic Need
Enable (Working in India)
Ethiopiaid
Fair Trade Shops (British Association for)
Fairtrade Foundation
Forest Peoples Programme
Friends of Peoples Close to Nature
Gambia Horse and Donkey Trust
Global Crop Diversity Trust
Global Dimension
Global Eye
HALO Trust

HIV InSite

HIV/Aids Alliance (International)

Homeless International

International Development (Department for)

International Monetary Fund

Islamic Relief

Jubilee Debt Campaign

Kids for Kids

Kiva

Labour Behind the Label

Lorna Young Foundation

Malaria No More UK

Mary's Meals

Médecins sans Frontières (UK)

Media for Development

Medical Trust (Britain-Nepal)

Mercy Corps

Nicaragua Solidarity Campaign

ONE International

One World Action

Operation Smile UK

Opportunity International UK

Overseas Development Institute

Oxfam

Panos Institute

People and Planet

Plan International UK

Practical Action

Restless Development

Room to Read

Save the Children (UK)

SCIAF

Shine a Light

Sight Savers International

Skillshare International

SOS Children

Stakeholder Forum

Survival International

TAPOL

Tearfund

Tools for Self Reliance

Tourism Concern

Traidcraft

TRóCAIRE

UNICEF UK

United Nations Association of the UK

Vision Aid Overseas

VSO

War on Want

Water Aid

Womankind Worldwide

World Development Movement

World Food Programme (United Nations)

World Health Organisation

World Vision UK

Y Care International

## Disability/Special Needs

1 Voice

Accessible Environments (Centre for)

Afasic

Arts Disability Wales

Artsline

Asian People's Disability Alliance

Back-up Trust

Bikers with a Disability (National Association for)

Blind (National Federation of the)

Blind (Royal National Institute of the)

Blind Golf Association (English)

Blind in Business

Blind People (Action for)

Blind Sport (British)

Blue Badge Network

Calvert Trust

Camp Mohawk

Canine Partners

Carers (The Princess Royal Trust For)

Changing Faces

Chess Association (Braille)

Child Growth Foundation

Children's Hope Foundation

Clapa

ClearVision Project

Conductive Education (The National Institute of)

Connect

Contact a Family

CP Sport

CROSSROADS Care

Cued Speech Association UK

Cycling Projects

Deaf (Commonwealth Society for the)

Deaf Association (British)

Deaf Broadcasting Council

Deaf Children's Society (National)

Deaf Education Through Listening and Talking

Deaf Sports Council (British)

Deafblind International

Deafblind Scotland

Deafblind UK

Deafblindness (A-Z to)

Deafness Research UK

Dial UK

Disability & Development (Action on)

Disability Action

Disability Alliance

Disability Law Service

Disability Pregnancy & Parenthood International

Disability Snowsport UK

Disability Sport (English Federation of)

Disability Sport (Events)

Disabled Children (Council for)

Disabled Living Foundation

Disabled Parents' Network

Disabled People's Council (UK)

Disfigurement Guidance Centre

Dogs for the Disabled

Douglas Bader Foundation

Down's Syndrome Association

Down's Syndrome Scotland

Dyslexia Action

Dyslexia Association (British)

Dyspraxia Foundation

Edward Lear Foundation

ENABLE

Enable (Working in India)

Equality and Human Rights Commission

Equality Britain

Gateway Award

Guide Dogs for the Blind Association

Hairline International

Handsel Trust

Hearing Dogs for Deaf People

Hypermobility Syndrome Association

Inclusion (National Development Team for) NDTi

Inclusive Education (Alliance for)

Inclusive Education (Centre for Studies on)

Independent Living Alternatives

IPSEA

Jubilee Sailing Trust

Learn To Sign

Learning Disabilities (British Institute of)

Let's Face It

Limbless Association

Listening Books

Makaton Vocabulary Development Project

Mencap

Mencap Cymru

Mencap Northern Ireland

Mental Health Foundation

Mobilise

Mobility Information Service

Multiple Sclerosis Society

Multiple Sclerosis Therapy Centres (Federation of)

Music and the Deaf

NBCS

Network '81

Newlife Foundation for Disabled Children

NOAH

Norwood

Operation Smile UK

Papworth Trust

Paralympic Association (British)

Parents for Inclusion

Partially Sighted Society

People First

Phab

RADAR

Rathbone

REMAP

Remploy

Ricability

Riding for the Disabled Association

RNIB National Library Service

RNID

Rona Sailing Project

RYA Sailability

Saving Faces

Scope

SeeAbility

Self Unlimited

Sense

Shopmobility (National Federation of)

Short Persons Support

Sibs

Signature

Skill: National Bureau for Students with Disabilities

Skills for Care

Sound Sense

Special Educational Needs & Disability Tribunal

Special Educational Needs (National Association for)

Special Needs Education (European Agency for Development in)

Special Olympics GB

SPIT

Sports Association for People with Learning Disabilities (UK)

Stammering Association (British)

Stammering Children (Michael Palin Centre for)

Support Dogs

Swimming Clubs for the Handicapped (National Association of)

TACT

TAG

Talking Newspaper Association

Thalidomide Society (UK)

Tourism for All

Transport for London

Treloar Trust

Tuberous Sclerosis Association

UPDATE

VoiceAbility

Volunteer Reading Help

WheelPower

Whizz-Kidz

Winvisible (Women with visible & invisible disabilities)

Wireless for the Blind Fund (British)

# Drugs and Substance Abuse

Addaction

Addiction (Action on)

ADFAM

Advisory Council on the Misuse of Drugs

Blenheim CDP

BNTL-Freeway

Cocaine Anonymous

Drug Education Forum

Drugs and Crime (UN Office on)

Drugs Forum (Scottish)

DrugScope

Families Anonymous

Frank

Freshfield Service

Hope UK

Know Cannabis

London Drug & Alcohol Network

Narcotics Anonymous UK

Release

ReSolv

Roofie Foundation

Tacade

Thesite

Tranquillisers, Antidepressants and Painkillers (Council for Information on)

Transform Drug Policy Foundation

Turning Point

Monetary Justice (Christian Council for)

MyBnk

New Economics Foundation

Pensions Ombudsman

Public Management and Policy Association

Save our Building Societies

Shared Interest Society Ltd

Smith Institute

Social & Economic Research (Institute for)

Treasury

World Bank

# Economics

Adam Smith Institute

Anglo-German Foundation for the Study of Industrial Society

Audit Commission

Audit Office (National)

Bank of England

Bankruptcy Advisory Service

Citizens Income Trust

Credit Unions (Association of British)

Currency converter

Economic & Social Research (National Institute of)

Extreme Inequality

Foreign Policy Centre

Independent Financial Adviser Promotion Ltd

International Monetary Fund

Letslink UK

Local Economic Strategies (Centre for)

Local Economy Policy Unit

# Education

100 Black Men of London

Academic Freedom & Academic Standards (Council for)

Alcohol Education and Research Council

Alexander Teachers (Professional Association of)

Alexander Technique (Society of Teachers of the)

Anne Frank Trust UK

Antidote: Campaign for Emotional Literacy

Art and Design (National Society for Education in)

Arts Education Network

ASDAN

Asiatic Society of Great Britain and Ireland (Royal)

Aspect

Associated Board of the Royal Schools of Music

Association of Colleges

Athletic Association (English Schools)

Awesome Library

Basic Skills Agency at NIACE

BBC Schools

BECTA

Bibliomania

Big Bus

Big Read (The)

Bilingualism, Languages, Literacies and Education Network

Bitesize: BBC revision web site

BKA

Black Students Alliance (National)

Black Training & Enterprise Group

Boarding Concern

Book Aid International

Book Power

Books Council (Welsh)

BOOKTRUST

Brainwave

BRIT School for Performing Arts and Technology

British Council

Business in the Community

CACHE

CAMFED International

Canon Collins Educational Trust for Southern Africa

Career Development Loans

Careers Research & Advisory Centre

Catholic Education Service

CfBT Education Trust

Chartered Surveyors Training Trust

Chess Association (English Primary Schools)

Children and War

Children's Book Groups (Federation of)

Chinese Arts Centre

Choir Schools Association

Christian Education

Christian Teachers (Association of)

CILT

Citizenship Foundation

Citizenship Teaching (Association for)

City and Guilds of London Institute

Classical Association

Clear Vision Trust

ClearVision Project

Coleg Harlech (WEA)

Common Purpose

Commonwealth Education Trust

Commonwealth Scolarships

Commonwealth Society (Royal)

Communities Empowerment Network

Conductive Education (The National Institute of)

Countryside Foundation for Education

Creative Partnerships

CREST Awards

CSV Education for Citizenship

Cult Information Centre

Dance Education & Training (Council for)

Daneford Trust

Dark Skies (Campaign for)

Deaf Education Through Listening and Talking

Development Education Association (DEA)

Development Education Project

Down's Syndrome Educational Trust

Drama (National)

Drama Schools (The Conference of)

Drama Training (National Council for)

Drug Education Forum

Dyslexia Action

Dyslexia Association (British)

Early Childhood Education (British Association for)

Early Years

Economics & Business Education Association

Eco-Schools

Edexel

Education & Culture (European Commission Directorate General)

Education & Industry (Centre for)

Education (Advisory Centre for)

Education (Department for)

Education and Training (Centre for the Study of)

Education Business Excellence (Institute for)

Education Consultants (Society of)

Education for Choice

Education Index (British)

Education of Adults (European Association for the)

Education of Travelling Communities (European Federation for the)

Education Otherwise

Education Statistics (USA National Center for)

Educational Psychologists (Association of)

Educational Recording Agency

e-Learning Foundation

EMI Music Sound Foundation

Employment & Learning Northern Ireland (Department for)

Engage

English and Media Centre

English Association

English Heritage Education

English Speaking Union

Enterprise Education Trust

Erasmus

ESU

Eurodesk

Every Child a Chance Trust

Exchange of Commonwealth Teachers (League for the)

Exploratorium

Fair Access (Office for)

Fairbridge

Farming & Countryside Education

fforwm

Field Studies Council

Film & Television Archive (Northern Region)

Film and Television School (National)

Film Education

Findhorn Foundation

Football Association (English Schools)

Fulbright Commission (The US-UK)

GCSE Answers

Geographical Association

Geological Society

Get Global!

Gifted Children (National Association for)

Gifted Children's Information Centre

Global Action Plan

Global Dimension

Global Ethics UK Trust (Institute for)

Global Eye

Governor's Association (National)

Graduate careers website

Greater London Enterprise

Headliners

Healthy Schools Programme (National)

Heartstone

Higher Education Funding Council for England

Historical Association

History World

HMRC Education Zone

Holocaust Educational Trust

Homework High

Hope UK

Human Rights Education Association

Human Scale Education

IATEFL

IDTA

Imaginate

Include

Inclusion (National Development Team for) NDTi

Inclusive Education (Alliance for)

Inclusive Education (Centre for Studies on)

Independent Schools Council

InfoSearcher.com

Innovation in Mathematics Teaching (Centre for)

Integrated Education (N. Ireland Council for)

International Baccalaureate Organization

IPSEA

ISTD

JANET

Japan Foundation London Language Centre

Kid Info School Subjects

Kids in museums

Language Awareness (Association for)

Language Learning (Association for)

learndirect

Learning (Campaign for)

Learning (Institute for)

Learning and Skills Development Agency Northern Ireland

Learning and Skills Improvement Service

Learning and Teaching Scotland

Learning Disabilities (British Institute of)

Learning Outside the Classroom

Learning Through Action Centre

Learning Zone

Left 'n' Write

Lifelong Learning

Lifetracks

Linguists (Chartered Institute of)

Literacy Association (National)

Literacy Association (UK)

Literacy in Primary Education (Centre for)

Literacy Trust (National)

Local History (British Association for)

London Schools Arts Service

Makaton Vocabulary Development Project

Mathematical Association

Mathematics (Centre for the Popularisation of)

Mentoring and Befriending Foundation

Met Office

Montessori Centre International

Music Council (National)

Music Educators (National Association of)

Muslim Schools UK (Association of)

NAACE

NABSS

National Extension College

Network '81

NFER

NHS Health Scotland

NIACE

NUS

OCR/Oxford Cambridge and RSA Examinations

Ofqual

OFSTED

Open & Distance Learning Quality Council

Open College of the Arts

Open University

Outdoor Learning (Institute for)

Parent Teacher Associations (National Confederation of)

Parents for Inclusion

Parliamentary Education Unit

Pastoral Care in Education (National Association for)

Personal Finance Education Group

Pharmaceutical Society (Royal)

Physical Education (Association for)

Physics (Institute of)

Placement Survival Guide

Pre-School Learning Alliance

Pre-School Play Association (Scottish)

Pre-School Playgroups Association (Wales)

Primary Education (Association for the Study of)

Primary Education (National Association for)

Pyramid

Qualifications and Curriculum Development Authority

Quality in Study Support and Extended Services

RADA

Real Education (Campaign for)

Religious Education (Professional Council for)

REonline

Room to Read

Royal College of Veterinary Surgeons

Royal Geographical Society

Royal Society

RSA

Ruskin College

School Councils UK

School Food Trust

School Governors (National Association of)

School Journey Association

School Librarianship (International Association of)

School Library Association

Schools Adjudicator (Office of the)

Schools Health Education Unit

Schools Music Association of Great Britain

SCIcentre

Science Education (Association for)

Science Education (Centre for)

Scottish Qualifications Authority

Sex Education Forum

Shakespeare Schools Festival

Simon Wiesenthal Centre

Skill: National Bureau for Students with Disabilities

Skills Funding Agency

Smallpeice Trust

Social Entrepreneurs (School for)

Social Sciences (Association for the Teaching of the)

Spanish Embassy Education Office

Spartacus Educational

Spatial Literacy

Special Educational Needs & Disability Tribunal

Special Educational Needs (National Association for)

Specialist Schools and Academies Trust

Spelling Society (English)

State Education (Campaign for)

Steiner Waldorf Education (European Council for)

Stephen Lawrence Charitable Trust

Storytelling (Society for)

Student Awards Agency for Scotland

Student Drama Festival (National)

Student Loans Company Ltd

Sundial Society (British)

Swimming

Tacade

Teacher Support Network

TeacherNet

Teachers of Mathematics (Association of)

Teaching Council for England (General)

Teaching Council for Wales (General)

Teaching English & Other Community Languages to Adults (National Association for)

Teaching of Drama (National Association for)

Teaching of English (National Association for the)

The Sikh Way

Third Age Trust

Topmarks

Training & Development Agency for Schools

Transforming Conflict

Treloar Trust

UCAS

UK Islamic Education Waqf

UNESCO

Uni4me

Unistats

University of the First Age

Values Education for Life (The Collegiate Centre for)

Victorian Society

Voices Foundation

Volunteer Reading Help

Winston Churchill Memorial Trust

Workers Educational Association

Working Men's College for Women & Men

WorkLife Support Limited

World Challenge Expeditions

Writers in Education (National Association of)

Year Out Group

Young Engineers

Young Enterprise

Young People's Learning Agency

Youth in Action

## Emergency aid

CAFOD

Christian Aid

Concern Worldwide

Disasters Emergency Committee

Echo

Islamic Relief

Médecins sans Frontières (UK)

Mercy Corps

MERLIN

Oxfam

Plan International UK

Save the Children (UK)

SCIAF

Tearfund

UNICEF UK

World Health Organisation

World Jewish Relief

World Vision UK

## Environment and Countryside

10:10

ACT ON CO2

African Conservation Experience

AirportWatch

Allotment and Leisure Gardeners Ltd. (National Society of)

Alternative Technology (Centre for)

Aluminium Packaging Recycling Organisation

An Taisce

Ancient Tree forum

Architecture and the Built Environment (Commission for)

Arthur Rank Centre

Basel Action Network (BAN)

Bat Conservation Trust

bikerecycling.net

Biological Diversity (Convention on)

Black Environment Network

Body Shop Foundation

Born Free Foundation

Botanic Garden of Wales (National)

Breathing places

BTCV

Butterfly Conservation

Byways & Bridleways Trust

CABE

Cadw

Carbon Neutral Company

CEH

Choose Climate

Churches Conservation Trust

Civic Society Initiative

CLA

Cleanair

Climate Change (Intergovernmental Panel on)

Committee on Climate Change

Common Ground

Communities in Rural England (Action with)

Community Composting Network

Conservation of Energy (Association for the)

Conservation of Plants & Gardens (National Council for the)

Corporate Watch

Countryside Alliance

Countryside Council for Wales

Countryside Foundation for Education

CPRE: Campaign to Protect Rural England

CTC

Cycling Campaign (London)

Dark Skies (Campaign for)

Deer Society (British)

Defra

Divers Marine Life Rescue (British)

Down to Earth

Earth First! Worldwide

EarthAction Network

Earthquake Locator (World Wide)

Earthwatch Europe

Ecological Society (British)

Ecology Building Society

Eco-Schools

Ecotourism Society (The International)

Eden Project

Energy Association (International)

Energy Foundation (National)

Energy Saving Trust

English Heritage

Environment & Nature Conservation (Young People's Trust for the)

Environment Agency

Environment and Development (International Institute for)

Environment Council

Environment Protection Agency (Scottish)

Environmental Investigation Agency

Environmental Law & Development (Foundation for International)

Environmental Law Foundation

Environmental Noise Maps

Environmental Pollution (Royal Commission on)

Environmental Protection UK

Environmental Transport Association

Farming & Countryside Education

Fauna & Flora International

Field Studies Council

Findhorn Foundation

Floodline

Forestry Commission

Forestry Society of England, Wales & N. Ireland (Royal)

Forum for the Future

Forward Scotland

Friends of the Earth

Froglife

Furniture Re-use Network

Gaia Foundation

Galapagos Conservation Trust

Garden History Society

Gardens Scheme Charitable Trust (National)

Geographic Society (National)

Geographical Association

Geological Society

Global Action Plan

Global Witness

Go4awalk

Green Alliance

Green Mark

Green Moves

Green Party

Greenpeace

Groundwork UK

Hawk & Owl Trust

Heat is Online

Hedgeline

Hurricane Center (National)

Indigenous Tribal Peoples of the Tropical Forests (International Alliance of)

INK

Inland Waterways Association

IUCN

Joint Nature Conservation Committee,

Keep Britain Tidy

Lake District (Friends of the)

Lake District National Park Authority

Lake District Weather Line

Landlife

Landmark Trust

Landscape Institute

LINK

Living Earth Foundation

Living Streets

London Green Belt Council

Marine Conservation Society

Marine Stewardship Council

Maritime & Coastguard Agency

Met Office

Meteorological Organization (World)

Meteorological Society (Royal)

Millennium Seed Bank

Mongabay.com

National Energy Action

National Forest Company

National Parks (Campaign for)

National Tidal and Sea Level Facility

National Trust

National Trust Working Holidays

Natural Death Centre

Natural England

Natural Environment Research Council

Natural Heritage (Scottish)

Noise Abatement Society

Northern Ireland Environment Link

Nuclear Tourist

Open Spaces Society

Ordnance Survey

Our Dynamic Earth

People and Planet

People's Trust for Endangered Species

Permaculture Association (Britain)

Pesticide Action Network UK

Pipedown

Plantlife

Preservation Trusts (UK Association of)

Primate Protection League (International)

Protection of Rural Wales (Campaign for the)

Rainforest Concern

Rainforest Foundation

Reclaim the Streets

Re-Cycle

Recycle for London

Recycle more

Recycle now campaign

Recycling Appeal

Red List of Endangered Species

RenewableUK

Rising Tide

Royal Geographical Society

Royal Horticultural Society

Royal Parks

Rural Communities (Commission for)

Rural Research (Centre for)

Rural Scotland (Association for the Protection of)

Save our Waterways

Schumacher UK

Scientific Exploration Society

Shark Alliance

Snow and Ice Data Center (National)

Soil Association

Stakeholder Forum

Steel Can Recycling Information Bureau

Stop Climate Chaos Coalition

Stop Climate Chaos Scotland

Surfers Against Sewage

SustainAbility

Telework Association

Thrive

Town & Country Planning Association

Town Planning Institute (Royal)

Transport & Environment (European Federation for)

Transport (Department for)

Tree Council

UK Climate projections

UKAEA

United Nations Environment Programme

Wales Environment Link

WalkScotland

Waste Watch

Waterways (British)

Weather Centre (BBC Online)

Whale & Dolphin Conservation Society
Wild Flower Society
Wildfowl & Wetlands Trust (WWT)
Wildlife and Countryside Link
Wildlife Trusts (Royal Society of)
Wind Energy Association (European)
Women's Environmental Network
Woodland Trust
World Land Trust
World Monuments Fund in Britain
WRAP
WWF-UK

## Equality issues

Black Training & Enterprise Group
Citizens Income Trust
Equality and Human Rights Commission
Equality Britain
Extreme Inequality
Fawcett Society
Friends, Families and Travellers
Left 'n' Write
ManKind Initiative
Migration Policy Group
Minority Rights Group International
Race Equality Foundation
Racism in Europe (Youth Against)
Room to Read
Short Persons Support
Stonewall
Tall Person's Club (GB & Ireland)

## Europe

Council of Europe
Council of Europe Youth
Education of Adults (European Association for the)
Erasmus
ESU
EU in the United Kingdom (European Commission)
Eurodesk
Europe Direct
Europe in the UK
European Central Bank
European Commission Agriculture and Rural Development
European Court of Justice
European Information Centres
European Investment Bank
European Movement
European Parliament (UK Office)
European Parliamentary Labour Party
European Trade Union Confederation
European Union
European Union Committee of the Regions
European Youth Card Association
European Youth Forum
European Youth Information and Counselling Agency
European Youth Music Week
France: culture and communications website
Franco British Council (British Section)
Franco-Scottish Society of Scotland
Freedom Association
Friedrich Ebert Foundation
Golf Association (European)
Individual Rights in Europe (Advice on)
Rail Europe
Special Needs Education (European Agency for Development in)
Wind Energy Association (European)

# Family

1 Voice
Adopted Children's Register
Birth Trauma Association
Bounty Healthcare Fund
Chance UK
Child Contact Centres (National Association of)
Children's Bureau (National)
Children's Service
Compassionate Friends
Conception & birth
Contact a Family
Cry-sis
Dad
Dad Talk
Dad's House
Daycare Trust
Disability Pregnancy & Parenthood International
Disabled Parents' Network
Donor Conception Network
Donor Family Network
Down's Heart Group
Elder Abuse (Action on)
Families Need Fathers
Family & Parenting Institute (National)
Family Action
Family Holiday Association
Family Planning Association
Family Rights Group
Family Search
Family Therapy (Institute of)
Fatherhood Institute
Fathers4justice Ltd

Find a Parent or Child
FreeBMD
Friendship Works
Full Time Mothers
Gamete Donation Trust (National)
General Register Office
Gingerbread
Grandparents Plus
Grandparents' Association
HELP
Home-Start
Honour Network (The)
It's not your fault
Lone Twin Network
Lucy Faithfull Foundation
ManKind Initiative
MATCH
Mosac
Mothers Union
National Childbirth Trust
Parenting UK
Parentline Plus
Parents & Abducted Children Together
Planned Parenthood Federation (International)
Prisoners' Families (Action for)
Prisoners' Families and Friends Service
Register Office for Northern Ireland (General)
Register Office for Scotland (General)
Relate
Relationships Scotland
Resolution
RESPECT
reunite
Sibs
Twins & Multiple Births Association
Working Families
Working with men
Young Father's Initiative

## Farming/Agriculture

Allotment and Leisure Gardeners Ltd. (National Society of)

City Farms & Community Gardens (Federation of)

CLA

Compassion in World Farming Trust

Countryside Alliance

Countryside Foundation for Education

Dairy Council (The)

Defra

Elm Farm Research Centre

Environment Agency

European Commission Agriculture and Rural Development

Farm Animal Welfare Council

Farmers' Markets (Scottish Association of)

Farmers' Retail & Markets Association (National)

Farming & Countryside Education

Farms for City Children

Food & Agricultural Organisation (United Nations)

Garden Organic

Global Crop Diversity Trust

Natural England

Rare Breeds Survival Trust

Rural Communities (Commission for)

Rural Research (Centre for)

Soil Association

Sustain

Viva!

Women's Food & Farming Union

WWOOF Association (International)

Young Farmers' Clubs (National Federation of)

## Food

Additives (Action on)

Agriculture and Horticulture Development Board

chewonthis.org.uk

Chocolate Society

Dairy Council (The)

Defra

Dietetic Association (British)

Egg Information Service (British)

Farmers' Markets (Scottish Association of)

Farmers' Retail & Markets Association (National)

Food & Agricultural Organisation (United Nations)

Food & Drink Federation

Food & Drug Administration (US)

Food Commission

Food Standards Agency

GM Freeze

Herb Society

IFST

Mary's Meals

Nutrition Foundation (British)

Nutrition Society

Optimum Nutrition (Institute for)

Overeaters Anonymous

School Food Trust

Sea Fish Industry Authority

Slow Food

Sustain

Tea Council Ltd.

Vegan Society

Vegetarian & Vegan Foundation

Vegetarian Society

Viva!

Women's Food & Farming Union

World Food Programme (United Nations)

# Government

10 Downing Street Website

Advisory Council on the Misuse of Drugs

Attorney General's Office

Audit Commission

Audit Office (National)

Business Link

Business, Innovation & Skills (Department for )

Cabinet Office

Cafcass

Central Office of Information

Charity Commission for England & Wales

CIA

Committee on Climate Change

Communities and Local Government (Department for)

Competition Commission

Criminal Cases Review Commission

Criminal Injuries Compensation Authority

Crown Estates

Defence (Ministry of)

DIALOG

DirectGov

Education (Department for)

Energy Association (International)

Environmental Pollution (Royal Commission on)

e-Parliament Initiative

EU in the United Kingdom (European Commission)

European Parliament (UK Office)

European Union

Fair Access (Office for)

Fair Trading (Office of)

FBI

Financial Ombudsman Service

Foreign and Commonwealth Office

Foreign and Commonwealth Office Travel Advice

Government Actuary's Department

Greater London Authority

Health & Social Services (N. Ireland Department of)

Health (Department of)

Hear From Your MP

HM Revenue and Customs

HMRC Education Zone

Home Office

House of Lords

Housing Ombudsman Service

Human Rights Commission (N. Ireland)

Intellectual Property Office

International Development (Department for)

Joint Nature Conservation Committee,

Justice (Ministry of)

Land Registry

Local Authorities (Convention of Scottish)

Local Economy Policy Unit

Local Government Association

Local Government Information Unit

Local Government Ombudsman (England)

Low Pay Commission

Maritime & Coastguard Agency

National Archives

National Archives of Scotland (NAS)

Northern Ireland Executive

Northern Ireland Office

Northern Ireland Ombudsman

Office for National Statistics

Office of Government Commerce

OFSTED

Parliament

Parliamentary and Health Service Ombudsman

Parliamentary Education Unit

Parliaments (Websites of National)

Passport Office

Pensions Ombudsman

PlanningAlerts.com

Postcomm (Postal Services Commission)

Privacy International

Public Services Ombudsman (Scottish)

Public Whip

Register Office for Northern Ireland (General)

Register Office for Scotland (General)

Schools Adjudicator (Office of the)

Scotland Office

Scottish Government

Scottish Parliament

Serious Fraud Office

TheyWorkForYou.com

Trading Standards Institute

Transparency International

Transport (Department for)

Treasury

UK Border Agency

US Department of State

Wales Office

Welsh Assembly Government

WriteToThem.com

# Health and Medicine

Abortion Rights

Active Birth Centre

Acupuncture Council (British)

Acupuncture Society (British Medical)

Additives (Action on)

AIDS Trust (National)

Albinism Fellowship

Alcohol & Health Research Unit

Alcohol Studies (Institute of)

Allergy UK

Alzheimer Scotland

Alzheimer's Research Trust

Alzheimer's Society

Anaphylaxis Campaign

Anthony Nolan Trust

Anxiety UK

ARC

Art Therapists (British Association of)

Arthritic Association

Arthritis Care

Arthritis Research UK

Arts in Therapy & Education (Institute for)

ASBAH

Asthma UK

Ataxia UK

Attend

Autistic Society (National)

AVERT

Baby Lifeline

Baby Milk Action

BackCare

BASIC

BBC Health

BEAT (Beat Eating Disorders)

Behavioural & Cognitive Psychotherapies (British Association of)

Better Seating (Campaign for)

Bibic

Bioethics (Nuffield Council on)

BirthChoice UK

Bladder and Bowel Foundation (B&BF)

Blood Donor Registration Line (National)

Blood Pressure Association

Body Positive

Bounty Healthcare Fund

Bowel Cancer UK

Brain & Spine Foundation

Breakthrough Breast Cancer

Breast Cancer Care

British Heart Foundation

British Medical Association

Brittle Bone Society

Cancer Research UK

Cancer Society (American)

CancerHelp UK

Cardiac Risk in the Young

Care Quality Commission

Carers UK

Casualties Union

Chain of Hope

Chernobyl Children's Life Line

chewonthis.org.uk

Child Brain Injury Trust

Child Growth Foundation

Children with Leukaemia

Children's Heart Federation

Chiropodists & Podiatrists (Institute of)

Chiropractic Association (British)

Chiropractic Patients' Association

Christian Lewis Trust

Cinnamon Trust

Clapa

CLICSargent

Climb

Colitis & Crohn's Disease (National Association for)

Complementary and Natural Medicine (Institute for)

Concord Media

CORE

COTS

CROSSROADS Care

Cystic Fibrosis Trust

Daisy Network

DEBRA

Dental Association (British)

Depression Alliance

Dermatologists (British Association of)

Diabetes UK

Dietetic Association (British)

Different Strokes

Disfigurement Guidance Centre

Don't lose the music

Donor Family Network

Down's Heart Group

Down's Syndrome Association

Down's Syndrome Medical Interest Group

Down's Syndrome Scotland

Dr Edward Bach Centre

Drinking Water Inspectorate

Dyspraxia Foundation

Eating problems service

Eczema Society (National)

Ellen MacArthur Trust

Embarrassing Problems

Endometriosis UK

Epilepsy (National Centre for Young People with)

Epilepsy (National Society for)

Epilepsy Action

ERIC – Education and Resources for Improving Childhood Continence

ETCO

Eyecare Trust

Fertility Friends

Fertility UK

First Steps to Freedom

FirstSigns

Fit for Travel

Food & Drug Administration (US)

Fragile X Society

Friends at the end

General Dental Council

General Medical Council

Genetic Alliance UK

GM Freeze

Gulf Veterans & Families Association (National)

Haemochromatosis Society

Haemophilia Society

HEADWAY

Health & Safety Executive

Health & Social Services (N. Ireland Department of)

Health (Department of)

Health Information Resources

Health Professions Council

Health Promotion Agency for Northern Ireland

Health Protection Agency

Health Research & Development (Foundation for Women's)

Healthtalkonline

Healthy Schools Programme (National)

Help – For a life without tobacco

Help the Hospices

Hereditary Breast Cancer Helpline

Herpes Viruses Association

HIFY-UK

High Blood Pressure Foundation

HIV InSite

HIV/Aids Alliance (International)

Holistic Therapists (Federation of)

Hospital Broadcasting Association

Human Fertilisation & Embryology Authority

Human Genetics Commission

Humane Research Trust

Huntington's Disease Association

Hyperactive Children's Support Group

Hypermobility Syndrome Association

IBS Helpline

Infant Deaths (Foundation for the Study of)

Infertility Network UK

Interact Worldwide

Jane Tomlinson Appeal

Jeans for Genes

Kidney Patient Association (British)

Kidney Research UK

King's Fund

Lavender Trust

Learning Disabilities (The Foundation for People with)

LEPRA

Let's Face It

Leukaemia and Lymphoma Research

Liver Trust (British)

Lung Foundation (British)

Lupus UK

Macmillan Cancer Support

Mafan Association UK

Malaria No More UK

Marfan Friends World

Marie Curie Cancer Care

Maternal & Childhealth Advocacy International (MCAI)

MDF The Bipolar Organisation

ME (Action for)

ME Association

Médecins sans Frontières (UK)

Medical Accidents (Action Against)

Medical Advisory Service

Medical Advisory Services for Travellers Abroad Ltd.

Medical Aid for Palestinians

Medical Conditions at School

Medical Foundation for the Care of Victims of Torture

Medical Helpline (General)

Medical Research Charities (Association of)

Medical Research Council

Medical Trust (Britain-Nepal)

MedicAlert Foundation

Medicines & Healthcare Products Regulatory Agency

Men's Health Helpline

Meningitis Research Foundation

Meningitis Trust

Mental Health (Scottish Association for)

MERLIN

Migraine Action Association

Migraine Trust

Miscarriage Association

Motor Neurone Disease Association

Mouth Cancer Foundation

Multiple Sclerosis Society

Multiple Sclerosis Therapy Centres (Federation of)

Multiple Sclerosis Trust

Muscular Dystrophy Campaign

Musculoskeletal Medicine (British Institute of)

Music Therapy (British Society for)

Narcolepsy Association UK (UKAN)

National Institute for Health and Clinical Excellence

NBCS

Netdoctor

Neurofibromatosis Association

Newlife Foundation for Disabled Children

NHS Careers

NHS Confederation

NHS Direct

NHS Health Scotland

NHS Support Federation

Nursing & Midwifery Council

Nutrition Foundation (British)

Obesity (International Association for the Study of) & Obesity TaskForce (International)

Obesity Forum (National)

Occupational Hygiene Society (British)

Orchid Cancer Appeal

Organ Donation

Organ Donation and Transplantation (International Registry of)

Osteopathic Council (General)

Osteoporosis Society (National)

Overeaters Anonymous

Pain Relief Foundation

Pain Society (British)

Pain Support

Palliative Care (National Council for)

Papworth Trust

PAPYRUS (Prevention of Suicides)

Parkinson's Disease Society

Parliamentary and Health Service Ombudsman

Patient Safety Agency (National)

Patient UK

Patients Association

Paul D'Auria Cancer Support Centre

Performing Arts Medicine (British Association for)

Personal Injury Lawyers (Association of)

Pets as Therapy

Physiotherapy (Chartered Society of)

Pilates Foundation

Pituitary Foundation

Pod Charitable Trust

Polio Fellowship (British)

Population Services International

Positively UK

Post Natal Illness

Premenstrual Syndrome (National Association for)

Professional Music Therapists (Association of)

Prostate Cancer Helpline

Psoriasis Association

Psychiatrists (Royal College of)

Psychotherapists (British Association of)

Psychotherapy (UK Council for)

PWSA (UK)

Raynaud's & Scleroderma Association

REACT

Red Cross (British)

Relatives & Residents Association

Restricted Growth Association

Roy Castle Lung Cancer Foundation

Royal Society of Medicine

SADS

Safer Medicines Campaign

Saint John Ambulance

Schools Health Education Unit

Scoliosis Association (UK)

Seriously Ill for Medical Research

Sexual Advice Association

Shiatsu Society (UK)

Shingles Support Society

Sick Children (Action for)

Sickle Cell Society

Sight Savers International

Skills for Care

Sleep Council

Smokefree (NHS)

Social Workers (British Association of)

Socialist Health Association

Sorted In 10

Sparks

Speech and Language Therapists (Royal College of)

Spinal Injuries Association

Spinal Injury Research, Rehabilitation & Reintegration (Association for)

Stillbirth & Neonatal Death Society

Stress Management Association (International)

Stroke Association

Sunsmart Campaign

Surgerydoor.co.uk

Tampon Alert (Alice Kilvert)

Teenage Cancer Trust

Tenovus

Terrence Higgins Trust

Thalidomide Society (UK)

The White Ribbon Alliance

Tinnitus Association (British)

Tisserand Aromatherapy Institute

Tommy's, the baby charity

Tranquillisers, Antidepressants and Painkillers (Council for Information on)

Tropical Diseases (Hospital for)

Tuberous Sclerosis Association

Vision Aid Overseas

Vitiligo Society

Voice for Choice

Voices in the Wilderness UK

WellBeing of Women

Wessex Cancer Trust

Williams Syndrome Foundation (UK)

Willow Foundation

World AIDS Day

World Health Organisation

Yoga (Iyengar Institute)

Young People with ME (Association of)

Your Life

Youthhealthtalk

# Heritage

1901 Census for England & Wales

An Taisce

Ancient Buildings (Society for the Protection of)

Ancient Monument Society

Ancient Tree forum

Antiquaries of London (Society of)

Archaeology (Council for British)

Archaeology Abroad

Archaeology Scotland

Archéire

Architectural Heritage Fund

Arms and Armour Society

Army Museum (National)

ArtWatch UK

Black History Month

Brontë Society

Cadw

Cambridge Past, Present & Future

Churches Conservation Trust

Civic Society Initiative

Community Pubs Foundation

Crown Estates

Culture, Media & Sport (Department for)

Cutty Sark Trust

English Heritage

Family Search

FreeBMD

Friends of Friendless Churches

Garden History Society

Gardens Scheme Charitable Trust (National)

Genealogists (Society of)

Georgian Group

Heraldry Society

Heraldry Society of Scotland

Heritage Lottery Fund

Heritage Railway Association

Historic Houses Association

Historic Scotland

Historical Association

Historical Maritime Society

History World

ICON

Landmark Trust

Local History (British Association for)

Museums (International Council of)

National Archives

National Archives of Scotland (NAS)

National Churches Trust

National Trust

Natural Heritage (Scottish)

Open-City

Oral History Society

Preservation Trusts (UK Association of)

Public Monuments & Sculpture Association

Royal Airforce Museum Cosford

Royal Airforce Museum London

Royal Naval Museum

Royal Parks

SCRAN

Sealed Knot Ltd.

Shakespeare Birthplace Trust

Sundial Society (British)

Surname Profiler

Theatres Trust

Twentieth Century Society

Vatican

Venice in Peril Fund

Victorian Society

Weights & Measures Association (British)

Women's Archive of Wales

Woodland Trust

Working Class Movement Library

World Monuments Fund in Britain

# Homeless and Housing

Albert Kennedy Trust

Alone in London

Big Issue

Borderline

Broadway

Building & Social Housing Foundation

Centrepoint

ChildHope UK

Community Self Build Agency

Crisis (UK)

Depaul International

Depaul Nightstop UK

Eaves Housing for Women

Ecology Building Society

Elderly Accommodation Counsel

Emmaus

Empty Homes Agency

Green Moves

Habitat for Humanity

Homeless International

Homeless Link

Housing (Chartered Institute of)

Housing (Confederation of Co-operative)

Housing Federation (National)

Housing Justice

Housing Ombudsman Service

Housing Policy (Centre for)

HousingCare.org

Joseph Rowntree Foundation

Net House Prices

PlanningAlerts.com

Refuge

Salvation Army

Shelter

Shine a Light

Simon Community

Squatters (Advisory Service for)

Tenant Participation Advisory Service for England

Town Planning Institute (Royal)

# Human Rights

Academic Freedom & Academic Standards (Council for)

African Initiatives

AMAR

Amnesty International

Anti-Slavery International

ARTICLE 19, The Global Campaign for Free Expression

Body Shop Foundation

Burma Campaign UK

Children's Rights

Children's Rights Alliance for England

Children's Society

Colombia Solidarity Campaign

Conscience

CRIN

Disability Action

EveryChild

Fair Trials International

Foreign Policy Centre

Forest Peoples Programme

Free the Children

Free Tibet Campaign

Freedom of Information (Campaign for)

Friends of Peoples Close to Nature

Global Witness

Gypsy Association

Howard League for Penal Reform

Human Fertilisation & Embryology Authority

Human Rights (British Institute of)

Human Rights (European Court of)

Human Rights Commission (N. Ireland)

Human Rights Education Association

Human Rights Policy (International Council on)

Human Rights Society

Human Rights Watch

Inclusive Education (Centre for Studies on)

Indigenous Tribal Peoples of the Tropical Forests (International Alliance of)

Individual Rights in Europe (Advice on)

Interact Worldwide

Interights

Islamic Human Rights Commission

JUSTICE

Kurdish Human Rights Project

Laogai Research Foundation

Liberty

Lilith Research and Development

Medical Aid for Palestinians

Medical Foundation for the Care of Victims of Torture

No Sweat

Ombudsman Association (British & Irish)

One World Action

Overseas Development Institute

Peace & Freedom (Women's International League for)

Peace Brigades International

Peace Pledge Union

People and Planet

Prisoners Abroad

Prisoners of Conscience Appeal Fund

Privacy International

Red Cross (British)

REDRESS

Refugee Council

Reporters sans Frontières

Simon Wiesenthal Centre

Solidar

Statewatch

Stonewall

Survival International

TAPOL

Tibet Society UK

Tibetan Nuns Project

Torture (Association for the Prevention of)

Torture (The World Organisation Against)

Transforming Conflict

UN High Commissioner for Human Rights
(Office of the)

United Nations Development Programme

Unlock Democracy

Voices in the Wilderness UK

Volunteer Action for Peace

War Resisters League

Womankind Worldwide

Women living under Muslim laws

World Civil Society Forum

World Development Movement

World Land Trust

# Industry and Employment

ACAS

Andrea Adams Trust

Anglo-German Foundation for the Study of
Industrial Society

Architects (Royal Institute of British)

Business, Innovation & Skills
(Department for )

Centre for Economic & Social Inclusion

Certification Office for Trade Unions and
Employers' Association

Children's Workforce Development Council

Community and Youth Workers Union

Co-operatives UK

Directors (Institute of)

Directory of Social Change

Education & Industry (Centre for)

Education and Training (Centre for the Study of)

Education of Travelling Communities
(European Federation for the)

Effective Dispute Resolution (Centre for)

Employment & Learning Northern Ireland
(Department for)

Employment Appeals Tribunal

Employment Research (Warwick Institute for)

Employment Rights (Institute of)

Employment Solicitors Online

Employment Studies (Institute for)

Employment Tribunals Service

Endeavour Training Limited

Engineering Council (UK)

Enterprise Education Trust

European Trade Union Confederation

Fawcett Society

Fitness Industry Association

Fredericks Foundation

Greater London Enterprise

Industrial Injuries Advisory Council

Jobcentre Plus

Labour Behind the Label

Labour Research Department

learndirect

Liberal Democrat Trade Unionists
(Association of)

Lifetracks

Mechanics Centre Ltd.

Motor Manufacturers & Traders Ltd. (Society of)

NHS Careers

No Sweat

Opportunity Now

Personnel & Development (Chartered
Institute of)

Practical Action

Public Concern at Work

Public Service Excellence (Association for)

Rathbone

REACH

Remploy

Safety Council Awards (British)

Sea Fish Industry Authority

Slivers of Time

Solidar

Tea Council Ltd.

Trade Union Rights (International Centre for)

Trade Unions Confederation (International)

Trades Union Congress

Travel and Tourism (Institute of)

Unite

Women and Manual Trades

Women's Engineering Society

Work Foundation

Workaholics Anonymous

Workers Educational Association

Working Families

Young Engineers

Young Enterprise

## Language

Alliance Française

Apples & Snakes

Arab-British Understanding (Council for)

Bilingualism, Languages, Literacies and Education Network

British Council

CILT

Cymdeithas yr Iaith Gymraeg

Daiwa Anglo-Japanese Foundation

English Association

English Speaking Union

Esperanto Association of Britain

Finnish Institute

Franco British Council (British Section)

Franco-Scottish Society of Scotland

Gaelic Books Council

Goethe Institut

Hispanic & Luso Brazilian Council

IATEFL

Italian Cultural Institute

Japan Foundation London Language Centre

Language Awareness (Association for)

Language Learning (Association for)

Linguists (Chartered Institute of)

Literacy in Primary Education (Centre for)

Makaton Vocabulary Development Project

Plain English Campaign

Scots Language Resource Centre

Spanish Embassy Education Office

Spanish Institute

Speakers Clubs (Association of)

Speech and Language Therapists (Royal College of)

Spelling Society (English)

Teaching English & Other Community Languages to Adults (National Association for)

Teaching of English (National Association for the)

Welsh Language Board (Bwrdd yr Iaith Gymraeg)

## Law

Advice Now

Advocacy After Fatal Domestic Abuse

Arbitrators (Chartered Institute of)

ARX Advocacy Resource Exchange

Attorney General's Office

Bar Council

Bar Pro Bono Unit and Bar in the Community

Black Police Association (National)

Cafcass

Catch22

Children are unbeatable

Children's Legal Centre

Citizenship and the Law (National Centre for)

Community Legal Advice

Court Service

Crime and Justice Studies (Centre for)

Crime Reduction

Crimestoppers

Criminal Cases Review Commission

Criminal Defence Service

Criminal Injuries Compensation Authority

Criminal Justice System

Crisis Counselling for Alleged Shoplifters

Crown Prosecution Service

Dignity in Dying

Disability Law Service

Domestic Violence (Campaign Against)

Drugs and Crime (UN Office on)

DVLA

Employment Solicitors Online

Environmental Law & Development (Foundation for International)

Environmental Law Foundation

European Court of Justice

Fair Trials International

Fathers4justice Ltd

Foreignprisoners.com

Friends at the end

Gun Control Network

Howard League for Penal Reform

Human Rights (European Court of)

Immigration & Asylum Tribunals Service

Immigration Law Practitioners Association

Immigration Services Commissioner (Office of the)

Independent Police Complaints Commission

Individual Rights in Europe (Advice on)

Interights

International Criminal Court

Interpol

Just for Kids

JUSTICE

Justice (Ministry of)

Law Centres Federation

Law Commission

Law Society of England & Wales

Legal Action Group

Legal Complaints Service

Legal Services Commission

Legal Services Ombudsman

Liberty

Magistrates Association

Metropolitan Police

Money Claim Online

Most Wanted

Old Bailey, London (Proceedings of) 1674 to 1834

Ombudsman Association (British & Irish)

Penal Reform International

Personal Injury Lawyers (Association of)

Police Federation (Scottish)

Police Federation of England & Wales

Police National Legal Database

Prison Advice & Care Trust (PACT)

Prison Reform Trust

Prison Studies (International Centre for)

Prisons and Probation Ombudsman for England and Wales

Probation Service (National)

Resolution

Rights of Women

Serious Fraud Office

Simple Free Law Advisor

Skills for Justice

SOCA (Serious Organised Crime Agency)

Solicitors for the Elderly

Special Educational Needs & Disability Tribunal

Statewatch

Trackoff

UNLOCK

Women Solicitors (Association of)

Youth Justice Board for England and Wales

## Library/Books/Publishing

American Library Association

ARKive

Art Library (National)

Authors' Licensing and Collecting Society

Bartleby.com

Bibliothèque Nationale de France

Big Read (The)

Bodleian Library

Book Aid International

Book Power

Book Trust (Scottish)

BookCrossing

Books Council (Welsh)

BOOKTRUST

British Library

British Library Sound Archive

Buddhist Society

Children's Book Groups (Federation of)

CILIP: the Chartered Institute of Library and
Information Professionals

ClearVision Project

Demos

Edinburgh International Book Festival

Editors and Proofreaders (Society for)

English PEN

Ethical Consumer Research Association &
ECRA Publishing Ltd.

Feminist Archive North

Folger Shakespeare Library

Frankfurt Book Fair

Gaelic Books Council

Hay Festival

Health Information Resources

Indexers (Society of)

Information Management (Association for)

InfoSearcher.com

INK

ipl2

Libraries for Life for Londoners

Library Campaign

Libri Trust

Listening Books

Literacy Association (UK)

London Library

Marx Memorial Library

Music Publishers Association

National Libraries (Friends of the)

National Library of Scotland

National Library of Wales

New Internationalist

Newspaper Library (British Library)

Nobel Internet Archive

People's Network

Poetry Library

Project Gutenberg

Psychical Research (Society for)

Questionpoint

Reading Agency

RNIB National Library Service

School Librarianship (International
Association of)

School Library Association

Searchlight Magazine

Seven Stories

Siobhan Dowd Trust

Storytelling (Society for)

Women in Publishing

Women's Archive of Wales

Women's Library

Working Class Movement Library

Writers' Guild of Great Britain

## Media

Adbusters
Advertising Association
Advertising Standards Authority
Al-Jazeera
BBC
BBC Backstage Tours
BBC News
BBC Online
BBC Schools
BBC Studio Audiences
BBC World Service
Blogger
British Film Institute
Broadcasting Trust (International)
Channel 4
Cinema & Popular Culture (The Bill Douglas Centre for the History of)
Commonwealth Broadcasting Association
Community Media Association
Concord Media
Deaf Broadcasting Council
Editors and Proofreaders (Society for)
Educational Recording Agency
English and Media Centre
Extreme Inequality
Film & Television Archive (Northern Region)
Film and Television School (National)
Film Classification (British Board of)
Film Education
Film London
First Light
Five
Hospital Broadcasting Association
Index on Censorship
Indexers (Society of)

INK
ITN
Learning Zone
Media Center (Independent)
Media for Development
Media Trust
MediaWise Trust
Movie Review Query Engine
New Internationalist
Newspaper Library (British Library)
Nominet UK
OFCOM
Paperboy
Phonepay Plus
photoLondon
Press and Broadcasting Freedom (Campaign for)
Press Association
Press Complaints Commission
Radio Society of GB
Recording Services (Association of Professional)
Reporters sans Frontières
S4C
Science Centre (Glasgow)
Sky
Talking Newspaper Association
UK Film Council
Undercurrents
Video Standards Council
Voice of the Listener and Viewer

## Mental Health

Action Postpartum Psychosis
Albany Trust
Anxiety Care
Anxiety UK

Behavioural & Cognitive Psychotherapies (British Association of)

Brainwave

CALM

Care Quality Commission

Child and Adolescent Mental Health (Association for)

Combat Stress

Depression Alliance

Down's Syndrome Educational Trust

Educational Psychologists (Association of)

First Steps to Freedom

Learning Disabilities (The Foundation for People with)

MDF The Bipolar Organisation

Mencap

Mencap Cymru

Mencap Northern Ireland

Mental Health (Scottish Association for)

Mental Health Foundation

Mental Welfare Commission for Scotland

MIND

No Panic

OCD Action

Office of the Public Guardian

PAPYRUS (Prevention of Suicides)

Psychological Society (British)

Psychotherapists (British Association of)

Psychotherapy (UK Council for)

Rethink

SANE

Seasonal Affective Disorder Association

SEBDA

Triumph over Phobia (TOP UK)

Turning Point

Women's Therapy Centre

Workaholics Anonymous

YoungMinds

# Money

Bank of England (Damaged and Mutilated Banknotes)

Career Development Loans

European Central Bank

Heritage Lottery Fund

International Monetary Fund

Jubilee Debt Campaign

Low Pay Commission

Moneysavingexpert.com

My Supermarket

MyBnk

Net House Prices

Office of the Public Guardian

Personal Finance Education Group

Slivers of Time

# Museums/Galleries

Apsley House Wellington Museum

Army Museum (National)

Ashmolean Museum

BALTIC

Bank of England Museum

Barbican Gallery

Beamish

Big Pit

British Museum

Bugatti Trust

Burrell Collection

Childhood (Museum of)

Courtauld Institute Gallery

Culture24

Cutty Sark Trust

Design Museum

Dulwich Picture Gallery

Eureka!

Fitzwilliam Museum

Football Museum (National)

Football Museum (Scottish)

Glass Centre (National)

Great buildings

Hayward Gallery

Henry Moore Foundation

Imperial War Museum

Imperial War Museum

Imperial War Museum

Imperial War Museum London

Institute of Contemporary Arts

Ironbridge Gorge Museum

Jewish Museum

Jodrell Bank Observatory

Kids in museums

London (Museum of)

London's Transport Museum

Lowry

Magna: science adventure centre

Manchester Museum

Maritime Museum (National)

Mining Museum (Scottish)

Museum Net

Museums (International Council of)

National Gallery

National Gallery of Scotland

National Media Museum

National Museum and Gallery Cardiff

National Portrait Gallery

Natural History Museum

People's History Museum

Railway Museum (National)

Royal Academy of Arts

Royal Airforce Museum Cosford

Royal Airforce Museum London

Royal Armouries Museum

Royal Institution & Michael Faraday Museum

Royal Naval Museum

Royal Observatory Greenwich

Royal Scottish Academy

Rugby Museum

Science and Industry in Manchester (Museum of)

Science Museum

Scotland (Museum of)

Scottish National Gallery of Modern Art

Scottish National Portrait Gallery

SCRAN

Seven Stories

Space Centre (National)

Tate Britain

Tate Liverpool

Tate Modern

Tate St Ives

The British Monarchy (The official website of)

The Deep

Vatican Museums & Sistine Chapel

Waterways Museum (National)

# Music

*refer also to the section on Dance Drama, Music & Performing Arts Schools*

Associated Board of the Royal Schools of Music

Barbershop Singers (British Association of)

BKA

Cello Society

Channel Arts Association

Children's Orchestra (National)

Choir Schools Association

CoMA

Don't lose the music

EMI Music Sound Foundation

English National Opera

European Youth Music Week

Festivals (British & International Federation of )

Guitar Foundation & Festivals (International)

Live Music Now!

London Charity Orchestra

London Symphony Orchestra

Making Music

Midi Music Company

Music and the Deaf

Music Council (National)

Music Educators (National Association of)

Music for Youth

Music Publishers Association

Music Therapy (British Society for)

Musicians (Incorporated Society of)

Musicians Union

Natural Voice

NODA

Orchestras (Association of British)

Passion for Jazz

Professional Music Therapists (Association of)

Raw Material Music and Media

Royal Academy of Music

Royal Opera

Schools Music Association of Great Britain

Scottish Opera

Songwriters, Composers and Authors (British Academy of)

Sound and Music

Sound Sense

SoundJunction

Suzuki Institute (British)

Voices Foundation

Welsh National Opera

Young Concert Artists Trust

Youth Choir of Great Britain (National)

Youth Music

Youth Music Theatre (National)

Youth Orchestra (National of GB)

# Older People

Age

Age Exchange

Anchor Trust

Contact the Elderly

Counsel and Care

Elder Abuse (Action on)

Elderly Accommodation Counsel

Elders (The)

Grandparents Plus

HousingCare.org

Pensioners Convention (National)

Policy on Ageing (Centre for)

Relatives & Residents Association

Ricability

Solicitors for the Elderly

Third Age Trust

# Politics

10 Downing Street Website

Adam Smith Institute

Bevan Foundation

Cabinet Office

Christian Socialist Movement

Citizenship (Institute for)

Civitas

Colombia Solidarity Campaign

Conscience

Conservative Party

Co-operative Party

Cuba Solidarity Campaign

Democracy and Electoral Assistance (International Institute for)

Demos

Elders (The)

Electoral Reform Services

Electoral Reform Society

EMILY'S LIST UK

European Parliamentary Labour Party

Fabian Society

Free Tibet Campaign

Freedom Association

Green Party

Hansard Society

Hear From Your MP

House of Lords

Labour Party

Labour Research Department

Labour Women's Network

Law Society of Scotland

Liberal Democrat Trade Unionists
(Association of)

Liberal Democrats

Make My Vote Count

Martin Luther King Center

Marx Memorial Library

Media Center (Independent)

Monetary Justice (Christian Council for)

Nicaragua Solidarity Campaign

No candidate deserves my vote

Operation Black Vote

Parliament

Plaid Cymru - The Party of Wales

Policy Studies (Centre for)

Policy Studies Institute

Political Studies Association

Public Policy Research (Institute for)

Public Whip

Racism and Fascism (Campaign Against)

Schumacher UK

Searchlight Magazine

Smith Institute

SNP

Social Democratic & Labour Party

Social Market Foundation

Socialist Health Association

Socialist Labour Party

Southern Africa (Action for)

TheyWorkForYou.com

Tibet Society UK

Unite Against Fascism

Unlock Democracy

USA President

Welsh Assembly Government

World Civil Society Forum

WriteToThem.com

# Poverty

Action Aid

Afghanaid

Birmingham Settlement

Brazil's Children Trust (Action for)

CARE International UK

Child Poverty Action Group

Chronic Poverty Research Centre

Church Action on Poverty

Comic Relief

Concern Worldwide

e-Learning Foundation

Ethiopiaid

Family Holiday Association

International Development (Department for)

Islamic Relief

Kiva

National Debtline

One World Action

Poverty (UK Coalition Against)

Practical Action

Shine a Light

Sustain

Taskforce for the Rural Poor (International)

TaxAid

War on Want

Water Aid

## Prisoners

Amnesty International
Crime and Justice Studies (Centre for)
English PEN
Foreignprisoners.com
Hibiscus
HM Prison Service
Howard League for Penal Reform
Human Writes
INQUEST
Inside Out Trust
Nacro
New Bridge
Penal Reform International
Prison Advice & Care Trust (PACT)
Prison Reform Trust
Prison Service NI
Prison Studies (International Centre for)
Prison Visitors (National Association of Official)
Prisoners Abroad
Prisoners of Conscience Appeal Fund
Prisoners' Advice Service
Prisoners' Families (Action for)
Prisoners' Families and Friends Service
Prisons and Probation Ombudsman for England and Wales
Probation Service (National)
SACRO
SOVA
UNLOCK
Women in Prison

## Race

100 Black Men of London
Anne Frank Trust UK
Artists Against Racism
Asian People's Disability Alliance
Black Environment Network
Black History Month
Black Police Association (National)
Black Students Alliance (National)
CEMVO
DIALOG
Equality and Human Rights Commission
Equality Britain
Ethnic Relations (Centre for Research in)
Football Unites, Racism Divides
Heartstone
Intermix
Kick It Out
Martin Luther King Center
NABSS
Operation Black Vote
Race Equality Foundation
Race Relations (Institute of)
Racism (National Assembly Against)
Racism and Fascism (Campaign Against)
Racism in Europe (Youth Against)
Runnymede Trust
Show Racism the Red Card
Stephen Lawrence Charitable Trust
UK New Citizen

# Refugees and Immigration

AMAR
Asylum Aid
Immigrants (Joint Council for the Welfare of)
Immigration & Asylum Tribunals Service
Immigration Advisory Service
Immigration Aid Unit (Greater Manchester)
Immigration Law Practitioners Association
Immigration Services Commissioner (Office of the)
Racism (National Assembly Against)
Refugee Council
Refugees & Exiles (European Council on)
Refugees (Student Action for)
Refugees (US Committee for)
UK Border Agency
UNHCR

# Relationships

Broken Rainbow
Dad's House
Divorced & Separated (National Council for the)
Family Therapy (Institute of)
Fatherhood Institute
Grandparents' Association
Honour Network (The)
Intermix
It's not your fault
Leap Confronting Conflict
MALE
ManKind Initiative
Relationships Scotland

RESPECT
Shared Parenting Information Group
Solo Clubs (National Federation of)
Young Father's Initiative

# Religion and Beliefs

Arthur Rank Centre
Astrological and Psychic Society (British)
Bible Society
British Jews ( Board of Deputies of)
Buddhist Centre, North London
Buddhist Information Network
Buddhist Society
Catholic Agency to Support Evangelisation
Catholic Education Service
Christian Education
Christian Socialist Movement
Christian Teachers (Association of)
Christians and Jews (Council of)
Church Army
Church Mission Society
Church of England
Church of England Education Division
Churches Together in Britain and Ireland
Clear Vision Trust
Cult Information Centre
Day One Christian Ministries
Evangelical Alliance
Findhorn Foundation
Hindu Universe – Hindu Resource Center
Humanist Association (British)
Inform
Integrated Education (N. Ireland Council for)
Inter Faith Network for the UK
Islamic Human Rights Commission
Jewish Women (League of)
Life
MAYC
Methodist Church

Muslim Schools UK (Association of)

Muslim Welfare House

Muslim Women's Helpline

National Churches Trust

Nil by Mouth

Quakers in Britain

Reform Judaism (Movement for)

Religious Education (Professional Council for)

REonline

Salvation Army

Secular Society (National)

Sikh Organisations UK (Network of)

Tearfund

The Sikh Way

Tibetan Nuns Project

Time for God

UK Islamic Education Waqf

United Reformed Church

Urban Saints

Vatican

Women living under Muslim laws

Young Christian Workers

Youth for Christ

## Research

1901 Census for England & Wales

Alcohol & Health Research Unit

Alcohol Education and Research Council

Atmospheric Research (US National Center for)

Australian Bureau of Statistics

AVERT

Biotechnology & Biological Sciences Research Council

Brain & Spine Foundation

Cancer Research UK

CEH

Cinema & Popular Culture (The Bill Douglas Centre for the History of)

Climb

Economic & Social Research (National Institute of)

Education Index (British)

Education Statistics (USA National Center for)

Elm Farm Research Centre

Ergonomics Society

Ethnic Relations (Centre for Research in)

Feminist Archive North

Fiscal Studies (Institute for)

Folger Shakespeare Library

Football Industry Group

Friedrich Ebert Foundation

Garden Organic

Government Actuary's Department

Health Research & Development (Foundation for Women's)

Human Genetics Commission

Humane Research Trust

Indian Census

International Affairs (Royal Institute of)

JANET

Jeans for Genes

Joseph Rowntree Foundation

King's Fund

Leukaemia and Lymphoma Research

Life (Centre for)

Linnean Society of London

Lucy Faithfull Foundation

Marine Life Study Society (British)

Medical Research Charities (Association of)

Medical Research Council

Meningitis Research Foundation

Mycological Society (British)

National Archives

National Archives of Scotland (NAS)

Natural Environment Research Council

New Economics Foundation

NFER

NOAH

Nobel Internet Archive

Ocean Mammal Institute

Old Bailey, London (Proceedings of) 1674
to 1834

Optimum Nutrition (Institute for)

Overseas Development Institute

Pain Relief Foundation

Policy Studies (Centre for)

Policy Studies Institute

Political Studies Association

Population Statistics

Psychical Research (Society for)

Public Management and Policy Association

Public Policy Research (Institute for)

Royal Institution & Michael Faraday Museum

Rural Research (Centre for)

Saferworld

Saving Faces

Seriously Ill for Medical Research

Snow and Ice Data Center (National)

Social & Economic Research (Institute for)

Social Issues Research Centre

Social Market Foundation

Soil Association

Stammering Children (Michael Palin Centre for)

Statistics New Zealand

Suzy Lamplugh Trust

Tommy's, the baby charity

UKAEA

Understanding Animal Research

Unistats

Vitiligo Society

WATCh?

WellBeing of Women

Worldometers

Young People in Focus

# Safety/Accidents/Injury

Airsafe.com

Arson Prevention Bureau

Back-up Trust

BASIC

Bibic

Bicycle Helmet Initiative Trust

Brake

Casualties Union

Child Accident Prevention Trust

Child Brain Injury Trust

Consumers International

Criminal Injuries Compensation Authority

Domestic Violence (Campaign Against)

Drinking Water Inspectorate

Ergonomics Society

Fire Brigade (London)

Fire Protection Authority

Firework Safety (National Campaign for)

Floodline

Food Commission

Food Standards Agency

Foreign and Commonwealth Office Travel
Advice

Get Safe Online

Global Road Safety (Campaign for)

HEADWAY

Health & Safety Executive

Heritage Railway Association

Industrial Injuries Advisory Council

Infant Deaths (Foundation for the Study of)

Internet Watch Foundation

Kidscape

Let's Face It

Lifeguard Skills

Lifesavers

Living Streets

London Hazards Centre

Medical Accidents (Action Against)

Medicines & Healthcare Products Regulatory Agency

Navigation (Royal Institute of)

Occupational Safety & Health (Institution of)

Personal Injury Lawyers (Association of)

Pesticide Action Network UK

Placement Survival Guide

Refuge

RoadPeace

RoSPA

Royal National Lifeboat Institution

Safety Council (British)

Safety Council Awards (British)

Simon Jones Memorial Campaign

SmartParent

Spinal Injuries Association

Spinal Injury Research, Rehabilitation & Reintegration (Association for)

sportscotland Avalanche Information Service

Surf Life Saving Association of GB

Sustrans

Sustrans Cymru

Sustrans Northern Ireland

Sustrans Scotland

Suzy Lamplugh Trust

Traffic Statistics (Global)

Transport Safety (Parliamentary Advisory Council for)

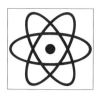

# Science

Anthropological Institute of GB & Ireland (Royal)

Astronomical Association (British)

Atmospheric Research (US National Center for)

Bioethics (Nuffield Council on)

Biological Diversity (Convention on)

Biology (Society of)

Biotechnology & Biological Sciences Research Council

Botanical Society of British Isles

CASE - Campaign for Science and Engineering

Chemistry (Royal Society of)

Climate Change (Intergovernmental Panel on)

Computer Society (British)

Computing Centre (National)

CREST Awards

Earthwatch Europe

Eden Project

Energy Foundation (National)

Exploratorium

FRAME

Genetic Alliance UK

Geological Survey (British)

Geological Survey (US)

Geologists Association

GM Freeze

Heat is Online

Human Genetics Commission

Intellect

Jodrell Bank Observatory

Life (Centre for)

Linnean Society of London

Magna: science adventure centre

Met Office

Meteorological Organization (World)

Millennium Seed Bank

Mongabay.com

Mycological Society (British)

Nuclear Tourist

Nutrition Society

Our Dynamic Earth

Pharmaceutical Society (Royal)

Physics (Institute of)

Popular Astronomy (Society for)

Psychical Research (Society for)

Royal Botanic Garden Edinburgh

Royal Botanic Gardens, Kew

Royal Institution & Michael Faraday Museum

Royal Observatory Greenwich

Royal Society

SCIcentre

Science and Industry in Manchester (Museum of)

Science Association (British)

Science Centre (Glasgow)

Science Education (Association for)

Science Education (Centre for)

Science in the Public Interest (Center for)

Science Museum

Science, Technology & the Arts (National Endowment for)

Scientists for Global Responsibility

Solar Energy Society

Space Agency (European)

Space Centre (National)

Telescope (Bradford Robotic)

UNESCO

Weights & Measures Association (British)

Women Into Science & Engineering (WISE)

World Space Week

## Sexual Issues

AIDS Trust (National)

Albany Trust

Albert Kennedy Trust

AVERT

Beaumont Society

Body Positive

Crossroads Women's Centre

HIFY-UK

HIV/Aids Alliance (International)

Lesbian and Gay Switchboard (London)

Lesbian Information Service

Lesbians & Gays (Families & Friends of)

likeitis.org

Lucy Faithfull Foundation

Mankind UK

Mermaids

PACE

Positively UK

Sexual Advice Association

Sorted In 10

Stonewall

Terrence Higgins Trust

Thesite

Your Life

## Sport and Leisure

Activity Holiday Association (British)

Adventure Activities Licensing Authority

Aikido Board (British)

Allotment and Leisure Gardeners Ltd. (National Society of)

Amateur Athletic Association

Amateur Boxing Association of England Ltd.

Amateur Boxing Scotland

Angling Trust

Archery GB

Arms and Armour Society

Army Cadet Force

Artistic Roller Skating (Federation of)

Athletic Association (English Schools)

Athletics Federations (International Association of)

Backpackers Club

Back-up Trust

Badminton England

Balloon and Airship Club (British)

Basketball Association (English)

BBC Backstage Tours

Bike Events

Bike Express (European)

Blind Golf Association (English)

Blind Sport (British)

Bowling Association Ltd (English Indoor)

Boys Brigade

British Rowing

Business in Sport & Leisure

Camping and Caravanning Club

Canoe Association (Scottish)

Canoe Union (British)

Caravan Club

Caving Association (British)

Ceroc

Chess Association (Braille)

Chess Association (English Primary Schools)

Chess Federation (English)

Chess Scotland

Chess Union (Ulster)

Chess Union (Welsh)

Child Protection in Sport Unit

Church Lads' and Church Girls' Brigade

Circus Sensible/Circus School

Circus Space

Cirdan Sailing Trust

Clubs for Young People (National Association of)

Commonwealth Games Federation

Countryside Alliance

CP Sport

Cricinfo

Cricket Board (England & Wales)

Croquet Association

Crown Green Bowling Association (British)

Crufts Dog Show

Cruising Association

CTC

Culture, Media & Sport (Department for)

Cyclenation

Cycling (British)

Cycling Association (Welsh)

Cycling Centre (National)

Cycling Projects

Cycling Union (International)

Cyclists' Federation (European)

Dancesport UK

Deaf Sports Council (British)

Disability Snowsport UK

Disability Sport (English Federation of)

Disability Sport (Events)

Elastic Rope Sports Association (British)

Ellen MacArthur Trust

England Hockey

England Squash & Racketball

Exercise, Movement and Dance Partnership

Family Holiday Association

Fell Runners Association

Fencing (British Academy of)

Fencing Association (British)

Fields in Trust – FIT

FIFA

Fitness Industry Association

Fitness League

Fitness N. Ireland

Flower Arranging Societies (National Association of)

Football Association

Football Association (English Schools)

Football Foundation

Football Industry Group

Football League (Scottish)

Football Museum (National)

Football Supporters Federation

Football Unites, Racism Divides

Girlguiding UK

Girls' Brigade

Girls' Venture Corps Air Cadets

Give Us Back Our Game

Gliding Association (British)

Go4awalk

Golf Association (European)

Gymnastics (British)

Handball Association (English)

Handball Association (Scottish)

Hang Gliding and Paragliding Association (British)

HELP

Hostelling (Internet Guide to)

Hostelling International

Ice Hockey UK

Ice Skating Association UK Ltd (National)

International Olympic Committee

Jewish Lads' & Girls' Brigade (JLGB)

Judo Association (British)

Judo Scotland

Ju-Jitsu Association GB National Governing Body (British)

Karate and Martial Art Schools (National Association of)

Karate Board (N. Ireland)

Karate Governing Body Ltd (Welsh)

Keep Fit Association

Kennel Club

Kick It Out

Kickboxing and Karate Association (World)

Kite Society of Great Britain

Lacrosse Association (English)

Ladies' Golf Union

Lake District Weather Line

Lawn Tennis Association

Lidos

Lifesavers

Long Distance Walkers Association

Marathon (Virgin London)

Marine Leisure Association (MLA)

Marine Society and Sea Cadets

Martial Association (Amateur)

MCC

Medau

Mountain Leader Training England

Mountaineering Council (British)

National Trust Holiday Cottages

Netball Association (All England)

Ocean Youth Trust

Olympic Association (British)

Orienteering Federation (British)

Outdoor Learning (Institute for)

Outward Bound Trust

Parachute Association (British)

Paralympic Association (British)

Photographic Society of Great Britain (Royal)

Physical Education (Association for)

Physical Recreation (Central Council of)

Pilates Foundation

Play England

PLAYLINK

Plus

Pony Club

Pool Association (English)

Professional Footballers Association

Professional Golfers' Association

Quilters' Guild of the British Isles

Ramblers' Association

Riding for the Disabled Association

Rifle Association (National)

Road Runners Club

Roller Hockey Association of England Ltd. (National)

Rona Sailing Project

Royal Botanic Garden Edinburgh

Royal Botanic Gardens, Kew

Royal Mint (British)

Rugby Football League

Rugby Football Union

Rugby Football Union for Women

RYA Sailability

Sand & Land Yacht Clubs (British Federation of)

Scottish Athletics Ltd

Scottish Cycling

Scout Association

Scrum.com

Sea Ranger Association

Sealed Knot Ltd.

Show Jumping Association (British)

Show Racism the Red Card

Ski Club of Great Britain

Skylight Circus Arts

Solo Clubs (National Federation of)

Sparks

Speakers Clubs (Association of)

Special Olympics GB

Sport England

Sport Northern Ireland

Sport Wales

Sports Association for People with Learning Disabilities (UK)

Sports Centre (Lilleshall National)

Sports Coach UK

Sports Leaders UK

SportsAid

sportscotland

sportscotland Avalanche Information Service

Sub Aqua Club (British)

Surf Life Saving Association of GB

Surfers Against Sewage

Surfing Association (British)

Swimming

Swimming Clubs for the Handicapped (National Association of)

Table Tennis Association (English)

Tai Chi Finder

Tai Chi Union for GB

Tall Ships Youth Trust

Tandem Club

Tour de France

Tourism for All

Triathlon Association (British)

UEFA

UK Sport

UK Youth

Universities and Colleges Sport (British)

Venuemasters

Volleyball Association (English)

Walking Federation (British)

Walkit

WalkScotland

Water Ski & Wakeboard (British)

Welsh Athletics

WheelPower

Wimbledon

Wind Sand & Stars

Windsurfing Association (UK)

Women's Bowling Federation (English)

Women's Golf Association (English)

Women's Sports & Fitness Foundation

Woodcraft Folk

Woodworking Federation (British)

World Cup

World Ju-Jitsu Federation (Ireland)

World Travel & Tourism Council

Yachting Association (Royal)

YMCA (National Council of)

Yoga (British Wheel of)

Yoga (Iyengar Institute)

Young Farmers' Clubs (National Federation of)

Youth Hostel Association (England & Wales) Ltd

Youth Sport Trust

YWCA England & Wales

# Technology

Access Art
Alternative Technology (Centre for)
BECTA
Bibliomania
Blogger
Computer Aid International
Computer Society (British)
Computers 4 Africa
Computing Centre (National)
Cyber Mentors
Design and Technology Association
e-Learning Foundation
Get Safe Online
Information Commissioner's Office
InfoSearcher.com
Intellect
Internet Watch Foundation
ipl2
Jodrell Bank Observatory
My Supermarket
Nominet UK
People's Network
Popular Astronomy (Society for)
Recording Services (Association of Professional)
Redundant Technology Initiative
Science, Technology & the Arts (National Endowment for)
Scientists for Global Responsibility
SmartParent
Space Agency (European)
Space Centre (National)
Specialist Schools and Academies Trust
TAG
Technology Means Business
Telephone Directories On Web
Telescope (Bradford Robotic)
Telework Association
UKAEA
Wired Safety
World Space Week

# Transport

Aeronautical Society (Royal)
Air Transport Users' Council
AirportWatch
Airsafe.com
Automobile Association (AA)
Balloon and Airship Club (British)
Better Transport (Campaign for)
Bicycle Helmet Initiative Trust
Bikers with a Disability (National Association for)
Blue Badge Network
Brake
Bus Users UK
CADD
Choose Climate
Community Rail Partnerships (Association of)
Community Transport Association
Cyclenation
Cycling Campaign (London)
Cycling Projects
DVLA
Environmental Transport Association
Global Road Safety (Campaign for)
Heritage Railway Association
Inland Waterways Association
Liftshare.com Ltd
Light Rail Transit Authority
Living Streets
Logistics and Transport in the UK (Chartered Institute of)
London Travel Information

Mobilise

Mobility Information Service

Motorvations Project

Multimap

Navigation (Royal Institute of)

Passenger Focus

Passenger Transport UK (Confederation of)

Port of London Authority

RAC

Rail Enquiries (National)

Rail Europe

Rail Regulation (Office of)

Railfuture

Reclaim the Streets

Road Haulage Association

RoadPeace

School Journey Association

Shopmobility (National Federation of)

Sustrans

Sustrans Cymru

Sustrans Northern Ireland

Sustrans Scotland

Traffic Statistics (Global)

Trainline

Transport & Environment (European Federation for)

Transport for London

Transport Safety (Parliamentary Advisory Council for)

WalesRails

Waterway Recovery Group

Couch Surfing Project

Country Holidays for Inner City Children

Currency converter

Cycling Union (International)

Ecotourism Society (The International)

Fit for Travel

Foreign and Commonwealth Office Travel Advice

Geographic Society (National)

Hostelling (Internet Guide to)

Journeywoman.com

London Travel Information

Multimap

Ordnance Survey

Passport Office

Royal Parks

Tour Operators (Association of Independent)

Tourism Concern

Tourism Offices Worldwide Directory

Travel and Tourism (Institute of)

Travel Warnings (US State Department)

Tropical Diseases (Hospital for)

Visit England

Visit London

Visit Scotland

Visit Wales

VisitBritain

WalesRails

Winston Churchill Memorial Trust

World Tourism Organization

World Travel & Tourism Council

Youth Hostel Association (England & Wales) Ltd

# Travel & Tourism

ABTA

Berlin - Info

Bike Express (European)

Brathay Exploration Group

Choose Climate

# Volunteers

Africa and Asia Venture
An Taisce
Army Cadet Force
ATD Fourth World
BOND
BTCV
Casualties Union
CEMVO
Chartered Surveyors Voluntary Service
Children in Need Appeal
Cinnamon Trust
Community Service Volunteers (CSV)
Community Transport Association
Contact the Elderly
Couch Surfing Project
Cross Cultural Solutions
CSV Education for Citizenship
Depaul Nightstop UK
Directory of Social Change
Do it
Friendship Works
Get connected
Girlguiding UK
Habitat for Humanity
International Service
IVS
Jewish Lads' & Girls' Brigade (JLGB)
Jewish Women (League of)
Lattitude Global Volunteering
Lesbians & Gays (Families & Friends of)
LINK
Mercy Corps
NOAH
Pets as Therapy
Prince's Trust (Head Office)

Prison Visitors (National Association of Official)
Project Trust
Quaker Voluntary Action
REACH
REMAP
Restless Development
Royal National Lifeboat Institution
RSVP/CSV
Self Unlimited
Simon Community
SOVA
Time for God
Toc H
Tools for Self Reliance
United Nations Volunteers
Voluntary Action (Wales Council for)
Voluntary Agencies (International Council of)
Voluntary and Community Action (National Association for)
Voluntary Arts Network
Voluntary Organisations (National Council for) (NCVO)
Voluntary Organisations (Scottish Council for)
Voluntary Youth Services (National Council for)
Volunteer Action for Peace
Volunteer Development Scotland
Volunteer Now
Volunteer Reading Help
Volunteering England
Volunteers For Rural India
VSO
Waterway Recovery Group
Working For A Charity
Worldwide Volunteering
WRVS
WWOOF Association (International)
Year Out Group
Young Enterprise
Youth Council (British)
Youth in Action

# War & Conflict

Abolition of War (Movement for the)

Aegis Trust

Army (British)

British Legion (Royal)

Campaign Against Arms Trade

Children and War

CND

Combat Stress

Conscience

Control Arms

Defence (Ministry of)

Echo

Elders (The)

Forgiveness Project

Gulf Veterans & Families Association (National)

HALO Trust

Imperial War Museum

Imperial War Museum

International Criminal Court

Landmine Action

Landmines (International Campaign to Ban)

Mine Action Service (UN)

Mines Advisory Group

Miracles

Navy (US)

Pax Christi

Peace Brigades International

Peace Pledge Union

Royal Air Force

Royal Navy

Saferworld

War Resisters League

# Women

Action Postpartum Psychosis

AIMS

Birth Trauma Association

Black Women for Wages for Housework

Black Women's Rape Action Project

Bowling Association Ltd (English Indoor)

Breast Cancer Care

Business & Professional Women UK Ltd

CAMFED International

Crossroads Women's Centre

Daisy Network

Eaves Housing for Women

EMILY'S LIST UK

Endometriosis UK

Feminist Archive North

Full Time Mothers

GFS Platform for Young Women

Health Research & Development (Foundation for Women's)

Hibiscus

Jewish Women (League of)

Journeywoman.com

Labour Women's Network

Ladies' Golf Union

Lavender Trust

Lilith Research and Development

Margaret Pyke Family Planning Centre

MATCH

Meet A Mum Association

Mothers Union

Muslim Women's Helpline

Opportunity Now

Peace & Freedom (Women's International League for)

Positively UK

Post-natal illness (Association for)

Premenstrual Syndrome (National Association for)

Rape Crisis

Refuge

Rights of Women

Rugby Football Union for Women

Sea Ranger Association

Tampon Alert (Alice Kilvert)

Winvisible (Women with visible & invisible disabilities)

Womankind Worldwide

Women (National Assembly of)

Women and Manual Trades

Women Entrepreneurs (British Association of)

Women in Prison

Women in Publishing

Women Into Science & Engineering (WISE)

Women living under Muslim laws

Women of Great Britain (National Council of)

Women Working Worldwide

Women's Archive of Wales

Women's Bowling Federation (English)

Women's Food & Farming Union

Women's Golf Association (English)

Women's Library

Women's Resource Centre

Women's Sports & Fitness Foundation

Women's Aid (Scottish)

Women's Clubs (National Association of)

Women's Engineering Society

Women's Environmental Network

Women's Institutes (National Federation of)

Women's National Commission

Women's Register (National)

Women's Therapy Centre

WRVS

YWCA England & Wales

# Organisations

Before contacting an organisation, check first whether your library has information. Most organisations which include British, National, International, Association, Society etc in their names have been placed in order by the key word in the name except where such a change would make the name unfamiliar or more difficult to find.

**1 Voice**
PO Box 559  Halifax HX1 2XT
Tel: 0845 330 7862
info@1voice.info
www.1Voice.info
Network and support for children and families using communication aids

**10 Downing Street Website**
www.number10.gov.uk
Interactive information from Prime Minister's Department

**100 Black Men of London**
The Bridge  12-16 Clerkenwell Road London EC1M 5PQ
Tel: 08701214100
info@100bmol.org.uk
Charity dedicated to the education, development and uplifting of our youth and the wider community

**10:10**
PO Box 64749  London  NW1W 8HE
020 7388 6688
hello@1010uk.org
www.1010global.org
www.1010uk.org
Project to unite every sector of British society behind one simple idea

**1901 Census for England & Wales**
www.1901censusonline.com

**24 hour museum** now see Culture24

**4Children**
City Reach  5 Greenwich View Place London E14 9NN
Helpline: 020 7512 2100
Tel: 020 7512 2112
info@4children.org.uk
www.4children.org.uk
National charity which promotes out of school hours child care

# A

**AAA** see Amateur Athletic Association

**ABA** see Amateur Boxing Association

**ABCUL** see Credit Unions (Association of British)

**Abolition of War (Movement for the)**
11 Venetia Road  London N4 1EJ
Tel: 01908 511948
email via website
www.abolishwar.org.uk

**Abortion** see also ARC, Education for Choice, Life, Unborn Children (Society for the Protection of)

**Abortion Campaign (National)** now see Abortion Rights

**Abortion Law Reform Association** now see Abortion Rights

**Abortion Rights**
18 Ashwin Street  London E8 3DL
Tel: 020 7923 9792
email via website
www.abortionrights.org.uk
Campaigns for equal access to safe, legal, free abortion on request

**ABSA** now see Arts & Business

**ABTA** Association of British Travel Agents
30 Park Street  London SE1 9EQ
Tel: 020 3117 0500
abta@abta.co.uk
www.abta.com

**Academic Freedom & Academic Standards (Council for)**
Tel: 01932 840928
johnfernandes500@googlemail.com
www.cafas.org.uk
dedicated to maintaining standards of integrity and practice in academia

**ACAS** Advisory Conciliation and Arbitration Service
Euston Tower  286 Euston Road  London NW1 3JJ
Helpline: 0845 7474 747
tel: 0207 396 0022
www.acas.org.uk
Industrial relations and employment enquiries

**ACCAC** see Qualifications, Curriculum and Assessment Authority for Wales

**Access Art**
info@accessart.org.uk
www.accessart.org.uk
Online workshops & arts educational activities for all ages

**Access & Mobility (London)** now see Transport for London

**Access to London Theatres** London Theatre Guide
  www.officiallondontheatre.co.uk/access
  Guide to West End Theatres for theatregoers with a disability

**Accessible Environments (Centre for)**
  70 South Lambeth Road  London SW8 1RL
  Tel: 020 7840 0125
  info@cae.org.uk
  www.cae.org.uk
  Advise on access to the built environment/ inclusive design

**ACRE** see Communities in Rural England (Action with)

**ACT ON CO2**
  Defra  Customer Contact Unit  Eastbury House  30 - 34 Albert Embankment
   London, SE1 7TL
  Energy saving advice line: 0800 512012
  Email via website
  http://actonco2.direct.gov.uk/home.html

**Action Aid**
  Chataway House  Leach Rd  Chard Somerset TA20 1FR
  Tel: 01460 238000
  supporterservices@actionaid.org
  www.actionaid.org.uk

**Action for Children**
  85 Highbury Park  London N5 1UD
  Tel: 020 7704 7000
  www.actionforchildren.org.uk
  Supports and speaks out for the most vulnerable children and young people in the UK

**Action for ME** see ME (Action for)

**Action for Sick Children** see Sick Children (Action for)

**Action for Southern Africa**  see Southern Africa (Action for)

**Action for Victims of Medical Accidents** see Medical Accidents (Action Against)

**Action Postpartum Psychosis**
  FREEPOST RSGT-YJEY-ZRREE  Room 225 Monmouth House  University Hospital of Wales  Heath Park  Cardiff  CF14 4XW
  Tel: 0292 074 2038
   app@app-network.org
  www.app-network.org
  Provides up to date research information to women and their families on Postpartum Psychosis – a severe mental illness which has a sudden onset in the first few weeks following childbirth

**Action on Addiction** see Addiction (Action on)

**Action on Elder Abuse** see Elder Abuse (Action on)

**Action Transport**
  Whitby Hall  Stanney Lane  Ellesmere Port CH65 9AE
  Tel: 0151 357 2120
  info@actiontransport theatre.co.uk
  www.actiontransporttheatre.co.uk
  Action Transport Theatre Company is an arts and ideas company creating work for, by and with young people

**Active Birth Centre**
  25 Bickerton Rd  London N19 5JT
  Tel: 020 7281 6760
  info@activebirthcentre.com
  www.activebirthcentre.com
  Education for active birth, professional training, water birth pool hire & sales

**Activity Holiday Association (British)**
  The Hollies  Oak Bank Lane  Hoole Village Chester CH2 4ER
  Tel: 01244 301342
  info@baha.org.uk
  www.baha.org.uk

**Acupuncture Council (British)**
  63 Jeddo Road  London W12 9HQ
  Tel: 020 8735 0400
  email via website
  www.acupuncture.org.uk
  Self-regulatory body for acupuncturists in the UK

**Acupuncture Society (British Medical)** BMAS
  BMAS House  3 Winnington Court Northwich  Cheshire CW8 1AQ
  Tel: 01606 786782
  admin@medical-acupuncture.org.uk
  www.medical-acupuncture.co.uk
  Professional organisation

**Adam Smith Institute**
  23 Great Smith St  London SW1P 3BL
  Tel: 020 7222 4995
  info@adamsmith.org
  www.adamsmith.org
  Free market think-tank

**Adbusters**
  www.adbusters.org
  Website providing a critical look at advertising

**ADD** see Disability & Development (Action on)

**Addaction**
  67-69 Cowcross St  London EC1M 6PU
  Tel: 020 7251 5860
  info@addaction.org.uk

www.addaction.org.uk
Helping individuals and communities
manage the effects of drug and alcohol
misuse

**Addiction (Action on)**
East Knoyle  Wiltshire SP3 6BE
Tel: 0845 126 4130
email via website
www.actiononaddiction.org.uk
Charity seeking out the causes of nicotine,
alcohol and drug addiction

**Additives (Action on)**
94 White Lion Street
London N1 9PF  London N1 9PF
info@actiononadditives.com
www.actiononadditives.com
Aims to list all the foods, drinks and
medicines which contain the additives linked
to hyperactivity in susceptible children

**ADFAM**
25 Corsham Street  London N1 6DR
Admin: 020 7553 7640
admin@adfam.org.uk
www.adfam.org.uk
National charity working with families
affected by drugs & alcohol

**Adopted Children's Register**
General Register Office  Adoption Section
Trafalgar Rd  Birkdale  Southport PR8 2HH
Tel: 0151 471 4830
www.direct.gov.uk/en/
Governmentcitizensandrights/
Registeringlifeevents/index.htm
Adoption certificates & access to birth
records. Contact Register for adoptions in
England and Wales

**Adoption and Fostering (British
Association for)**
Saffron House  6-10 Kirby Street  London
EC1N 8TS
Tel: 0207 421 2600
Tel: 0292 076 1155 Cymru
Tel: 0121 753 2001 Central England
Tel: 0113 289 1101 Northern England
Tel: 0131 220 4749 Scotland
mail@baaf.org.uk
www.baaf.org.uk

**Adoption and Fostering Information Line**
www.adoption.org.uk

**Adoption UK**
46 The Green  South Bar Street  Banbury
Oxon OX16 9AB
Helpline: 0844 848 7900
Tel: 01295 752240 (Admin)
email via website
www.adoptionuk.org

Supporting adoptive families before, during
and after adoption

**Adult Continuing Education (National
Institute of)**  see NIACE

**Adult Education** see also NIACE,
learndirect, Third Age Trust, Workers
Educational Association

**Adventure Activities Licensing Authority**
44 Lambourne Cres  Llanishen  Cardiff CF14
5GG
Tel: 029 20 755 715
info@aala.org.uk
www.aala.org.uk
Inspects providers of adventure activities
as per The Adventure Activities Licensing
Regulations 1996

**Advertising Association**
7th Floor North  Artillery House  11-19
Artillery Row  London SW1P 1RT
Tel: 020 7340 1100
aa@adassoc.org.uk
www.adassoc.org.uk
Federation of trade bodies

**Advertising Standards Authority**
Mid City Place  71 High Holborn  London
WC1V 6QT
Tel: 020 7492 2222
enquiries@asa.org.uk
www.asa.org.uk
Regulates content of non-broadcast
advertisements

**Advice** see thematic guide - Counselling

**Advice Now**
www.advicenow.org.uk
Comprehensive legal information from a
variety of leading services

**Advice UK**
6th Floor  63 St. Mary Ave  London EC3A
8AA
Tel: 020 7409 5700
mail@adviceuk.org.uk
www.adviceuk.org.uk
Umbrella organisation. Membership
organisation of independent social welfare
law advice centres

**Advisory Council on the Misuse of Drugs**
Home Office  3rd Floor Seacole Building  2
Marsham Street  London SW1P 4DF
020 7035 0454
ACMD@homeoffice.gsi.gov.uk
www.homeoffice.gov.uk/drugs/acmd
Independent expert body that advises
government on drug related issues in the
UK.

## Advocacy After Fatal Domestic Abuse
AAFDA
Edith Stevens House  77/78 Bridge Street
Swindon SN1 1BT
Helpline: 07768 386922 if you need
immediate assistance
info@aafda.org.uk
www.aafda.org.uk
Practical and emotional support after fatal
domestic abuse incidents

## Advocates for Animals see Onekind

## Aegis Trust
4 Pinchin Street  London E1 1SA
Tel: 020 7481 1011
office@aegistrust.org
www.aegistrust.org
An independent, international organisation,
dedicated to eliminating genocide.

## AENA see Netball Association (All England)

## Aeronautical Society (Royal)
4 Hamilton Place  London W1J 7BQ
Tel: 020 7670 4300
raes@raes.org.uk
www.aerosociety.com
A professional institution dedicated to the
Global Aerospace Community

## Afasic
1st Floor  20 Bowling Green Lane  London
EC1R 0BD
Helpline: 0845 355 5577
Tel: 020 7490 9410
info@afasic.org.uk
www.afasic.org.uk
www.afasicengland.org.uk
Representing children & young adults with
speech, language and communication
impairments

## Afghanaid
56 - 64 Leonard Street  London EC2A 4LT
Tel: 020 7065 0825
info@afghanaid.org.uk
www.afghanaid.org.uk
UK based charity working alongside Afghan
communities

## Africa and Asia Venture
10 Market Place  Devizes SN10 1HT
Tel: 01380 729009
av@aventure.co.uk
www.aventure.co.uk
Volunteer projects and adventure for four
months in gap year in the developing world

## Africa Centre
38 King Street  Covent Garden  London WC2E
8JT
Tel: 020 7836 1973
email via website

www.africacentre.org.uk
Promoting African arts, culture, opinion and
business

## Africa Now
The Old Music Hall  106-108 Cowley Road
Oxford OX4 1JE
Tel: 01865 403265
info@africanow.org
www.africanow.org
Supports local business initiatives and provides
access to basic services in Kenya & Zimbabwe

## African Conservation Experience
Unit 1, Manor Farm  Churchend Lane
Charfield  Wotton-under-edge  GL12 8LJ
Tel: 0845 5200 888
email via website
www.conservationafrica.net
Gives volunteers the opportunity to
experience conservation work in Southern
Africa and to provide financial support and
information for conservation projects

## African Initiatives
Brunswick Court  Brunswick Square  Bristol
BS2 8PE
Tel: 0117 915 0001
info@african-initiatives.org.uk
www.african-initiatives.org.uk
Promotes right to participate in decisions
affecting communities in Africa

## Africans Unite Against Child Abuse
Unit 3D/F Leroy House  436 Essex Road
London N1 3QP
Tel: 0844 660 8607
email via website
www.afruca.org

## Age UK
York House  207-221 Pentonville Rd
London N1 9UZ
Tel: 0800 169 6565
Tel: 0800 107 8977
contact@ageuk.org.uk
www.ageuk.org.uk
Age UK is the new force combining Age
Concern  and Help the Aged

## &  Cymru
Ty John Pathy  13-14 Neptune Court
Vanguard Way  Cardiff CF24 5PJ
Helpline: 0800 169 6565
Tel: 029 20 431555
enquiries@agecymru.org.uk
www.ageuk.org.uk/cymru

## &  Northern Ireland
3 Lower Cres  Belfast BT7 1NR
Helpline: 02890 325055
Tel: 02890 245729
info@ageni.org
www.ageuk.org.uk/northern-ireland

**& Scotland**
Causewayside House  160 Causewayside
Edinburgh EH9 1PR
Scottish helpline for older people: 0845 125
9732
Tel: 0845 833 0200
enquiries@
ageconcernandhelptheagedscotland.org.uk
www.ageuk.org.uk/scotland

**Age Concern** Now see Age

**Age Exchange**
The Reminiscence Centre  11 Blackheath
Village  London SE3 9LA
Tel: 020 8318 9105
administrator@age-exchange.org.uk
www.age-exchange.org.uk
Works in all areas of reminiscence

**Ageing (Centre for Policy on)** see Policy
on Ageing (Centre for)

**Ageing (Research Info)** see Help the Aged

**Agriculture and Horticulture
Development Board**
Stoneleigh Park  Kenilworth  Warwickshire
CV8 2TL
Tel: 0247 669 2051
info@ahdb.org.uk
www.ahdb.org.uk
Helps improve the efficiency and
competitiveness of various agriculture and
horticulture sectors within the UK. October
2010: future under review

**Ahimsa**
6 Victoria Place  Millbay Road  Plymouth
PL1 3LP
Tel: 01752 660330
nicky@ahimsasaferfamilies.co.uk
www.ahimsasaferfamilies.co.uk
Specialist help for men with a history of
violence. Support for their partners

**AIDS Trust (National)**
New City Cloisters  196 Old St  London
EC1V 9FR
Tel: 020 7814 6767
info@nat.org.uk
www.nat.org.uk
The UK's leading independent policy and
campaigning voice on HIV and AIDS

**AIDS/HIV** see also African AIDS Helpline,
AVERT, Body Positive, Healthwise, HIFY-
UK, HIV/Aids Alliance (International), People
Living with HIV & AIDS, PACE, Playing
Safely, Positively UK, Terrence Higgins
Trust, Youthlink Wales

**Aikido Board (British)**  BAB
general@bab.org.uk
www.bab.org.uk

**AIMS** Association for Improvements in the
Maternity Services
5 Ann's Court  Grove Rd  Surbiton  Surrey
KT6 4BE
Helpline: 0300 365 0663
Tel: 020 8390 9534
chair@aims.org.uk
www.aims.org.uk
Advice and information network for parents'
choices in childbirth

**Air Cadets** see Girls' Venture Corps Air
Cadets

**Air Transport Users' Council** AUC
CAA House  45-59 Kingsway  London
WC2B 6TE
Tel: 020 7240 6061
admin@auc.org.uk
www.auc.org.uk

**AirportWatch**
Broken Wharf House  2 Broken Wharf
London EC4V 3DT
Tel: 020 7248 2227
info@airportwatch.org.uk
www.airportwatch.org.uk
Opposes airport expansion across the UK

**Airsafe.com** Safety information for the
airline passenger
www.airsafe.com

**AITO** see Tour Operators (Association of
Independent)

**Al-Anon Alateen**
Al-Anon Family Groups (UK & Eire) 61 Great
Dover St  London SE1 4YF
Confidential Helpline: 020 7403 0888
enquiries@al-anonuk.org.uk
www.al-anonuk.org.uk
Al-Anon offers understanding & support
for families & friends of problem drinkers.
Alateen is for 12 & 20 year olds who have
been affected by someone else's drinking,
usually that of a parent

**Al-Jazeera**
http://english.aljazeera.net
English language web site of the Arab news
service, based in Qatar

**Albany Trust**
c/o The Art of Health and Yoga  239a
Balham High Road  London SW17 7BE
Tel: 020 8767 1827
info@albanytrust.org
www.albanytrust.org.uk
A professional therapy service offering
emotional, sexual and/or psychological help

**Albert Kennedy Trust**
Hatton Sq  Unit 305a  16/16a Baldwins
Gardens  London EC1N 7RJ
Tel: 020 7831 6562

contact@akt.org.uk
www.akt.org.uk
Supporting lesbian, gay and bisexual young people who are homeless or living in hostile environments

**&**

4th Floor, Princess House  105-107 Princess Street  Manchester M1 6DD
Tel: 0161 228 3308
contact@akt.org.uk
www.akt.org.uk
Provides supported lodgings, placements and/or mentors to young lesbian/gay/bisexual people who are homeless/fleeing abuse and/or harassment because of their sexuality

**Albinism** see also NOAH - National Organization for Albinism and Hypopigmentation

### Albinism Fellowship
PO Box 77  Burnley BB11 5GN
Tel: 01282 771900
email via website
www.albinism.org.uk
Advice and support

### Alcohol Concern
64 Leman Street  London E1 8EU
Tel: 020 7264 0510
contact@alcoholconcern.org.uk
www.alcoholconcern.org.uk
Provides information and comment on alcohol issues

### Alcohol & Drug Education (Advisory Council for) see Tacade

### Alcohol Education and Research Council
Eliot House (EH 1.4),  10 – 12 Allington Street, LONDON SW1E 5EH
020 7808 7150
Develops research based evidence to inform and influence policy and practice and help people and organisations to address alcohol issues. October 2010 will become a charity. Change of name expected.

### Alcohol Focus Scotland
2nd Floor  166 Buchanan Street  Glasgow G1 2LW
Tel: 0141 572 6700
enquiries@alcohol-focus-scotland.org.uk
www.alcohol-focus-scotland.org.uk
Dedicated to raising awareness of, and reducing the significant health and social harm caused by alcohol.

### Alcohol & Health Research Unit
http://hsc.uwe.ac.uk/net/research/Default.aspx?pageid=228
Research programme - UK lead on a number of international projects on alcohol and other drugs.

### Alcohol Studies (Institute of)
12 Caxton St  London SW1H 0QS
Tel: 020 7222 4001
info@ias.org.uk
www.ias.org.uk

### Alcoholics Anonymous
PO Box 1  10 Toft Green  York YO1 7NJ
Helpline: 0845 7697 555
www.alcoholics-anonymous.org.uk

### Alexander Teachers (Professional Association of)
Room 706  The Big Peg, 120 Vyse St  Birmingham B18 6NF
Tel: 01743 236 195
info@paat.org.uk
www.paat.org.uk

### Alexander Technique (Society of Teachers of the)
1st Floor  Linton House  39-51 Highgate Rd  London NW5 1RS
Tel: 020 7482 5135
office@stat.org.uk
www.stat.org.uk

**Alice Kilvert Tampon Alert** see Tampon Alert (Alice Kilvert)

**Allergies** see also Anaphylaxis Campaign

### Allergy UK
Planwell House  Lefa Business Park  Edgington Way  Sidcup, Kent  DA14 5BH
Tel: 01322 619898
info@allergyuk.org
www.allergyuk.org

**Alliance for Inclusive Education** see Inclusive Education (Alliance for)

### Alliance Française
1 Dorset Street  London NW1 6PU
Tel: 020 7723 6439
info@alliancefrancaise.org.uk
www.alliancefrancaise.org.uk
French classes/diplomas in French as a foreign language & language skills consultancy, some social and cultural activities

### Allotment and Leisure Gardeners Ltd. (National Society of)
O'Dell House  Hunters Road  Corby NN17 5JE
Tel: 01536 266 576
natsoc@nsalg.org.uk
www.nsalg.org.uk
Advice on setting up an allotment user group

### Alone in London
Unit 6  48 Provost Street  N1 7SU
Tel: 020 7278 4224
enquiries@als.org.uk
www.als.org.uk

Assists the single young homeless under 26 in London

**Alopecia** see Hairline International

**Alternative Technology (Centre for)**
Machynlleth  Powys SY20 9AZ
Tel: 01654 705950
www.cat.org.uk
Environmental demonstration centre open to visitors

**Aluminium Packaging Recycling Organisation**
1 Brockhill Court  Brockhill Lane  Redditch B97 6RB
Tel: 01527 597757
info@alupro.org.uk
www.alupro.org.uk
Info packs, educational materials

**Alzheimer Scotland**
22 Drumsheugh Gardens  Edinburgh EH3 7RN
Helpline: 0808 808 3000
Tel: 0131 243 1453
alzheimer@alzscot.org
www.alzscot.org
Helping people with dementia and their carers and families in Scotland

**Alzheimer's Research Trust**
The Stables  Station Road  Cambridge CB22 5LR
Tel: 01223 843899
enquiries@alzheimers-research.org.uk
www.alzheimers-research.org.uk
Leading UK research charity for Alzheimer's disease and related dementias. Provides free information on dementia

**Alzheimer's Society**
Devon House  58 St Katharine's Way
London E1W 1LB
Helpline: 0845 300 0336
Tel: 020 7425 3500
enquiries@alzheimers.org.uk
www.alzheimers.org.uk

**AMAR**
Hope House  45 Great Peter Steet  London SW1P 3LT
Tel: 020 7799 2217
london@amarfoundation.org
www.amarappeal.com

**Amateur Athletic Association**
PO Box 557  Chichester PO19 9DS
Tel: 01928 733 067
www.aaa-athletics.org
Governing body of amateur athletics

**Amateur Boxing Association of England Ltd.**
The English Institute of Sport  Coleride Road Sheffield S9 5DA
Tel: 0114 2235654
info@abae.co.uk
www.abae.co.uk

**Amateur Boxing Scotland**
5 Nasmyth Court  Houston Industrial Estate Livingston EH54 5EG
Tel: 0845 241 7016
email via website
www.amateurboxingscotland.co.uk
Promotes boxing as physical exercise for boys and girls

**Amateur Theatre Network** see Theatre Network (The Amateur)

**American Library Association**
www.ala.org

**Amnesty International**
17-25 New Inn Yard  London EC2A 3EA
Tel: 020 7033 1500
Textphone 020 7033 1664
sct@amnesty.org.uk
www.amnesty.org.uk
Campaigns for prisoners of conscience, against the use of torture & the death penalty

**An Taisce** National Trust for Ireland
Tailor's Hall  Back Lane  Dublin 8
Tel: 00 353 1 454 1786
info@antaisce.org
www.antaisce.org
An environmental voluntary organisation concerned with the preservation of buildings, landscapes and natural heritage

**Anaphylaxis Campaign**
PO Box 275  Farnborough  Hants GU14 6SX
Helpline: 01252 542029
Tel: 01252 546100
info@anaphylaxis.org.uk
www.anaphylaxis.org.uk/
www.allergyinschools.org.uk
Fighting for people with life-threatening allergies, providing education, information and support

**Anchor Trust**
2nd Floor  25 Bedford Street  London WC2E 9ES
Tel: 0845 140 2020
email via website
www.anchor.org.uk
working with older people and providing residential care homes

**Ancient Buildings (Society for the Protection of)**
37 Spital Sq  London E1 6DY
Tel: 020 7377 1644
info@spab.org.uk

www.spab.org.uk
Campaigns to save threatened buildings, gives advice on repair and runs courses

## Ancient Monument Society
St Ann's Vestry Hall  2 Church Entry  London EC4V 5HB
Tel: 020 7236 3934
office@ancientmonumentssociety.org.uk
www.ancientmonumentssociety.org.uk
Study and conservation of historic buildings of all ages and types

## Ancient Tree forum
www.woodland-trust.org.uk/ancient-tree-forum

## Andrea Adams Trust
Shalimar House  24 Derek Avenue  Hove East Sussex BN3 4PF
Tel: 01273 389412
mail@andreaadamsconsultancy.com
www.andreaadamstrust.org
Support and advice on workplace bullying to individuals and organisations

## Angling Trust
Eastwood House  6 Rainbow Street Leominster  Herefordshire  HR6 8DQ
Tel: 0844 7700616
admin@anglingtrust.net
www.anglingtrust.net
Represent all game, coarse and sea anglers and angling in England

## Anglo-German Foundation for the Study of Industrial Society
34 Belgrave Square  London SW1X 8DZ
Tel: 020 7823 1123
ap@agf.org.uk
www.agf.org.uk
Creating sustainable growth in Europe

## Animal Aid
The Old Chapel  Bradford St  Tonbridge Kent TN9 1AW
Tel: 01732 364546
info@animalaid.co.uk
www.animalaid.org.uk
Campaigns against animal abuse and for a cruelty-free lifestyle

## Animal Aid Youth
www.animalaid.org.uk/h/n/YOUTH/HOME/
Youth section of Animal Aid

## Animal Defenders
Millbank Tower  Millbank  London SW1P 4QP
Tel: 020 7630 3340
info@ad-international.org
www.ad-international.org
Welfare and conservation group currently campaigning to end use of animals in circuses

## Animal Health (National Office of)
3 Crossfield Chambers  Gladbeck Way Enfield EN2 7HF
Tel: 020 8367 3131
noah@noah.co.uk
www.noah.co.uk
Represents the UK animal medicines industry

## Animal Health Trust
Lanwades Park  Kentford  Suffolk CB8 7UU
Tel: 01638 751000
info@aht.org.uk
www.aht.org.uk
Registered charity which aims to advance veterinary science

## Animal Rescue (International)
Lime House  Regency Close  Uckfield  East Sussex TN22 1DS
Tel: 01825 767688
info@internationalanimalrescue.org
www.iar.org.uk
Registered charity in UK, USA, India and Malta dedicated to the rescue and rehabilitation of suffering animals

## Animal Rescuers (UK)
www.animalrescuers.co.uk
Directory of UK rescue centres

## Animal Research (Understanding) see
Understanding Animal Research

## Animal Welfare Trust (National)
Tyler's Way  Watford By Pass  Watford  Herts WD25 8WT
Tel: 020 8950 0177
email via web
www.nawt.org.uk/
Operates rescue centres for unwanted, ill-treated and abandoned animals and birds. No healthy animal is ever put to sleep

## Animals in Medical Experiments (Fund for the Replacement of) see FRAME

## Anne Frank Trust UK
Star House  104/108 Grafton Road  London NW5 4BA
Tel: 020 7284 5858
info@annefrank.org.uk
www.annefrank.org.uk
Exhibitions and educational programmes on citizenship and social responsibility to counter bigotry and racism. Organises the Anne Frank Awards for Moral Courage

## Antenatal Results and Choices see ARC

## Anthony Nolan Trust
Unit 2-3 Heathgate Place  75 - 87 Agincourt Rd  London NW3 2NU
Tel: 0303 303 0303
info@anthonynolan.org.uk
www.anthonynolan.org.uk

Co-ordinates donation of bone marrow for treatment of disease

**Anthropological Institute of GB & Ireland (Royal)**
50 Fitzroy St  London W1T 5BT
Tel: 020 7387 0455
admin@therai.org.uk
www.therai.org.uk

**Anti-Bullying Network**
Simpson House  52 Queen Street  Edinburgh EH2 3NS
info@antibullying.net
www.antibullying.net
Network set up by The Scottish Executive so that teachers, parents and young people in Scotland could share ideas about how bullying should be tackled

**Anti-Nazi League** now see Unite Against Fascism

**Anti-Slavery International**
Thomas Clarkson House  The Stableyard Broomgrove Road  London SW9 9TL
Tel: 020 7501 8920
info@antislavery.org
www.antislavery.org
Campaigns for the elimination of slavery, child labour, debt bondage, forced labour, trafficking people. Educational materials available

**Anti-Snaring Campaign (National)**
NASC  PO BOX 3058  Littlehampton  West Sussex  BN16 3LG
Tel: 05601 716524
info@antisnaring.org.uk
www.antisnaring.org.uk

**Anti-Vivisection Society (National)**
Millbank Tower  Millbank  London SW1P 4QP
Tel: 020 7630 3340
email via website
www.navs.org.uk
Campaigns to end all animal experiments

**Antidote: Campaign for Emotional Literacy**
Cityside House  3rd Floor  40 Adler St London E1 1EE
Tel: 020 7247 3355
emotional.literacy@antidote.org.uk
www.antidote.org.uk
Advice, consultancy and workshops for schools, colleges & other organisations

**Antiquaries of London (Society of)**
Burlington House  Piccadilly  London W1J 0BE
Tel: 020 7479 7080
Tel: 020 7479 7084 (Library – to make appointments)

Tel: 020 7479 7088 (Museum - collection enquiries)
admin@sal.org.uk
www.sal.org.uk
Fellowship of antiquaries. Has a library for scholars to which access is by appointment

**Anxiety Care**
Cardinal Heenan Centre  326 High Rd  Ilford IG1 1QP
Helpline: 020 8478 3400
Tel: 020 8262 8891
enquiries@anxietycare.org.uk
www.anxietycare.org.uk
Deals with anxiety, phobias and obsessive compulsive disorders

**Anxiety UK**
Zion Community Resource Centre  339 Stretford Rd  Hulme  Manchester M15 4ZY
Tel: 0844 4775 774
Tel: 0161 227 9898
info@anxietyuk.org.uk
www.anxietyuk.org.uk
Provides information & support for people suffering from anxiety disorders

**Ape Alliance**
www.4apes.com
An international coalition of organisations and individuals, working for the conservation and welfare of apes

**Apples & Snakes**
The Albany  Douglas Way  London SE8 4AG
Tel: 0845 521 3460
info@applesandsnakes.org
www.applesandsnakes.org
Promotes performance poetry as a social and cross-cultural activity

**APRS** see Recording Services (Association of Professional)

**APRS** see Rural Scotland (Association for the Protection of)

**Apsley House Wellington Museum**
149 Piccadilly  Hyde Park Corner  London W1J 7NT
Tel: 020 7499 5676
http://www.apsleyhouseguide.co.uk/
One of London's finest Georgian buildings, former home of the Duke of Wellington

**AQA**  Assessment and Qualifications Alliance
31-33 Springfield Av   Harrogate HG1 2HW
Exam support: 0844 209 6614
Tel: 01423 840 015
mailbox@aqa.org.uk
www.aqa.org.uk
Largest unitary awarding body in the UK

**&**
Devas St  Manchester M15 6EX
Tel: 0161 953 1180
www.aqa.org.uk

**&**
Stag Hill House  Guildford GU2 7XJ
Tel: 01483 506 506
www.aqa.org.uk

**Arab-British Understanding (Council for)**
CAABU
1 Gough Square  London EC4A 3DE
Tel: 020 7832 1321
email via website
www.caabu.org

**Arbitration** see ACAS

**Arbitrators (Chartered Institute of)**
CIArb  12 Bloomsbury Square  London
WC1A 2LP
Tel: 020 7421 7444
info@ciarb.org
www.ciarb.org
Professional organisation for arbitrators,
mediators and adjudicators

**ARC** Antenatal Results and Choices
73 Charlotte St  London W1T 4PN
Helpline: 020 7631 0285
Tel: 020 7631 0280
info@arc-uk.org
www.arc-uk.org
Information and support to parents throughout
antenatal testing

**Arc Theatre for Change**
The Malthouse Studios  62-76 Abbey Road
Essex IG11 7BT
Tel: 020 8594 1095
email via website
www.arctheatre.com

**Archaeology Abroad**
31-34 Gordon Sq  London WC1H 0PY
Tel: 020 8537 0849
arch.abroad@ucl.ac.uk
www.britarch.ac.uk/archabroad
Information about fieldwork opportunities
outside the UK

**Archaeology (Council for British)**
St Mary's House  66 Bootham  York YO30 7BZ
Tel: 01904 671417
email via website
www.britarch.ac.uk

**Archaeology Scotland**
Suite 1a  Stuart House  Eskmills  Station Road
Musselburgh EH21 7PB
Tel: 0845 872 3333
info@archaeologyscotland.org.uk
www.archaeologyscotland.org.uk

**Archéire**
Email via website
www.archeire.com

Archéire is a website dedicated to the
promotion of Irish architecture

**Archery GB**
Lilleshall National Sports Centre  Nr Newport
Shropshire TF10 9AT
Tel: 01952 677888
enquiries@archerygb.org
www.archerygb.org
The governing body for the sport of archery
in Great Britain and Northern Ireland

**Architects (Royal Institute of British)** RIBA
66 Portland Place  London W1B 1AD
Tel: 020 7580 5533
info@inst.riba.org
www.architecture.com

**Architectural Heritage Fund**
Alhambra House  27-31 Charing Cross Road
London WC2H 0AU
Tel: 020 7925 0199
ahf@ahfund.org.uk
www.ahfund.org.uk
Loans and grants to charities to preserve
historic buildings

**Architecture and the Built Environment
(Commission for)**
1 Kemble Street  London WC2B 4AN
020 7070 6700
info@cabe.org.uk
CABE is the government's advisor on
architecture, urban design and public space.
October 2010: future under consideration.
Government looking at options for reform

**Architecture Foundation**
Ground Floor East  136-148 Tooley Street
London  SE1 2TU
Tel: 020 7084 6767
mail@architecturefoundation.org.uk
www.architecturefoundation.org.uk
Aims to promote the importance of high
quality contemporary architecture & urban
design

**ARKive**
Wildscreen  Ground Floor
 The Rackhay  Queen Charlotte Street  Bristol
BS1 4HJ
Tel : 0117 328 5950
arkive@wildscreen.org.uk
www.arkive.org
Images of life on earth. The world's centralised
digital library of films, photographs and
associated recordings of species

**Arms and Armour Society**
PO Box 10232  London SW19 2ZD
armsandarmour.soc@btinternet.com
www.armsandarmour.net
A learned society for the study and
preservation of arms and armour

**Army (British)**
www.army.mod.uk

**Army Cadet Force**
www.armycadets.com
National voluntary youth organisation

**Army Museum (National)**
Royal Hospital Road  Chelsea  London  SW3 4HT
020 7881 2455 (information line)
020 7730 0717 (switchboard)
info@national-army-museum.ac.uk
www.national-army-museum.ac.uk

**Aromatherapy** see also Tisserand Aromatherapy Institute

**Arson Prevention Bureau**
Tel : 020 7216 7522
www.arsonpreventionbureau.org.uk
Funded by UK insurers to reduce the incidence and costs of arson

**Art and Design (National Society for Education in)**
3 Masons Wharf  Potley Lane  Corsham Wiltshire  SN13 9FY
Tel: 01225 810134
info@nsead.org

www.nsead.org
If you teach art, craft or design in primary or secondary schools, or in further or higher education
- especially teacher educators - the National Society for Education in Art & Design (NSEAD) site is for you:

**Art Fund**
Millais House  7 Cromwell Place  London SW7 2JN
Tel: 020 7225 4800
info@artfund.org
www.artfund.org
The UK's leading art charity, it enriches museums and galleries with works of art

**Art Library (National)**
Victoria and Albert Museum  South Kensington Cromwell Road  London SW7 2RL
Tel: 020 7942 2000
vanda@vam.ac.uk
www.vam.ac.uk/nal/
A major public reference library & the V&A's curatorial department for the art, craft & design of the book

**Art Therapists (British Association of)**
24-27 White Lion Street  London N1 9PD
Tel: 020 7686 4216
info@baat.org
www.baat.org

**Arthritic Association**
One Upperton Gardens  Eastbourne  East Sussex BN21 2AA
Tel: 01323 416550
Freephone: 0800 652 3188
info@arthriticassociation.org.uk
www.arthriticassociation.org.uk
Offers a natural drug free Home Treatment programme to help arthritis sufferers

**Arthritis Care**
18 Stephenson Way  London NW1 2HD
Helpline: 0808 800 4050
Helpline for young people with arthritis: 0808 808 2000
Tel: 020 7380 6500
info@arthritiscare.org.uk
www.arthritiscare.org.uk

**Arthritis Research UK**
Copeman House  St Mary's Gate  Chesterfield Derbyshire S41 7TD
Tel: 0300 790 0400
enquiries@arthritisresearchuk.org
www.arthritisresearchuk.org
Aims to advance the understanding, prevention and treatment of arthritis & related conditions

**Arthur Rank Centre**
Stoneleigh Park  Warwickshire  CV8 2LZ
Tel: 024 7685 3060
admin@arthurrankcentre.org.uk
www.arthurrankcentre.org.uk
National rural resources unit for the churches

**ARTICLE 19, The Global Campaign for Free Expression**
Free Word Centre  60 Farringdon Road London EC1R 3GA
Tel: 020 7324 2500
info@article19.org
www.article19.org
Human rights organisation which campaigns globally for freedom of expression and information

**Artistic Roller Skating (Federation of)**
10 The Broadway  Thatcham  Berks RG19 3JA
Tel: 01635 877322
office@fars.co.uk
www.fars.co.uk

**Artists Against Racism**
aarcharity@gmail.com
www.artistsagainstracism.com

**Arts and Business**
Nutmeg House  60 Gainsford St  Butler's Wharf  London SE1 2NY
Tel: 020 7378 8143
contactus@artsandbusiness.org.uk
www.aandb.org.uk

Helps business people support the arts & the arts inspire business people

**Arts Council England**
14 Great Peter Street  SW1P 3NQ
Tel: 0845 300 6200
Email via website
www.artscouncil.org.uk
National development agency for the arts in England, distributing public money from government & the national lottery

**& East**
Eden House  48-49 Bateman St  Cambridge CB2 1LR
Tel: 0845 300 6200
Email via website
www.artscouncil.org.uk

**& East Midlands**
St Nicholas Ct  25-27 Castle Gate  Nottingham NG1 7AR
Tel: 0845 300 6200
Email via website
www.artscouncil.org.uk

**& North East**
Central Square  Forth St  Newcastle upon Tyne NE1 3PJ
Tel: 0845 300 6200
Email via website
www.artscouncil.org.uk

**& North West**
The Hive  49 Lever Street  Manchester M1 1FN
Tel: 0845 300 6200
Email via website
www.artscouncil.org.uk

**& South East**
Sovereign House  Church St  Brighton BN1 1RA
Tel: 0845 300 6200
Email via website
www.artscouncil.org.uk

**& South West**
Senate Court  Southernhay Gardens  Exeter EX1 1UG
Tel: 0845 300 6200
Email via website
www.artscouncil.org.uk

**& West Midlands**
82 Granville St  Birmingham B1 2LH
Tel: 0845 300 6200
Email via website
www.artscouncil.org.uk

**& Yorkshire**
21 Bond St  Dewsbury WF13 1AX
Tel: 0845 300 6200
Email via website
www.artscouncil.org.uk

**& N. Ireland**
Arts Council of Northern Ireland  77 Malone Road  Belfast BT9 6AQ
Tel: 028 9038 5200
info@artscouncil-ni.org
www.artscouncil-ni.org

**& Wales** Cyngor Celfyddydau Cymru
Bute Plate  Cardiff  CF10 5AL
Tel: 0845 8734 900
Minicom: 029 2045 1023
info@artswales.org.uk
www.artswales.org.uk

**& Wales** (Mid and West Wales Office)
6 Gardd Llydaw  Jackson's Lane  Carmarthen SA31 1QD
Tel: 01267 234248
info@artswales.org.uk
www.artswales.org.uk
The Arts Council of Wales is the organisation responsible for distributing Welsh Assembly Government and National Lottery funding to the arts in Wales

**& Wales** North Wales Office
36 Prince's Drive  Colwyn Bay LL29 8LA
Tel: 01492 533440
info@artswales.org.uk
www.artswales.org.uk

**& Scottish**
12 Manor Place  Edinburgh EH3 7DD
Help Desk: 0845 603 6000
Tel: 0131 226 6051
help.desk@scottisharts.org.uk
www.scottisharts.org.uk
Provides info, funding and development to the arts in Scotland

**Arts Disability Wales**
Sbectrwm  Bwlch Rd  Fairwater  Cardiff CF5 3EF
Tel: 029 20 551040
post@dacymru.com
www.dacymru.com
Training & info service

**Arts Education Network**
www.artsed.net
Reference tool on the state of the arts in schools

**Arts in Therapy & Education (Institute for)**
2-18 Britannia Row  London N1 8PA
Tel: 020 7704 2534
info@artspsychotherapy.org
www.artspsychotherapy.org
Qualification in integrative arts psychotherapy and child therapy

**Arts Marketing Association**
7a Clifton Court  Clifton Rd  Cambridge CB1 7BN
Tel: 01223 578078
info@a-m-a.co.uk

www.a-m-a.org.uk
Works to improve professional development and the status of arts professionals

**Arts (National Campaign for the)**
1 Kingly Street  London W1B 5PA
Tel: 020 7287 3777
Email via website
www.artscampaign.org.uk

**Arts (Royal Academy of)** see Royal Academy of Arts

**Artsline**
21 Pine Court  Wood Lodge Gardens Bromley  BR1 2WA
Tel: 020 7388 2227
ceo@artsline.org.uk
www.artsline.org.uk
Advice service for disabled people on access to the arts and entertainment

**Artswork**
23 Basepoint  Anderson Road  Southampton SO14 5FE
Tel: 02380 682 535
info@artswork.org.uk
www.artswork.org.uk
Youth arts development agency

**ArtWatch UK**
Tel: 020 8216 3492
information@artwatch.org.uk
www.artwatch.org.uk
Campaigning body of artists & art historians opposed to the damaging effects of modern, invasive restorations on our artistic heritage

**Arvon Foundation** The Foundation for Writing
Free Word  60 Farringdon Road  London EC1R 3GA
Tel: 020 7324 2554
london@arvonfoundation.org
www.arvonfoundation.org
Runs residential creative writing courses for adults and groups of young people at centres in Devon, Shropshire, W. Yorkshire and Inverness

**ARX Advocacy Resource Exchange**
Portman House  53 Millbrook Road East Southampton SO15 1HN
Tel: 02380 234 904
enquiries@advocacyresource.org.uk
www.advocacyresource.org.uk
A resource agency supporting local advocacy schemes by providing training, information and advice

**ASBAH** Association for Spina Bifida & Hydrocephalus
ASBAH House  42 Park Road  Peterborough Cambs. PE1 2UQ
Tel: 0845 450 7755
helpline@asbah.org
www.asbah.org

Provides information, advice and support on hydrocephalus and spina bifida

**ASDAN**
Wainbrook House  Hudds Vale Rd  St George Bristol BS5 7HY
Tel : 0117 9411126
info@asdan.org.uk
www.asdan.org.uk
Lifeskills programmes and qualifications for a variety of learners

**ASH** Action on Smoking and Health
First Floor  144-145 Shoreditch High Street London E1 6JE
Tel: 020 7739 5902
enquiries@ash.org.uk
www.ash.org.uk

**ASH Scotland** Action on Smoking and Health
8 Frederick St  Edinburgh EH2 2HB
Tel: 0131 225 4725
ashscotland@ashscotland.org.uk
www.ashscotland.org.uk

**Ashmolean Museum**
Beaumont St  Oxford OX1 2PH
Tel: 01865 278002
www.ashmolean.org/

**Asian People's Disability Alliance**
Suite 1A, 3rd Floor  Alperton House Bridgewater Road  Wembley  Middlesex HA0 1EH
Tel: 020 8903 2231
apdmcha@aol.com
www.apda.org.uk

**Asiatic Society of Great Britain and Ireland (Royal)**
14 Stephenson Way  London NW1 2HD
Tel: 020 7388 4539
email via website
www.royalasiaticsociety.org
Encourages and facilitates Asian Studies and is Britain's senior learned society in the field

**Aslib** see Information Management (Association for)

**Aspect** The Association of Professionals in Education and Children's Trusts
Woolley Hall  Wakefield  West Yorkshire WF4 2JR
Tel: 01226 383 428
info@aspect.org.uk
www.aspect.org.uk
Professional association and trade union

**Assessment and Qualifications Alliance** see AQA

**Associated Board of the Royal Schools of Music**
24 Portland Place  London W1B 1LU

Tel: 020 7636 5400
Email via website
www.abrsm.org

**Association for the Protection of Rural Scotland** see Rural Scotland (Association for the Protection of)

**Association of Colleges** AOC
2-5 Stedham Place  London WC1A 1HU
Tel: 020 7034 9900
enquiries@aoc.co.uk
www.aoc.co.uk
Promotes the interests of further education colleges in England and Wales.

**Asthma UK**
Summit House  70 Wilson Street  London EC2A 2DB
Advice Line: 0800 121 62 44
Tel: 020 7786 4900
info@asthma.org.uk
www.asthma.org.uk
Independent UK charity

**Astrological and Psychic Society (British)**
PO Box 5687  Springfield  Milton Keynes MK6 3WZ
Tel: 01908 260 122
info@baps.ws
www.baps.ws

**Astronomical Association (British)**
Burlington House  Piccadilly  London W1J 0DU
Tel: 020 7734 4145
Email via website
www.britastro.org

**Astronomy** see Dark Skies (Campaign for), Popular Astronomy (Society for)

**Asylum** see also Immigration & Asylum Tribunals Service

**Asylum Aid**
Club Union House  253-254 Upper Street London N1 1RY
Tel: 020 7354 9631
Advice line number: 020 7354 9264
info@asylumaid.org.uk
www.asylumaid.org.uk
Free advice & legal representation to refugees and asylum-seekers. Campaigns for their rights

**Ataxia UK**
Lincoln House  Kennington Park  1-3 Brixton Road  London SW9 6DE
Helpline: 0845 644 0606
Tel: 0207 582 1444
office@ataxia.org.uk
www.ataxia.org.uk
National charity working with and for people affected by Friedreich's and other cerebellars ataxias

**ATD Fourth World**
48 Addington Sq  London SE5 7LB
Tel: 020 7703 3231
atd@atd-uk.org
www.atd-uk.org
Aims to eradicate extreme poverty. Organises summer volunteering opportunities in Europe and long term volunteer work worldwide

**Athletic Association (English Schools)**
email via website
www.esaa.net
Governing body of schools athletics in England

**Athletics** see also Amateur Athletic Association, Scottish Athletics Ltd., UK Sport

**Athletics Federations (International Association of)** IAAF
17 Rue Princesse Florestine  BP 359  MC-98007  Monaco
Tel: +00 377 93 10 88 88
info@iaaf.org
www.iaaf.org

**Atmospheric Research (US National Center for)**
www.ncar.ucar.edu

**Atomic Energy Authority** see UKAEA

**ATSS** see Social Sciences (Association for the Teaching of the)

**Attend**
11-13 Cavendish Square  London W1G 0AN
Tel: 0845 4500285
info@attend.org.uk
www.attend.org.uk
Independent local charities which care for and support people disadvantaged by illness, age or disability

**Attorney General's Office**
20 Victoria Street  London  SW1H 0NF
Tel: 020 7271 2492
correspondenceunit@attorneygeneral.gsi.gov.uk
www.attorneygeneral.gov.uk

**Audit Commission**
1st Floor  Millbank Tower  Millbank  London SW1P 4HQ
Tel: 020 7828 1212
Tel: 0844 798 1212
public-enquiries@audit-commission.gov.uk
www.audit-commission.gov.uk
Helps to improve public services and promotes the best use of public money. October 2010 The Secretary of State for Communities and Local Government announced plans to disband the Audit

Commission. The intention is to have new arrangements in place for auditing England's local public bodies by 2012/13. The audit practice will be done by private companies

**Audit Office (National)**
157-197 Buckingham Palace Road  London SW1W 9SP
Tel: 020 7798 7000
enquiries@nao.gsi.gov.uk
www.nao.gov.uk
Monitors central government spending

**Australian Bureau of Statistics**
www.abs.gov.au

**Authors' Licensing and Collecting Society**
The Writers' House  13 Haydon Street EC3N 1DB
Tel: 020 7264 5700
alcs@alcs.co.uk
www.alcs.co.uk

**Autistic Society (National)**
393 City Rd  London EC1V 1NG
Helpline: 0845 070 4004
Tel: 020 7833 2299
nas@nas.org.uk
www.autism.org.uk
Helpline, information service and support services

**Automobile Association (AA)**
Member Administration  Contact Centre Lambert House  Stockport Road  Cheadle SK8 2DY

Tel: 0870 600 0371
Textphone: 0800 328 2810
www.theaa.com

**Avalanche Info. Service** see sportscotland Avalanche Info. Service

**AVERT**
4 Brighton Rd  Horsham  West Sussex RH13 5BA
Tel: 01403 210202
info@avert.org
www.avert.org
Charity involved in HIV/AIDS education, research and care projects worldwide

**Avicultural Society**
c/o Paul Boulden  Arcadia  The Mounts  East Allington  Devon TQ9 7QJ
admin@avisoc.co.uk
www.avisoc.co.uk

**Award Scheme** see ASDAN Educational Limited

**Awesome Library**
www.awesomelibrary.org
American educational website

# B

**BAAF** see Adoption and Fostering (British Association for)

**BAB** see Aikido Board (British)

**BABCP** see Behavioural & Cognitive Psychotherapies (British Association of)

**Baby Greenhouse**
admins@baby-greenhouse.co.uk
www.baby-greenhouse.co.uk
Online magazine on pregnancy and birth

**Baby Lifeline**
Empathy Enterprise Building  Bramston Crescent  Tile Hill  Coventry CV4 9SW
Tel: 02476 422135
info@babylifeline.org.uk
www.babylifeline.org.uk
Supports the care of pregnant mothers & newborn babies

**Baby Milk Action**
34 Trumpington Street  Cambridge CB2 1QY
Tel: 01223 464420
Email via website
www.babymilkaction.org
Aims to save infant lives & end avoidable suffering caused by inappropriate infant feeding

**Babyworld**
www.babyworld.co.uk
Online magazine and discussion group

**Baccalaureate** see International Baccalaureate Organization

**Bach Centre** see Dr Edward Bach Centre

**Back-up Trust**
Jessica House  Red Lion Square  191 Wandsworth High Street  SW18  4LS
Tel: 020 8875 1805
firstname@backuptrust.org.uk
www.backuptrust.org.uk
Works with people paralysed through spinal cord injury to rebuild self confidence and independence

**BackCare** National Charity for healthier backs
16 Elmtree Rd  Teddington TW11 8ST
Helpline: 0845 130 2704
Tel: 020 8977 5474
email via website
www.backcare.org.uk

**Backpackers Club**
inforequest@backpackersclub.co.uk
www.backpackersclub.co.uk
A club for the lightweight camper, who travels on foot, by bicycle, canoe or cross-country ski

**BACUP** now see Macmillan Cancer Support

**Badminton England**
National Badminton Centre  Milton Keynes MK8 9LA
Tel: 01908 268400
enquiries@badmintonengland.co.uk
www.badmintonengland.co.uk

**Ballet** see also Birmingham Royal Ballet, Bolshoi Ballet, English National Ballet, London Children's Ballet, National Youth Ballet, Northern Ballet, Royal Academy of Dance, Royal Ballet, Scottish Ballet & see thematic guide Dance and also section on Dance, Drama, Music & Performing Arts Schools

**Ballet Organization (British)**
Woolborough House  39 Lonsdale Rd Barnes  London SW13 9JP
Tel: 020 8748 1241
info@bbo.org.uk
www.bbo.org.uk
A teaching and examining society for ballet, jazz, modern and tap

**Balloon and Airship Club (British)**
Cushy Dingle  Watery Lane  Llanishen Monmouthshire  NP16 6QT
information@bbac.org
www.bbac.org

**BALTIC**  The Centre for Contemporary Art
Gateshead Quays  South Shore Rd Gateshead NE8 3BA
Tel: 0191 478 1810
info@balticmill.com
www.balticmill.com

**Banana Link**
Suite 201 Sackville Place  44-48 Magdalen Street  Norwich NR3 1JU
Tel: 01603 765670
info@bananalink.org.uk
www.bananalink.org.uk
Working towards a fair and sustainable banana industry

**Bank of England**
Threadneedle St  London EC2R 8AH
Tel: 020 7601 4444
Tel: 020 7601 4878 (public enquiries)
enquiries@bankofengland.co.uk
www.bankofengland.co.uk

**Bank of England (Damaged and Mutilated Banknotes)**
The Manager, Dept MN,
  Bank of England,  King Street  Leeds  LS1 1HT
Tel: 0113 244 1711
http://www.bankofengland.co.uk/banknotes/damaged_banknotes.htm

**Bank of England Museum**
Threadneedle St  (Entrance in Bartholomew Lane)  London EC2R 8AH
Tel: 020 7601 5545
museum@bankofengland.co.uk
www.bankofengland.co.uk/museum
Free presentations for groups

**Banking Ombudsman** see Financial Ombudsman Service

**Bankruptcy Advisory Service**
PO Box 155  Knaresborough  North Yorkshire HG5 0UE
Tel: 01423 862114
gill@bankruptcyadvisoryservice.co.uk
www.bankruptcyadvisoryservice.co.uk

**Bar Council**
289-293 High Holborn  London WC1V 7HZ
Tel: 020 7242 0082
Email via website
www.barcouncil.org.uk
Regulatory & representative body for barristers in England & Wales

**Bar Pro Bono Unit and Bar in the Community**
289–293 High Holborn  London WC1V 7HZ
Tel: 020 7611 9500 (Bar Pro Bono Unit)
enquiries@barprobono.org.uk
www.barprobono.org.uk
Free legal advice and representation in deserving cases where Legal Aid is not available

**Barbershop Singers (British Association of)**
email via website
www.singbarbershop.com
Promoting the enjoyment of harmony singing

**Barbican Gallery**
Barbican Centre  Silk St  London EC2Y 8DS
Tel: 020 7638 8891
Group Bookings: 020 7382 7211
Main Switchboard: 020 7638 4141
info@barbican.org.uk
www.barbican.org.uk

**Barnardo's**
Tanners Lane  Barkingside  Ilford IG6 1QG
Tel: 020 8550 8822
email via website
www.barnardos.org.uk

**Bartleby.com**
www.bartleby.com/
Hundreds of out-of-copyright books, all digitised and free

**Basel Action Network (BAN)**
inform@ban.org
www.ban.org
Confronting the toxic trade (toxic wastes, products and technologies) and its devastating impacts.

**BASIC** Brain & Spinal Injury Centre
554 Eccles New Rd  Salford M5 5AP
National Helpline: 0870 750 0000
Tel: 0161 707 6441
www.basiccharity.org.uk

**Basic Skills Agency at NIACE**
20 Princess Road West  Leicester LE1 6PT
Tel: 0116 204 4200
Tel: 0116 204 4201
Email via website
www.niace.org.uk
The lead agency for literacy, numeracy and basic skills

**Basketball Association (English)**
PO Box 3971  Sheffield S9 9AZ
Tel: 0114 284 1060
info@englandbasketball.co.uk
www.englandbasketball.co.uk
Governing body

**BASPCAN** British Association for the Study and Prevention of Child Abuse and Neglect
17 Priory St  York YO1 6ET
Tel: 01904 613605
baspcan@baspcan.org.uk
www.baspcan.org.uk
Multi-disciplinary association disseminating research and training to professionals working on child abuse and neglect

**Bat Conservation Trust**
15 Cloisters House  8 Battersea Park Rd London SW8 4BG
Helpline: 0845 1300 228
Tel: 020 7627 2629
enquiries@bats.org.uk
www.bats.org.uk

**Battersea Dogs Home**
4 Battersea Park Rd  London SW8 4AA
Tel: 020 7622 3626
info@battersea.org.uk
www.battersea.org.uk

**BBC**
www.bbc.co.uk

**BBC Backstage Tours**
email via website
www.bbc.co.uk/showsandtours/tours

**BBC Health**
www.bbc.co.uk/health/conditions
Access to information about a wide range of illnesses and conditions

**BBC News**
Email via website
http://news.bbc.co.uk

**BBC Online**
www.bbc.co.uk
Covers all BBC programmes plus sections on business, health, lifestyle, science

**BBC Schools**
Email via website
www.bbc.co.uk/schools

**BBC Studio Audiences**
www.bbc.co.uk/tickets/
Apply for free tickets to watch live & recorded TV shows

**BBC World Service**
email via website
www.bbc.co.uk/worldservice

**BDA** see Dyslexia Association (British)

**Beamish**
Beamish Museum  Beamish  Co. Durham DH9 0RG
Tel: 0191 370 4000
museum@beamish.org.uk
www.beamish.org.uk
Recreates Northern life in the early 1800s and 1900s.

**BEAT (Beat Eating Disorders)**
103 Prince of Wales Rd  Norwich NR1 1DW
Tel: 01603 619090
Head Office: 0300 123 3355
info@b-eat.co.uk
www.b-eat.co.uk
Raises awareness & offers support to people affected by eating disorders

**Beaumont Society**
27 Old Gloucester St  London WC1N 3XX
Helpline: 01582 412 220
email@beaumontsociety.org.uk
www.beaumontsociety.org.uk
Self-help group for transsexuals, crossdressers and their families

**BECTA** British Educational Communications & Technology Agency
Milburn Hill Rd Science Park  Coventry CV4 7JJ
Tel: 024 7641 6994
customerservices@becta.org.uk
www.becta.org.uk
Government lead agency for Information and Communications Technology in education. October 2010: the body is to be closed and some of its functions transferred to the Department for Education

**Befrienders International**
www.befrienders.org
Worldwide organisation providing emotional support

**Behavioural & Cognitive Psychotherapies (British Association of)**
BABCP
BABCP Imperial House, Hornby Street, BURY, BL9 5BN
Tel: 0161 705 4304
babcp@babcp.com
www.babcp.com

**Benefits Agency** see Work & Pensions (Department for)

**Benesh Institute of Choreology**
c/o Royal Academy of Dance 36 Battersea Sq London SW11 3RA
Tel: 020 7326 8000
info@rad.org.uk
www.benesh.org
Training organisation and governing body of Benesh movement notation system

**Bereavement Network (London)**
61 Philpot Street London E1 2JH
info@bereavement.org.uk
www.bereavement.org.uk
Forum for bereavement issues in Greater London. Referral line for bereavement support.

**Berlin - Info**
www.berlin-info.de
Comprehensive information about Berlin in either German or English

**BESO** now see VSO

**Better Seating (Campaign for)**
www.betterseating.org
Information about the importance of chair design

**Better Transport (Campaign for)**
16 Waterside 44-48 Wharf Road London N1 7UX
Tel: 020 7566 6480
info@bettertransport.org.uk
www.bettertransport.org.uk
Sustainable transport campaign aiming to reduce car dependence

**Bevan Foundation**
Innovation Centre
Festival Drive Ebbw Vale Blaenau Gwent NP23 8XA
Tel: 01495 356 702
info@bevanfoundation.org
www.bevanfoundation.org
Radical Welsh think tank concerned with social justice

**BFI** see British Film Institute

**BHF** see British Heart Foundation

**Bibic**
Knowle Hall Bridgwater Somerset TA7 8PJ
Tel: 01278 684060
info@bibic.org.uk

www.bibic.org.uk
Works to help maximise the potential of children with conditions affecting behaviour, sensory processing, communication, social, motor and learning abilities.

**Bible Society**
Stonehill Green Westlea Swindon SN5 7DG
Tel: 01793 418 222
email via website
www.biblesociety.org.uk

**Bibliomania**
www.bibliomania.com
Literary texts (particularly those set for exams) available online

**Bibliothèque Nationale de France**
Email via website
www.bnf.fr
Web page giving information about the National Library of France in French and in English

**Bicycle Helmet Initiative Trust**
51 Milford Rd Reading RG1 8LG
Tel: 0118 958 3585
BHIT@dial.pipex.com
www.bhit.org
Promoting and educating about the need to wear bicycle helmets

**Big Bus**
Sherston Software Angel House Sherston Wiltshire SN16 0LH
Tel: 01666 843200
support@sherston.co.uk
www.thebigbus.com
Fun interactive learning for 3-11 year-olds

**Big Issue**
1-5 Wandsworth Road Vauxhall London SW8 2LN
Tel: 020 7526 3200
info@bigissue.coom
www.bigissue.com

**Big Lottery Fund**
1 Plough Place London EC4A 1DE
Tel: 0845 410 2030
Tel: 020 7211 1800
Textphone: 0845 602 1659
Tel: 0300 500 5050
general.enquiries@biglotteryfund.org.uk
www.biglotteryfund.org.uk
Lottery distribution organisation awarding funds for community projects

**Big Pit** National Coal Museum
Blaenafon Torfaen NP4 9XP
Tel: 01495 790 311
Email via website
www.museumwales.ac.uk/en/bigpit

**Big Read (The)**
info@campaignforeducation.org
www.campaignforeducation.org/bigread/
Campaign against illiteracy and for a decent
education for all

**Bike Events**
PO Box 2127  Bristol BS99 7LN
Email via website
www.bike-events.com
Organises charity bike rides

**Bike Express (European)**
3 Newfield Lane  South Cave  Hull  Hu15
2JW
Tel: 01430 422 111
info@bike-express.co.uk
www.bike-express.co.uk
In co-operation with CTC offers cyclists
convenient transport methods to favourite
cycling areas in France and beyond

**Bike Links** see Cycling Projects

**bikerecycling.net**
39 Magdalen Rd  Oxford OX4 1RB
email via website
www.bikerecycling.net
A directory of bicycle recycling and re-use
projects in the UK, with links and a brief
description of each.

**Bikers with a Disability (National
Association for)**
Unit 20 The Bridgewater Centre  Robson
Avenue  Urmston  Manchester M41 7TE
Tel: 0844 415 4849
nabd@nabd.org.uk
www.nabd.org.uk
Helps disabled people to enjoy the freedom
and independence of motorcycling

**Bilingualism, Languages, Literacies and
Education Network** (blen)
35 Connaught Rd  London N4 4NT
Tel: 020 7281 8686
ask@blen-education.org.uk
www.blen-education.org.uk

**Bill Douglas Centre for the History of
Cinema & Popular Culture** see Cinema &
Popular Culture

**Bioethics (Nuffield Council on)**
28 Bedford Square  London WC1B 3JS
Tel: 020 7681 9619
cjoynson@nuffieldbioethics.org
www.nuffieldbioethics.org
Examining ethical issues around developments
in medicine and biology

**Biological Diversity (Convention on)**
Secretariat  413 St Jacques St  suite 800
Montreal,  QC H2Y 1N9
Tel: 001 514 288 2220

secretariant@cbd.int
www.cbd.int

**Biology (Society of)**
9 Red Lion Court  London EC4A 3EF
Tel: 020 7936 5900
email via website
www.societyofbiology.org

**Biotechnology & Biological Sciences
Research Council**
Polaris House  North Star Avenue  Swindon
Wiltshire  SN2 1UH
Tel: 01793 413200
email via website
www.bbsrc.ac.uk/life
Explores the science & issues of modern
biological research

**Bird Council (British)**
Hampstead House  Condover Road  West
Heath  Birmingham B31 3QY
Tel: 0121 476 5999
info@britishbirdcouncil.com
www.britishbirdcouncil.com

**Birmingham Royal Ballet**
Thorp St  Birmingham B5 4AU
Tel: 0121 245 3500
info@brb.org.uk
www.brb.org.uk

**Birmingham Settlement**
Birmingham Settlement
Units 4-7 Alma House
Newtown Shopping Centre  Birmingham B19
2AB
Tel: 0121 250 3000
www.birminghamsettlement.org.uk
A multi-purpose inner city charity tackling
social disadvantage

**Birth Defects Foundation** see Newlife
Foundation for Disabled Children

**Birth Trauma Association** Helping people
traumatised by childbirth
PO Box 671  Ipswich  Suffolk  IP1 9AT
email via website
www.birthtraumaassociation.org.uk
Support for women suffering from Post Natal
Post Traumatic Stress Disorder (PTSD) or birth
trauma

**BirthChoice UK**
info@BirthChoiceUK.com
www.birthchoiceuk.com
To help make the right decisions about where
to have a baby

**BIS** see Business Innovation & Skills
(Department for) BIS

**Bitesize: BBC revision web site**
www.bbc.co.uk/schools/bitesize/
For KS2, 3 & 4 / Standard Grade

**BKA** British Kodaly Academy
c/o 13 Midmoor Road  London SW19 4JD
Tel: 01638 601664
enquiries@britishkodalyacademy.org
www.britishkodalyacademy.org
Musical literacy through singing

**Black Environment Network**
1st Floor  60 High St  Llanberis  Gwynedd
LL55 4EU
Tel: 0207 921 4339

ukoffice@ben-network.org.uk
www.ben-network.org.uk
Networking organisation working for full ethnic
participation in the built & natural environment

**Black History Month**
www.black-history-month.co.uk

**Black Police Association (National)**
PO Box 15690
Tamworth  Staffordshire  United Kingdom
B77 9HZ
Tel: 07971 162821
Email via website
www.nationalbpa.com

**Black Students Alliance (National)**
c/o NAAR (National Assembly Against Racism)
28 Commercial Street  London E1 6LS
Tel: 020 7247 9907
info@naar.org.uk
www.naar.org.uk

**Black Training & Enterprise Group**
2nd Floor  Lancaster House  31-33 Islington
High Street  London N1 9LH
Tel: 020 7843 6110
info@bteg.co.uk
www.bteg.co.uk
Seeks to ensure fair access and outcomes for
black communities in employment, enterprise
and regeneration

**Black Women for Wages for Housework**
contact Crossroads Women's Centre
Crossroads Women's Centre  230a Kentish
Town Road  London NW5 2AB
Tel: 020 7482 2496
allwomencount@crossroadswomen.net
www.allwomencount.net

**Black Women's Rape Action Project**
contact Crossroads Women's Centre
Crossroads Women's Centre  230a Kentish
Town Road  London NW5 2AB
Tel: 020 7482 2496
allwomencount@crossroadswomen.net
www.allwomencount.net

**Bladder and Bowel Foundation (B&BF)**
SATRA Innovation Park  Rockingham Road
Kettering  Northants NN16 9JH
Nurse helpline: 0845 345 0165

Tel: 01536 533255
info@bladderandbowelfoundation.org
www.bladderandbowelfoundation.org
The UK's largest advocacy charity providing
information and support for all types of
bladder and bowel related problems, including
incontinence, prostate problems, constipation
and Diverticular Disease, for patients, their
families, carers and healthcare professionals

**Blenheim CDP**
Head Office
66 Bolton Crescent  London SE5 0SE
Tel: 020 7582 2200
info@blenheimcdp.org.uk
www.blenheimcdp.org.uk
Advice and support to drug users at 3
locations in London area

**Blind** see also Deafblind UK, Guide
Dogs for the Blind Association, Listening
Books, Partially Sighted Society, Sense,
RNIB National Library Service, Sight
Savers International, Talking Newspaper
Association, Wireless for the Blind Fund
(British)

**Blind Golf Association (English)**
email via website
www.blindgolf.co.uk

**Blind in Business**
4th floor  1 London Wall Buildings  London
EC2M 5PG
Tel: 020 7588 1885
info@blindinbusiness.org.uk
www.blindinbusiness.co.uk
Improving education & employment
prospects of young visually impaired people

**Blind (National Federation of the)**
Sir John Wilson House  215 Kirkgate
Wakefield WF1 1JG
Tel: 01924 291 313
nfbuk@nfbuk.org
www.nfbuk.org
Campaigning organisation for a better quality
of life for blind and partially sighted people

**Blind (National Library for the)** see RNIB
National Library Service

**Blind People (Action for)**
14-16 Verney Rd  London SE16 3DZ
Helpline: 0303 123 9999
Tel: 020 7635 4800
Email via website
www.actionforblindpeople.org.uk
Employment support, hotels, supported
housing, out-of-school clubs for visually
impaired children, grants, information and
advice

## Blind (Royal National Institute of the)
RNIB

105 Judd St  London WC1H 9NE
Helpline: 0303 123 9999.
Tel: 020 7388 1266
helpline@rnib.org.uk
www.rnib.org.uk
Information, support & advice for anyone with a serious sight problem

## Blind Sport (British)

Pure Offices, Plato Close  Tachbrook Park Leamington Spa  Warwickshire
 CV34 6WE.
Tel: 01926 424247
info@britishblindsport.org.uk
www.britishblindsport.org.uk
Encourages blind and partially sighted children and adults to take part in sport and recreation

## Bliss – the premature baby charity

9 Holyrood Street  London Bridge  London SE1 2EL
Advice Line: 0500 618 140
Tel: 020 7378 1122
information@bliss.org.uk
www.bliss.org.uk

## Blogger

www.blogger.com
A site to help you create and manage a weblog

## Blood Donor Registration Line (National)

Tel: 0300 123 2323
Email via website
www.blood.co.uk

## Blood Pressure Association

60 Cranmer Terrace  London SW17 0QS
Blood Pressure Information Line:  0845 241 0989
Tel: 020 8772 4994
info@bpassoc.org.uk
www.bpassoc.org.uk
Information and support to the general public on problems of high blood pressure

## Blue Badge Network

198 Wolverhampton St  Dudley DY1 1DZ
Tel: 01384 257001
headoffice@bluebadgenetwork.org
www.bluebadgenetwork.org
Assists disabled people, and their families to integrate with society to overcome access problems. Seeks to maintain the integrity and validity of the concessionary parking permit

## Blue Cross

Shilton Rd  Burford  Oxon OX18 4PF
Tel: 01993 822 651
info@bluecross.org.uk
www.bluecross.org.uk
Animal welfare charity

**BMA** see British Medical Association

**BMAS** see Acupuncture Society (British Medical)

**BNTL-Freeway** British National Temperance League

30 Keswick Road  Worksop S81 7PT
Tel: 01909 477882
bntl@btconnect.com
www.bntl.org
The 'Freeway' newsletter provides drug and alcohol resources based around the national curriculum

## Boarding Concern

email via website
www.boardingconcern.org.uk
Represents people who have concerns about the practice of boarding education for the young and the effect on these people as adults. This website offers a voice and provides information and support to ex-boarders, current boarders and those thinking of boarding

**Boardsailing Association (UK)** now see Windsurfing Association

## Bodleian Library

Main Enquiry Desk  Bodleian Library  Broad Street  Oxford OX1 3BG
Tel: 01865 277162
reader.services@bodleian.ox.ac.uk
www.bodleian.ox.ac.uk/bodley
Main research library of the University of Oxford and copyright deposit library

## Body Positive

39 Russell Road  Whalley Range Manchester M16 8DH
Helpline: 0161 882 2202
Tel: 0161 882 2200
info@bpnw.org.uk
www.bpnw.org.uk
Service provider for people affected and infected by HIV/AIDS

## Body Shop Foundation

Watermead  Littlehampton   West Sussex BN17 6LS
Tel: 01903 844 039
bodyshopfoundation@thebodyshop.com
www.thebodyshopfoundation.org
Human/civil rights projects, animals & environment. No unsolicited requests for support

## Bolshoi Ballet

www.bolshoi.ru/en

**BOND** (British Overseas NGOs for Development)
Regent's Wharf  8 All Saints Street  London N1 9RL
Tel: 020 7837 8344
Email via website
www.bond.org.uk
The UK's broadest network of voluntary organisations working in international development

**Book Aid International**
39-41 Coldharbour Lane  Camberwell London SE5 9NR
Tel: 020 7733 3577
info@bookaid.org
www.bookaid.org
Works in partnership with organisations in developing countries to support their work in literacy, education, training and publishing.

**Book Fair** see Frankfurt Book Fair

**Book Festival** see Edinburgh International Book Festival, Hay Festival

**Book Power**
120 Pentonville Road  London N1 9JN
Tel:  020 7843 1938
info@bookpower.org
www.bookpower.org
Making available the best, most relevant textbooks to university and vocational students in low-income countries at prices which students and their institutions' libraries can afford

**Book Trust (Scottish)**
Sandeman House  Trunk's Close  55 High St Edinburgh EH1 1SR
Tel: 0131 524 0160
info@scottishbooktrust.com
www.scottishbooktrust.com
Scotland's national agency for readers and writers. Provides key services to readers, writers and the educational sector

**BookCrossing**
www.bookcrossing.com
Encourages readers to leave books for others in a public place and tracks their progress via the web

**Books Council (Welsh)**
Castell Brychan  Aberystwyth  Ceredigion SY23 2JB
Tel: 01970 624151
castellbrychan@wbc.org.uk
www.wbc.org.uk
www.gwales.com
National body which provides a focus for the publishing industry in Wales

**BOOKTRUST**
Book House  45 East Hill  London SW18 2QZ
Tel: 020 8516 2977
query@booktrust.org.uk
www.booktrust.org.uk
www.booktrustchildrensbooks.org.uk
Book information service, reading resource centre, book prizes, projects and National Children's Book Week

**Border and Immigration Agency** now see UK Border Agency

**Borderline**
37 King Street  Covent Garden  London WC2E 8JS
Tel: 0800 174 047
Tel: 0845 456 2190
Email via website
www.borderline-uk.org
Advice, information & support to homeless Scots in London

**Born Free Foundation**
3 Grove House  Foundry Lane  Horsham RH13 5PL
Tel: 01403 240 170
info@bornfree.org.uk
www.bornfree.org.uk
International wildlife charity which promotes conservation and compassionate education and investigates animal suffering

**Botanic Garden of Wales (National)**
Llanarthne  Carmarthenshire SA32 8HG
Tel: 01558 668 768
info@gardenofwales.org.uk
www.gardenofwales.org.uk

**Botanic Gardens** see Royal Botanic Gardens, Edinburgh & Kew

**Botanical Society of British Isles**
c/o Dept of Botany  Natural History Museum Cromwell Rd  London SW7 5BD
coordinator@bsbi.org.uk
www.bsbi.org.uk

**Bounty Healthcare Fund**
healthcarefund@bounty.com
www.bounty.com/charity
Raises funds for good causes which make family life easier

**Bowel Cancer UK**
7 Rickett St  London SW6 1RU
Helpline: 0800 8 40 35 40
Tel: 020 7381 9711
admin@bowelcanceruk.org.uk
www.bowelcanceruk.org.uk

**Bowling** see also Crown Green Bowling Association (British), Womens' Bowling Federations (English)

## Bowling Association Ltd (English Indoor)

David Cornwell House  Bowling Green
Leicester Road  Melton Mowbray LE13 0FA
Tel: 01664 481900
enquiries@eiba.co.uk
www.eiba.co.uk
National governing body for indoor level
green bowls in England

**Boxing** see Amateur Boxing Association
of England Ltd., Amateur Boxing Scotland
Ltd.

## Boys Brigade

Felden Lodge  Felden  Hemel Hempstead
HP3 0BL
Tel: 01442 231 681
enquiries@boys-brigade.org.uk
www.boys-brigade.org.uk
Uniform youth organisation for children and
young people

**BPAS** British Pregnancy Advisory Service
20 Timothys Bridge Road  Stratford
Enterprise Park  Stratford-upon-Avon CV37 9BF
Actionline: 08457 30 40 30
Tel: 0870 365 5050
info@bpas.org
www.bpas.org
Non-profit making charity offering advice
and treatment for unplanned pregnancy and
fertility control

**Brain Injuries** see BASIC, BIBIC, Child
Brain Injury Trust, HEADWAY

**Brain & Spinal Injury Centre** see BASIC

## Brain & Spine Foundation

3.36 Canterbury Court  Kennington Park  1-3
Brixton Road  London SW9 6DE
Helpline: 0808 808 1000
Tel: 020 7793 5900
info@brainandspine.org.uk
www.brainandspine.org.uk
A registered charity supporting neuroscience
research projects. Offers information service
and education

## Brainwave

Huntworth Gate  Bridgwater  Somerset TA6
6LQ
Tel: 01278 429 089
Email via website
www.brainwave.org.uk
Therapy & rehabilitation for children with
special needs

## Brake

PO Box 548  Huddersfield HD1 2XZ
Helpline: 0845 603 8570
Tel: 01484 559 909
brake@brake.org.uk
www.brake.org.uk
Road safety organisation

## Brandon Centre

26 Prince of Wales Rd  London NW5 3LG
Tel: 020 7267 4792
reception@brandon-centre.org.uk
www.brandon-centre.org.uk
Counselling, psychotherapy and
contraceptive advice for 12-21 year olds

## Brathay Exploration Group

Brathay Hall  Ambleside  Cumbria LA22 0HP
Tel: 015394 33942
admin@brathayexploration.org.uk
www.brathayexploration.org.uk
Expeditions in wild parts of the world for 16-
25 year olds

## Brazil's Children Trust (Action for)

Level 4, 53 Frith Street  London W1D 4SN
Tel: 020 7494 9344
info@abctrust.org.uk
www.abctrust.org.uk
Aims to relieve suffering, maintain and
educate deprived, children, young people
and their families

## Breakthrough Breast Cancer

3rd Floor Weston House  246 High Holborn
London WC1V 7EX
Freephone Info Line: 08080 100 200
Tel: 020 7025 2400
info@breakthrough.org.uk
www.breakthrough.org.uk

## Breast Cancer Care

5-13 Great Suffolk Street  London SE1 0NS
Helpline: 0808 800 6000
Textphone: 0808 800 6001
info@breastcancercare.org.uk
www.breastcancercare.org.uk
National organisation offering support and
information

**Breastfeeding** see La Leche League

## Breathing places

BBC Learning Campaigns  MC4 A5  Media
Centre  201 Wood Lane  London W12 7TQ
Email via website
www.bbc.co.uk/breathingplaces
Areas that have been or are being
transformed by the public to create an oasis
for people and wildlife, including insects,
birds, plants and mammals

## BRIT School for Performing Arts and Technology

60 The Crescent  Croydon  CR0 2HN
Tel: 020 8665 5242
admin@brit.croydon.sch.uk
www.brit.croydon.sch.uk

## British Association for the Advancement of Science (BA) now see Science Association (British)

## British Council

Bridgewater House  58 Whitworth Street
Manchester M1 6BB
Tel: 0161 957 7755
general.enquiries@britishcouncil.org
www.britishcouncil.org/
Cultural, educational & technical co-operation between Britain & other countries

## British Film Institute BFI

21 Stephen St  London W1T 1LN
Tel: 020 7255 1444
Email via website
www.bfi.org.uk

## British Heart Foundation

Greater London House  180 Hampstead
Road  London NW1 7AW
Heart Information Line: 0300 330 3311
Tel: 020 7554 0000
internet@bhf.org.uk
www.bhf.org.uk
Leading heart research charity

## British Jews ( Board of Deputies of)

6 Bloomsbury Square  London WC1A 2LP
Tel: 020 7543 5400
info@bod.org.uk
www.bod.org.uk
Elected representative body of the British
Jewish community.

## British Legion (Royal)

199 Borough High Street  London SE1 1AA
Legionline: 08457 725 725
Tel: 020 3207 2100
email via website
www.britishlegion.org.uk
Safeguarding the welfare, interests and
memory of those who have served in the
Armed Forces

## British Library

96 Euston Rd  London NW1 2DB
Tel: 020 7412 7333
development@bl.uk
www.bl.uk

## British Library Sound Archive

96 Euston Rd  London NW1 2DB
Tel: 020 7412 7676
email via website
www.bl.uk/soundarchive
Holds recordings of popular, classical &
world and traditional music, oral history,
drama and literature and wildlife sounds

## British Medical Association BMA

BMA House  Tavistock Sq  London WC1H
9JP
Tel: 020 7387 4499
Email via website
www.bma.org.uk
Voluntary professional association for
doctors

## British Museum

Great Russell St  London WC1B 3DG
Tel: 020 7323 8000
information@britishmuseum.org
www.britishmuseum.org

## British Pregnancy Advisory Service see
BPAS

## British Rowing

6 Lower Mall  Hammersmith  London W6
9DJ
Tel: 020 8237 6700
info@britishrowing.org
www.britishrowing.org
Governing body for rowing in GB

## British Standards Institute BSI

389 Chiswick High Rd  London W4 4AL
Tel: 020 8996 9001
cservices@bsigroup.com
www.bsigroup.com
National body producing standards and
technical regulations for industry and small
businesses

## Brittle Bone Society

Grant-Paterson House  30 Guthrie St
Dundee DD1 5BS
Helpline: 08000 28 24 59
Tel: 01382 204446
contact@brittlebone.org
www.brittlebone.org
Promotes research & supports people with
osteogenesis imperfecta and their families

## Broadcasting Standards Commission
now see OFCOM

## Broadcasting Trust (International)

CAN Mezzanine  32-6 Loman Street  London
SE1 0EH
Tel: 020 7922 7940
mail@ibt.org.uk
www.ibt.org.uk
Educational charity & independent TV
production company specialising in
development, environment and human rights
issues

## Broadway

15 Half Moon Court
Bartholomew Close  London
EC1A 7HF
Tel: 020 7710 0550
reception@broadwaylondon.org
broadway.jamkit.com
Support & rehousing services to homeless
people in London

## Broken Rainbow

J414 Tower Bridge Business Complex  100
Clements Rd  London
SE16 4DG

Helpline: 0300 999 5428
Tel: 08452 60 55 60
mail@broken-rainbow.org.uk
www.broken-rainbow.org.uk/
Support for lesbian, gay, bisexual and
transgender (LGBT) people experiencing
domestic violence

**Brontë Society**
Brontë Parsonage Museum  Haworth
Keighley  West Yorkshire BD22 8DR
Tel: 01535 642 323
info@bronte.org.uk
www.bronte.info

**Brook**
421 Highgate Studios  53-79 Highgate Rd
London NW5 1TL
Tel: 0808 802 1234 (Young People's Helpline)
Tel: 020 7284 6040
admin@brook.org.uk
www.brook.org.uk
Free sexual health & contraceptive advice
service for young people under 25

**Brooke Hospital for Animals**
The Brooke  30 Farringdon Street  London
EC4A 4HH
Tel: 0203 012 3456
Email via website
www.thebrooke.org
Healthy working animals for the world's
poorest communities. Operating in
Egypt, India, Jordan and Pakistan, and in
Afghanistan, Kenya and Guatemala

**BSES Expeditions**
Royal Geographical Society  1 Kensington
Gore  London SW7 2AR
Tel: 020 7591 3141
info@bses.org.uk
www.bses.org.uk
Runs adventure and research expeditions for
16-20 year olds

**BSI** see British Standards Institute

**BTCV**
Sedum House  Mallard Way  Doncaster DN4
8DB
Tel: 01302 388883
information@btcv.org.uk
www.btcv.org.uk
Working with people to bring about positive
environmental change

**BTCV Scotland**
Balallan House  24 Allan Park  Stirling FK8
2QG
Tel: 01786 479697
scotland@btcv.org.uk
www.btcv.org.uk
Scottish environmental conservation charity

**BTEC** see Edexel

**BUAV** see Vivisection (British Union for the
Abolition of)

**Buddhist Centre, North London**
72 Holloway Rd  Islington  London N7 8JG
Tel: 020 7700 1177
via website
www.northlondonbuddhistcentre.com

**Buddhist Information Network**
www.buddhanet.net

**Buddhist Society**
58 Eccleston Sq  London SW1V 1PH
Tel: 020 7834 5858
info@thebuddhistsociety.org
www.thebuddhistsociety.org
Centre teaching Buddhism and meditation.
Also large Buddhist library and bookshop

**Budgerigar Society**
Spring Gardens  Northampton NN1 1DR
Tel: 01604 624549
www.budgerigarsociety.com

**Bugatti Trust**
Prescott Hill  Gotherington  Cheltenham
Gloucestershire GL52 9RD
Tel: 01242 677201
Email via website
www.bugatti-trust.co.uk
To preserve and make available for study the
works of Ettore Bugatti

**Building & Social Housing Foundation**
Memorial Square  Coalville  Leicestershire
LE67 3TU
Tel: 01530 510444
bshf@bshf.org
www.bshf.org
Carries out research into low cost housing
around the world

**Building Societies** see also Ecology
Building Society, Financial Ombudsman
Service, Save our Building Societies

**Building Societies Members Association**
49 Clifford Avenue  Taunton  Somerset TA2
6DL
Tel: 01823 321 304
Info@building-societies-members.org.uk
www.building-societies-members.org.uk
Fighting to maintain mutuality &
accountability of the building societies to
their members

**Bully Free Zone**
50 Chorley New Road
 Bolton  BL1 4AP
Tel: 01204 454 958
office@bullyfreezone.co.uk
www.bullyfreezone.co.uk
Provide a service for children and young
people who have issues around bullying

**Bullying** see also Andrea Adams Trust, Anti Bullying Network, Childline, Kidscape, Stop Text Bullying

**Bullying Online**
702 Windsor House Cornwall Road Harrogate HG1 2PW
help@bullying.co.uk
www.bullying.co.uk

**Bungee Jumping** see Elastic Rope Sports Association (British)

**Burma Campaign UK**
28 Charles Square London N1 6HT
Tel: 020 73244710
info@burmacampaign.org.uk
www.burmacampaign.org.uk
Human rights & democracy in Burma

**Burrell Collection**
Pollok Country Park 2060 Pollokshaws Rd Glasgow G43 1AT
Tel: 0141 287 0047
museums@glasgowlife.org.uk
www.glasgowmuseums.com

**Bus Users UK**
PO Box 2950 Stoke on Trent ST4 9EW
Tel: 01782 442855
enquiries@bususers.org
www.bususers.org

**Business, Enterprise and Regulatory Reform (Department for)** now see Business Innovation & Skills (Department for) BIS

**Business in Sport & Leisure** BISL
Tel: 020 8255 3782
info@bisl.org
www.bisl.org
Umbrella organisation for private sector companies

**Business in the Community**
137 Shepherdess Walk London N1 7RQ
Tel: 020 7566 8650
information@bitc.org.uk
www.bitc.org.uk
Companies across the UK committed to improving their positive impact on society

**Business, Innovation & Skills (Department for )**
1 Victoria St London SW1H 0ET
Tel: 020 7215 5000
Minicom: 020 7215 6740
email via website
www.bis.gov.uk/

**Business Link**
Tel: 0845 600 9 006
minicom Tel 0845 606 2666
email via website
www.businesslink.gov.uk
Practical advice for business

**Business & Professional Women UK Ltd**
74 Fairfield Rise Billericay Essex CM12 9NU
Tel: 01277 623 867
hq@bpwuk.co.uk
www.bpwuk.co.uk
Lobbying training and networking organisation for working women

**Business Shop Network (Scottish)**
Tel: 0845 609 6611
www.bgateway.com
Information and start-up service for small and medium enterprise companies

**Business & Technology Education Council (BTEC)** see Edexel

**Butterfly Conservation**
Manor Yard East Lulworth Wareham Dorset BH20 5QP
Tel: 01929 400 209
info@butterfly-conservation.org
www.butterfly-conservation.org
UK charity taking action to save butterflies, moths and their habitats

**Buy nothing day**
bndpress@googlemail.com
www.buynothingday.co.uk
Challenges consumer culture. Takes place on the last Saturday in November

**Byways & Bridleways Trust**
PO Box 117 Newcastle upon Tyne NE3 5YT
editor@bbtrust.org.uk
www.bbtrust.org.uk

# C

**CAAT** see Campaign Against Arms Trade

**CABE** Commission for Architecture & the Built Environment
1 Kemble Street London WC2B 4AN
Tel: 020 7070 6700
info@cabe.org.uk
www.cabe.org.uk
Ensures quality of new buildings

**Cabinet Office**
70 Whitehall
London SW1A 2AS
Tel: 020 7276 1234
Email via website
www.cabinetoffice.gov.uk

**CACHE** Council for Awards in Children's Care and Education
Apex House 81 Camp Road St Albans Hertfordshire AL1 5GB
Tel: 0845 347 2123
info@cache.org.uk
www.cache.org.uk

**CADD** Campaign Against Drinking &
Driving
 PO Box 62  Brighouse  West Yorkshire HD6
 3YY
 Helpline: 0845 123 5542
 Tel: 0845 1235541
 Tel: 0845 123 5543
 cadd@scard.org.uk
 www.cadd.org.uk

**Cadw**
 Welsh Assembly Government  Plas Carew
 Unit 5/7 Cefn Coed  Parc Nantgarw  Cardiff
 CF15 7QQ
 Tel: 01443 336000
 cadw@wales.gsi.gov.uk
 www.cadw.wales.gov.uk
 Protects and conserves the ancient
 monuments and historic buildings in Wales

**CAF** see Charities Aid Foundation

**Cafcass** Children and Family Court
Advisory Support Service
 6th Floor  Sanctuary Buildings  Great Smith
 Street  London SW1P 3BT
 Tel: 0844 353 3350
 webenquiries@cafcass.gsi.gov.uk
 www.cafcass.gov.uk
 October 2010: Future under consideration as
 part of a review of the family justice system
 reporting in 2011.

**CAFOD** Catholic Agency for Overseas
Development
 Romero House  55 Westminster Bridge
 Road  London  SE1 7JB
 Tel: 020 7733 7900
 cafod@cafod.org.uk
 www.cafod.org.uk

**CALM** Campaign Against Living Miserably
 Tel: 0800 58 58 58
 info@thecalmzone.net
 www.thecalmzone.net
 Encourages young men aged 15 to 35 in
 Manchester, Merseyside and Bedfordshire
 to open up and talk about their problems.
 Helpline open to all ages and sexes

**Calvert Trust** Kielder
 Kielder Water  Hexham   Northumberland
 NE48 1BS
 Tel: 01434 250232
 email via website
 www.calvert-trust.org.uk

**&**
 Wistlandpound  Kentisbury   Barnstaple
 North Devon EX31 4SJ
 Tel: 01598 763221
 email via website
 www.calvert-trust.org.uk/exmoor/
 Activity holidays for people of all abilities

**&**
 Little Crosthwaite  Keswick  Cumbria CA12
 4QD
 Tel/minicom: 017687 72255
 email via website
 www.calvert-trust.org.uk

**Cambridge Past, Present & Future**
 Wandlebury Ring  Gog Magog Hills
 Babraham  Cambridge CB22 3AE
 Tel: 01223 243830
 email via website
 www.cambridgeppf.org
 Aims to protect the character, amenities,
 historic buildings and settings of Cambridge
 and its surroundings.

**CAMFED International** Campaign for
Female Education
 22 Millers Yard  Mill Lane  Cambridge CB2
 1RQ
 Tel: 01223 362648
 info@camfed.org
 www.camfed.org
 Supporting the education of girls in Africa

**Camp Mohawk**
 Highfield Lane  Crazies Hill  Wargrave
 Berkshire RG10 8PU
 Tel: 0118 940 4045
 camp_mohawk@hotmail.com
 http://www.campmohawkuk.btik.com/
 A unique and very caring camp offering day
 care for brain damaged and autistic children
 from all over England.

**Campaign Against Arms Trade** CAAT
 11 Goodwin St  Finsbury Park  London N4
 3HQ
 Tel: 020 7281 0297
 enquiries@caat.org.uk
 www.caat.org.uk

**Campaign Against Drinking & Driving**
see CADD

**Campaign Against Living Miserably** see
CALM

**Campaign for Nuclear Disarmament** see
CND

**Campaign for the Protection of Rural
Wales** see Protection of Rural Wales
(Campaign for the)

**Campaign to Protect Rural England** see
CPRE

**Camping and Caravanning Club**
 Greenfields House  Westwood Way
 Coventry CV4 8JH
 Tel: 0845 130 7631
 Tel: 024 7647 5448
 email via website
 www.campingandcaravanningclub.co.uk

The largest and longest established membership organisation for all types of camping and caravanning

**CAMRA** Campaign for Real Ale
230 Hatfield Rd  St Albans AL1 4LW
Tel: 01727 867201
camra@camra.org.uk
www.camra.org.uk
To promote and preserve full-flavoured, distinctive beers, ciders and perries and the best features of the pub

**Canals** see Inland Waterways Association

**Cancer** see also Bowel Cancer UK, Breakthrough Breast Cancer, Breast Cancer Care, Children with Leukaemia, Christian Lewis Trust, CLICSargent, Core, Hereditary Breast Cancer Helpline, Leukaemia & Lymphoma Research, Macmillan Cancer Support, Marie Curie Cancer Care, Orchid Cancer Appeal, Prostate Cancer Helpline, Roy Castle Lung Cancer Foundation, Tenovus

**Cancer and Leukaemia in Childhood** see CLICSargent

**Cancer BACUP** now see Macmillan Cancer Support

**Cancer Research UK**
PO Box 123  Lincoln's Inn Fields  London WC2A 3PX
Tel: 020 7242 0200
email via website
www.cancerresearchuk.org

**Cancer Resource Centre** now see Paul D'Auria Cancer Support Centre

**Cancer Society (American)**
email via website
www.cancer.org

**CancerHelp UK**
Nurse: 0808 800 4040
cancerhelpuk@cancer.org.uk
www.cancerhelp.org.uk
Information website from Cancer Research UK

**Canine Defence League** see Dogs Trust

**Canine Partners**
Mill Lane  Heyshott  Midhurst  West Sussex GU29 0ED
Tel: 08456 580 480
email via website
www.caninepartners.co.uk
Trains assistance dogs for disabled people

**Canoe Association of N. Ireland**
Unit 2, Rivers Edge  13-15 Ravenhill Road Belfast BT6 8DN
Tel: 02890738884
office@cani.org.uk
www.cani.org.uk

**Canoe Association (Scottish)**
Caledonia House  South Gyle  Edinburgh EH12 9DQ
Tel: 0131 317 7314
general.office@canoescotland.org
www.canoescotland.org
National Governing Body for canoe sport in Scotland

**Canoe Union (British)**
18 Market Place  Bingham  Nottingham NG13 8AP
Tel: 0845 3709 500
Tel: 0300 0119 500
Info@bcu.org.uk
www.bcu.org.uk
Governing body of sport for canoe & kayak in the UK

**Canoe Wales**
Canolfan Tryweryn  Frongoch  Bala Gwynedd LL23 7NU
Tel: 01678 521083
welsh.canoeing@virgin.net
www.welsh-canoeing.org.uk

**Canoeing Association (Welsh)** now see Canoe Wales

**Canon Collins Educational Trust for Southern Africa** CCETSA
22 The Ivories  6 Northampton St  London N1 2HY
Tel: 020 7354 1462
info@canoncollins.org.uk
www.canoncollins.org.uk

**Captive Animals' Protection Society**
PO Box 4186  Manchester M60 3ZA
Tel: 0845 330 3911
info@captiveanimals.org
www.captiveanimals.org
Campaigns against use of animals in circuses & zoos

**Caravan Club**
East Grinstead House  East Grinstead  West Sussex RH19 1UA
Tel: 01342 326944
enquiries@caravanclub.co.uk
www.caravanclub.co.uk

**Caravanning** see also Camping & Caravanning Club

**Carbon Neutral Company**
Bravington House  2 Bravington Walk  Regent Quarter  Kings Cross  London N1 9AF
Tel: 020 7833 6000
email via website
www.carbonneutral.com
Plants trees to offset carbon emissions

**Cardiac Risk in the Young** CRY
Unit 7  Epsom Downs Metro Centre Waterfield, Tadworth  Surrey KT20 5LR

Tel: 01737 363222
cry@c-r-y.org.uk
www.c-r-y.org.uk
Campaigning for ECG testing in schools and sports clubs. Offers counselling to bereaved families and funds research into heart disease

**CARE** now see Self Unlimited

**Care Council for Wales** Cyngor Gofal Cymru
South Gate House  Wood Street  Cardiff CF10 1EW
Tel: 029 2022 6257
info@ccwales.org.uk
www.ccwales.org.uk

**Care for the Wild International**
The Granary  Tickfold Farm  Kingsfold RH12 3SE
Tel: 01306 627900
info@careforthewild.com
www.careforthewild.com
Charity dedicated to protecting wild animals

**Care in the Community** see Zito Trust

**CARE International UK**
10-13 Rushworth Street  London SE1 0RB
Tel: 020 7934 9334
email via website
www.careinternational.org.uk
Development charity helping world's poorest and most vulnerable people

**Care Not Killing**
PO Box 56322  London SE1 8XW
Tel: 020 7234 9680
info@carenotkilling.org.uk
www.carenotkilling.org.uk
Promoting more and better palliative care and ensuring that existing laws against euthanasia and assisted suicide are not weakened or repealed

**Care Quality Commission**
Citygate  Gallowgate  Newcastle upon Tyne NE1 4PA
Tel: 03000 616161
enquiries@cqc.org.uk
www.cqc.org.uk/
Independent regulator of health and social care in England. Aims to make sure better care is provided for everyone, whether that's in hospital, in care homes, in people's own homes, or elsewhere

**Career Development Loans**
email via website
www.lifelonglearning.co.uk/cdl
A deferred repayment loan providing individuals with help to fund vocational education or learning

**Careers Research & Advisory Centre** CRAC
2nd Floor  Sheraton House  Castle Park Cambridge CB3 0AX
Tel: 01223 460277
email via website
www.crac.org.uk

**Carers** see CROSSROADS Care

**Carers (The Princess Royal Trust For)**
Charles Oakley House  125 West Regent Street  Glasgow  G2 2SD
Tel: 0141 221 5066
infoscotland@carers.org
www.carers.org
96 centres in UK providing information for carers

&
Unit 14  Bourne Court  Southend Road Woodford Green  Essex IG8 8HD
Tel: 0844 800 4361
info@carers.org
www.carers.org
Information, advice and support

**Carers UK**
20 Great Dover Street  London SE1 4LX
Carersline: 0808 808 7777 (freefone)
Tel: 020 7378 4999
info@carersuk.org
www.carersuk.org
Information and advice on all aspects of caring

**CASE - Campaign for Science and Engineering**
Gordon House
 29 Gordon Square  London   WC1H 0PP
Tel: 020 7679 4995
info@sciencecampaign.org.uk
www.sciencecampaign.org.uk
An independent campaign for effective policies for science, engineering, technology and medicine and a proper appreciation of their cultural and economic importance

**Cash Machines (World Wide Locator of)**
http://visa.via.infonow.net/locator/global/

**Casualties Union**
PO Box 1942  London E17 6YU
Tel: 08700 780590
hq@casualtiesunion.org.uk
www.casualtiesunion.org.uk
Recruits volunteers to act as casualties in first aid and rescue practice

**Cat Fancy (Governing Council of the)**
5 Kings Castle Business Park  The Drove Bridgewater  Somerset TA6 4AG
Tel: 01278 427 575
info@gccfcats.org

www.gccfcats.org
Registers pedigree cats

**Catch22**
Churchill House  142-146 Old Street
London EC1V 9BW
Tel: 020 7336 4800
information@catch-22.org.uk
www.catch-22.org.uk
National charity that works with young
people who find themselves in difficult
situations

**Catholic Agency to Support
Evangelisation**
39 Eccleston Square  London SW1V 1BX
Tel: 0207 901 4863
 info@caseresources.org.uk
www.caseresources.org.uk

**Catholic Education Service**
39 Eccleston Sq  London SW1V 1BX
Tel: 0207 901 1900
general@cesew.org.uk
www.cesew.org.uk
Educational agency of The Catholic Bishops
Conference of England and Wales

**Cats Protection**
National Cat Centre
 Chelwood Gate  Sussex
 RH17 7TT
National helpline: 03000 12 12 12
Tel: 08707 708 649
helpline@cats.org.uk
www.cats.org.uk
UK's oldest and largest feline charity offering
rescue, rehabilitation and rehoming services

**Caving Association (British)**
The Old Methodist Chapel  Great Hucklow
Buxton SK17 8RG
www.british-caving.org.uk

**CCETSA** see Canon Collins Educational
Trust for Southern Africa

**CEE**  see Environmental Education (Council
for)

**CEH** Centre for Ecology & Hydrology
NERC Headquarters  Polaris House  North
Star Avenue  Swindon  Wilts SN2 1EU
Tel: 01491 692371
enquiries@ceh.ac.uk
www.ceh.ac.uk
Environmental research

**Cello Society**
www.cello.org
Non profit society run by cellists for cellists

**CEMVO** Council of Ethnic Minority
Voluntary Sector Organisations
www.cemvo.org.uk
Charity for the social regeneration of Black &
Minority Ethnic Communities

**Census** see 1901 Census for England &
Wales, Family Search, FreeBMD, Indian
Census, National Archives, Office for
National Statistics, Register Office for N.
Ireland, Register Office for Scotland

**Central Office of Information** COI
Hercules House  Hercules Rd  London SE1
7DU
Tel: 020 7928 2345
email via website
www.coi.gov.uk
October 2010: future under review

**Centre for Alternative Technology** see
Alternative Technology (Centre for)

**Centre for Economic & Social Inclusion**
Camelford House  3rd Floor  89 Albert
Embankment  London SE1 7TP
Tel: 020 7582 7221
info@cesi.org.uk
www.cesi.org.uk

**Centre for Studies on Inclusive
Education** see Inclusive Education (Centre
for Studies on)

**Centrepoint**
Central House  25 Camperdown Street
London E1 8DZ
Tel: 0845 466 3400
email via website
www.centrepoint.org.uk
Runs emergency shelters and
accommodation in Greater London for
homeless young people (16-25)

**Ceroc**
77 Fernhead Road  London W9 3EA
Tel: 020 8969 4401
email via website
www.ceroc.com
Fusion of jive and salsa

**Certification Office for Trade Unions and
Employers' Association**
22nd Floor Euston Tower  286 Euston Road
London NW1 3JJ
Tel: 020 7210 3734
info@certoffice.org
www.certoffice.org
October 2010: Will merge with the Central
Arbitration Committee, which also works
with Trade Unions and employers.

**CF Appointments Ltd.**  also trading as
Charity and Fundraising Appointments Ltd
52-54 Gracechurch Street  London EC3V
0EH
Tel: 020 7220 0180
enquiries@cfappointments.com
www.cfappointments.com
Fills senior executive positions for charities
and not-for-profit organisations etc

## CfBT Education Trust
60 Queens Road  Reading  Berkshire RG1 4BS
Tel: 0118 902 1000
enquiries@cfbt.com
www.cfbt.com
An education consultancy and service organisation which aims to provide education for public benefit both in the UK and internationally.

## Chain of Hope
South Parade   Chelsea  London SW3 6NP
Tel: 020 7351 1978
info@chainofhope.org
www.chainofhope.org
Chain of Hope exists to provide children suffering from life-threatening disease with the corrective surgery and treatment to which they do not have access

## Chambers of Commerce (British)
65 Petty France  London SW1H 9EU
Tel: 020 7654 5800
info@britishchambers.org.uk
www.britishchambers.org.uk

## Chance UK
2nd Floor, London Fashion Centre  89-93 Fonthill Rd  London N4 3JH
Tel: 020 7281 5858
admin@chanceuk.com
www.chanceuk.com
Early intervention in the lives of vulnerable children, to build a brighter future. Solution focused mentoring for children aged 5-11 years.

## Changemakers
Ground Floor  Zetland House  5-25 Scrutton Street  London EC2A 4HJ
Tel: 020 7033 6970
info@changemakers.org.uk
www.changemakers.org.uk
A charity which encourages young people to tackle issues of concern to themselves, their community and to the world in which they live

## Changing Faces
The Squire Centre  33-37 University Street London WC1E 6JN
Tel: 0845 4500 275
info@changingfaces.org.uk
www.changingfaces.org.uk
Advice & counselling for children and adults with disfigurements and promotion of public awareness

## Channel 4
PO Box 1058  Belfast BT1 9DU
Tel: 0845 076 0191
email via website
www.channel4.com

## Channel 5 see Five

## Channel Arts Association
The Ariel Studios  Mullacott Cross  Ilfracombe Devon EX34 8ND
Tel: 01271 862701
www.ariel.org.uk
Studio/rehearsal space and digital recording studio

## Charities Aid Foundation CAF
25 Kings Hill Avenue  Kings Hill  West Malling Kent ME19 4TA
Tel: 03000 123 000
enquiries@cafonline.org
www.cafonline.org
CAF is the not for profit organisation which is committed to effective giving, providing a range of specialist services to donors, companies and charities in the UK and internationally

## CharitiesDirect.com
www.charitiesdirect.com
A guide to UK charities

## Charity Appointments see CF Appointments Ltd.

## Charity Choice
www.charitychoice.co.uk
Online Guide to Charities in the UK

## Charity Commission for England & Wales
PO Box 1227  Liverpool  L69 3UG
Tel: 0845 3000218
email via website
www.charity-commission.gov.uk
Registers, supervises and advises charities. Provides free publications and runs an outreach and education programme

## Charter 88 now see Unlock Democracy

## Chartered Management Institute
Management House  Cottingham Rd  Corby NN17 1TT
Tel: 01536 204222
enquiries@managers.org.uk
www.managers.org.uk
Professional organisation

## Chartered Surveyors (Royal Institute of) RICS
RICS   Parliament Square  London   SW1P 3AD
Tel: 0870 333 1600
contactrics@rics.org
www.rics.org
Professional body for surveyors

## Chartered Surveyors Training Trust
16th Floor
The Tower Building  11 York Road London  SE1 7NX

Tel: 0207 871 0454
cstt@cstt.org.uk
www.cstt.org.uk
Encourages young people to become
chartered surveyors via other routes than
university

**Chartered Surveyors Voluntary Service**
Parliament Square  London  SW1P 3AD
Tel: 0870 333 1600
contactrics@rics.org.uk
www.rics.org
Works with Citizen's Advice Bureaux when a
chartered surveyor can't be afforded

**Chemistry (Royal Society of)**
Burlington House  Piccadilly  London W1J 0BA
Tel: 020 7437 8656
email via website
www.rsc.org

**Chernobyl Children's Life Line**
Courts  61 Petworth Rd  Haslemere  Surrey
GU27 3AX
Tel: 01428 642 523
email via website
www.chernobylchildlifeline.org
Supports child victims of radioactivity and
organises recuperative visits to the UK

**Chess Association (Braille)**
customerservices@braillechess.org.uk
www.braillechess.org.uk

**Chess Association (English Primary Schools)**
www.epsca.org.uk

**Chess Federation (English)**
The Watch Oak  Chain Lane  Battle  East
Sussex TN33 0YD
Tel: 01424 775222
office@englishchess.org.uk
www.englishchess.org.uk

**Chess Scotland**
www.chessscotland.com

**Chess Union (Ulster)**
www.ulsterchess.org

**Chess Union (Welsh)**
www.welshchessunion.co.uk

**chewonthis.org.uk** Honest information
about the food you eat
www.chewonthis.org.uk
Committed to providing well-researched
and independent information about food
and health. Their campaigns and research
are not funded by government or the food
industry.

**Child Abuse** see also Africans Unite
Against Child Abuse, Barnardo's, Chance
UK, Child Protection in Sport Unit,
ChildLine, Children 1st, NSPCC

**Child Abuse and Neglect (British Association for the Study and Prevention of)** see BASPCAN

**Child Accident Prevention Trust**
Canterbury Court  1-3 Brixton Road  London
SW9 6DE
Tel: 020 7608 3828
safe@capt.org.uk
www.capt.org.uk

**Child Advocacy International** now
see Maternal & Childhealth Advocacy
International MCAI

**Child and Adolescent Mental Health (Association for)**
St Saviour's House  39-41 Union St  London
SE1 1SD
Tel: 020 7403 7458
www.acamh.org.uk
Professional organisation

**Child Bereavement Trust**
Aston House  West Wycombe  High
Wycombe  Bucks HP14 3AG
Tel: 01494 446648
enquiries@childbereavement.org.uk
www.childbereavement.org.uk
Helps bereaved families by providing
training, resources and support to
professionals.

**Child Brain Injury Trust**
Unit 1  The Great Barn  Baynards Green
Farm  Nr Bicester  Oxfordshire OX27 7SG
Helpline: 0845 6014939
Tel: 01869 341075
info@cbituk.org
www.cbituk.org

**Child Contact Centres (National Association of)**
Minerva House  Spaniel Row  Nottingham
NG1 6EP
Tel: 0845 4500 280
Landline (cheaper for mobiles) 0115 948
4557
contact@naccc.org.uk
www.naccc.org.uk
Supports Child Contact Centres, where
children of separated families can have
contact with family members

**Child Death Helpline**
Freephone 0800 282986
Additional Freephone number for ALL
mobiles
0808 800 6019
contact@childdeathhelpline.org
www.childdeathhelpline.org.uk

## Child Growth Foundation
2 Mayfield Ave  Chiswick  London W4 1PW
Tel: 020 8995 0257
info@childgrowthfoundation.org
www.childgrowthfoundation.org
Supports sufferers of growth disorders and
their families

## Child Poverty Action Group
94 White Lion St  London N1 9PF
Tel: 020 7837 7979
staff@cpag.org.uk
www.cpag.org.uk

## Child Protection in Sport Unit CPSU
NSPCC National Training Centre  3 Gilmour
Close  Beaumont Leys  Leicester LE4 1EZ
Tel: 0116 234 7278
cpsu@nspcc.org.uk
www.thecpsu.org.uk
Offers advice to sports professionals,
volunteers, parents and children as part of a
long-term strategy for ending child abuse

### & Northern Ireland
NSPCC  Block 1  Jennymount Business
Park  North Derby Street  Belfast BT15 3HN
Tel: 02890 351 135
cpsu@nspcc.org.uk
www.thecpsu.org.uk

### & Cymru/Wales
Diane Engelhardt House,  Treglown Court,
Dowlais Road  Cardiff CF24 5LQ
Tel: 0844 892 0290
cpsuwales@nspcc.org.uk
www.thecpsu.org.uk

### & Scotland
Children 1st  Sussex House  61 Sussex
Street  Kinning Park  Glasgow G41 1DY
Tel: 0141 418 5674
cpinsport@children1st.org.uk
www.thecpsu.org.uk

## Child Rights Information Network see CRIN

## Childbirth Trust see National Childbirth Trust

## Childcare see Daycare Trust

## Childcare Link
http://childcarefinder.direct.gov.uk/
childcarefinder/
Government website with useful information
about childcare & childcare facilities

## Childhood (Alliance for)
Kidbrooke Park  Forest Row  East Sussex
RH18 5JA
Tel: 01342 827792
info@alliancechildhood.org
www.alliancechildhood.org
Partnership of individuals and organisations
committed to each child's inherent right

to a healthy, developmentally appropriate
childhood

## Childhood Bereavement Network
8 Wakley Street  London EC1V 7QE
Tel: 020 7843 6309
cbn@ncb.org.uk
www.childhoodbereavementnetwork.org.uk
A national, multi-professional federation of
organisations and individuals working with
bereaved children and young people.

## Childhood (Museum of) at Bethnal Green
Cambridge Heath Road  London E2 9PA
Tel: 020 8983 5200
Group Bookings: 020 8983 5205
moc@vam.ac.uk
www.vam.ac.uk/moc/

## ChildHope UK
Development House  56-64 Leonard Street
London EC2A 4LT
Tel: 020 7065 0950
info@childhope.org.uk
www.childhope.org.uk
Working with street children worldwide

## ChildLine
Weston House  42 Curtain Road  London
EC2A 3NH
Helpline: 0800 1111
Tel: 020 7825 2775
info@nspcc.org.uk
www.childline.org.uk

## Childlink Adoption Society
10 Lion Yard  Tremadoc Rd  London SW4
7NQ
Tel: 020 7501 1700
enquiries@adoptchildlink.org.uk
www.adoptchildlink.org.uk

## CHILDREN 1ST Royal Scottish Society for Prevention of Cruelty to Children
83 Whitehouse Loan  Edinburgh EH9 1AT
Helpline: 0808 800 2222 (Parentline Scotland)
Tel: 0131 446 2300
info@children1st.org.uk
www.children1st.org.uk

## Children and Family Court Advisory Support Service see Cafcass

## Children and War A Peace Pledge Union project
1 Peace Passage  London N7 OBT
Tel: 020 7424 9444
Email via website
www.ppu.org.uk
Education & awareness on disarmament,
conflict resolution

## Children are unbeatable
www.childrenareunbeatable.org.uk
An alliance of organisations against hitting
children

**Children in Need Appeal** BBC
P O Box 1000  London W12 7WJ
www.bbc.co.uk/pudsey

**Children in Scotland**
Princes House  5 Shandwick Place
Edinburgh EH2 4RG
Tel: 0131 228 8484
info@childreninscotland.org.uk
www.childreninscotland.org.uk
National agency for voluntary, statutory and
professional organisations and individuals
working with children and their families in
Scotland

**Children of Alcoholics (National
Association for)**  NACOA
PO Box 64  Fishponds  Bristol BS16 2UH
Helpline: 0800 358 3456
Tel: 0117 924 8005
admin@nacoa.org.uk
www.nacoa.org.uk
Support and advice to children of alcoholics
and to professionals

**Children with Leukaemia**
51 Great Ormond St  London WC1N 3JQ
Tel: 020 7404 0808
info@leukaemia.org
www.leukaemia.org

**Children's Book Groups (Federation of)**
2 Bridge Wood View  Horsforth  Leeds LS18 5PE
Tel: 0113 2588 910
info@fcbg.org.uk
www.fcbg.org.uk
Parents, teachers, librarians and publishers
promoting good children's books

**Children's Bureau (National)**
8 Wakley St  London EC1V 7QE
Tel: 020 7843 6000
enquiries@ncb.org.uk
www.ncb.org.uk
Promotes interests and wellbeing of all
children and young people

**Children's Care & Education (Council for
Awards in)** see CACHE

**Children's Commissioner for England**
1 London Bridge  London SE1 9BG
Tel: 0844 800 9113
info.request@childrenscommissioner.gsi.
gov.uk
www.childrenscommissioner.gov.uk
Promoting the views and best interests of all
children and young people. October 2010
under review.

**Children's Express** now see Headliners

**Children's Heart Federation**
Level One
  2-4 Great Eastern Street  London EC2A
3NW

Helpline: 0808 808 5000
Tel: 020 7422 0630
Email via website
www.childrens-heart-fed.org.uk
For families of children with heart conditions

**Children's Hope Foundation**
15 Palmer Place  London N7 8DH
Tel: 020 7700 6855
info@childrenshopefoundation.org
www.childrenshopefoundation.org.uk
Helps children with special needs

**Children's Legal Centre**
University of Essex  Wivenhoe Park
Colchester  Essex CO4 3SQ
Child Law Advice Line Freephone: 08088
020 008
Community Legal Advice: 0845 345 4345
Young Person's Freephone: 0800 783 2187
Tel: 01206 877 910
clc@essex.ac.uk
www.childrenslegalcentre.com
Free and confidential legal advice on issues
affecting children

**Children's Literature (National Centre for
Research in)**
School of Arts
  Digby Stuart College  Roehampton
University  Roehampton Lane  London
SW15 5PH
Tel: 020 8392 3000
email via website
/www.roehampton.ac.uk/researchcentres/
ncrcl/

**Children's Medical Research Charity** now
see Sparks

**Children's Orchestra (National)**
57 Buckingham Road  Weston-Super-Mare
BS24 9BG
Tel: 01934 418855
mail@nco.org.uk
www.nco.org.uk
For children between the ages of 7-14 years

**Children's Play Initiative** now see Play
England

**Children's Rights**
www.child-abuse.com/childhouse/
A web page set up by United Nations High
Commissioner for Human Rights

**Children's Rights Alliance for England**
CRAE
94 White Lion St  London N1 9PF
Tel: 020 7278 8222
info@crae.org.uk
www.crae.org.uk
Promoting the fullest implementation of the UN
convention on rights of the child.

## Children's Scrapstore
Scrapstore House  21 Sevier Street  Bristol
BS2 9LB
Tel: 0117 908 5644
enquiries@childrensscrapstore.co.uk
www.childrensscrapstore.co.uk
Clean and safe waste products from industry as
a resource for children's art and play activities.
Directory of scrapstores.

## Children's Service
The Cambridge Family Mediation Service  3rd
Floor, Essex House
 71 Regent St  Cambridge CB2 1AB
Tel: 01223 576 308
families@cambridgefms.co.uk
www.cambridgefms.co.uk
Helping children (6-19 yrs) to adjust to
separation or divorce

## Children's Society
Edward Rudolf House  Margery St  London
WC1X 0JL
Tel: 0845 300 1128
supporteraction@childrenssociety.org.uk
www.childrenssociety.org.uk
A Christian, social justice organisation
concerned with children at risk on the streets,
children in trouble with the law, disabled
children and young refugees

## Children's Workforce Development Council
2nd Floor  City Exchange  11 Albion Street
LEEDS   LS1 5ES
0113 244 6311
email via website
www.cwdcouncil.org.uk
Advises and works in partnership with
organisations and people involved with children
to join up the way different agencies work,
and bring consistency to the way children
and young people are listened to and looked
October 2010: Status under review

## Chinese Arts Centre
Market Buildings  Thomas Street
Manchester M4 1EU
Tel: 0161 832 7271
Email via website
www.chinese-arts-centre.org
UK agency for Chinese arts, culture and
creativity

## Chiropodists & Podiatrists (Institute of)
27 Wright St  Southport PR9 0TL
Tel: 01704 546141
secretary@iocp.org.uk
www.iocp.org.uk

## Chiropodists & Podiatrists (The Society of)
1 Fellmonger's Path  Tower Bridge Rd
London SE1 3LY
Tel: 020 7234 8620

Email via website
www.feetforlife.org

## Chiropractic (Anglo-European College of)
13-15 Parkwood Rd  Bournemouth BH5 2DF
Tel: 01202 436200
email via website
www.aecc.ac.uk

## Chiropractic Association (British)
59 Castle Street  Reading RG1 7SN
Tel: 0118 950 5950
enquiries@chiropractic-uk.co.uk
www.chiropractic-uk.co.uk

## Chiropractic Patients' Association
8 Centre One  Lysander Way  Old Sarum
Park  Salisbury SP4 6BU
Tel: 01722 415 027
backs@chiropatients.org.uk
www.chiropatients.org.uk
Supports chiropractic patients and seeks to
make treatment more widely available

## Chocolate Society
Unit B1 Southgate  Commerce Park  Frome
BA11 2RY
Tel: 01373 473335
email via website
www.chocolate.co.uk
Promotes the consumption and enjoyment
of the finest chocolates

## Choir Schools Association
The Information Officer  Windrush  Church
Road  Market Weston  Diss, Norfolk IP22
2NX
Tel: 01359 221333
info@choirschools.org.uk
www.choirschools.org.uk
Provides advice to prospective pupils and
bursary help where applicable

**Choirs** see also youngchoirs.net, Youth
Choir of Great Britain (National)

## Choose Climate
www.chooseclimate.org
Details the science of climate change & the
effects of air travel

## Christian Aid
35 Lower Marsh  Waterloo  London SE1 7RL
Tel: 020 7620 4444
info@christian-aid.org
www.christianaid.org.uk

## Christian Education
1020 Bristol Road  Selly Oak  Birmingham
B29 6LB
Tel: 0121 472 4242
enquiries@christianeducation.org.uk
www.christianeducation.org.uk

**Christian Lewis Trust** Children's Cancer
Charity
  62 Walter Road  Swansea SA1 4PT
  Tel: 01792 480 500
  enquiries.christianlewistrust.org
  www.christianlewistrust.org.uk

**Christian Socialist Movement**
  PO Box 65108  London SW1P 9PQ
  Tel: 020 7783 1590
  info@thecsm.org.uk
  www.thecsm.org.uk

**Christian Teachers (Association of)**
  94a London Rd  St Albans AL1 1NX
  Tel: 01727 840 298
  act@christians-in-education.org.uk
  www.christian-teachers.org.uk

**Christians and Jews (Council of)**
  Godliman House
  21 Godliman Street
  London  EC4V 5BD
  Tel: 0207 015 5160
  cjrelations@ccj.org.uk
  www.ccj.org.uk

**Chronic Poverty Research Centre**
  Institute for Development Policy and
  Management  School of Environment and
  Development  University of Manchester
  Humanities Bridgeford Street  Manchester
  M13 9PL
  Tel: 0161 275 2810
  www.chronicpoverty.org

**Church Action on Poverty**
  Third floor Dale House  35 Dale Street
  Manchester M1 2HF
  Tel: 0161 236 9321
  info@church-poverty.org.uk
  www.church-poverty.org.uk
  Aiming to raise awareness about the causes,
  extent and impact of poverty in the UK

**Church Army**
  Marlowe House  109 Station Rd  Sidcup
  Kent DA15 7AD
  Tel: 0300 123 2113
  info@churcharmy.org.uk
  www.churcharmy.org.uk

**Church Lads' and Church Girls' Brigade**
  2 Barnsley Rd  Wath-upon-Dearne
  Rotherham S63 6PY
  Tel: 01709 876 535
  brigadesecretary@clcgb.org.uk
  www.clcgb.org.uk
  A uniformed young people and children's
  organisation within the Church of England

**Church Mission Society**
  Watlington Road  Cowley  Oxford OX4 6BZ
  Tel: 0845 620 1799
  info@cms-uk.org

  www.cms-uk.org
  Sends UK personnel to other countries, in
  partnership with churches

**Church of England**
  www.cofe.anglican.org

**Church of England Education Division**
  The Church of England National Offices
  Church House  Great Smith St  London
  SW1P 3AZ
  Tel: 020 7898 1000
  webmaster@c-of-e.org.uk
  www.cofe.anglican.org

**Churches** see also Cathedral Camps

**Churches Conservation Trust**
  1 West Smithfield  London EC1A 9EE
  020 7213 0660
  central@tcct.org.uk
  www.visitchurches.org.uk
  National charity protecting historic churches
  at risk

**Churches Together in Britain and Ireland**
  39 Eccleston Square  London SW1V 1BX
  Tel: 0207 901 4890
  info@ctbi.org.uk
  www.ctbi.org.uk

**CIA** Central Intelligence Agency
  Email via website
  www.cia.gov
  US government agency

**CILIP: the Chartered Institute of Library
and Information Professionals**
  7 Ridgmount St  London WC1E 7AE
  Tel: 020 7255 0500
  Textphone: 020 7255 0505
  info@cilip.org.uk
  www.cilip.org.uk
  Professional body for Information Managers
  and Librarians.

**CILIPS: Chartered Institute of Library
and Information Professionals in
Scotland**
  1st Floor Building C  Brandon Gate
  Leechlee Rd  Hamilton ML3 6AU
  Tel: 01698 458 888
  slic@slainte.org.uk
  www.slainte.org.uk

**CILT** National Centre for Languages
  3rd Floor  111 Westminster Bridge Road
  London SE1 7HR
  Tel: 08456 12 5885
  info@cilt.org.uk
  www.cilt.org.uk

## Cinema & Popular Culture (The Bill Douglas Centre for the History of)
University of Exeter  The Old Library  Prince of Wales Rd  Exeter EX4 4SB
Tel: 01392 264321
bdc@exeter.ac.uk
www.billdouglas.org
Museum & academic research centre

## Cinnamon Trust
10 Market Square  Hayle TR27 4HE
Tel: 01736 757 900
admin@cinnamon.org.uk
www.cinnamon.org.uk
Provides volunteers to help care for the pets of elderly or terminally ill people

## Circus see also Skylight Circus Arts

## Circus Sensible/Circus School
18, Church Street  Ashton under Lyne,  OL6 6XE
Mobile: 07958 780246
papaclive@yahoo.com
www.circussensible.co.uk
Britain's smallest tented circus. Performance & teaching of circus skills in schools, youth clubs etc.

## Circus Space
Coronet St  Hoxton  London N1 6HD
Tel: 020 7729 9522
reception@thecircusspace.co.uk
www.thecircusspace.co.uk
Circus training & production venue offering the only BA circus degree in the UK

## Cirdan Sailing Trust
3 Chandlers Quay  Fullbridge  Maldon Essex CM9 4LF
Tel: 01621 851 433
info@cirdansailing.com
www.cirdansailing.com
Adventure sailing for groups of all abilities of 10 years+

## Citizens Advice
Myddelton House  115-123 Pentonville Rd London N1 9LZ
www.citizensadvice.org.uk
www.adviceguide.org.uk
Independent advice, policy and campaigning charity. For local CAB, see phone book or websites

## Citizens Income Trust
PO Box 26586  London SE3 7WY
Tel: 020 8305 1222
info@citizensincome.org
www.citizensincome.org
Research and education on the feasibility of a citizen's income: an unconditional income for every citizen

## Citizenship and the Law (National Centre for)
Galleries of Justice  High Pavement  The Lace Market  Nottingham NG1 1HN
Tel: 0115 952 0555
info@nccl.org.uk
www.nccl.org.uk/
Runs learning programmes

## Citizenship Foundation
63 Gee Street  London EC1V 3RS
Tel: 020 7566 4141
info@citizenshipfoundation.org.uk
www.citizenshipfoundation.org.uk
Educational charity promoting citizenship education

## Citizenship (Institute for)
Clifford's Inn  Fetter Lane  London  EC4A 1BZ
Tel: 020 7841 5159
info@citizen.org.uk
www.citizen.org.uk
Promotes informed, active citizenship and greater participation in democracy

## Citizenship Teaching (Association for)
63 Gee Street  London EC1V 3RS
Tel: 020 7566 4133
info@teachingcitizenship.org.uk
www.teachingcitizenship.org.uk

## City and Guilds of London Institute
1 Giltspur St  London EC1A 9DD
Tel: 0844 543 0000
www.cityandguilds.com
Awarding body for vocational qualifications, NVQs and GNVQs

## City Farms & Community Gardens (Federation of)
The Green House  Hereford St  Bedminster Bristol BS3 4NA
Tel: 01179 231 800
admin@farmgarden.org.uk
www.farmgarden.org.uk
Supports, promotes and represents city farms and community gardens throughout the UK

## Civic Society Initiative
Unit 101  82 Wood Street  The Tea Factory Liverpool L1 4DQ
Tel: 0151 708 9920
admin@civicsocietyinitiative.org.uk
www.civicsocietyinitiative.org.uk
Restores & enhances the urban environment

## Civil Liberties see also thematic guide Human Rights

## Civil Liberties (National Council for) see Liberty

**Civitas**
First Floor  55 Tufton Street  Westminster London SW1P 3QL
Tel: 0207 799 6677
info@civitas.org.uk
www.civitas.org.uk
Independent health, education and social policy think tank.

**CLA** Country Land and Business Association
16 Belgrave Sq  London SW1X 8PQ
Tel: 020 7235 0511
mail@cla.org.uk
www.cla.org.uk
A membership organisation and lobby group representing rural land and business owners

**Clapa** Cleft Lip & Palate Association
First Floor  Green Man Tower  332B Goswell Road  London EC1V 7LQ
Tel: 020 7833 4883
info@clapa.com
www.clapa.com
CLAPA provides information and support for all those with and affected by cleft lip and/ or palate.

**Classical Association**
Office Administrator  Senate House  Malet St  London WC1E 7HU
Tel: 020 7862 8706
office@classicalassociation.org
www.classicalassociation.org

**Clean Air & Environmental Protection (National Society for)**  see Environmental Protection UK

**Cleanair** Campaign for a Smoke Free Environment
33 Stillness Rd  London SE23 1NG
Tel: 0181 690 4649
www.ezme.com/cleanair/
Raises awareness about the dangers of smoking

**Clear Vision Trust**
16-20 Turner Street  Manchester M4 1DZ
Tel: 0161 839 9579
clearvision@clear-vision.org
www.clear-vision.org
Supports the teaching of Buddhism in schools

**ClearVision Project**
61 Princes Way  London SW19 6JB
Tel: 020 8789 9575
info@clearvisionproject.org
www.clearvisionproject.org
Postal lending library of children's books suitable for sharing by sighted and visually impaired

**Cleft Lip & Palate Association** see Clapa

**CLICSargent**  Caring for children with cancer
Griffin House  161 Hammersmith Rd
London W6 8SG
Child Cancer Helpline: 0800 197 0068
Tel: 0845 301 0031

helpline@clicsargent.org.uk
www.clicsargent.org.uk
Offers professional, practical and financial help to young people up to 21 years diagnosed with cancer, and their families

**Climate** see also Choose Climate, Global Climate Coalition, Met Office, Meteorological Organization (World), Meteorological Society (Royal), Rising Tide

**Climate Change (Intergovernmental Panel on)**
c/o World Meteorological Organization  7 bis Avenue de la Paix  C.P. 2300  CH- 1211 Geneva 2, Switzerland
Tel: 00 41 22 730 8208 / 54 / 84
ipcc-sec@wmo.int
www.ipcc.ch/
Assessment of factual information on all aspects of climate change

**Climate projections** see Climate projections

**Climb** Children Living with Inherited Metabolic Diseases
Climb Building  176 Nantwich Rd  Crewe CW2 6BG
Tel: 0845 241 2172 & 0800 652 3181
Tel: 0845 241 2173
info.svcs@climb.org.uk
www.climb.org.uk
Support and information for families and professionals covering over 700 metabolic disorders

**Clubs for Young People (National Association of)**
371 Kennington Lane  London SE11 5QY
Tel: 020 7793 0787
office@clubsforyoungpeople.org.uk
www.clubsforyoungpeople.org.uk

**CND** Campaign for Nuclear Disarmament
Mordechai Vanunu House  162 Holloway Rd
London N7 8DQ
Tel: 020 7700 2393
enquiries@cnduk.org
www.cnduk.org
Non-political, peace educational material & speakers

**CND (Scottish)**
15 Barrland St  Glasgow G41 1QH
Tel: 0141 423 1222

scnd@banthebomb.org
www.banthebomb.org

**Co-operative Party**
77 Weston Street  London SE1 3SD
Tel: 020 7367 4150
Email via website
www.party.coop
Political wing of co-operative movement

**Co-operatives UK**
Holyoake House  Hanover St  Manchester
M60 0AS
Tel: 0161 246 2900
Email via website
www.uk.coop
Information and advice on employee
ownership, innovative co-operatives, social
enterprise and mutual businesses

**Coaching Foundation (National)** see
Sports Coach UK

**Coal Museum (National)** see Big Pit

**Cocaine Anonymous**
PO Box 46920  London E2 9WF
Tel: 0800 612 0225
From UK Mobile Phones
800 612 0225

info@cauk.org.uk
www.cauk.org.uk

**COI** see Central Office of Information (COI)

**Coleg Harlech (WEA)**
Harlech  Gwynedd LL46 2PU
Tel: 01766 781900
info@fc.harlech.ac.uk
www.harlech.ac.uk
Adult education residential college. Full time
& short courses

**Colitis & Crohn's Disease (National
Association for)**
4 Beaumont House  Sutton Rd  St Albans
Herts AL1 5HH
Tel: 01727 830 038
enquiries@CrohnsAndColitis.org.uk
www.nacc.org.uk

**Colombia Solidarity Campaign**
PO Box 8446  London N17 6NZ
info@colombiasolidarity.org.uk
www.colombiasolidarity.org.uk

**CoMA** Contemporary Music-making for
Amateurs
RICH MIX  35 - 47 Bethnal Green Road
London E1 6LA
Tel: 020 7739 4680
admin@coma.org
www.coma.org
Promotes participation in contemporary
music through commissions, music
ensembles and training

**Combat Stress** Ex-Services Mental Welfare
Society
Tyrwhitt House  Oaklawn Road  Leatherhead
Surrey KT22 0BX
Tel: 01372 587000
contactus@combatstress.org.uk
www.combatstress.org.uk
Rebuilding the lives of veterans who suffer
from injury of the mind

**Combined Youth Clubs** see young@now

**Comic Relief**
5th Floor  89 Albert Embankment  London
SE1 7TP
Tel: 020 7820 5555
info@comicrelief.com
www.comicrelief.com

**Committee on Climate Change**
4th Floor, Manning House,  22 Carlisle Place,
London,      SW1P 1JA
0207 592 1553
enquiries@theccc.gsi.gov.uk
www.theccc.org.uk
Independent advisors to the UK Government
on tackling and preparing for climate change

**Common Ground**
Gold Hill House  21 High St  Shaftesbury
Dorset SP7 8JE
Tel: 01747 850820
info@commonground.org.uk
www.commonground.org.uk
www.england-in-particular.info
Environmental charity; encourages
people to value everyday places and local
distinctiveness

**Common Purpose**
Discovery House  28-42 Banner St  London
EC1Y 8QE
Tel: 020 7608 8100
enquiries@commonpurpose.org.uk
www.commonpurpose.org.uk
Independent educational organisation

**Commonwealth Broadcasting
Association**
17 Fleet St  London EC4Y 1AA
Tel: 020 7583 5550
Email via website
www.cba.org.uk
Working for quality broadcasting throughout
the Commonwealth

**Commonwealth Education Trust**
New Zealand House  80 Haymarket  London
SW1Y 4TQ
Tel: 020 7024 9822
information@cet1886.org
www.cet1886.org/
Principal objective is to advance education
in the Commonwealth

**Commonwealth Games Federation**
2nd Floor  138 Piccadilly  London W1J 7NR
Tel: 020 7491 8801
info@thecgf.com
www.thecgf.com

**Commonwealth Institute** now see
Commonwealth Education Trust

**Commonwealth Scolarships**
Woburn House, 20-24 Tavistock Square
 20-24 Tavistock Square   London WC1H
9HF
Tel: 0207 380 6700
email via website
www.cscuk.org.uk
Offers opportunities to Commonwealth
citizens to study in the UK and to identify UK
citizens to study overseas

**Commonwealth Society for the Deaf**  see
Deaf (Commonwealth Society for the)

**Commonwealth Society (Royal)**
25 Northumberland Ave  London WC2N 5AP
Tel: 020 7766 9200
info@thercs.org
www.thercs.org
Promotes and educates about the
Commonwealth. Provides a multicultural
meeting place. Does not give out grants or
sponsorship

**Commonwealth Teachers** see Exchange
of Commonwealth Teachers (League for
the)

**Commonwealth Youth Exchange Council**
7 Lion Yard  Tremadoc Road  London SW4
7NQ
Tel: 020 7498 6151
Email via website
www.cyec.org.uk
Promotes educational exchanges for 15-25
year olds from Britain and their partners in
the Commonwealth

**Communities and Local Government
(Department for)**
Eland House  Bressenden Place  London
SW1E 5DU
Tel: 0303 444 0000
Email via website
www.communities.gov.uk

**Communities Empowerment Network**
Office 7  Boardman House  64 Broadway
Stratford EI5 1NT
Tel: 020 8432 0531
post@compowernet.org
www.compowernet.org
Provides support for people experiencing
mistreatment and disadvantage in education

**Communities in Rural England (Action
with)** ACRE
Somerford Court  Somerford Rd  Cirencester
GL7 1TW
Tel: 01285 653477
acre@acre.org.uk
www.acre.org.uk
A national charity supporting sustainable
rural community development

**Community and Youth Workers Union**
Transport House  211 Broad Street
Birmingham B15 1AY
Tel: 0121 643 6221
Email via website
www.cywu.org.uk
Trade union for youth, community, play
workers, mentors and personal advisers.

**Community Composting Network**
67 Alexandra Rd  Sheffield S2 3EE
Tel: 0114 258 0483
info@communitycompost.org
www.communitycompost.org
Advice & support

**Community Dance (Foundation for)**
LCB Depot  31 Rutland Street  Leicester
LE1 1RE
Tel: 0116 253 3453
info@communitydance.org.uk
www.communitydance.org.uk
National development agency

**Community Foundation Network**
12 Angel Gate
 320-326 City Road  London EC1V 2PT
Tel: 020 7713 9326
network@communityfoundations.org.uk
www.communityfoundations.org.uk
National network linking, promoting and
supporting over 60 community foundations
throughout the UK

**Community Fund** see Big Lottery Fund

**Community Justice National Training
Organisation** see Skills for Justice

**Community Legal Advice**
Tel: 0845 345 4345
Tel: 0800 0856 643
email via website
www.communitylegaladvice.org.uk
Offers free, confidential and independent
legal advice for residents of England and
Wales

**Community Matters**
12-20 Baron St  Islington  London N1 9LL
Tel: 020 7837 7887
Advice: 0845 847 4253

Email via website
www.communitymatters.org.uk
National federation of community
organisations

**Community Media Association**
15 Paternoster Row  Sheffield S1 2BX
Tel: 0114 279 5219
cma@commedia.org.uk
www.commedia.org.uk
Aims to facilitate the development of
community based communications media
for empowerment, cultural expression,
information & entertainment

**Community Pubs Foundation**
230 Hatfield Road  St Albans  Herts AL1
4LW
Tel: 01727 867201
communitypubs@camra.org.uk
www.communitypubs.org
Prevents the loss of, or inappropriate
alterations to, a public house of community,
architectural or historical importance

**Community Rail Partnerships
(Association of)**
Rail and River Centre  Canal Side
Slaithwaite Civic Hall  15a New Street
Slaithwaite  Huddersfield HD7 5AB
Tel: 01484 847790
info@acorp.uk.com
www.acorp.uk.com
Association of organisations promoting links
between railways and local communities

**Community Self Build Agency**
Swale Foyer  Bridge Road  Sheerness  Kent
ME12 1RH
Tel: 01795 663 073
info@communityselfbuildagency.org.uk
www.communityselfbuildagency.org.uk
Aims to create more opportunities for people
to acquire the knowledge and skills to build
their own homes, focussing particularly on
those in housing need

**Community Service Volunteers (CSV)**
237 Pentonville Rd  London N1 9NJ
Tel: 020 7278 6601
www.csv.org.uk
Creates opportunities for everyone to play
an active part in their community

**Community Transport Association**
Highbank  Halton St  Hyde SK14 2NY
Tel: 0845 1306195
Tel: 0161 351 1475
info@ctauk.org
www.ctauk.org
Co-ordinating body for voluntary and
community transport

**Companion Animal Studies (Society for)**
The Blue Cross  Shilton Rd  Burford  Oxon
OX18 4PF
Tel: 01993 825597
Email via website
www.scas.org.uk

**Compassion in World Farming Trust**
River Court  Mill Lane  Godalming  Surrey
GU7 1EZ
Tel: 01483 521 950
Email via website
www.ciwf.org

**Compassionate Friends**
53 North St  Bristol BS3 1EN
Helpline: 0845 123 2304
Tel: 0845 120 3785
info@tcf.org.uk
www.tcf.org.uk
Support and friendship for bereaved parents
and their families, through the loss of a child
of any age and through any circumstance

**Competition Commission**
Victoria House  Southampton Row  London
WC1B 4AD
Tel: 020 7271 0100
Tel: 020 7271 0243 (Public enquiries)
Press Office: 020 7271 0242
info@cc.gsi.gov.uk
www.competition-commission.org.uk
October 2010:Government will consult in the
new year on a merger with the competition
functions of the Office of Fair Trading

**Complementary and Natural Medicine
(Institute for)**
Can-Mezzanine  32-36 Loman Street
London SE1 0EH
Tel: 0207 922 7980
info@icnm.org.uk
www.i-c-m.org.uk
Provides register of practitioners' names and
a list of courses

**Complementary Medicine Association
(British)**
PO Box 5122  Bournemouth BH8 0WG
Tel: 0845 345 5977
office@bcma.co.uk
www.bcma.co.uk
Umbrella organisation. Has a practitioners
register

**Computer Aid International**
Unit 10  Brunswick Industrial Park
Brunswick Way  London N11 1JL
Tel: 020 8361 5540
info@computeraid.org
www.computeraid.org
Recycles computer equipment for use in
developing world

## Computer Society (British)
1st Floor, Block D  North Star House  North Star Ave  Swindon SN2 1FA
Tel: 01793 417424
Tel: 0845 300 4417
Email via website
www.bcs.org.
Professional and learned society for the IT profession

## Computers see also BECTA, Free Computers for Education, !ntellect, NAACE, Recycle-IT! Ltd

## Computers 4 Africa
Raglan House, St. Peters St  St Peter's Street  Maidstone  Kent ME16 0ST
Tel: 03000 112233
Tel: 01622 808897
Tel: 01622 750323
contact-us@computers4africa.org.uk
www.computers4africa.org.uk

## Computing Centre (National)
The Flint Glass Works  64 Jersey Street  Manchester  M4 6JW
Tel: 0845 519 1055
info@ncc.co.uk
www.ncc.co.uk

## Conception & birth Taking the stress out of expectancy
41 Portesbery Road  Camberley  Surrey GU15 3TA
Tel: 01276 21386

info@conceptionandbirth.com
www.conceptionandbirth.com
Support to help women and their partners overcome the emotional challenges as they move through the various stages from conception to birth, postnatal recovery and into early parenthood

## Concern Worldwide
52-55 Lower Camden Street,  Dublin 2 Republic of Ireland
Tel: 00 353 1417 7700
Email via website
www.concern.net
Aims to enable absolutely poor people to achieve major improvements in their lives

## Concord Media (Concord Video & Film Council)
Tel: 01473 726012
sales@concordmedia.org.uk
www.concordmedia.co.uk
Hires & sells videos concerned with social welfare, counselling, health & medical education and domestic violence

## Conductive Education (The National Institute of)
Email via website
www.conductive-education.org.uk
Teaches children and adults with movement disabilities the skills and practical techniques they need to control their bodies

## Connect
16-18 Marshalsea Rd  Southwark  London SE1 1HL
Tel: 020 7367 0840
info@ukconnect.org
www.ukconnect.org
The communication disability network

## Connect Youth now see Youth in Action

## Connexions
Tel: 0808 0013219
Email via website
www.connexions-direct.com
Government support & advice service for 13-19 year olds

## Conscience
Archway Resource Centre  1B Waterlow Rd London N19 5NJ
Tel: 020 7561 1061
info@conscienceonline.org.uk
www.conscienceonline.org.uk/
Campaigns for the right for those ethically opposed to war to have the military part of their taxes spent on peace-building initiatives

## Conservation see thematic guide - Environment and Countryside & Heritage

## Conservation (Institute of ) see ICON

## Conservation of Energy (Association for the)
Westgate House  2A Prebend St  London N1 8PT
Tel: 020 7359 8000
Email via website
www.ukace.org

## Conservation of Plants & Gardens (National Council for the)
Plant Heritage  12 Home Farm,  Loseley Park,  Guildford  GU3 1HS
Tel: 01483 447 540
info@plantheritage.org.uk
www.nccpg.com
Charity responsible for National Plant Collection Scheme

## Conservation Volunteers (British Trust for ) see BTCV

## Conservative Party
30 Millbank  London SW1P 4DP
Tel: 020 7222 9000
email via website
www.conservatives.com

**Consumer Affairs (Research Institute for)**
see Ricability

**Consumer Council (National)** now see
Consumer Focus

**Consumer Credit Counselling Service**
Wade House  Merrion Centre  Leeds LS2
8NG
Helpline: 0800 138 1111
Email via website
www.cccs.co.uk
Charity funded by the financial services
industry specialising in debt management
plans

**Consumer Direct**
Tel: 0845 404 05 06
Minicom users: 08451 28 13 84
Welsh-speaking adviser: 08454 04 05 05
email via website
www.consumerdirect.gov.uk
Government-funded telephone and online
service offering information and advice on
consumer issues

**Consumer Focus**
4th Floor  Artillery House  Artillery Row
London SW1P 1RT
Tel: 020 77997900
contact@consumerfocus.org.uk
www.consumerfocus.org.uk
October 2010: Government  decided to
transfer at least some  functions to Citizens
Advice and Citizens Advice Scotland.
It is likely to be 2012 before the necessary
legislative measures take effect.

**Consumers' Association** see Which?

**Consumers International**
24 Highbury Cres  Islington  London N5 1RX
Tel: 020 7226 6663
consint@consint.org
www.consumersinternational.org
Defends the rights of all consumers,
especially the poorest, by international
campaigning

**Contact a Family**
209-211 City Rd  London EC1V 1JN
Freephone Helpline for parents and families:
0808  808 3555
Tel: 020 7608 8700 Textphone: 0808 808
3556
info@cafamily.org.uk
www.cafamily.org.uk
Supporting families who care for children with
any disability or health condition including
rare disorders

**Contact the Elderly**
15 Henrietta St  Covent Garden
  London WC2E 8QG
Tel: 020 7240 0630

info@contact-the-elderly.org.uk
www.contact-the-elderly.org.uk
Links volunteers with isolated elderly people
for monthly outings

**Contemporary Art Society**
11-15 Emerald Street  London WC1N 3QL
Tel: 020 7831 1243
info@contemporaryartsociety.org
www.contempart.org.uk
Promotes collection of contemporary art
and acquires works by living artists for gift to
public collections in UK

**Continence Foundation** now see Bladder
and Bowel Foundation

**ContinYou**
Unit C1 Grovelands Court  Grovelands Estate
Longford Rd  Exhall  Coventry CV7 9NE
Tel: 024 7658 8440
info.coventry@continyou.org.uk
www.continyou.org.uk
Works in education, health, economic and
community regeneration nationally and
internationally

**Control Arms**
info@controlarms.org
www.controlarms.org
Control Arms is a campaign jointly run by
Amnesty International, IANSA and Oxfam

**CORE**
Freepost
  LON4268  London  NW1 0YT

Tel: 020 7486 0341
info@corecharity.org.uk
www.corecharity.org.uk
Information for people with digestive
problems from food poisoning to bowel
cancer. Medical research

**Corporate Watch**
c/o Freedom Press  Angel Alley  84b
Whitechapel High Street  London E1 7QX
Tel: 0207 426 0005
contact@corporatewatch.org
www.corporatewatch.org.uk
Research into corporate behaviour &
structure

**Cot Death** see Infant Deaths (Foundation for
the Study of)

**COTS** Surrogacy in the UK
Moss Bank  Manse Road  Lairg  IV27 4EL
Tel: 0844 414 0181
Tel: 01549 402777
robin@surrogacy.org.uk
www.surrogacy.org.uk
Providing advice, help and support to
surrogates and intended parents

**Cottage and Rural Enterprises Ltd.** now see Self Unlimited

**Couch Surfing Project**
www.couchsurfing.com
Helping to make connections around the world by offering some sort of accommodation to travellers

**Council for Advancement of Communication with Deaf People** now see Signature

**Council of Ethnic Minority Voluntary Sector Organisations** see CEMVO

**Council of Europe**
Head Office  Avenue de l'Europe  F - 67075 Strasbourg Cedex
  France
Tel: 00 33 03 88 41 20 00
visites@coe.int
www.coe.int

**Council of Europe Youth**
youth@coe.int
www.coe.int/youth
An international meeting place for youth organisations

**Counsel and Care**
Twyman House  16 Bonny St  London NW1 9PG
Advice Line: 0845 300 7585 (Mon-Fri 10am-1pm)
Tel: 020 7241 8555 (Admin)
Email via website
www.counselandcare.org.uk
Advice for older people & their carers, research & campaigns about ageing and quality of care in care homes

**Counselling & Psychotherapy (British Association for)**
BACP House  15 St John's Business Park Lutterworth  Leicestershire LE17 4HB
Tel: 01455 883300
bacp@bacp.co.uk
www.bacp.co.uk
Promotion of counselling & training of counsellors

**Country Holidays for Inner City Children** CHICKS
Moorland Retreat  Bonnaford  Brentor Tavistock  Devon PL19 0LX
Tel: 01822 811020
Email via website
www.chicks.org.uk/
Provides free respite breaks for disadvantaged children aged between 8 and 15 regardless of race or religion

**Country Landowners Association** see CLA

**Countryside Alliance**
The Old Town Hall  367 Kennington Rd London SE11 4PT
Tel: 020 7840 9200
Email via website
www.countryside-alliance.org.uk

**Countryside Council for Wales**
Maes y Ffynnon  Penrhosgarnedd  Bangor Gwynedd LL57 2DW
Tel: 0845 1306229
Enquiries@ccw.gov.uk
www.ccw.gov.uk
Advises the government on conservation matters in Wales

**Countryside Foundation for Education**
PO Box  8  Hebden Bridge  West Yorkshire HX7 5YJ
Tel: 01422 885566
info@countrysidefoundation.org.uk
www.countrysidefoundation.org.uk
Promotes an understanding of the countryside as a living, working environment and the problems facing those responsible for its management

**Court Service**
www.hmcourts-service.gov.uk/
Runs most of the courts and tribunals in England & Wales

**Courtauld Institute Gallery**
Courtauld Institute of Art  Somerset House The Strand  London WC2R 0RN
Tel: 020 7872 0220
www.courtauld.ac.uk

**CP Sport**
5 Heathcoat Building  Nottingham Science Park  University Boulevard  Nottingham NG7 2QJ
Tel: 0115 925 7027
info@cpsport.org
www.cpsport.org
Provides opportunities for people with cerebral palsy

**CPRE: Campaign to Protect Rural England**
128 Southwark St  London SE1 0SW
Tel: 020 7981 2800
info@cpre.org.uk
www.cpre.org.uk
Campaigning charity which promotes the beauty, tranquility and diversity of rural England

**CPSU** see Child Protection in Sport Unit

**CPT** see Passenger Transport UK (Confederation of)

**CRAC** see Careers Research & Advisory Centre

**CRAE** see Children's Rights Alliance for England

**Crafts Council**
44A Pentonville Rd  London N1 9BY
Tel: 020 7806 2500
reference@craftscouncil.org.uk
www.craftscouncil.org.uk
Promotes British contemporary crafts and provides services to craftspeople and the public

**Creative Partnerships**
Great North House  Sandyford Road Newcastle upon Tyne  NE1 8ND
Tel: 0844 811 2145
enquiries@cceengland.org
www.creative-partnerships.com
Supports school children in deprived areas in developing creativity and participating in cultural activities. Funded by The Arts Council

**Credit Unions (Association of British)** ABCUL
Holyoake House  Hanover St  Manchester M60 0AS
Tel: 0161 832 3694
info@abcul.org
www.abcul.org
Main trade association for credit unions (financial co-operatives)

**Cremation Society of Great Britain**
1st Floor Brecon House  16/16A Albion Place Maidstone  Kent ME14 5DZ
Tel: 01622 688292/3
info@cremation.org.uk
www.srgw.demon.co.uk/CremSoc/
Promotion of cremation

**CREST Awards**
c/o The British Science Association Wellcome Wolfson Building  165 Queen's Gate  London SW7 5HD
Tel: 0870 770 7101
email via website
www.britishscienceassociation.org/web/ccaf/CREST/
Awards for creativity in science and technology

**Cricinfo**
www.cricinfo.com/
Cricket information website

**Cricket** see also MCC

**Cricket Board (England & Wales)** ECB
Lord's Cricket Ground  London NW8 8QZ
Tel: 020 7432 1200
www.ecb.co.uk
Governing body

**Crime and Justice Studies (Centre for)**
King's College London  Strand  London WC2R 2LS
Tel: 020 7848 1688
info@crimeandjustice.org.uk
www.crimeandjustice.org.uk
Non-campaigning body for all concerned with criminal justice

**Crime Concern** now see Catch22

**Crime Reduction**
www.crimereduction.gov.uk/ideas.htm
Government site offers up to date information on news, ideas and initiatives regarding the reduction of crime

**Crimestoppers**
Apollo House  66A London Rd  Morden Surrey SM4 5BE
Tel: 0800 555 111 (for public to give info about crime anonymously)
email via website
www.crimestoppers-uk.org
Only charity in the UK helping to solve crimes

**Criminal Cases Review Commission**
Alpha Tower  Suffolk St Queensway Birmingham B1 1TT
Tel: 0121 633 1800
info@ccrc.gov.uk
www.ccrc.gov.uk

**Criminal Defence Service**
Legal Services Commission  4 Abbey Orchard Street  London  SW1P 2BS
Helpline: 0845 345 4345
Tel: 0207 783 7000
www.legalservices.gov.uk/criminal.asp

**Criminal Injuries Compensation Authority**
Tay House  300 Bath Street  Glasgow G2 4LN
Freephone: 0800 358 3601
email via website
www.cica.gov.uk

**Criminal Justice System** for England and Wales
OCJRenquiry@cjs.gsi.gov.uk
www.cjsonline.org
The criminal justice system online

**CRIN** Child Rights Information Network
East Studio  2 Pontypool Place  London SE1 8QF
Tel: 020 7401 2257
info@crin.org
www.crin.org
Global network coordinating information and promoting action on child rights

**Crisis Counselling for Alleged Shoplifters**
PO Box 147  Stanmore  Middlesex HA7 4PQ
Helpline: 020 8954 8987

**Crisis (UK)**
66 Commerical St  London E1 6LT
Tel: 0844 251 0111
enquiries@crisis.org.uk
www.crisis.org.uk

Provides year round services for homeless people and publishes research

**Croquet Association**
c/o Cheltenham Croquet Club  Old Bath Rd  Cheltenham GL53 7DF
Tel: 01242 242318
caoffice@croquet.org.uk
www.croquet.org.uk

**Cross Cultural Solutions**
Tower Point   44 North Road  Brighton BN1 1YR
Tel: 0845 458 2781 / 2782
Tel: 01273 666392
infouk@crossculturalsolutions.org
www.crossculturalsolutions.org
Operates international volunteer programmes

**CROSSROADS Care**
Tel: 0845 450 0350
email via website
www.crossroads.org.uk
Support for carers and the people they care for

**Crossroads Women's Centre**
230a Kentish Town Road  London NW5 2AB or  PO Box 287  London NW6 5QU
Tel: 020 7482 2496 (voice/minicom) (manned Mon-Fri 1.30pm-4pm)
allwomencount@crossroadswomen.net
www.allwomencount.net
Base for a number of organisations covering a wide range of women's issues

**Crown Estates**
16 New Burlington Place  London W1S 2HX & 6 Bell's Brae  Edinburgh EH4 3BJ
Tel: 020 7851 5000
Tel: 0131 260 6070 (Edinburgh Office)
enquiries@thecrownestate.co.uk
www.crownestate.co.uk
Manages land belonging to the Crown

**Crown Green Bowling Association (British)**
94 Fishers Lane  Pensby  Wirral CH61 8SB
Tel: 0151 648 5740
email via website
http://talkingbowls.sports.officelive.com/default.aspx

**Crown Prosecution Service**
www.cps.gov.uk
Will merge with Revenue and Customs Prosecution Office

**Cruel Sports Ltd (League Against)**
New Sparling House  Holloway Hill  Godalming
 Surrey  GU7 1QZ
Tel: 01483 524 250
info@league.org.uk
www.league.org.uk

Campaigning for the welfare of animals involved in sport

**Crufts Dog Show**
The Kennel Club  1-5 Clarges St  London W1J 8AB
Tickets: 0844 444 9944
Tel: 0844 463 3980
Email via website
www.crufts.org.uk
Annual canine spectacular

**Cruising Association**
CA House  1 Northey St  Limehouse Basin  London E14 8BT
Tel: 020 7537 2828
email via website
www.cruising.org.uk
A worldwide association of cruising boaters with headquarters in London containing an extensive library

**Cruse Bereavement Care**
PO Box 800  Richmond TW9 2RG
Helpline: 0844 477 9400
Tel: 020 8939 9530
info@cruse.org.uk
www.crusebereavementcare.org.uk
Support groups, advice & practical information

**CRY** see Cardiac Risk in the Young

**Cry-sis**
BM Cry-sis  London WC1N 3XX
Helpline: 08451 228 669
www.cry-sis.org.uk
Support for families with excessively crying, sleepless & demanding children

**CSET** see Education and Training (Centre for the Study of)

**CSV Education for Citizenship**
237 Pentonville Road  London N1 9NJ
Tel: 020 7278 6601
information@csv.org.uk
www.csv.org.uk
Promotes and supports citizenship in schools, colleges and universities through active community involvement

**CTC** The UK's national cyclists' organisation
Parklands  Railton Rd  Guildford GU2 9JX
Tel: 0844 736 8450
Direct line: 01483 238 337
cycling@ctc.org.uk
www.ctc.org.uk
For cycling of all kinds in the UK

**Cuba Solidarity Campaign**
c/o UNITE Woodberry  218 Green Lanes
London N4 2HB
Tel: 020 8800 0155
office@cuba-solidarity.org.uk
www.cuba-solidarity.org.uk

**Cued Speech Association UK**
9 Jawbone Hill  Dartmouth  Devon TQ6 9RW
Tel: 01803 832 784 (voice and textphone)
info@cuedspeech.co.uk
www.cuedspeech.co.uk
Cued Speech overcomes the problems of
lip-reading and thus enables deaf children
and adults to understand full spoken
language.

**Cult Information Centre**
BCM Cults  London WC1N 3XX
Tel: 0845 4500 868
www.cultinformation.org.uk
Help and information for families and friends
of people involved in cults. Gives talks and
offers information to media and researchers

**Culture, Media & Sport (Department for)**
2-4 Cockspur St  London SW1Y 5DH
Tel: 020 7211 6000
enquiries@culture.gov.uk
www.culture.gov.uk

**Culture24**
Culture24
  Office 4  28 Kensington Street  Brighton
BN1 4AJ
Tel: 01273 623266
info@culture24.org.uk
www.culture24.org.uk
Enables a search of many UK museums by
different criteria

**Currency converter**
www.xe.com/ucc/

**Curriculum and Assessment Authority
for Wales** now see Qualifications,
Curriculum and Assessment Authority for
Wales

**Curvature of the spine** see Scoliosis
Association (UK)

**Customs and Excise** see HM Revenue
and Customs

**Cutty Sark Trust**
2 Greenwich Church St  London SE10 9BG
Tel: 020 8858 2698
enquiries@cuttysark.org.uk
www.cuttysark.org.uk
To conserve and display the clipper ship
'Cutty Sark'

**Cyber Mentors**
Units 1 + 4  Belvedere Road  London SE19
2AT
Tel:  0208 771 3377

admin@beatbullying.org
www.cybermentors.org.uk
Supports all young people affected by
bullying and uses social networking to allow
young people at different levels to mentor
each other.

**Cyclenation**
2 Newhams Row  London  SE1 3UZ
email via website
www.cyclenation.org.uk

**Cycling** see also Bike Express (European),
CTC, Sustrans, Tandem Club

**Cycling Association (Welsh)**
www.welshcycling.org

**Cycling (British)**
Stuart St  Manchester M11 4DQ
Tel: 0161 274 2000
info@britishcycling.org.uk
www.britishcycling.org.uk

**Cycling Campaign (London)**
2 Newhams Row  London SE1 3UZ
Tel: 020 7234 9310
Email via website
www.lcc.org.uk

**Cycling Centre (National)**
Stuart St  Manchester M11 4DQ
Tel: 0161 223 2244
admin@nationalcyclingcentre.com
www.nationalcyclingcentre.com
Centre for training in track racing cycling
and other sports events

**Cycling Projects**
Priory Court  Buttermarket Street
Warrington WA1 2NP
Tel: 01925 234 213
ian.tierney@cycling.org.uk
www.cycling.org.uk
Runs several community cycling projects:-
Bikelinks, Cycle Lifestyle – using cycles to
reduce social exclusion & to improve health;
Wheels for All! – cycling for people with
differing needs

**Cycling Union (International)** Union
Cycliste Internationale
International Cycling Union (UCI)
  Ch. de la Mêlée 12  1860 Aigle  Switzerland
Tel: 00 41 24 468 5811
admin@uci.ch
www.uci.ch
Develops and promotes all aspects of
cycling

**Cyclists' Federation (European)**
Rue Franklin, 28  1000 Brussels, Belgium
Tel: 0032 2 880 92 74
office@ecf.com
www.ecf.com

**Cyclists Touring Club** now see CTC

**Cymdeithas Clychoedd Chwarae Cyn-ysgol Cymru** see Pre-School Playgroups Association (Wales)

**Cymdeithas Ddrama Cymru** see Drama Association of Wales

**Cymdeithas y Cerddwyr** see Ramblers Association Wales

**Cymdeithas yr Iaith Gymraeg** Welsh Language Society
Ystafell 5  Y Cambria  Rhodfa'r Mor
Aberystwyth SY23 2AZ
Tel: 01970 624501
swyddfa@cymdeithas.org
http://cymdeithas.org/

**Cyngor Celfyddydau Cymru** see Arts Council of Wales

**Cyngor Gofal Cymru** see Care Council for Wales

**Cystic Fibrosis Trust**
11 London Rd  Bromley  Kent BR1 1BY
Support helpline: 0300 373 1000
Tel: 020 8464 7211
enquiries@cftrust.org.uk
www.cftrust.org.uk

# D

**Dad**
www.dad.info
To give dads a free and permanent source of the information they're likely to need - from pregnancy, birth and babies to financial, legal and education info - from a dad's perspective

**Dad Talk**
www.dadtalk.co.uk

**Dad's House**
5 Kensington Square  London W8 5EP
www.dadshouse.co.uk
Helping single fathers in the UK

**Dairy Council (The)**
93 Baker Street  London W1U 6QQ
Tel: 020 7467 2629
info@dairycouncil.org.uk
www.milk.co.uk
Represents farmers and processors

**Daisy Network**
PO Box 183  Rossendale  BB4 6WZ
daisy@daisynetwork.org.uk
www.daisynetwork.org.uk
Nationwide support group for women who have suffered a premature menopause

**Daiwa Anglo-Japanese Foundation**
13-14 Cornwall Terrace  London NW1 4QP
Tel: 020 7486 4348
office@dajf.org.uk
www.dajf.org.uk
Charity supporting links between Britain & Japan. Scholarships, grant-giving and cultural events

**DAN** see Disabled People's Direct Action Network

**Dance Council (British)**
240 Merton Road  South Wimbledon
London SW19 1EQ
Tel: 020 8545 0085
secretary@british-dance-council.org
www.british-dance-council.org
Governing body for ballroom dancing in Great Britain

**Dance Education & Training (Council for)**
Old Brewer's Yard
17-19 Neal Street  Covent Garden
London WC2H 9UY
Tel: 020 7240 5703
info@cdet.org.uk
www.cdet.org.uk
Provides a list of accredited dance courses & can offer advice on obtaining grants & careers advice

**Dance Teachers Alliance (UKA)**
Centenary House  38-40 Station Rd
Blackpool FY4 1EU
info@ukadance.co.uk
www.ukadance.co.uk

**Dance UK**
The Urdang  The Old Finsbury Town Hall
Rosebery Avenue  London EC1R 4QT
Tel: 020 7713 0730
info@danceuk.org
www.danceuk.org
Membership organisation for professional dancers, choreographers, teachers and dance managers

**Danceconsortium**
www.worldwidedanceuk.com

**Dancesport UK**
www.dancesport.uk.com
Resource on competitive Ballroom Dancing

**Daneford Trust**
45-47 Blythe St  London E2 6LN
Tel: 020 7729 1928
info@danefordtrust.org
www.danefordtrust.org
Educational & working exchanges for 18-28 year olds (from London only) in Africa, Asia & the Caribbean

**Dark Skies (Campaign for)**
www.britastro.org/dark-skies
The British Astronomical Association's
campaign explores the issues about light
pollution and includes educational projects

**DATA** see Design and Technology
Association

**DATA** now see ONE

**Data Protection Registrar** see Information
Commissioner's Office

**David Sheldrick Wildlife Trust**
Unit 19  Brook Willow Farm  Woodlands
Road  Leatherhead KT22 0AN
Tel: 01372 844 608
infouk@sheldrickwildlifetrust.org
www.sheldrickwildlifetrust.org
Dedicated to the preservation and protection
of Africa's wilderness and its denizens,
particularly endangered species

**Day One Christian Ministries**
Ryelands Road  Leominster  Herefordshire
HR6 8NZ
Tel: 01568 613740
info@dayone.co.uk
www.lordsday.co.uk

**Daycare Trust**
2nd Floor  Novas Contemporary Urban
Centre  73-81 Southwark Bridge Road
London SE1 0NQ

Information line: 0845 872 6251
Tel: 0845 872 6260 (020 7940 7510)
info@daycaretrust.org.uk
www.daycaretrust.org.uk
Charity which campaigns for and offers
information and advice on childcare

**Deaf** see also Betterhearing, Cued Speech
Association UK, Hearing Dogs for Deaf
People, Learn To Sign, Music and the
Deaf, RNID, Sense, Signature, SPIT,
Telecommunications Action Group

**Deaf Association (British)**
10th Floor  Coventry Point  Market Way
Coventry CV1 1EA
Tel: 02476 550936
Textphone: 02476 550393
headoffice@bda.org.uk
www.bda.org.uk

**Deaf Broadcasting Council**
pennybes@aol.com
www.deafcouncil.org.uk/dbc
A consumer organisation representing deaf
TV viewers

**Deaf Children's Society (National)**
15 Dufferin St  London EC1Y 8UR
Freephone Helpline: 0808 800 8880
Tel: 020 7490 8656 voice and text

ndcs@ndcs.org.uk
helpline@ndcs.org.uk
www.ndcs.org.uk

**Deaf (Commonwealth Society for the)**
34 Buckingham Palace Rd  London SW1W
0RE
Tel: 020 7233 5700
admin@sound-seekers.org.uk
www.sound-seekers.org.uk
Supports the needs of deaf children in the
developing countries of the Commonwealth

**Deaf Education Through Listening and
Talking** DELTA
The Con Powell Centre  Alfa House  Molesey
Road  Walton on Thames  Surrey KT12 3PD
Tel: 0845 108 1437
enquiries@deafeducation.org.uk
www.deafeducation.org.uk
Members are parents of deaf children,
teachers of the Deaf, etc. Provides
information and advice on the Natural Aural
Approach to the education of deaf children

**Deaf Sports Council (British)**
email via website
www.britishdeafsportscouncil.org.uk

**Deafblind International**
www.deafblindinternational.org
World association promoting services for
deafblind people

**Deafblind Scotland**
21 Alexandra Ave  Lenzie  Glasgow G66
5BG
Tel: 0141 777 6111 (voice/text)
info@deafblindscotland.org.uk
www.deafblindscotland.org.uk

**Deafblind UK**
National Centre for Deafblindness  John
& Lucille van Geest Place  Cygnet Rd
Hampton  Peterborough PE7 8FD
Helpline: 0800 132 320
Tel/Minicom: 01733 358 100
info@deafblind.org.uk
www.deafblind.org.uk
Assists people who are losing their
sight and hearing and raises awareness
of deafblindness through educational
programmes

**Deafblindness (A-Z to)**
www.deafblind.com

**Deafness Research UK**
330/332 Gray's Inn Rd  London WC1X 8EE
Helpline: 0808 808 2222
Tel: 020 7833 1733
text 020 7915 1412
contact@deafnessresearch.org.uk
www.deafnessresearch.org.uk
National medical research charity

**DEBRA**
Debra House 13 Wellington Business Park Dukes Ride Crowthorne Berks RG45 6LS
Tel: 01344 771961
debra@debra.org.uk
www.debra.org.uk
Supports people living with all forms of epidermolysis bullosa (EB) and funds research into the condition

**Deer Society (British)**
The Walled Garden Burgate Manor Fordingbridge Hampshire SP6 1EF
Tel: 01425 655434
h.q@bds.org.uk
www.bds.org.uk

**Defence (Ministry of)** MoD
Main Building Whitehall London SW1A 2HB
Tel: 020 7218 9000
email via website
www.mod.uk

**Defra** Department for Environment, Food & Rural Affairs
Eastbury House 30 - 34 Albert Embankment London SE1 7TL
Tel: 08459 33 55 77
helpline@defra.gsi.gov.uk
http://ww2.defra.gov.uk/

**Delinquency (Institute for the Study and Treatment of)** see Crime and Justice Studies (Centre for)

**Dementia** see Alzheimer

**Democracy and Electoral Assistance (International Institute for)** IDEA
Strömsborg SE-103 34 Stockholm Sweden
Tel: 00 46 8 698 3700
Email via website
www.idea.int

**Demos**
3rd Floor Magdalen House 136 Tooley Street London SE1 2TU
Tel: 0845 458 5949
hello@demos.co.uk
www.demos.co.uk
Political think-tank & publisher

**Dental Association (British)**
64 Wimpole St London W1G 8YS
Tel: 020 7935 0875
enquiries@bda.org
www.bda.org
National professional association for dentists

**Depaul International**
291-299 Borough High Street London SE1 1JG
Tel: 0207 939 1220
depaul@depauluk.org

www.depauluk.org
Largest charity for young homeless people in the UK. Affiliated body for over 50 Nightstop schemes nationwide

**Depaul Nightstop UK**
The Resource Centre Oxford Street Whitley Bay Newcastle NE26 1AD
email via website
www.depaulnightstopuk.org
Provides safe emergency accommodation for homeless young people aged 16-25 in the homes of approved volunteers

**DEPIS** see Drug Education & Prevention Information Service

**Depression** see also Journeys, MDF The Bipolar Association

**Depression Alliance**
20 Great Dover Street London SE1 4LX
Tel: 0845 1232 320
information@depressionalliance.org
www.depressionalliance.org
Information and support

**Depression Alliance Cymru** now see Journeys

**Depression Alliance Scotland**
11 Alva Street Edinburgh EH2 4PH
Helpline: 0845 123 23 20
Tel: 0131 467 3050
info@dascot.org
www.dascot.org

**Dermatologists (British Association of)**
Willan House 4 Fitzroy Sq London W1T 5HQ
Tel: 020 7383 0266
admin@bad.org.uk
www.bad.org.uk

**Design** see also Art & Design (National Society for Education in), Better Seating (Campaign for), Inventors (British Institute of)

**Design and Artists Copyright Society**
33 Great Sutton Street London EC1V 0DX
Tel: 020 7336 8811
info@dacs.org.uk
www.dacs.org.uk

**Design and Technology Association** DATA
16 Wellesbourne House Walton Rd Wellesbourne Warwickshire CV35 9JB
Tel: 01789 470007
info@data.org.uk
www.data.org.uk
Professional association

**Design Council**
34 Bow Street  London WC2E 7DL
020 7420 5200
email via website
www.designcouncil.org.uk
Aims to Help Britain use design to build a
stronger economy and improve everyday
life October 2010: No longer receiving
Government funding but the Design Council
will retain its charitable status and be an
independent not-for profit organisation
incorporated by Royal Charter.

**Design Museum**
Shad Thames   London SE1 2YD
Tel: 020 7403 6933
info@designmuseum.org
www.designmuseum.org

**Development Education Association
(DEA)**
Can Mezzanine  32-36 Loman Street
London SE1 OEH
Tel: 020 7922 7930
dea@dea.org.uk
www.dea.org.uk
Promotes understanding of global and
development issues

**Development Education Project**
Laurel Cottage  799 Wilmslow Road
Manchester M20 2RR
Tel: 0161 921 8020
info@dep.org.uk
www.dep.org.uk
Support and training to teachers

**Development in Special Needs Education
(European Agency for)** see Special
Needs Education (European Agency for
Development in)

**Developments**
Email via website
www.developments.org.uk/
Website about development issues run by
the DFID  linking to their magazine of the
same name

**Diabetes UK**
10 Parkway  London NW1 7AA
Careline: 0845 120 2960
Tel: 020 7424 1000
info@diabetes.org.uk
www.diabetes.org.uk
Caring for those living with diabetes

**Dial UK**
St Catherine's   Tickhill Rd  Doncaster DN4
8QN
Tel/Textphone: 01302 310123
informationenquiries@dialuk.org.uk
www.dialuk.info

Provides services and support to over 150
disability advice centres

**DIALOG**  Diversity in Action in Local
Government
Local Government Improvement and
Development  Layden House  76-86 Turnmill
St  London EC1M 5LG
Tel: 020 7296 6880
ihelp@local.gov.uk
www.idea.gov.uk
Works to address issues of equality and
diversity to deliver best practice in local
government

**Dietetic Association (British)**
5th Floor  Charles House  148-9 Great
Charles St   Queensway  Birmingham B3
3HT
Tel: 0121 200 8080
info@bda.uk.com
www.bda.uk.com
Professional association and trade union for
state registered dieticians

**Different Strokes**
9 Canon Harnett Court  Wolverton Mill
Milton Keynes MK12 5NF
Tel: 0845 130 7172
Email via website
www.differentstrokes.co.uk
A charity for younger stroke survivors for
the purposes of active self-help and mutual
support

**Digestive Disorders Foundation** see
CORE

**Dignity in Dying**
181 Oxford Street  London W1D 2JT
Tel: 020 7479 7730
info@dignityindying.org.uk
www.dignityindying.org.uk/

**DIPEx** see Healthtalkonline and
Youthhealthtalk

**Direct Labour Organisations
(Association of)** see Public Service
Excellence (Association for)

**Direct Marketing Association**
DMA House  70 Margaret St  London W1W 8SS
Tel: 020 7291 3300
info@dma.org.uk
www.dma.org.uk
Trade association

**DirectGov**
www.direct.gov.uk
Links to all government websites

**Directors (Institute of)**
116 Pall Mall  London SW1Y 5ED
Tel: 020 7766 8866
enquiries@iod.com
www.iod.com

## Directory of Social Change

24 Stephenson Way  London NW1 2DP
Tel: 020 7391 4800
08450 77 77 07 (Customer services team)
enquiries@dsc.org.uk
www.dsc.org.uk
Information and training for the voluntary sector.

## Disability Action

Portside Business Park  189 Airport Rd West
Belfast BT3 9ED
Tel: 028 9029 7880
hq@disabilityaction.org
www.disabilityaction.org
Northern Ireland organisation which works to ensure that people with disabilities attain their full rights as citizens

## Disability Alliance

Universal House  88-94 Wentworth St
London E1 7SA
Tel: 020 7247 8776
office@disabilityalliance.org
www.disabilityalliance.org
Provides information on benefits through publications, training and website

## Disability & Development (Action on)

ADD
Vallis House  57 Vallis Rd  Frome  Somerset
BA11 3EG
Tel: 01373 473064
Email via website
www.add.org.uk
Charity working in Africa and Asia to help people with disabilities

## Disability Law Service

Ground Floor  39-45 Cavell St  London E1 2BP
Tel: 020 7791 9800
Minicom: 020 7791 9801
advice@dls.org.uk
www.dls.org.uk
Free and confidential legal advice to disabled people and their carers

## Disability Pregnancy & Parenthood International

Unit F9  89/93 Fonthill Rd  London N4 3JH
Tel: 0800 018 4730
Text: 0800 018 9949
info@dppi.org.uk
www.dppi.org.uk
Information service for disabled parents and their professional allies

## Disability & Rehabilitation see RADAR

## Disability Rights Commission  now see Equality and Human Rights Commission

## Disability Snowsport UK

Administration Office  Cairngorm Mountain
Via Aviemore  Inverness-shire PH22 1RB
Tel: 01479 861272
admin@disabilitysnowsport.org.uk
www.disabilitysnowsport.org.uk
Providing snowsports for all disabilities.
Qualified instructors and helpers attend on lessons/activity weeks

## Disability Sport (English Federation of)

SportPark - Loughborough University
3 Oakwood Drive  Loughborough
Leicestershire LE11 3QF
Tel: 01509 227750
federation@efds.co.uk
www.efds.co.uk
National body

## Disability Sport (Events)

Belle Vue Leisure Centre  Pink Bank Lane
Manchester M12 5GL
Tel: 0161 953 2499
info@dse.org.uk
www.disabilitysport.org.uk
Co-ordinates 14 national/international and over 200 regional multi-disability sporting events

## Disabled Children (Council for)

8 Wakley Street  London EC1V 7QE
Tel: 020 7843 1900
cdc@ncb.org.uk
www.ncb.org.uk
Umbrella body for the disabled children's sector in England, with links to the other UK nations

## Disabled Drivers' Association now see Mobilise

## Disabled Living Foundation

380-384 Harrow Rd  London W9 2HU
Helpline: 0845 130 9177 (Textphone) 020 7432 8009
Tel: 020 7289 6111
info@dlf.org.uk
www.dlf.org.uk
Offers advice and information on equipment and daily living for people with disabilities, older people and carers

## Disabled Parents' Network

81 Melton Road  West Bridgford
Nottingham  NG2 8EN
Disabled Parents Helpline & General
Enquiries: 0300 3300 639
Tel: 0870 241 0450
information@disabledparentsnetwork.org.uk
www.disabledparentsnetwork.org.uk
Organisation of disabled parents offering support to disabled parents

**Disabled People's Council (UK)**
Stratford Advice Arcade  107-109 The Grove
Stratford   London, E15 1HP
Tel: 020 8522 7433
ceo@ukdpc.net
www.ukdpc.net
National umbrella organisation

**Disabled Persons Housing Service Ltd**
see HoDis

**Disablement Information** see Dial UK

**Disasters Emergency Committee**
1st Floor  43 Chalton Street  London NW1
1DU
Tel: 020 7387 0200
info@dec.org.uk
www.dec.org.uk
Co-ordinates national appeals for response to
major overseas disasters

**Disfigurement Guidance Centre**
PO Box 7  Cupar  Fife KY15 4PF
Tel: 01337 870 281
Tel: 01334 839084
www.timewarp.demon.co.uk/dgc.html
www.skinlaserdirectory.org.uk
A range of services to provide support for
disfigured people and their families. Also
publishes directory of skin laser clinics

**Dispute Resolution** see Effective Dispute
Resolution (Centre for)

**Divers Marine Life Rescue (British)**
Lime House  Regency Close  Uckfield  East
Sussex TN22 1DS
Tel:  01825 765546
info@bdmlr.org.uk
www.bdmlr.org.uk
Organisation ready to respond immediately
to any marine disaster or marine mammal
stranding anywhere in the UK

**Diversity in Action in Local Government**
see DIALOG

**Divorce** see also Children's Service,
Families Need Fathers, Fathers4Justice, It's
not your fault, Relate

**Divorced & Separated (National Council
for the)**
68 Parkes Hall Road  Woodsetton  Dudley
DY1 3SR
Tel: 07041 478120
Email via website
www.ncds.org.uk
Helps divorced, separated and widowed
people

**Do it**
First Floor  50 Featherstone Street,  London,
EC1Y 8RT
020 7250 5700

Email via website
www.do-it.org.uk
Database detailing ways in which you can
volunteer to help your local community or
people further afield

**Do-it** Volunteering made easy
www.do-it.org.uk
A searchable central database about all
aspects of volunteering

**Dogs** see also Battersea Dogs' Home,
Canine Partners, Crufts Dog Show, Guide
Dogs for the Blind Association, Hearing
Dogs for Deaf People, Kennel Club, Lost
Doggies UK, Pets as Therapy, Support Dogs

**Dogs for the Disabled**
The Frances Hay Centre  Blacklocks Hill
Banbury  Oxon OX17 2BS
Tel: 01295 252600
info@dogsforthedisabled.org
www.dogsforthedisabled.org
Provides trained assistance dogs to help
disabled people

**Dogs Trust**
17 Wakley St  London EC1V 7RQ
Tel: 020 7837 0006
Email via website
www.dogstrust.org.uk

**Domain names** see Nominet

**Domestic Violence (Campaign Against)**
CADV
PO Box 2371  London E1 5NQ
Freephone 24 Hour National Domestic
Violence Helpline Phone: 0808 2000 247
Tel: 020 8520 5881
enquiries@cadv.org.uk
www.cadv.org.uk

**Don't lose the music**
RNID  19-23 Featherstone Street  London
EC1Y 8SL
Telephone/Textphone: 020 7296 8142
dontlosethemusic@rnid.org.uk
www.dontlosethemusic.com
A campaign run by RNID to protect people
against hearing loss caused by listening to
too-loud music.

**Donkey Breed Society**
The Hermitage  Pootings  Edenbridge  Kent
TN8 6SD
Tel: 01732 864414
societysecretary@donkeybreed society.
co.uk
www.donkeybreedsociety.co.uk

**Donkey Sanctuary**
Sidmouth  Devon EX10 0NU
Tel: 01395 578222
email via website

www.thedonkeysanctuary.org.uk
Registered charity working worldwide for
donkeys

## Donor Conception Network
PO Box 7471   Nottingham NG3 6ZR
Tel: 0208 245 4369
enquiries@dcnetwork.org
www.donor-conception-network.org/
Self-help network of over 1,300 families
created with the help of donated eggs,
sperm or embryos; couples and individuals
seeking to found a family this way; and adults
conceived using a donor

## Donor Family Network
PO Box 13825  Birmingham B42 9DJ
Tel: 0845 680 1954
info@donorfamilynetwork.co.uk
www.donorfamilynetwork.co.uk
Supports donor families and promotes
awareness of organ donation

## Douglas Bader Foundation
45 Dundale Road  Tring  Herts HP23 5BU
Tel: 01442 826662
douglasbaderfdn@btinternet.com
www.douglasbaderfoundation.co.uk
Sports Centre mainly for disabled people

**Down to Earth** International Campaign for
Ecological Justice in Indonesia
Greenside Farmhouse  Hallbankgate
Cumbria CA8 2PX
Tel: 016977 46266
dte@gn.apc.org
http://dte.gn.apc.org
Environmental group, indigenous rights, land
and natural resources

## Down's Heart Group
PO Box 4260  Eaton Bray   Dunstable  Beds
LU6 2ZT
Tel: 0844 288 4800
info@dhg.org.uk
www.dhg.org.uk
Support and information for families who
have a member with Down's Syndrome  and
congenital heart defects

## Down's Syndrome Association
Langdon Down Centre  2a Langdon Park
Teddington TW11 9PS
Tel: 0845 2300372
info@downs-syndrome.org.uk
www.downs-syndrome.org.uk

## Down's Syndrome Educational Trust
The Sarah Duffen Centre  Belmont St
Southsea  Hampshire PO5 1NA
Tel: 023 9285 5330
enquiries@downsed.org
www.downsed.org

## Down's Syndrome Medical Interest Group
Children's Centre  City Hospital Campus
Nottingham NG5 1PB
0115 9627658 ext 31158/7
info@dsmig.org.uk
www.dsmig.org.uk
Network of doctors from the UK and Republic
of Ireland

## Down's Syndrome Scotland
158/160 Balgreen Road  Edinburgh EH11
3AU
Tel: 0131 313 4225
info@dsscotland.org.uk
www.dsscotland.org.uk

**Downing Street** see 10 Downing Street
Website

## Dr Edward Bach Centre
Mount Vernon  Bakers Ln  Brightwell-cum-
Sotwell  Oxon OX10 0PZ
Tel: 01491 834678
email via website
www.bachcentre.com
Flower based remedies, information,
education & manufacture. Referral to
practitioners

## Dragonfly Society (British)
23 Bowker Way  Whittlesey  Peterborough
PE7 1PY
bdssecretary@dragonflysoc.org.uk
www.dragonflysoc.org.uk

**Drama** see also National Drama, NODA,
RADA, Student Drama Festival (National),
Student Theatre Company (National),
Teaching of Drama (National Association
for the), Theatre Council (Independent),
Theatre for Children and Young People
(International Association), Youth Theatres
(National Association of)

**Drama Association of Wales** Cymdeithas
Ddrama Cymru
The Old Library  Singleton Rd  Splott  Cardiff
CF24 2ET
Tel: 029 2045 2200
info@dramawales.org.uk
www.dramawales.org.uk

## Drama (National)
secretary@nationaldrama.co.uk
www.nationaldrama.co.uk
Professional association for drama
educators

## Drama Schools (The Conference of)
PO Box 34252  London NW5 1XJ
info@cds.drama.ac.uk
www.drama.ac.uk
The 22 leading drama schools in UK with
most courses accredited by National Council
for Drama Training

### Drama Training (National Council for)
NCDT
249 Tooley Street  London   SE1 2JX
Tel: 020 7407 3686
info@ncdt.co.uk
www.ncdt.co.uk
Provides a list of accredited drama courses
& can offer advice on obtaining grants &
careers advice

### Dramatic Need
info@dramaticneed.org
www.dramaticneed.org
Sends international volunteers from
the creative arts to South Africa to host
workshops with children living in rural
communities.

### Drawing (The Campaign for)
7 Gentleman's Row  Enfield EN2 6PT
Tel: 020 8351 1719
info@campaignfordrawing.org
www.campaignfordrawing.org
Organises events to promote drawing,
including 'The Big Draw' in October UK-wide

### Drink Helpline (National)
Drinkline: Freefone 0800 917 8282 (9am-11pm
Mon-Fri, 6am-11pm Sat, Sun) Voicemail
available outside above hours
Free confidential advice about alcohol related
problems

### drinkaware.co.uk
Samuel House  6 St Albans St  London  SW1Y
4SQ
Tel: 020 7766 9900
Email via website
www.drinkaware.co.uk
Useful information about alcohol and drinking

### Drinking & Driving see CADD

### Drinking Water Inspectorate
Room M03, 55 Whitehall  London SW1A 2EY
Tel:  0300 068 6400
dwi.enquiries@defra.gsi.gov.uk
www.dwi.gov.uk

### Drug Education Forum
c/o Mentor UK  4th Floor  74 Great Eastern
Street  London   EC2A 3JG
Tel: 020 7739 8494
email via website
www.drugeducationforum.com
Online forums for those involved in drug
education. In particular to those interested in
the development of policy and practice

### Drugs and Crime (UN Office on)
Email via website
www.unodc.org

### Drugs Forum (Scottish)
91 Mitchell Street  Glasgow G1 3LN

Tel: 0141 221 1175
enquiries@sdf.org.uk
www.sdf.org.uk
National non government agency for policy
and information work

### Drugs Helpline (National) now see Frank

### DrugScope
Prince Consort House  Suite 204 (2nd Floor)
109/111 Farringdon Road  London EC1R 3BW
Tel: 020 7520 7550
info@drugscope.org.uk
www.drugscope.org.uk
Centre of expertise on drugs which works to
inform policy development and reduce drug
related risk

### DTI see Business, Enterprise and Regulatory Reform (Department for)

### Duke of Edinburgh's Award
Gulliver  House  Madeira Walk  Windsor SL4
1EU
Tel: 01753 727400
info@DofE.org
www.dofe.org
A programme of leisure activities for young
people aged 14-25. Registered charity

### Dulwich Picture Gallery
Gallery Rd  London SE21 7AD
Tel: 020 8693 5254
email via website
www.dulwichpicturegallery.org.uk

### DVLA
Swansea  SA6 7JL
Tel: 0300 790 6801 (Drivers enquiries)
Textphone: 0300 123 1278
email via website
www.dft.gov.uk/dvla/

### Dyslexia Action
Park House  Wick Rd  Egham  Surrey TW20
0HH
Tel: 01784 222300
info@dyslexiaaction.org.uk
www.dyslexiaaction.org.uk

### Dyslexia Association (British) BDA
Unit 8, Bracknell Beeches  Old Bracknell
Lane  Bracknell RG12 7BW
Helpline: 0845 251 9002
Tel: 0845 251 9003
admin@bdadyslexia.org.uk  helpline@
bdadyslexia.org.uk
www.bdadyslexia.org.uk

### Dyspraxia Foundation
8 West Alley  Hitchin  Herts SG5 1EG
Tel: 01462 454 986
Tel: 01462 455 016
dyspraxia@dyspraxiafoundation.org.uk
www.dyspraxiafoundation.org.uk

### Dystrophic Epidermolysis see DEBRA

# E

## e-Learning Foundation
3000 Hillswood Drive  Hillswood Business Park
Chertsey  Surrey KT16 0RS
Tel: 01932 796036
info@e-learningfoundation.com
www.e-learningfoundation.com
Helps schools give access to IT to their most
deprived students and their  families

## e-Parliament Initiative
www.e-parl.net
A world parliament on the internet to link
parliamentarians into Action Networks

## Early Childhood Education (British Association for)
136 Cavell St  London E1 2JA
Tel: 020 7539 5400
office@early-education.org.uk
www.early-education.org.uk
Works to improve educational provision for
children from birth to 8 years

## Early Years The organisation for young children
6c Wildflower Way
  Apollo Road  Boucher Road  Belfast BT12 6TA
Tel: 028 9066 2825
email via website
www.early-years.org

## Earth First! Worldwide
greg7@EarthFirst.org
www.earthfirst.org

## EarthAction Network
contact@earthaction.org
www.earthaction.org
A global action alert network

## Earthquake Locator (World Wide)
http://tsunami.geo.ed.ac.uk/local-bin/quakes/
mapscript/home.pl
Website giving locations and other details of
recent earthquakes

## Earthwatch Europe
Mayfield House  256 Banbury Rd  Oxford OX2
7DE
Tel: 01865 318 838
info@earthwatch.org.uk
www.earthwatch.org/europe
An environmental charity supporting scientific
field research

## Eating Disorders see BEAT

## Eating problems service
Tel: 020 7602 0862
post@eatingproblems.org
www.eatingproblems.org

## Eaves Housing for Women
Unit 2.03, Canterbury Court   1-3 Brixton Rd
London SW9 6DE
Tel: 020 7735 2062
post@eaveshousing.co.uk
www.eaves4women.co.uk
Support housing and refuge accommodation
for homeless women and women escaping
domestic violence plus other violence against
women projects

## ECB see Cricket Board (England & Wales)

## Echo
http://ec.europa.eu/echo
European Union's humanitarian arm, providing
emergency assistance and relief to the victims
of natural disaster or armed conflict worldwide

## ECIS see Engineering Careers Information Service

## Eco-Schools
Eco-Schools  Keep Britain Tidy, Elizabeth
House  The Pier, Wigan
  WN3 4EX
Tel: 01942 612621
eco-schools@keepbritaintidy.org
www.eco-schools.org.uk
Promotes environmental awareness & has a
scheme of awards

## Ecological Society (British)
Charles Darwin House
  12 Roger Street  London, WC1N 2JU

Tel: 0207 685 2500
info@BritishEcologicalSociety.org
www.britishecologicalsociety.org

## Ecology see also CEH

## Ecology Building Society
7 Belton Road  Silsden  Nr. Keighley
W.Yorks BD20 0EE
Tel: 0845 674 5566
info@ecology.co.uk
www.ecology.co.uk
Ethical savings and green mortgages
for properties in need of renovation and
ecological new builds

## Economic & Social Research (National Institute of)
2 Dean Trench St  Smith Square London,
SW1P 3HE
Tel: 020 7222 7665
enquiries@niesr.ac.uk
www.niesr.ac.uk

## Economics & Business Education Association
The Forum  277 London Road  Burgess Hill RH15 9QU
Tel: 01444 240150
office@ebea.org.uk
www.ebea.org.uk
Subject association for teachers

## Ecotourism Society (The International)
www.ecotourism.org
Not for profit organisation concerned with ecotourism

## ECRA Publishing see Ethical Consumer Research Association

## Eczema Society (National)
Hill House  Highgate Hill  London N19 5NA
Patients Helpline: 0800 089 1122
Tel: 020 7281 3553 (office & membership)
helpline@eczema.org
info@eczema.org
www.eczema.org

## Eden Project
Bodelva  St Austell  Cornwall PL24 2SG
Tel: 01726 811911
email via website
www.edenproject.com
Centre for plants & a new scientific institute

## Edexel
190 High Holborn  London WC1V 7BH
emai via website
www.edexcel.org.uk
Examining & awarding body

## Edinburgh International Book Festival
5a Charlotte Square  Edinburgh EH2 4DR
Tel: 0131 718 5666
admin@edbookfest.co.uk
www.edbookfest.co.uk
Organises the world's largest book festival in Charlotte Square Gardens every August

## Edinburgh International Festival Society
The Hub, Castlehill  Edinburgh UK  EH1 2NE
Tel: 0131 473 2099
Email via website
www.eif.co.uk
A festival of the arts taking place every August

## Editors and Proofreaders (Society for)
Erico House  93–99 Upper Richmond Road Putney  London SW15 2TG
Tel: 020 8785 5617
administration@sfep.org.uk
www.sfep.org.uk

## Education (Advisory Centre for)
1C Aberdeen Studios  22 Highbury Grove London N5 2DQ
Adviceline: 0808 800 5793
Tel: 020 7704 3370

Exclusion Line: 020 7704 9822
enquiries@ace-ed.org.uk
www.ace-ed.org.uk
Supports and advises parents whose children aged 5-16 have problems in school

## Education and Training (Centre for the Study of) CSET
Department of Educational Research
County South  Lancaster University
Lancaster LA1 4YD
Tel: 01524 592679
d.daglish@lancaster.ac.uk
www.lancs.ac.uk/fss/centres/cset
Researches education, training & careers

## Education Business Excellence (Institute for)
188 Main St  New Greenham Park
Thatcham  Berks RG19 6HW
Tel: 01635 279914
office@iebe.org.uk
www.iebe.org.uk
Provides links between the worlds of business and education to offer young people a rewarding and realistic introduction to the world of work

## Education Consultants (Society of)
Floor 5 Amphenol Business Centre  Thanet Way  Whitstable  Kent CT5 3JF
Tel: 0845 345 7932
administration@sec.org.uk
www.sec.org.uk
Network of individual consultants working under a code of practice

## Education & Culture (European Commission Directorate General)
eac-info@ec.europa.eu
http://ec.europa.eu/dgs/education_culture/index_en.htm

## Education (Department for)
Castle View House  East Lane  Runcorn
Cheshire  WA7 2GJ
Tel: 0870 000 2288
Typetalk: 18001 0870 000 2288
email via website
www.education.gov.uk

## Education Extra now see ContinYou

## Education for Choice
The Resource Centre  356 Holloway Road London N7 6PA
Tel/fax: 020 7700 8190
efc@efc.org.uk
www.efc.org.uk/
Provides educational materials about abortion

**Education in Art and Design (National Society for)** see Art and Design (National Society for Education in)

**Education Index (British)**
Brotherton Library  University of Leeds  Leeds LS2 9JT
Tel: 0113 343 5525
bei@leeds.ac.uk
www.leeds.ac.uk/bei/
An index to the contents of 300 education and training journals

**Education & Industry (Centre for)**
University of Warwick  Coventry CV4 7AL
Tel: 0247 652 3909
cei@warwick.ac.uk
www2.warwick.ac.uk/fac/soc/cei
Centre of expertise in education, especially work related learning

**Education of Adults (European Association for the)** EAEA
www.eaea.org

**Education of Travelling Communities (European Federation for the)** EFECOT
efecot@efecot.net
www.efecot.net
Aims to create and promote education adapted to the particular needs of occupational travellers

**Education Otherwise**
125 Queen Street  Sheffield  South Yorkshire S1 2DU
Helpline: 0845 4786345
email via website
www.education-otherwise.org
For families who want to educate children outside the school system

**Education & Research Networking Association (UK)** see JANET

**Education Statistics (USA National Center for)**
Email via website
http://nces.ed.gov
Collects & analyses data about the USA & other nations. Part of the USA Dept of Education

**Educational Communications & Technology Agency (British)** see BECTA

**Educational Psychologists (Association of)**
4 The Riverside Centre  Frankland Lane Durham DH1 5TA
Tel: 0191 384 9512
enquiries@aep.org.uk
www.aep.org.uk

**Educational Recording Agency**
New Premier House  150 Southampton Row London WC1B 5AL
Tel: 020 7837 3222
era@era.org.uk
www.era.org.uk
Licenses UK educational establishments to record TV & radio programmes for non commercial educational use

**Educational Visits & Exchanges** see British Council, Commonwealth Youth Exchange Council, Daneford Trust, Education & Training Group, Fulbright Commission, Youth in Action

**Edward Lear Foundation**
info@learfoundation.org.uk
www.learfoundation.org.uk
Disability arts think tank

**EFECOT** see Education of Travelling Communities (European Federation for the)

**Effective Dispute Resolution (Centre for)**
70 Fleet Street  London EC4Y 1EU
Tel: 020 7536 6000
info@cedr.com
www.cedr.com
Aims to encourage cost-effective resolution and prevention techniques

**Egg Information Service (British)**
52A Cromwell Road  London SW7 5BE
Tel: 0207 052 8899
www.britegg.co.uk
Represents 'Lion' egg producers. Provides leaflets and information about eggs

**EIRIS** Experts in Responsible Investment Solutions
80-84 Bondway  London SW8 1SF
Tel: 020 7840 5700
info@eiris.org
www.eiris.org
Researches the social and environmental aspects of companies. Provides general ethical investment information (non financial) to the public

**Elastic Rope Sports Association (British)**
33a Canal Street  Oxford OX2 6BQ
Tel: 01865 311179
info@bersa.org
http://www.bungeezone.com/orgs/bersa.shtml
Certification body for bungee jumping

**Elder Abuse (Action on)**
PO Box 60001  Streatham SW16 9BY
Helpline: 0808 808 8141
Tel: 020 8835 9280
enquiries@elderabuse.org.uk
www.elderabuse.org.uk
For anyone concerned about abuse of an older person

**Elderly Accommodation Counsel**
Promoting choice for older people
3rd Floor  89 Albert Embankment  London SE1 7TP

Tel: 020 7820 1343
enquiries@eac.org.uk
www.eac.org.uk
Aims to help older people make informed choices about meeting their housing and care needs

**Elders (The)**
The Elders Foundation  PO BOX 60837
London W6 6GS
Email via website
www.theelders.org
The Elders are an independent group of eminent global leaders, brought together by Nelson Mandela, who offer their collective influence and experience to support peace building, help address major causes of human suffering and promote the shared interests of humanity.

**Electoral Reform Services**
The Election Centre  33 Clarendon Rd  London N8 0NW
Tel: 020 8365 8909
enquiries@electoralreform.co.uk
www.electoralreform.co.uk

**Electoral Reform Society**
Thomas Hare House
 6 Chancel St  London SE1 0UU
Tel: 020 7928 1622
ers@electoral-reform.org.uk
www.electoral-reform.org.uk
Campaigns to strengthen democracy through changes to the voting system

**Electricity Regulation** see Gas & Electricity Markets (Office of)

**Ellen MacArthur Trust**
Cowes Waterfront - Venture Quays  Castle Street  East Cowes  Isle of Wight PO32 6EZ
Tel: 01983 297750
info@ellenmacarthurtrust.org
www.ellenmacarthurtrust.org
Introduces children suffering from cancer or leukaemia to the joys of sailing on the sea

**Elm Farm Research Centre**
Hamstead Marshall  Nr Newbury  Berks RG20 0HR
Tel: 01488 658298
elmfarm@organicresearchcentre.com
www.efrc.com
Organic farming centre, advisory & research body

**Embarrassing Problems**
Health Press Limited  Elizabeth House
 Queen Street  Abingdon  Oxford OX14 3LN
Tel: 01235 523233
info@healthpress.co.uk
www.embarrassingproblems.com

A doctor's website that deals with health problems that can be difficult to discuss

**EMDP** see Exercise, Movement and Dance Partnership

**EMI Music Sound Foundation**
27 Wrights Lane  London W8 5SW
Tel: 020 7795 7000
enquiries@emimusicsoundfoundation.com
www.emimusicsoundfoundation.com
Independent charity providing funds for music education

**EMILY'S LIST UK**
11 Well House Road  Leeds  West Yorkshire LS8 4BS
enquiries@emilyslist.org.uk
www.emilyslist.org.uk
Provides financial support for women members of the Labour Party seeking public office

**Emmaus**
76 - 78 Newmarket Road  Cambridge, CB5 8DZ
Tel: 01223 576103
contact@emmaus.org.uk
www.emmaus.org.uk
Emmaus Communities offer homeless men and women a home, work and the chance to rebuild their self-respect in a supportive, community environment.

**Emotional literacy** see Antidote: Campaign for Emotional Literacy

**Employment Appeals Tribunal**
Audit House  58 Victoria Embankment London EC4Y 0DS
Tel: 020 7273 1041
londoneat@tribunals.gsi.gov.uk
www.employmentappeals.gov.uk

**Employment & Learning Northern Ireland (Department for)**
Adelaide House  39-49 Adelaide Street Belfast BT2 8FD
Tel: 028 9025 7777
del@nics.gov.uk
www.delni.gov.uk

**Employment Research (Warwick Institute for)**
University of Warwick  Gibbet Hill Rd Coventry CV4 7AL
Tel: 024 7652 3283
ier@warwick.ac.uk
www2.warwick.ac.uk/fac/soc/ier
A leading research centre in the field of labour market analysis

**Employment Rights (Institute of)**
50-54 Mount Pleasant  Liverpool L3 5SD
Tel: 0151 702 6925
office@ier.org.uk

www.ier.org.uk
Independent think tank specialising in employment and trade union law

**Employment Solicitors Online**
Email via website
www.employment-solicitors.co.uk

**Employment Studies (Institute for)**
Sovereign House  Church Street  Brighton BN1 1UJ
Tel: 01273 763400
directors.office@employment-studies.co.uk
www.employment-studies.co.uk
Independent research and consultancy, employment and human resources issues

**Employment Tribunals Service**
Enquiry Line: 0845 795 9775
Minicom: 0845 757 3722
email via website
www.employmenttribunals.gov.uk

**Empty Homes Agency**
Downstream Building  1 London Bridge London SE1 9BG
Tel: 020 7022 1870
info@emptyhomes.co.uk
www.emptyhomes.com
Campaigns to bring empty buildings in the UK back into use.

**ENABLE**
2nd Floor  146 Argyle Street  Glasgow G2 8BL
Tel: 0141 226 4541
enable@enable.org.uk
www.enable.org.uk
Charity for people with learning disabilities & their families in Scotland

**Enable (Working in India)**
35 Stileham Bank  Milborne St Andrew Blandford Forum  Dorset DT11 0LE
Tel:  01258 837546
mail@enable-india.org.uk
www.enable-india.org.uk
Supports disabled children in South India

**ENCAMS** now see Keep Britain Tidy

**Endeavour Training Limited**
Units 5 & 6 Sheepbridge Centre Sheepbridge Lane  Chesterfield S41 9RX
Tel: 01246 454 957
email via website
www.endeavour.org.uk
Providing personal development training for young people

**Endometriosis UK**
50 Westminster Palace Gardens  Artillery Row  London SW1P 1RR
Helpline: 0808 808 2227
Tel: 020 7222 2781
enquiries@endometriosis-uk.org

www.endometriosis-uk.org
Information and support

**Energy Association (International)**
info@iea.org
www.iea.org
Intergovernmental body committed to advancing security of energy supply, economic growth and environmental sustainability

**Energy Charity** see National Energy Action

**Energy Foundation (National)**
Davy Avenue  Knowlhill  Milton Keynes MK5 8NG
Tel: 01908 665555
info@nef.org.uk
www.nef.org.uk
Charity providing advice and information on energy efficiency and renewable energy

**Energy Saving Trust**
Free energy saving advice: 0800 512 012
Tel: 020 7222 0101
Email via website
www.energysavingtrust.org.uk

**Energywatch** now see Consumer Focus

**Engage** The National Association for Gallery Education
35-47 Bethnal Green Road  London E1 6LA
Tel: 020 7729 5858
info@engage.org
www.engage.org
Promotes understanding and enjoyment of the visual arts

**Engineering Council (UK)**
246 High Holborn  London WC1V 7EX
Tel: 020 3206 0500
email via website
www.engc.org.uk
Regulates the engineering profession in the UK and runs the register of Chartered Engineers, Incorporated Engineers & Engineering Technicians

**England Hockey**
Bisham Abbey National Sports Centre Marlow  Buckinghamshire SL7 1RR
Tel: 01628 897500
info@englandhockey.org
www.englandhockey.co.uk

**England Squash & Racketball**
National Squash Centre  Sportcity Manchester M11 3FF
Tel: 0161 231 4499
enquiries@englandsquashandracketball.com
www.englandsquashandracketball.com
The governing body for squash in England

**England & Wales Cricket Board** see Cricket Board (England & Wales)

**English and Media Centre**
18 Compton Terrace  London N1 2UN
Tel: 020 7359 8080
info@englishandmedia.co.uk
www.englishandmedia.co.uk
Good practice in teaching English and media via INSET and publications and website resources.

**English Association**
University of Leicester  University Rd
Leicester LE1 7RH
Tel: 0116 252 3982
engassoc@le.ac.uk
www.le.ac.uk/engassoc/

**English Heritage**
1 Waterhouse Square  138-142 Holborn
London EC1N 2ST
Customer Service: 0870 3331181
Tel: 020 7973 3000
Tel: 0870 333 1181
customers@english-heritage.org.uk
www.english-heritage.org.uk
Official government agency which manages historic buildings & ancient monuments. English Heritage Education Provides resource material and free educational visits to English Heritage sites

**English Heritage Education**
1 Waterhouse Square  138-142 Holborn
London EC1N 2ST
Tel: 0870 333 1181
Educational visits: Tel: 0207 499 5676
www.english-heritage.org.uk/education

**English Language** see English Speaking Union, IATEFL (International Association of Teachers of English as a Foreign Language), Plain English Campaign, Teaching of English (National Association for the)

**English National Ballet**
Markova House  39 Jay Mews  London SW7 2ES
Tel: 020 7581 1245
comments@ballet.org.uk
www.ballet.org.uk

**English National Opera**
London Coliseum  St Martin's Lane  London WC2N 4ES
Tel: 020 7836 0111
feedback@eno.org
www.eno.org
Performs all opera in English

**English PEN**
Free Word Centre  60 Farringdon Road
London EC1R 3GA
Tel: 020 7324 2535
enquiries@englishpen.org
www.englishpen.org
Promotes literature, upholds writers' freedoms and campaigns against the persecution of writers for stating their views

**English Speaking Union**
Dartmouth House  37 Charles St  London W1J 5ED
Tel: 020 7529 1550
esu@esu.org
www.esu.org
Creates international understanding and promotes human achievement through the widening use of the English language

**English Touring Theatre**
25 Short St  London SE1 8LJ
Tel: 020 7450 1990
admin@ett.org.uk
www.ett.org.uk
Touring productions of clarity and style throughout the UK

**ENO** see English National Opera

**Enterprise Education Trust**
Enterprise House  1-2 Hatfields  London SE1 9PG
Tel: 020 7620 0735
info@enterprise-education.org.uk
www.enterprise-education.org.uk
Brings business to life for students, aged 14 to 19.

**Entomologists' Society (Amateur)**
PO Box 8774  London SW7 5ZG
email via website
www.amentsoc.org

**Entrepreneurs** see Social Entrepreneurs (School for)

**Enuresis Resource & Information Centre** see ERIC – Education and Resources for Improving Childhood Continence

**Environment Agency**
National Customer Contact Centre  PO Box 544  Rotherham  S60 1BY
Tel: 0870 8506506
Tel: 0800 807060 (Incidents & emergencies)
Tel: 0845 988 1188 (Floodline 24hr)
enquiries@environment-agency.gov.uk
www.environment-agency.gov.uk
October 2010: Body retained but functions subject to review

**Environment and Development (International Institute for)**
3 Endsleigh St  London WC1H 0DD
Tel: 020 7388 2117
info@iied.org
www.iied.org

## Environment Council
www.the-environment-council.org.uk
Helps stakeholders to find sustainable solutions to environmental issues

## Environment, Food & Rural Affairs (Department for) see Defra

## Environment & Nature Conservation (Young People's Trust for the)
3A Market Square  Crewkerne  Somerset TA18 7LE
Tel: 01460 271717
info@ypte.org.uk
www.ypte.org.uk
An environmental education charity providing information on the environment and the need for sustainability

## Environment Protection Agency (Scottish) SEPA
Erskine Court  Castle Business Park  Stirling FK9 4TR
SEPA's Pollution Hotline - 0800 80 70 60.
SEPA's Floodline service - 0845 988 1188
Tel: 01786 457700
Email via website
www.sepa.org.uk

## Environmental Investigation Agency
62-63 Upper St  London N1 0NY
Tel: 020 7354 7960
ukinfo@eia-international.org
www.eia-international.org
Non-governmental organisation investigating and exposing the illegal trade in endangered species

## Environmental Law & Development (Foundation for International) FIELD
3 Endsleigh Street  London WC1H 0DD
Tel: 020 7872 7200
field@field.org.uk
www.field.org.uk
Legal assistance in environmental and sustainable development

## Environmental Law Foundation
2-10 Princeton Street  London WC1R 4BH
Tel: 020 7404 1030
info@elflaw.org
www.elflaw.org
National UK charity linking communities and individuals to legal and technical expertise to prevent damage to the environment

## Environmental Noise Maps
http://services.defra.gov.uk/wps/portal/noise
Maps of noise from roads, rail and industry in England

## Environmental Pollution (Royal Commission on)
Room 108  55 Whitehall  London SW1A 2EY
Tel: 0300 068 6474
enquiries@rcep.org.uk
www.rcep.org.uk
October 2010: the body is to be abolished and will formally close by the end of March 2011

## Environmental Protection UK
44 Grand Parade  Brighton BN2 9QA
Tel: 01273 878770
admin@environmental-protection.org.uk
www.environmental-protection.org.uk
Environmental protection charity

## Environmental Transport Association
68 High St  Weybridge KT13 8RS
Freephone: 0800 212 810
eta@eta.co.uk
www.eta.co.uk
Environmental breakdown company and lobby for a sustainable transport system

## Epilepsy Action
New Anstey House  Gate Way Drive  Yeadon Leeds LS19 7XY
Helpline: 0808 800 5050
Tel: 0113 210 8800
helpline@epilepsy.org.uk
epilepsy@epilepsy.org.uk
www.epilepsy.org.uk

## Epilepsy (National Centre for Young People with)
St Piers Lane  Lingfield  Surrey RH7 6PW
Confidential enquiry line 01342 831342
Tel: 01342 832243
enquiry@ncype.org.uk
www.ncype.org.uk
Runs courses for teachers and other education professionals.

## Epilepsy (National Society for)
Chesham Lane  Chalfont St Peter  Bucks SL9 0RJ
Helpline: 01494 601400
Tel: 01494 601300
Email via website
www.epilepsysociety.org.uk
Charity providing epilepsy research, treatment, assessment, care, info and training

## Epilepsy Scotland
48 Govan Rd  Glasgow G51 1JL
Helpline: 0808 800 2200
Tel: 0141 427 4911
enquiries@epilepsyscotland.org.uk
www.epilepsyscotland.org.uk

## Equal Opportunities Commission now see Equality and Human Rights Commission

## Equality and Human Rights Commission
Offices in Manchester, London, Cardiff and Glasgow – see website
Tel: 0845 604 6610 textphone 0845 604 6620 England

Tel: 0845 604 5510 textphone 0845 604 5520
Scotland
Tel: 0845 604 8810 textphone 0845 604 8820
Wales
Tel: 0161 829 8100 (non helpline calls only)
info@equalityhumanrights.com
englandhelpline@equalityhumanrights.com
wales@equalityhumanrights.com
scotland@equalityhumanrights.com
www.equalityhumanrights.com
Independent statutory body established
to help eliminate discrimination, reduce
inequality, protect human rights and to build
good relations. October 2010: body to be
retained but substantially changed.

## Equality Britain
Tel: 0151 707 6688
Email via website
www.equalitybritain.co.uk
Ethnic Britain was re-launched in 2007
as Equality Britain. Equality Britain strives
to continue working to help eliminate
discrimination, promote equality and diversity
and protect human rights, ensuring that
everyone has a fair chance to participate in
society.

## Erasmus
British Council  1 Kingsway Cardiff  CF10
3AQ
Tel: 029 2092 4311
erasmus@britishcouncil.org
www.britishcouncil.org/erasmus
European exchange programme for higher
education

## Ergonomics Society
Elms Court  Elms Grove  Loughborough LE11
1RG
Tel:  01509 234904
iehf@ergonomics.org.uk
www.ergonomics4schools.com
www.ergonomics.org.uk
Promoting ergonomics and supporting
professionals using information about people
to design for comfort, efficiency & safety

## ERIC – Education and Resources for Improving Childhood Continence
36 Old School House  Britannia Rd
Kingswood  Bristol BS15 8DB
Helpline: 0845 370 8008
Tel: 0117 960 3060
info@eric.org.uk
www.eric.org.uk
Information, support and resources on
childhood bedwetting and daytime wetting

**ERYICA** see European Youth Info. and
Counselling Agency

## Esperanto Association of Britain
Esperanto House  Station Rd  Barlaston
Stoke-on-Trent ST12 9DE
Tel: 0845 230 1887
eab@esperanto-gb.org
www.esperanto-gb.org
Promotes international auxiliary language

**ESU** European Students' Union
Tel: 00 32 2502 23 62
Email via website
www.esib.org
Represents the 10 million students across
Europe to European Institutions such as the
Parliament

**ETCO** European Transplant Coordinators
Organisation
http://www.europeantransplantcoordinators.
org/clinical-resources/irodat/
Promotes organ and tissue donation in all
member countries

## Ethical Consumer Research Association & ECRA Publishing Ltd.
Unit 21  41 Old Birley St  Manchester M15
5RF
Tel: 0161 226 2929
Email via website
www.ethicalconsumer.org
Publishers of ethical consumer magazine

**Ethical Investment Research Service** now
see EIRIS

## Ethiopiaid
PO Box 31052  London SW1X 9WB
Tel: 020 7201 9981
ethiopiaid@reed.co.uk
www.ethiopiaid.org.uk
Fundraising for projects in and around Addis
Ababa

## Ethnic Relations (Centre for Research in)
University of Warwick  Coventry CV4 7AL
Tel: 024 7652 4869
email via website
www2.warwick.ac.uk/fac/soc/crer

## EU in the United Kingdom (European Commission)
Europe House  32 Smith Square  London
SW1P 3EU
Tel: 020 7973 1992
jonathan.scheele at ec.europa.eu
http://ec.europa.eu/unitedkingdom/index_
en.htm
Access to Scotland, Northern Ireland and
Wales Offices via this website

**Eureka!**  The National Children's Museum
Discovery Road  Halifax HX1 2NE
Tel: 01422 330069
Education & Group Bookings: 01422 330012
info@eureka.org.uk

www.eureka.org.uk
Hands on museum for children aged birth to twelve

**Eurodesk**
British Council  10 Spring Gardens  London SW1A 2BN
Tel: 020 7389 4030
eurodeskuk@britishcouncil.org
www.eurodesk.org.uk
Europe-wide information service on European opportunities for young people

**Eurogroup for Animals**
6 rue des Patriotes  1000 Brussels  Belgium
Tel: 00 32 3 740 08 20
info@eurogroupforanimals.org
www.eurogroupforanimals.org

**Europe (Council of)** see Council of Europe

**Europe Direct**
Freefone: 00 800 6 7 8 9 10 11
email via website
http://ec.europa.eu/europedirect/index_en.htm
Information service from European commission

**Europe in the UK**
www.europe.org.uk
EU information with sections on news, culture, youth and education

**European Central Bank**
info@ecb.europa.eu
www.ecb.int
Website links to the sites of each national central bank

**European Commission Agriculture and Rural Development**
http://ec.europa.eu/agriculture/index_en.htm

**European Court of Justice**
Email via website
http://curia.europa.eu

**European Information Centres**
centres@euro-info.org.uk
www.euro-info.org.uk
Provides local access to a range of specialist information & advisory services to help companies develop their business in Europe

**European Investment Bank**
98-100, boulevard Konrad Adenauer  L-2950 Luxembourg
Tel: 00 352 43 79 1
Tel: 00 352 43 79 22000 (General Information)
Email via website
www.eib.org

**European Movement**
Southbank House  Black Prince Road London SE1 7SJ
Tel: 0203 176 0543
emoffice@euromove.org.uk
www.euromove.org.uk
Pro-European campaigning

**European Parliament (Office in Scotland)**
The Tun  4 Jackson's Entry  Holyrood Rd Edinburgh EH8 8PJ
Tel: 0131 557 7866
epedinburgh@europarl.europa.eu
www.europarl.org.uk

**European Parliament (UK Office)**
2 Queen Anne's Gate  London SW1H 9AA
Tel: 020 7227 4300
eplondon@europarl.europa.eu
www.europarl.org.uk

**European Parliamentary Labour Party**
EPLP
2 Queen Anne's Gate  London SW1H 9AA
Tel: 020 7222 1719
info@eurolabour.org.uk
www.eurolabour.org.uk

**European Students' Union** see ESU

**European Trade Union Confederation**
International Trade Union House (ITUH)
Boulevard Roi Albert II, 5
 B-1210 Brussels  Belgium
Tel: 00 32 02 224 0411
etuc@etuc.org
www.etuc.org

**European Transplant Coordinators Organisation** see ETCO

**European Union**
http://europa.eu

**European Union Committee of the Regions**
Bâtiment Jacques Delors  Rue Belliard 99-101  B - 1040 Brussels - Belgium
Tel: 00 32 2282 2211
info@europa.eu
www.europa.eu

**European Youth Card Association**
Spitálska 27  811 08 Bratislava  Slovakia
Tel: 00 421 2 529 21 655
mail@eyca.org
www.euro26.org
Central office of 'Euro under 26' Youth Card Organisations

**European Youth Forum**
Rue Joseph II straat 120  B-1000 Brussels Belgium
Tel: 00 32 22 30 6490
Email via website
www.youthforum.org

**European Youth Information and Counselling Agency** ERYICA
26 Place de la Gare   L-1616 Luxembourg
Tel: 00 352 24873992
email via website
www.eryica.org
European umbrella organisation for national youth info & counselling networks

**European Youth Music Week**
www.eymw.org
Partnership between youngorchestras.com (UK) and Internationaler Arbeitskreis fuer Musik e.V. (IAM) (Germany)

**Euthanasia** see Dignity in Dying, Human Rights Society

**Evangelical Alliance**
Whitefield House   186 Kennington Park Rd
London SE11 4BT
Tel: 020 7207 2100
info@eauk.org
www.eauk.org

**Every Child a Chance Trust**
2, Bath Place   Rivington Street   London EC2A 3DB
Tel: 0207 749 5162
admin@everychildachancetrust.org
www.everychildachancetrust.org
Aims to unlock the educational potential of socially disadvantaged children through the development and promotion of evidence-based, early intervention programmes.

**Every Child Matters**
www.dcsf.gov.uk/everychildmatters
A shared programme of change to improve outcomes for all children and young people

**EveryChild**
4 Bath Place   Rivington St   London EC2A 3DR
Tel: 020 7749 2468
email via website
www.everychild.org.uk
Promotes reformed childcare systems in central and eastern Europe and the former Soviet Union to give every child a proper home

**Everyman Project**
1a Waterlow Road   London N19 5NJ
Adviceline: 0207 263 8884
everymanproject@btopenworld.com
www.everymanproject.co.uk
Counselling programme for men who wish to change violent behaviour, and helpline for anyone affected by abuse or violence from men

**Ex-Offenders (National Association of)**
see UNLOCK

**Exchange of Commonwealth Teachers (League for the)**
60 Queens Road   Reading RG1 4BS
Tel: 0118 902 1171
www.lect.org.uk

**Exchanges** see also British Council, Commonwealth Youth Exchange Council, Daneford Trust, Education & Training Group, Fulbright Commission, Youth in Action

**Exclusion** see also Communities Empowerment Network, Include, Social Exclusion Unit

**Exercise, Movement and Dance Partnership** EMDP
1 Grove House   Foundry Lane   Horsham
West Sussex RH13 5PL
Tel: 01403 266000
info@emdp.org
www.emdp.info
Governing body

**Expeditions** see Brathay Exploration Group, BSES Expeditions, Raleigh International, Scientific Exploration Society, Wind Sand & Stars

**Exploratorium**
www.exploratorium.edu
Large & informative science centre website

**Extension College** see National Extension College

**Extreme Inequality**
http://extremeinequality.org
Network of journalists trying to look beyond conventional economics

**Eyecare Trust**
PO Box 804   Aylesbury   Bucks HP20 9DF
Tel: 0845 129 5001
info@eyecaretrust.org.uk
www.eyecaretrust.org.uk

# F

**Fabian Society**
11 Dartmouth St   London SW1H 9BN
Tel: 020 7227 4900
Tel: 020 7227 4917
info@fabians.org.uk
www.fabians.org.uk
Left of centre think tank

**Facial Disfigurement** see Changing Faces, Disfigurement Guidance Centre, Let's Face It, Operation Smile UK, Saving Faces

**Facsimile Preference Service**
DMA House
70 Margaret Street   London   W1W 8SS
FPS Registration line: 0845 070 0702

Tel:020 7291 3330 (Complaints Department)
fps@dma.org.uk
www.fpsonline.org.uk
Set up to help people being bothered by
unwanted and commercial sales faxes

### Fair Access (Office for)
Northavon House  Coldharbour Lane  Bristol
BS16 1QD
Tel: 0117 931 7171
enquiries@offa.org.uk
www.offa.org.uk
Helps people from poor backgrounds go
to university. October 2010: Future under
consideration

### Fair Play for Children Association
32 Longford Road  Bognor Regis PO21 1AG
Tel: 0845 330 7635
administration@fairplayforchildren.net
www.fairplayforchildren.org
Advice & information on play issues &
protecting children at play

### Fair Trade Shops (British Association for) BAFTS
66 Longstomps Avenue   Chelmsford CM2
9LA
Tel: 07866 759201
info@bafts.org.uk
www.bafts.org.uk

Campaigns for fair trade. List of shops and
info leaflet on receipt of sae

### Fair Trading (Office of)
Fleetbank House  2-6 Salisbury Square
London EC4Y 8JX
Tel: 020 7211 8000
OFT Enquiries and Reporting Centre 08457
22 44 99
enquiries@oft.gsi.gov.uk
www.oft.gov.uk
October 2010: future under review. Merger
with Competition Commission being
considered

### Fair Trials International
3rd Floor  59 Carter Lane  London EC4V 5AQ
Tel: 020 7762 6400
email via website
www.fairtrials.net
Seeks to help EU citizens accused of a crime
in countries other than their own. There is no
charge for this service

### Fairbridge
207 Waterloo Rd  London SE1 8XD
Tel: 020 7928 1704
info@fairbridge.org.uk
www.fairbridge.org.uk
Gives disadvantaged young people the
confidence, skills and motivation to change
their lives

### Fairtrade Foundation
3rd Floor  Ibex House  42-47 Minories
London EC3N 1DY
Tel: 020 7405 5942
email via website
www.fairtrade.org.uk
Awards Fairtrade Mark

### Families Anonymous
Doddington & Rollo Community Assoc.
Charlotte Despard Avenue  Battersea
London SW11 5HD
Helpline: 0845 1200 660
office@famanon.org.uk
www.famanon.org.uk
Support for the families and friends of drug
users

### Families Need Fathers
134 Curtain Rd  London EC2A 3AR
National helpline: 0300 0300 363
Tel: 020 7613 5060
fnf@fnf.org.uk
www.fnf.org.uk
Maintaining a child's contact with both
parents after family break-up

### Family Action
501-505 Kingsland Road  London E8 4AU
Tel: 020 7254 6251
email via website
www.family-action.org.uk
UK's leading family charity, supporting over
45,000 families every year. Tackle some of
the most complex and difficult issues facing
families today – including domestic abuse,
mental health problems, learning disabilities
and severe financial hardship

### Family Holiday Association
16 Mortimer St  London W1T 3JL
Tel: 020 7436 3304
info@FamilyHolidayAssociation.org.uk
www.fhaonline.org.uk
Addresses issues of poverty and
disadvantage through increasing access to
holidays and other recreational activities

### Family Mediation Scotland now see
Relationships Scotland

### Family & Parenting Institute (National)
430 Highgate Studios  53-79 Highgate Rd
London NW5 1TL
Tel: 020 7424 3460
info@familyandparenting.org
www.familyandparenting.org
Independent charity working to support
parents in bringing up their children, to
promote the well-being of families and to
make society more family friendly

**Family Planning Association**
50 Featherstone Street London EC1Y 8QU
Helpline England: 0845 122 8690
Helpline Northern Ireland: 0845 122 8687
general@fpa.org.uk
www.fpa.org.uk
The UK's leading sexual health charity working to improve the sexual health and reproductive rights and choices of people throughout the UK

**Family Records Centre** now see National Archives

**Family Rights Group**
Second Floor The Print House 18 Ashwin St London E8 3DL
Free confidential advice service: 0808 801 0366
Tel: 020 7923 2628
office@frg.org.uk
www.frg.org.uk
Advice by letter or telephone to families whose children are involved with social services

**Family Search**
email via website
www.familysearch.org
Internet genealogy service run by The Church of Jesus Christ of Latter Day Saints

**Family Service Units** see Investing in Families

**Family Therapy (Institute of)**
24-32 Stephenson Way London NW1 2HX
Tel: 020 7391 9150
info@iftnet.plus.com
www.instituteoffamilytherapy.org.uk
Training in family & couple therapy and clinical services

**Family Welfare Association** now see Family Action

**Faramir Sailing Trust** see Cirdan Sailing Trust

**Farm Animal Welfare Council** FAWC
FAWC Secretariat Area 8B, 9 Millbank c/o 17 Smith Square LONDON, SW1P 3JR
Tel: 020 7238 5016 / 5124/ 6340
fawcsecretariat@defra.gsi.gov.uk
www.fawc.org.uk
Independent advisory body which keeps under review the welfare of farm animals on agricultural land, at market, in transit and at the place of slaughter. October 2010: this body will cease to receive funding but will be reconstituted as a committee of experts.

**Farmers' Markets (Scottish Association of)**
email via website
www.scottishfarmersmarkets.co.uk
Information on markets in Scotland

**Farmers' Retail & Markets Association (National)** FARMA
12 Southgate Street Winchester SO23 9EF
Tel: 0845 458 8420
info@farma.org.uk
www.farma.org.uk
Information on where and when markets are held

**Farming & Countryside Education** FACE
Arthur Rank Centre Stoneleigh Park Warwickshire CV8 2LG
Tel: 024 7685 8261
Email via website
www.face-online.org.uk
A one-stop shop for all information and educational materials about food, farming and the countryside

**Farms for City Children**
Bridge House 25 Fore Street Oakhampton Devon EX20 1DL
Tel: 01837 55823
email via website
www.farmsforcitychildren.co.uk
Aims to provide young children from urban areas with a week in which they work actively and purposefully on a farm

**Fatherhood Institute**
Horsingtons Yard

Tiverton Place
Lion Street Abergavenny NP7 5PN
Tel: 0845 634 1328
mail@fatherhoodinstitute.org
www.fatherhoodinstitute.org
Seeks to promote positive relationships between men & their children

**Fathers** see also Families Need Fathers

**Fathers Direct** now see Fatherhood Institute

**Fathers4justice Ltd**
office@fathers-4-justice.org
www.fathers-4-justice.org

**Fauna & Flora International**
4th Floor Jupiter House Station Road Cambs CB1 2JD
Tel: 01223 571000
info@fauna-flora.org
www.fauna-flora.org
Conservation worldwide of threatened species

**FAWC** see Farm Animal Welfare Council

**Fawcett Library** see Women's Library

**Fawcett Society**
1-3 Berry Street  London EC1V 0AA
Tel: 020 7253 2598
Email via website
www.fawcettsociety.org.uk
Campaigning for equality between women and men at work, in the home and in public life

**FBI** Federal Bureau of Investigation
www.fbi.gov
US government agency

**Feline Advisory Bureau**
Taeselbury  High St  Tisbury  Wilts SP3 6LD
Tel: 01747 871 872

information@fabcats.org
www.fabcats.org

**Fell Runners Association**
www.fellrunner.org.uk

**Female Education** see CAMFED International

**Feminist Archive North**
www.feministarchivenorth.org.uk/
feministarchivesouth/index.htm
Holds a wide variety of material relating to the Women's Liberation Movement (WLM) from 1969 to the present. The Archive has gone into storage, care of the University of Bristol, who will eventually rehouse it.

**Feminist Archive South**
The Archive has gone into storage, care of the University of Bristol, who will eventually rehouse it
www.feministarchivenorth.org.uk/
feministarchivesouth/index.htm
National and international material of the second wave of feminism (roughly 1960-2000)

**Fencing Association (British)**
1 Baron's Gate  33-35 Rothschild Road
London W4 5HT
Tel: 020 8742 3032
headoffice@britishfencing.com
www.britishfencing.com

**Fencing (British Academy of)**
secretary@baf-fencing.org
www.baf-fencing.org

**Fertility** see also Fertility Friends, Human Fertilisation & Embryology Authority, Infertility Network UK

**Fertility Friends**
Email via website
www.fertilityfriends.co.uk
A self help community for those experiencing infertility

**Fertility UK** The National Fertility Awareness & Natural Family Planning Service UK
Bury Knowle Health Centre  207 London Rd
Headington  Oxford OX3 9JA
admin@fertilityuk.org
www.fertilityuk.org

**Festivals (British & International Federation of )**
Festivals House  198 Park Lane  Macclesfield SK11 6UD
Tel: 01625 428297 / 611578
info@federationoffestivals.org.uk
www.federationoffestivals.org.uk
Umbrella body for festivals of the performing arts in the UK and beyond

**FFLAG** see Lesbians & Gays (Families and Friends of)

**fforwm**
CollegesWales  Unit 7, Cae Gwyrdd,
Greenmeadow Springs Business Park
Tongwynlais  Cardiff CF15 7AB
Tel: 029 2052 2500
hello@collegeswales.ac.uk
www.collegeswales.ac.uk
National organisation representing the 23 further education (FE) colleges and two FE institutions in Wales

**FIELD** see Environmental Law & Development (Foundation for International)

**Field Sports Society (British)** now see Countryside Alliance

**Field Studies Council**
Preston Montford  Montford Bridge
Shrewsbury SY4 1HW
Tel: 01743 852100
Tel: 0845 3454071 (Local rate phone call - UK only)
enquiries@field-studies-council.org
www.field-studies-council.org
Charity works with schools and individuals through network of centres to bring environmental understanding to all

**Fields in Trust – FIT**
15 Crinan Street  London  N1 9SQ
Tel: 0207 427 2110
info@fieldsintrust.org
www.fieldsintrust.org
Responsible for acquiring, protecting and improving playing fields and play space, especially for children and those with disabilities

**& Cymru**
Welsh Institute of Sport  Sophia Gardens
Cardiff CF11 9SW
Tel: 029 20334 935
cymru@fieldsintrust.org
www.fieldsintrust.org

## & Scotland
Dewar House  Claverhouse  Staffa Place
Dundee DD2 3SX
Tel: 01382 817 427
scotland@fieldsintrust.org
www.fieldsintrust.org

## FIFA
FIFA-Strasse 20  P.O. Box 8044 Zurich
Switzerland
Tel: 0041 43 2227777
Email via website
www.fifa.com
International governing body for football

## Film and Television School (National)
NFTS
Beaconsfield Studios  Station Rd
Beaconsfield  Bucks HP9 1LG
Tel: 01494 671234
info@nfts.co.uk
www.nfts.co.uk
MA/Diploma courses in professional
disciplines for film and television. Short
courses for freelancers

## Film Classification (British Board of)
3 Soho Square  London W1D 3HD
Tel: 020 7440 1570
feedback@bbfc.co.uk
www.bbfc.co.uk

## Film Council see UK Film Council

## Film Education
91 Berwick Street  London W1F 0BP
Tel: 020 7292 7330
email via website
www.filmeducation.org
A link between the film industry & education

## Film Institute (British) see British Film
Institute

## Film London
Suite 6.10  The Tea Building  56 Shoreditch
High Street  London E1 6JJ
Tel: 020 7613 7676
info@filmlondon.org.uk
www.filmlondon.org.uk
Regional media development agency

## Film & Television Archive (Northern
Region)
School of Arts and Media  University of
Teesside  Middlesbrough  Tees Valley  TS1
3BA
Tel: 01642 384022
enquiries@nrfta.org.uk
www.nrfta.org.uk

## Film & Video Development Agency now
see Film London

## Financial Advisers Promotion see
Independent Financial Advisers Promotion

## Financial Ombudsman Service
South Quay Plaza  183 Marsh Wall  London
E14 9SR
Helpline: 0800 0 234 567 free for people
phoning from a fixed line 0300 123 9 123
free for mobile-phone users who pay a
monthly charge for calls to numbers starting
01 or 02
Tel: 020 7964 1000
complaint.info@financial-ombudsman.org.uk
www.financial-ombudsman.org.uk

## Financial Services Authority
25 The North Colonnade  Canary Wharf
London E14 5HS
Consumer Helpline: 0845 606 1234
Tel: 020 7066 1000
consumer.queries@fsa.gov.uk
www.fsa.gov.uk
Regulatory body

## Find a Parent or Child
www.findaparentorchild.co.uk
Reuniting parents and children

## Findhorn Foundation
Communications  Findhorn Foundation  The
Park  Findhorn  IV36 3TZ
Tel: 01309 690311
enquiries@findhorn.org
www.findhorn.org
Spiritual community, educational centre and
thriving ecovillage

## Finnish Institute
35-36 Eagle St  London WC1R 4AQ
Tel: 020 7404 3309
info@finnish-institute.org.uk
www.finnish-institute.org.uk

## Fire Brigade (London)
169 Union Street  London  SE1 0LL
tel: 020 8555 1200
info@london-fire.gov.uk
www.london-fire.gov.uk
Full listings and links to all the fire brigades
in the UK

## Fire Protection Authority
London Road  Moreton in Marsh  Glos GL56
0RH
Tel: 01608 812500
fpa@thefpa.co.uk
www.thefpa.co.uk
Organises fire protection seminars. 'Fire
Prevention' often covers school fire issues

## Firework Safety (National Campaign for)
Tel: 020 7836 6703
ncfs@cgsystems.co.uk
www.cgsystems.co.uk/ncfs
Licensing and training for the use of
fireworks in the UK

**First Light**
Studio 28  Fazeley Studios  191 Fazeley
Street  Birmingham B5 5SE
Tel: 0121 224 7511
info@firstlightonline.co.uk
www.firstlightonline.co.uk
Funding and development agency for film-
making by under 18s

**First Steps to Freedom**
PO Box 476  Newquay  TR7 1WQ
Helpline: 0845 120 2916
General enquiries: 0845 841 0619
first.steps@btconnect.com
www.first-steps.org/
Support for sufferers from stress related
disorders and their carers

**FirstSigns** (Self-Injury Guidance & Network
Support)
email via website
www.firstsigns.org.uk
Online, user-lead voluntary organisation
founded to raise awareness about self-injury
and provide information and support to
people of all ages affected by self-injury

**Fiscal Studies (Institute for)**
7 Ridgmount St  London WC1E 7AE
Tel: 020 7291 4800
mailbox@ifs.org.uk
www.ifs.org.uk
Independent research into UK public policy.

**Fishing** see Marine Stewardship Council,
Sea Fish Industry Authority

**Fishing Hurts**
www.fishinghurts.com

**Fit for Travel**
www.fitfortravel.scot.nhs.uk
Travel health information for people travelling
abroad from NHS Scotland

**Fitness Industry Association**
Castlewood House  77-91 New Oxford
Street  London WC1A 1PX
Tel: 020 7420 8560
email via website
www.fia.org.uk
Non-profit making trade association for the
entire health and fitness industry

**Fitness League**
6 Station Parade  Sunningdale  Berkshire
SL5 0EP
Tel: 01344 874787
info@thefitnessleague.com
www.thefitnessleague.com
Teaches rhythmic exercise to music

**Fitness N. Ireland**
The Robinson Centre  Montgomery Rd
Belfast BT6 9HS
Tel 028 9070 4080

fitnessni@aol.com
www.fitnessni.org
Governing body for fitness instructors

**Fitzwilliam Museum**
Trumpington St  Cambridge CB2 1RB
Tel: 01223 332900
Education: 01223 332993
Group Bookings: 01223 332904
fitzmuseum-enquiries@lists.cam.ac.uk
www.fitzmuseum.cam.ac.uk

**Five**
Customer Services  Five Television  22 Long
Acre  London WC2E 9LY
Tel: 020 7421 7270
Tel: 0845 705 0505 (Programme info)
customerservices@five.tv
www.five.tv

**Floodline**
National Customer Contact Centre  PO Box
544  Rotherham S60 1BY
Floodline: 0845 988 1188 (24 hour service)
Tel: 08708 506 506
enquiries@environment-agency.gov.uk
www.environment-agency.gov.uk
24 hr advice & info

**Flower Arranging Societies (National
Association of)**
Osborne House  12 Devonshire Sq  London
EC2M  4TE
Tel: 020 7247 5567
flowers@nafas.org.uk
www.nafas.org.uk

**Folger Shakespeare Library**
www.folger.edu
Independent research library located on
Capitol Hill in Washington, DC

**Food & Agricultural Organisation (United
Nations)**
Viale delle Terme di Caracalla  00153 Rome,
Italy
Tel: 00 39 065 7051
FAO-HQ@fao.org
www.fao.org

**Food Alliance (National)** see Sustain

**Food Commission**
94 White Lion St  London N1 9PF
Tel: 020 7837 2250
info@foodmagazine.org.uk.
www.foodmagazine.org.uk
Independent consumer organisation
campaigning for safer, healthier food.
Publishes food magazine, posters and reports

**Food & Drink Federation**
6 Catherine St  London WC2B 5JJ
Tel: 020 7836 2460
Email via website

www.fdf.org.uk
Trade organisation for the food manufacturing industry

**Food & Drug Administration (US)**
www.fda.gov

**Food Science & Technology (Institute of)**
see IFST

**Food Standards Agency**
Aviation House  125 Kingsway  London WC2B 6NH
Helpline: 020 7276 8829
Tel: 020 7276 8000 (switchboard)
helpline@foodstandards.gsi.gov.uk
www.food.gov.uk
Provision of advice/information on food safety issues to consumers

**Food Standards Agency (Northern Ireland)**
10 A-C Clarendon Road  Belfast BT1 3BG
Tel: 028 9041 7700
infosani@foodstandards.gsi.gov.uk
www.food.gov.uk

**Food Standards Agency (Scotland)**
St Magnus House  6th Floor  25 Guild St
Aberdeen AB11 6NJ
Tel: 01224 285100
scotland@foodstandards.gsi.gov.uk
www.food.gov.uk

**Food Standards Agency (Wales)**
11th Floor  South Gate House  Wood Street
Cardiff CF10 1EW
Tel: 029 2067 8999
wales@foodstandards.gsi.gov.uk
www.food.gov.uk

**Football** see also FIFA, Kick It Out, Professional Footballers Association, Safe Standing, Show Racism the Red Card, Sociology of Sport (Centre for), World Cup

**Football Association**
Customer relations: 0844 980 8200
email via website
www.thefa.com
Governing body of football in England

**Football Association (English Schools)**
4 Parker Court  Staffordshire Technology Park
ST18 0WP
Tel: 01785 785970
office@esfa.co.uk
www.esfa.co.uk

**Football Association (Irish)**
20 Windsor Avenue  Belfast BT9 6EG
Tel: 028 9066 9458
info@irishfa.com
www.irishfa.com

**Football Association (Scottish)** SFA
Hampden Park  Glasgow G42 9AY
Tel: 0141 616 6000

info@scottishfa.co.uk
www.scottishfa.co.uk

**Football Foundation**
Whittington House  19-30 Alfred Place
London  WC1E 7EA
Tel: 0845 345 4555
enquiries@footballfoundation.org.uk
www.footballfoundation.org.uk
Funds football and other sporting facilities

**Football Industry Group**
Management School  University of Liverpool
Liverpool L69 7ZH
Tel: 0151 795 3103
football@liverpool.ac.uk
www.liv.ac.uk/footballindustry
Conducts academic research into the social, economic, historical, business, cultural and political aspects of football in the UK and abroad

**Football League Ltd**
Football League Operations Centre  Edward VII Quay  Navigation Way  Preston PR2 2YF
Tel: 0844 463 1888
enquiries@football-league.co.uk
www.football-league.co.uk
The central administrative office of the clubs in The Championship, League One, League Two and the Coca Cola Football League

**Football League (Scottish)** SFL
The National Stadium  Hampden Park
Glasgow. G42 9EB.
Tel: 0141 620 4160
info@scottishfootballleague.com
www.scottishfootballleague.com

**Football Museum (National)**
Tel: 0161 870 9275
enquiries@nationalfootballmuseum.com
www.nationalfootballmuseum.com/
Temporarily closed to the general public. Opening in Manchester's Urbis building late 2011

**Football Museum (Scottish)**
Hampden Park  Glasgow  G42 9BA
Tel: 0141 616 6139
info@scottishfootballmuseum.org.uk
www.scottishfootballmuseum.org.uk

**Football Research** see also Sociology of Sport (Centre for)

**Football Supporters Federation**
info@fsf.org.uk.
www.fsf.org.uk

**Football Unites, Racism Divides**
The Stables Connexions Centre  Sharrow Lane  Sheffield S11 8AE
Tel: 0114 2553156
enquiries@furd.org
www.furd.org

## Foreign and Commonwealth Office
King Charles St  London SW1A 2AH
Tel: 020 7008 1500
Email via website
www.fco.gov.uk

## Foreign and Commonwealth Office Travel Advice
King Charles Street  London  SW1A 2AH
Tel: 020 7008 1500 (for assistance abroad and also for friends and relatives abroad)
TravelAdvicePublicEnquiries@fco.gov.uk
www.fco.gov.uk/en/travel-and-living-abroad/travel-advice-by-country/
Advice to British Nationals on whether it is safe to travel abroad

## Foreign Policy Centre
Suite 11, 2nd Floor  23-28 Penn Street
London N1 5DL
Tel: 020 7729 7566
events@fpc.org.uk
www.fpc.org.uk
Research into business ethics, foreign policy, human rights and international economics

## Foreignprisoners.com
Email via website
www.usp.com.au/fpss
Volunteer internet based, prison advocacy service to families whose loved ones are interned

## Forest Peoples Programme
1C Fosseway Business Centre  Stratford Road  Moreton in Marsh  GL56 9NQ
Tel: 01608 652893
info@forestpeoples.org
www.forestpeoples.org
Works to assist tribal tropical forest peoples to protect their rights and livelihood

## Forest School Camps
enquiries@fsc.org.uk
www.fsc.org.uk
Camping for boys & girls 6-17 years

## Forestry Commission
231 Corstorphine Road  Edinburgh EH14 5NE
Tel: 0845 3673787
enquiries@forestry.gsi.gov.uk
www.forestry.gov.uk
Government department for forestry in England, Scotland & Wales. October 2010 body retained but likely to be substantially changed.

## Forestry Society of England, Wales & N. Ireland (Royal)
102 High St  Tring  Herts HP23 4AF
Tel: 01442 822028
rfshq@rfs.org.uk
www.rfs.org.uk

## Forgiveness Project
3rd Floor, 38 Buckingham Palace Road
London SW1W 0RE
Tel: 0207 821 0035
info@theforgivenessproject.com
www.theforgivenessproject.com
An organisation working with grassroots projects in the fields of conflict resolution, reconciliation and victim support

## Forum for the Future
Overseas House  19-23 Ironmonger Row
London EC1V 3QN
Tel: 020 7324 3630
info@forumforthefuture.org
www.forumforthefuture.org/
Charity with mission to achieve sustainability taking a positive solutions orientated approach

## Forward Scotland
The Lodge  Earlsgate House  St Ninian's Road  Stirling  Scotland FK8 2HE
Tel: 05600 010560
enquiries@forward-scotland.org.uk
www.forward-scotland.org.uk
Promotes sustainable development

## Fostering see also thematic guide Adoption and Fostering

## Fostering Network  London Office
87 Blackfriars Road  London  SE1 8HA
Tel: 020 7620 6400
info@fostering.net
www.fostering.net
Charity for everyone involved in fostering

## & Belfast
Unit 10  40 Montgomery Road  Belfast  BT6 9HL
Tel:  028 9070 5056
ni@fostering.net
www.fostering.net/northern-ireland

## & Cardiff
1 Caspian Point  Pierhead Street  Cardiff Bay CF10 4DQ
Tel: 029 2044 0940
wales@fostering.net
www.fostering.net/wales/

## & Glasgow
Ingram House, 2nd Floor  227 Ingram Street Glasgow  G1 1DA
Tel: 0141 204 1400
scotland@fostering.net
www.fostering.net/scotland/

## Foundation For Peace
Peace Centre  Peace Drive  Great Sankey Warrington  Cheshire WA5 1HQ
Tel: 01925 581231
info@foundation4peace.org
www.foundation4peace.org

Conflict resolution and citizenship projects for young people

**Foyer Federation**
3rd Foor  5-9 Hatton Wall  London EC1N 8HX
Tel: 020 7430 2212
inbox@foyer.net
www.foyer.net
National umbrella organisation for Foyers: affordable accommodation, training & support for disadvantaged young people

**Fragile X Society**
Rood End House  6 Stortford Road  Great Dunmow  Essex CM6 1DA
Tel: 01371 875100
info@fragilex.org.uk
www.fragilex.org.uk
Supports those affected by the most common cause of inherited learning disability

**FRAME** Fund for the Replacement of Animals in Medical Experiments
Russell & Burch House  96-98 North Sherwood St  Nottingham NG1 4EE
Tel: 0115 958 4740
frame@frame.org.uk
www.frame.org.uk
Researches alternatives to animal testing

**France: culture and communications website**
www.culture.fr

**Franco British Council (British Section)**
Franco-British Council, British Section Victoria Chambers  16-18 Strutton Ground  London SW1P 2HP
Tel: 020 7976 8380
info@francobritishcouncil.org.uk
www.francobritishcouncil.org.uk
To promote better understanding between Britain & France and exchanges between British and French schools by means of a £5,000 prize

**Franco-Scottish Society of Scotland**
Association Franco-Ecossaise
127 Dundee Road  Broughty Ferry  Dundee DD5 1DU
mcmperom@tiscali.co.uk
www.franco-scottish.org.uk
To foster educational, cultural and social activities between France & Scotland

**Frank** Drugs Helpline (National)
Tel: 0800 77 66 00 (24hr freefone)
Email via website
www.talktofrank.com
Advice, information and support to anyone affected by drugs

**Frankfurt Book Fair**
info@book-fair.com
www.frankfurt-book-fair.com

**Fredericks Foundation**
Fredericks House  39 Guildford Road Lightwater  Surrey GU18 5SA
Tel: 01276 472 722
mail@fredericksfoundation.net
www.fredericksfoundation.org
Helps disadvantaged people of any age to realise their potential, often by helping them to start their own business

**Free the Children**
www.freethechildren.com
Children under 18 years old helping children to end abuse and exploitation

**Free Tibet Campaign**
28 Charles Square  London N1 6HT
Tel: 020 7324 4605
mail@freetibet.org
www.freetibet.org
Campaigning for an end to the Chinese occupation of Tibet

**FreeBMD**
http://freebmd.rootsweb.com
Free online access to transcribed records of births, marriages and deaths in England and Wales

**Freecycle**
www.freecycle.org
A grassroots movement of people who are giving (& getting) stuff for free in their own towns

**Freedom Association**
Richwood House  1 Trinity School Lane Cheltenham  Gloucestershire GL52 2JL
Tel: 0845 833 9626
jane@tfa.net
www.tfa.net
A pressure group campaigning for limited government & for individual freedom

**Freedom of Information (Campaign for)**
Suite 102  16 Baldwins Gardens  London EC1N 7RJ
Tel: 020 7831 7477
admin@cfoi.demon.co.uk
www.cfoi.org.uk

**Freegle**
www.ilovefreegle.org
National grassroots organisation of people who are giving and receiving free unwanted items in their immediate communities

**Freshfield Service**
Helpline: 0500 241952
www.freshfieldservice.co.uk
Confidential counselling & advice for drug users & their families

**Friedreich's Ataxia Group** now see Ataxia
UK

**Friedrich Ebert Foundation**
London Office 66 Great Russell Street
London WC1B 3BN
Tel: 020 70250990
info@feslondon.net
www.feslondon.org.uk
German political social democratic
foundation

**Friends at the end**
11 Westbourne Gardens GLASGOW
G12 9XD
Tel: 0141 334 3287
info@friends-at-the-end.org.uk
Friends at the End is a members' democratic
society, dedicated to promoting knowledge
about end-of-life choices and dignified death.

**Friends, Families and Travellers**
Advice & Information Unit Community Base
113 Queens Rd Brighton BN1 3XG
Tel: 01273 234 777
fft@gypsy-traveller.org
www.gypsy-traveller.org
Advice and support for Gypsies and
Travellers and information about the Traveller
community

**Friends of Friendless Churches**
St Ann's Vestry Hall 2 Church Entry London
EC4V 5HB
Tel: 020 7236 3934
office@friendsoffriendlesschurches.org.uk
www.friendsoffriendlesschurches.org.uk
Campaigns for the preservation of ancient
and beautiful but redundant churches

**Friends of Peoples Close to Nature**
email via website
www.fpcn-global.org
A network of people concerned with survival
of savage tribal peoples especially hunter-
gatherers

**Friends of the Earth**
26-28 Underwood St London N1 7JQ
Tel: 020 7490 1555
Email via website
www.foe.co.uk/
Environmental pressure group and charity

**Friends of the Earth Scotland**
Thorn House 5 Rose Street Edinburgh EH2
2PR
Tel: 0131 243 2700
email via website
www.foe-scotland.org.uk
Campaigning for environmental justice, a
decent environment for all and a fair share of
the earth's resources

**Friends United Network** now see
Friendship Works

**Friendship Works**
Studio 442 Highgate Studios 53-79
Highgate Rd London NW5 1TL
Tel: 020 7485 0900
info@friendshipworks.org.uk
www.friendshipworks.org.uk
Links volunteers to isolated children from
lone parent families who are lacking positive,
regular attention

**Froglife**
2A Flag Business Exchange
Vicarage Farm Road Fengate
Peterborough PE1 5TX
Tel: 01733 558844
Tel: 01733 558960 (Wildlife Information
Service)
info@froglife.org
www.froglife.org
Conservation and promotion of native
reptiles & amphibians to benefit biodiversity
and people

**Fulbright Commission (The US-UK)**
Battersea Power Station 188 Kirtling Street
London SW8 5BN
Tel: 020 7498 4010
programmes@fulbright.co.uk
www.fulbright.co.uk
An information service on studying in the US

**Full Time Mothers**
PO Box 43690 London SE22 9WN
Tel: 020 8653 8768
http://ftmuk.wordpress.com/
Supports full time mothers and campaigns
for policy changes

**Fund for Animal Welfare (International)**
87-90 Albert Embankment London SE1 7UD
Tel: 020 7587 6700
info-uk@ifaw.org
www.ifaw.org

**Fur Trade** see PETA Europe Ltd., Respect
for Animals

**Furniture Re-use Network**
48-54 West Street St Philips Bristol BS2
0BL
donation hotline: 0845 602 8003

Tel: 0117 954 3571
info@frn.org.uk
www.frn.org.uk
Co-ordinating body for furniture recycling
projects in UK

**Further Education National Training
Organisation** see Lifelong Learning UK

# G

### G-Nation
www.g-nation.co.uk
Works with young people throughout the
UK to show them how they can change the
world by giving

### Gaelic Books Council
22 Mansfield St  Glasgow G11 5QP
Tel: 0141 337 6211
Email via website
www.gaelicbooks.org
Supports Gaelic publishing with grants and
services and has its own bookshop

### Gaia Foundation
6 Heathgate Place  Agincourt Road  London
NW3 2NU
Tel: 020 7428 0055
info@gaianet.org
www.gaiafoundation.org
The Gaia Foundation works towards cultural
and biological diversity, ecological justice
and Earth democracy

### Galapagos Conservation Trust
5 Derby St  London W1J 7AB
Tel: 020 7629 5049
gct@gct.org
www.savegalapagos.org

### Gambia Horse and Donkey Trust
Brewery Arms Cottage  Stane Street  Ockley
Surrey  RH5 5TH
Tel: 01306 627568
heather@gambiahorseanddonkey.org.uk
www.gambiahorseanddonkey.org.uk
Ensuring that the horses and donkeys on
which farmers depend are well cared for

### Gamblers Anonymous & Gam-Anon
CVS Building   5 Trafford Court  Off Trafford
Way  Doncaster DN1 1PN
Tel: 020 7384 3040
email via website
www.gamblersanonymous.org.uk
Help for compulsive gamblers and their
families

### GAMCARE
2nd Floor  7-11 St John's Hill   London
SW11 1TR
Helpline: 0845 6000 133
Tel: 020 7801 7000
info@gamcare.org.uk
www.gamcare.org.uk
A charity dealing with the social impact of
gambling

### Gamete Donation Trust (National)
Confidential helpline: 0845 226 9193
info@ngdt.co.uk
www.ngdt.co.uk

Information mainly for those considering
becoming an egg or sperm donor but also
for health professionals and those requiring
treatment with donor eggs or sperm

### Gap Activity Projects now see Lattitude
Global Volunteering

### Garden History Society
70 Cowcross St  London EC1M 6EJ
Tel: 020 7608 2409
enquiries@gardenhistorysociety.org
www.gardenhistorysociety.org
Promotes the study of the history of
gardening, landscape gardening and
horticulture. Encourages conservation,
advises on restoration and supports
the development of parks, gardens and
designed landscapes

### Garden Organic
Coventry  Warwickshire  United Kingdom
CV8 3LG
Tel: 02476 303517
enquiry@gardenorganic.org.uk
www.gardenorganic.org.uk
Researching and promoting organic
gardening, farming and food

### Gardens see also Allotment and Leisure
Gardeners Ltd. (National Society of),
Botanic Garden of Wales (National), City
Farms & Community Gardens (Federation
of), Community Composting Network,
Conservation of Plants & Gardens
(National Council for the), Historic Houses
Association, Landscape Institute, Royal
Botanic Gardens, Thrive

### Gardens Scheme Charitable Trust (National)
Hatchlands Park  East Clandon  Guildford
GU4 7RT
Tel: 01483 211535
webmaster@ngs.org.uk
www.ngs.org.uk
Opening gardens of quality, character and
interest to the public for charity

### Gas & Electricity Markets (Office of)
OFGEM
9 Millbank  London SW1P 3GE
Tel: 020 7901 7000
consumeraffairs@ofgem.gov.uk
www.ofgem.gov.uk
Regulatory body for gas and electricity
markets, protects customers' interests
and encourages competition. Independent
advisors to the UK Government on tackling
and preparing for climate change. October
2010: Future under review

## GASP - Smoke Free Solutions
Unit 9   Parkway Trading Estate  St
Werburghs  Bristol  BS2 9PG
Tel 0117 955 0101
gasp@gasp.org.uk
www.gasp.org.uk
Educational resources and consultancy

## Gateway Award
Mencap  3rd Floor  Delta View  2309 -
2311Coventry Road  Birmingham B26 3PG
Tel: 0121 722 5900
Gateway.award@mencap.org.uk
www.mencap.org.uk/landing.asp?id=1624
Recreation, education resources for people
with learning disabilities

**Gay Issues** see thematic guide - Sexual
Issues

## GCSE Answers
www.gcse.com

## Genealogists (Society of)
14 Charterhouse Buildings  Goswell Rd
London EC1M 7BA
Tel: 020 7251 8799
genealogy@sog.org.uk
www.sog.org.uk

## General Dental Council
37 Wimpole St  London W1G 8DQ
Tel: 020 7887 3800
Tel: 0845 222 4141
information@gdc-uk.org
www.gdc-uk.org

## General Medical Council GMC
Regent's Place,  350 Euston Rd  London
NW1 3JN
Tel: 0845 357 8001 (Switchboard)

Tel: 0161 923 6602 (Contact Cente)
gmc@gmc-uk.org
www.gmc-uk.org
Governing body for doctors in UK

## General Register Office
Certificate Services Section  PO Box 2
Southport  PR8 2JD
Text phone: Typetalk
18001 08456 037 788
Certificate Information line:
0845 603 7788
certificate.services@ips.gsi.gov.uk
www.direct.gov.uk/en/
Governmentcitizensandrights/
Registeringlifeevents/index.htm
Order birth, marriage, death, civil
partnership, stillbirth or adoption certificates

## Genetic Alliance UK
Unit 4D, Leroy House,   436 Essex Rd
London N1 3QP
Tel: 020 7704 3141

mail@geneticalliance.org.uk
www.geneticalliance.org.uk
Umbrella group for charities concerned with
human genetic disorders

**Genetics** see also Human Genetics
Commission, Jeans for Genes

**Genocide** see Aegis Trust

## Geographic Society (National)
www.nationalgeographic.com
American non-profit scientific and
educational organisation

## Geographical Association
160 Solly St  Sheffield S1 4BF
Tel: 0114 296 0088
info@geography.org.uk
www.geography.org.uk
National subject teaching association for
geography teachers in the UK

**Geographical Society (Royal)** see Royal
Geographical Society

## Geological Society
Burlington House  Piccadilly  London W1J
0BG
Tel: 020 7434 9944
Email via website
www.geolsoc.org.uk
Professional & learned society for working
geologists

## Geological Survey (British)
Kingsley Dunham Centre
  Keyworth  Nottingham NG12 5GG
Tel: 0115 936 3100 (switchboard)
Tel: 0115 936 3143 (enquiries helpdesk)
enquiries@bgs.ac.uk
www.bgs.ac.uk

## Geological Survey (US)
www.usgs.gov

## Geologists Association
Burlington House  Piccadilly  London W1J
0DU
Tel: 020 7434 9298
geol.assoc@btinternet.com
www.geologists.org.uk

## Georgian Group
6 Fitzroy Sq  London W1T 5DX
Tel: 0871 750 2936
office@georgiangroup.org.uk
www.georgiangroup.org.uk
Architectural group

## Get connected
Helpline:  0808 808 4994
Email via website
www.getconnected.org.uk
Runaway children can call free to talk to
trained volunteers

## Get Global!
www.getglobal.org.uk
Support and training for teachers involved in global citizenship

## Get Safe Online
www.getsafeonline.org/
Protect yourself against internet threats. The site is sponsored by government and leading businesses working together to provide a free, public service

## GFS Platform for Young Women
Unit 2, Angel Gate  326 City Road  London EC1V 2PT
Tel: 020 7837 9669
info@gfsplatform.org.uk
www.gfsplatform.org.uk
Support for young women in community projects

## Gifted Children (National Association for)
Suite 1.2  Challenge House  Sherwood Drive  Bletchley  Bucks MK3 6DP
Tel: 0845 450 0295 or 01908 646433
amazingchildren@nagcbritain.org.uk
www.nagcbritain.org.uk

## Gifted Children's Information Centre
Hampton Grange  21 Hampton Lane  Solihull B91 2QJ
Tel: 0121 705 4547
petercongdon@blueyonder.co.uk
www.dyslexiabooks.biz/
Assessment, guidance and legal help for children with special needs eg gifted dyslexics, ADHD, Aspberger's Syndrome

## Gingerbread Association for Lone Parent Families
255 Kentish Town Road
  London NW5 2LX

Single parent helpline: 0808 802 0925
Tel: 020 7428 5400
info@gingerbread.org.uk
www.gingerbread.org.uk

## Girlguiding UK
17-19 Buckingham Palace Rd  London SW1W 0PT
Freephone: 0800 1695901 (info about recruitment into all parts of Guide Movement)
Tel: 020 7834 6242
chq@girlguiding.org.uk
www.girlguiding.org.uk
UK's largest voluntary organisation for girls and young women with around 600,000 members

## Girls' Brigade
The Girls' Brigade England & Wales  PO Box 196, 129 Broadway, Didcot Oxfordshire, OX11 8XN.
Tel: 01235 510425
gbco@girlsbrigadeew.org.uk
www.girlsb.org.uk

## Girls' Venture Corps Air Cadets
1 Bawtry Gate  Sheffield  S9 1UD
Tel: 0114 2448405
gvcac@toucansurf.com
www.gvcac.org.uk
A uniformed organisation for girls aged 11-20 years. With interests in aviation, adventure and travel.

## Give Us Back Our Game
email via website
www.footy4kids.co.uk
Dedicated to bringing back the fun into football

**GLAD** see Disability (Greater London Action on)

## Glass Centre (National)
Liberty Way  Sunderland SR6 0GL
Tel: 0191 515 5555
info@nationalglasscentre.com
www.nationalglasscentre.com

## Gliding Association (British)
3rd Floor  Kimberley House  Vaughan Way Leicester LE1 4SE
Tel: 01162 531051
office@gliding.co.uk
www.gliding.co.uk
National governing body

## Global Action Plan
9-13 Kean Street  London  WC2B 4AY
Tel: 020 7420 4444
Email via website
www.globalactionplan.org.uk
Aims to engage people in practical solutions to environmental & social problems.

## Global Crop Diversity Trust
info@croptrust.org
www.croptrust.org
Organisation set up to ensure the conservation and availability of crop diversity for food security worldwide

## Global Dimension
info@globaldimension.org.uk.
www.globaldimension.org.uk
Department for International Development educational website on global development issues

## Global Ethics UK Trust (Institute for)
6 Dyers Buildings  Holborn  London  EC1N 2JT
Tel: 020 7405 5709
igeuk@globalethics.org.uk

www.globalethics.org.uk
Works in citizenship education, business ethics and public policy

**Global Eye**
www.globaleye.org.uk
Aims to increase awareness of development issues. Web version of the magazine Global Eye, written for schools by Worldaware on behalf of the Dept for International Development

**Global Road Safety (Campaign for)**
http://www.makeroadssafe.org/Pages/home.aspx
Campaigns for safer roads

**Global Witness**
6th Floor, Buchanan House   30 Holborn London   EC1N 2HS
Tel: 0207 4925820
mail@globalwitness.org
www.globalwitness.org
Focuses on areas where profits from environmental exploitation fund human rights abuses

**Globe Theatre** see Shakespeare's Globe Theatre

**GM** see GM Freeze

**GM Freeze**
50 South Yorkshire Buildings  Silkstone Common  Barnsley S75 4RJ
Tel: 0845 217 8992
eve@gmfreeze.org
www.gmfreeze.org
Campaigning for a moratorium on the introduction of GM food, feed and animals in the UK

**GMC** see General Medical Council

**Go4awalk**
www.go4awalk.com
Website for walkers and hikers

**Goethe Institut** German Cultural Centre
Churchgate House  56 Oxford St  Manchester M1 6EU
Tel: 0161 237 1077
info@manchester.goethe.org
www.goethe.de/manchester
Contact office for information on aspects of Germany, its culture and language

**Goethe-Institut London**
50 Princes Gate  Exhibition Rd  London SW7 2PH
Tel: 020 7596 4000
info@london.goethe.org
www.goethe.de/london
Promotes German language & culture abroad

**Golf** see also Blind Golf Association (English), Ladies' Golf Union, Professional Golfers' Association, Women's Golf Association (English)

**Golf Association (European)**
Place de la Croix-Blanche 19  CH-1066 Epalinges  Switzerland
Tel: 00 41 21785 7060
info@ega-golf.ch
www.ega-golf.ch

**Gorilla Organisation**
110 Gloucester Av  London NW1 8HX
Tel: 020 7483 2681
info@gorillas.org
www.gorillas.org
Protects gorillas

**Government Actuary's Department**
Finlaison House  15-17 Furnival Street London  EC4A 1AB
Tel: 020 7211 2601
enquiries@gad.gov.uk
www.gad.gov.uk

**Government Websites** see DirectGov

**Governor's Association (National)**
Ground Floor  36 Great Charles Street Birmingham  B3 3JY
Tel: 0121 237 3780
governorhq@nga.org.uk
www.nga.org.uk
Representing the interests of school governing bodies to government and other agencies

**Governors & Managers (National Association of)** see School Governors (National Association of)

**Graduate careers website**
www.prospects.ac.uk

**Grandparents' Association**
Moot House  The Stow  Harlow CM20 3AG
Helpline: 0845 434 9585
Tel: 01279 428040
info@grandparents-association.org.uk
www.grandparents-association.org.uk

**Grandparents Plus**
18 Victoria Park Square  Bethnal Green London   E2 9PF
Tel: 020 8981 8001
info@grandparentsplus.org.uk
www.grandparentsplus.org.uk
Promotes the vital role of grandparents and the extended family in children's lives, particularly where parents are no longer able to care for their children.

## Great buildings
www.greatbuildings.com
Data and illustrations of many significant buildings worldwide

## Greater London Authority
City Hall  The Queens Walk  More London
 London SE1 2AA
Tel: 020 7983 4100
mayor@london.gov.uk
www.london.gov.uk

## Greater London Enterprise
New City Court  20 St Thomas Street
London SE1 9RS
Tel: 020 7403 0300
info@gle.co.uk
www.gle.co.uk
Training & support for young people who are thinking of starting their own business

## Green Alliance
36 Buckingham Palace Rd  London SW1W 0RE
Tel: 020 7233 7433
ga@green-alliance.org.uk
www.green-alliance.org.uk
Promotes sustainable development by ensuring that the environment is at the heart of decision making

## Green Mark
GLE Consulting  New City Court  20 St Thomas Street  London SE1 9RS
Tel: 020 7940 1562
green.mark@gle.co.uk
www.greenmark.co.uk
Environmental management and sustainable development. Environmental training & consultancy for the public & private sectors

## Green Moves
Orchard Cottage
 Charlynch
 Somerset
 TA5 1BL
Tel: 0845 0944663
enquiries@greenmoves.com
www.greenmoves.com
A website dedicated to advertising homes for sale that are more energy efficient than conventional homes.

## Green Party
1a Waterlow Rd  London N19 5NJ
Tel: 020 7272 4474
office@greenparty.org.uk
www.greenparty.org.uk
Political party committed to social justice and ecological sustainability

## Greenpeace
Canonbury Villas  London N1 2PN
Tel: 020 7865 8100
info@uk.greenpeace.org
www.greenpeace.org.uk

## Groundwork UK
Lockside  5 Scotland Street  Birmingham
B1 2RR
Tel: 0121 236 8565
info@groundwork.org.uk
www.groundwork.org.uk
Working in partnership to improve local environments & contribute to economic & social regeneration

## Guide Dogs for the Blind Association
Burghfield Common  Reading RG7 3YG
Tel: 0118 983 5555
guidedogs@guidedogs.org.uk
www.gdba.org.uk
www.guidedogs.org.uk

## Guitar Foundation & Festivals (International)
phil@igf.org.uk
www.igf.org.uk

## Gulf Veterans & Families Association (National)
Building E, Office 8
 Chamberlain Business Centre  Chamberlain Road  Hull  HU8 8HL
Tel: 0845 257 4853
info@ngvfa.org.uk
www.ngvfa.com/

## Gun Control Network
PO Box 11495  London N3 2FE
Crimestoppers 0800 555 111
contact@gun-control-network.org
www.gun-control-network.org
Working towards a tighter control of firearms and a gun-free environment

## Gutenberg see Project Gutenberg

## Gymnastics (British)
Ford Hall  Lilleshall National Sports Centre
Newport  Shrops TF10 9NB
Tel: 0845 129 7129
information@british-gymnastics.org
www.british-gymnastics.org
Governing body

## Gypsy Association
info@gypsy-association.com
www.gypsy-association.com
www.gypsy-association.co.uk
Information, advice, liaison & support

# H

## Habitat for Humanity
46 West Bar Street  Banbury  OX16 9RZ
Tel: 01295 264240
SupporterServices@habitatforhumanity.org.uk
www.habitatforhumanity.org.uk
International development organisation that builds homes with volunteers and people in need.

## Hadley Centre for Climate Prediction and Research see Met Office

## Haemochromatosis Society
Hollybush House  Hadley Green Road  Barnet, Herts  EN5 5PR
Tel: 020 8449 1363
info@haemochromatosis.org.uk
www.haemochromatosis.org.uk
Support for sufferers from this common genetic iron overload disorder

## Haemophilia Society
First Floor  Petersham House  57a Hatton Garden  London EC1N 8JG
Helpline: 0800 018 6068
Tel: 020 7831 1020
info@haemophilia.org.uk
www.haemophilia.org.uk

## Hairline International
Lyons Court  1668 High Street  Knowle, Nr Solihull  West Midlands B93 0LY
www.hairlineinternational.com/
The Alopecia Patients Society

## HALO Trust
Carronfoot  Thornhill  Dumfies DG3 5BF
Tel: 01848 331100
mail@halotrust.org
www.halotrust.org
Mine clearance and bomb disposal in the developing world

## Hamster Council (National)
Email via website
www.hamsters-uk.org

## Handball Association (English)
Unit G3  Barton Hall Estate  Hardy Street  Eccles  Manchester M30 7NB
Tel: 0161 707 8983
www.englandhandball.com
National governing body for Handball and Beach Handball in England

## Handball Association (Scottish)
National Sports Centre Inverclyde  Burnside Road  Largs  Scotland KA30 8RW
Tel: 01475 687820
AnneMclaughlin@hotmail.co.uk
www.scottishhandball.com

## Handsel Trust
Parks Farm  Clifford  Herefordshire HR3 5HH
Tel: 01497 831550
enquiries@handseltrust.org
www.handseltrust.org
Support for parents of children with disabilities

## Hang Gliding and Paragliding Association (British)
The Old Schoolroom  Loughborough Rd  Leicester LE4 5PJ
Tel: 0116 2611322
office@bhpa.co.uk
www.bhpa.co.uk

## Hansard Society
40-43 Chancery Lane  London WC2A 1JA
Tel: 020 7438 1222
hansard@lse.ac.uk
www.hansardsociety.org.uk
Educational charity to promote effective parliamentary democracy

## HAPPA Horses and Ponies Protection Association
Taylor Building, Shores Hey Farm  Black House Lane  Halifax Road  Briercliffe  Nr Burnley  Lancashire BB10 3QU
Tel: 01282 455992
www.happa.org.uk
Equine welfare

## Hawk & Owl Trust
PO Box 400  Bishops Lydeard  Taunton TA4 3WH
Tel: 0844 984 2824
enquiries@hawkandowl.org
www.hawkandowl.org
Protect & conserve wild birds of prey & their habitats

## Hay Festival
The Drill Hall  25 Lion Street  Hay-on-Wye HR3 5AD
Tel: 01497 822 620 (admin)
admin@hayfestival.com
www.hayfestival.com
Book festival

## Hayward Gallery
Southbank Centre
Belvedere Rd  Belvedere Road  London SE1 8XX
Tel: 0844 875 0073 (info & telephone booking)
Tel: 020 7960 4200 (switchboard)
customer@southbankcentre.co.uk
www.southbankcentre.co.uk/venues/hayward-gallery

## Headliners
Rich Mix  35-47 Bethnal Green Road  London E1 6LA

Tel: 020 7749 9360
enquiries@headliners.org
www.headliners.org
Out of school development and learning
programme through journalism for young
people aged 8-18

**Headlong Theatre**
34-35 Berwick Street  London W1F 8RP
Tel: 020 74780270
info@headlongtheatre.co.uk
www.headlongtheatre.co.uk

**HEADWAY**  The Brain Injury Association
Bradbury House  190 Bagnall Road
 Old Basford  Nottingham  Nottinghamshire
NG6 8SF
Free helpline: 0808 800 2244
Tel: 0115 924 0800
enquiries@headway.org.uk
www.headway.org.uk
Support for brain injury survivors and their
families

**Healing Organisations (Confederation of)**
www.confederation-of-healing-organisations.
org
To make contact & distant healing available on
NHS & in private medicine

**Health (Department of)**
Richmond House  79 Whitehall  London SW1A
2NS
Tel: 020 7210 4850
Minicom: 020 7210 5025
Email via website
www.dh.gov.uk

**Health Development Agency** see National
Institute for Health and Clinical Excellence

**Health Information Resources**
www.library.nhs.uk

**Health Professions Council**
Park House  184 Kennington Park Road
London  SE11 4BU
Tel: 020 7582 0866
See website for email
www.hpc-uk.org
Training, performance and conduct for 13
health professions (excluding doctors and
nurses). Check online if a health professional is
registered

**Health Promotion Agency for Northern
Ireland**
18 Ormeau Avenue  Belfast BT2 8HS
Tel: 028 9031 1611
info@hpani.org.uk
www.healthpromotionagency.org.uk
Supports those working in the areas of health
promotion and public health in Northern Ireland

**Health Protection Agency**
7th Floor Holborn Gate  330 High Holborn
London WC1V 7PP
Tel: 020 7759 2700 or 2701
 HPA.enquiries@hpa.org.uk
www.hpa.org.uk
October 2010: To be abolished as part of
the creation of a new national public health
service

**Health Research & Development
(Foundation for Women's)** FORWARD
Suite 2.1 Chandelier Building  2nd Floor  8
Scrubs Lane  London NW10 6RB
Tel: 0208 960 4000
Email via website
www.forwarduk.org.uk
International NGO acting for the health,
wellbeing and rights of African women &
girls

**Health & Safety Executive**
Redgrave Court  Merton Road  Bootle
Merseyside L20 7HS
Info Line: 0845 345 0055
Minicom: 0845 408 9577
hse.infoline@connaught.plc.uk
www.hse.gov.uk
October 2010: Body retained but functions
being scrutinised.

**Health Service Ombudsman** now
see Parliamentary and Health Service
Ombudsman

**Health & Social Services (N. Ireland
Department of)**
Castle Buildings  Stormont  Belfast BT4 3SQ
Tel: 028 9052 0500
webmaster@dhsspsni.gov.uk
www.dhsspsni.gov.uk

**Healthtalkonline**
DIPEx  PO Box 428  Witney  Oxon OX28
9EU
info@healthtalkonline.org
www.healthtalkonline.org
Unique database of personal and patient
experiences

**Healthy Schools Programme (National)**
Helpline: 0845 601 7848
support@healthyschools.gov.uk
www.healthyschools.gov.uk
Offers support for schools to equip young
people with the knowledge to make
informed health choices

**Hear From Your MP**
www.hearfromyourmp.com
Allows constituents to sign up to get emails
from their local MP about local issues

## Hearing Dogs for Deaf People
The Grange  Wycombe Rd  Saunderton
Princes Risborough  Bucks HP27 9NS
Tel: 01844 348 100
 info@hearingdogs.org.uk
www.hearingdogs.org.uk
Training dogs to alert their deaf owners to
specific sounds

## Heart Foundation (British) see British
Heart Foundation

## Heartstone
Mayfield  High Street  Dingwall  Ross-shire
IV15 9SS
Tel: 01349 865400
info@heartstone.co.uk
www.heartstone.co.uk/
Uses story, fiction and photojournalism to
challenge racism and intolerance

## Heat is Online
www.heatisonline.org
Extreme weather worldwide

## Hedgehog Preservation Society (British)
Hedgehog House  Dhustone  Ludlow
Shropshire SY8 3PL
Tel: 01584 890801
info@britishhedgehogs.org.uk
www.britishhedgehogs.org.uk

## Hedgeline
Tel: 01455 890649
http://freespace.virgin.net/clare.h/
Aims for the statutory control of hedge
nuisance

## HELP Holiday Endeavour for Lone Parents
25 Brook Street  Hemswell  Gainsborough
 DN21 5UJ
Tel: 01427 668717
janice@help.fslife.co.uk
www.helphols.co.uk
Offers reduced cost holidays to lone parent
families

## Help – For a life without tobacco
www.help-eu.com

## Help the aged now see Age

## Help the Hospices
Hospice House  34-44 Britannia St  London
WC1X 9JG
Tel: 020 7520 8200
info@helpthehospices.org.uk
www.helpthehospices.org.uk
Worldwide link for information about
hospice/palliative care

## Henry Doubleday Research Association
see Garden Organic

## Henry Moore Foundation
Dane Tree House  Perry Green  Herts SG10
6EE
Tel: 01279 843 333
Email via website
www.henry-moore.org
Registered charity

## Heraldry Society
PO Box 772  Guildford  Surrey GU3 3ZX
Tel: 01483 237373
honsecheraldrysociety@googlemail.com
www.theheraldrysociety.com

## Heraldry Society of Scotland
25 Craigentinny Crescent  Edinburgh EH7
6QA
Tel: 0131 5532232
info@heraldry-scotland.co.uk
www.heraldry-scotland.co.uk

## Herb Society
Sulgrave Manor  PO Box 946  Northampton
NN3 0BN
Tel: 0845 491 8699

info@herbsociety.org.uk
www.herbsociety.org.uk

## Herbalists see Medical Herbalists (National
Institute of)

## Hereditary Breast Cancer Helpline
Helpline: 01629 813000
canhelp@btopenworld.com

## Heritage Lottery Fund
7 Holbein Place  London  SW1W 8NR
020 7591 6042/44
enquire@hlf.org.uk
www.hlf.org.uk
Gives grants to support heritage:  museums,
parks and historic places, archaeology,
natural environment and cultural traditions

## Heritage Railway Association
www.heritagerailways.com
A trade organisation for heritage railways

## Herpes Viruses Association
41 North Road  London N7 9DP
Tel: 0845 123 2305
info@herpes.org.uk
www.herpes.org.uk
Gives help and advice to people with herpes
viruses. Enclose sae for information

## Hi8us First Light Now see First Light

## Hibiscus Female Prisoners Welfare Project
12 Angel Gate  320 City Road  London
EC1V 2PT
Tel: 020 7278 7116
fpwphibiscus@aol.com
http://fpwphibiscus.org.uk

**Hideout**
www.thehideout.org.uk
National website supporting children and
young people living with domestic violence

**HIFY-UK** Health Initiatives for Youth
26 Bedford House  Solon New Road
London SW4 7NS
Tel: 0207 733 9391
clint.walters@btinternet.com
Supports HIV positive youth

**High Blood Pressure Foundation**
Dept. of Medical Sciences  Western General
Hospital  Edinburgh EH4 2XU
Tel: 0131 332 9211
hbpf@hbpf.org.uk
www.hbpf.org.uk
Increasing awareness of dangers of high
blood pressure

**Higher Education Funding Council for
England**
Northavon House  Coldharbour Lane  Bristol
BS16 1QD
Tel: 0117 931 7317
hefce@hefce.ac.uk
www.hefce.ac.uk
Distributes public funding for teaching and
research and related activities in universities
and colleges.

**Hindu Universe – Hindu Resource Center**
www.hindunet.org

**Hispanic & Luso Brazilian Council**
Canning House  2 Belgrave Sq  London
SW1X 8PJ
Tel: 020 7235 2303
enquiries@canninghouse.org
 www.canninghouse.com
A focal point for the Spanish & Portuguese
speaking worlds: commercial, cultural,
educational and diplomatic.

**Historic Houses Association**
2 Chester St  London SW1X 7BB
Tel: 020 7259 5688
info@hha.org.uk
www.hha.org.uk
Representative body for private owners of
historic houses, parks and gardens

**Historic Monuments (Welsh)** see Cadw

**Historic Scotland**
Longmore House  Salisbury Place
Edinburgh EH9 1SH
Tel: 0131 668 8600
hs.website@scotland.gsi.gov.uk
www.historic-scotland.gov.uk

**Historical Association**
59A Kennington Park Rd  London SE11 4JH
Tel: 020 7735 3901
enquiry@history.org.uk
www.history.org.uk

**Historical Manuscripts Commission** see
National Archives

**Historical Maritime Society**
2 Mount Zion  Brownbirks Street  Cornholme
Todmorden  Lancashire  OL14 8PG
Tel:  01706 819248
grog@tesco.net
www.hms.org.uk
UK based historical research and re-
enactment group recreating the Royal Navy

**History World**
Email via website
www.historyworld.net
Site run by Bamber Gascoigne covering in
1 million words 400 separate histories and
4000 key events

**HIV InSite**
http://hivinsite.ucsf.edu/
Up-to-date information on HIV/AIDS
treatment and prevention

**HIV/AIDS** see also African AIDS Helpline,
AIDS Trust (National), AVERT, Body
Positive, Healthwise, HIFY-UK, PACE,
People Living with HIV & AIDS, Positively
UK, Terrence Higgins Trust, Youthlink Wales

**HIV/Aids Alliance (International)**
Supporting community action on AIDS in
developing countries
1st and 2nd Floor Preece House  91-101
Davigdor Road  Hove BN3 1RE
Tel: 01273 718900
mail@aidsalliance.org
www.aidsalliance.org

**HM Prison Service**
Parliamentary, Correspondence and Briefing
Unit  HM Prison Service Headquarters
Cleland House  Page Street  London, SW1P
4LN
Email via website
www.hmprisonservice.gov.uk

**HM Revenue and Customs**
Helpline: 0845 010 9000
www.hmrc.gov.uk
Advice on VAT, excise & customs

**HMRC Education Zone**
www.hmrc.gov.uk/education-zone/index.htm

**Holiday Care** see Tourism for All

**Holiday Endeavour for Lone Parents**  see
HELP (Holiday Endeavour for Lone Parents)

**Holidays** see also Activity Holiday Association (British), Calvert Trust, Family Holiday Association, Jubilee Sailing Trust, Landmark Trust, National Trust Holiday Cottages, National Trust Working Holidays

## Holistic Therapists (Federation of)
18 Shakespeare Business Centre  Hathaway Close  Eastleigh  Hampshire SO50 4SR
Tel: 0844 875 20 22
info@fht.org.uk
www.fht.org.uk
Professional body representing over 20,000 professional therapists offering massage, aromatherapy, reflexology, beauty and fitness therapies.

## Holocaust Educational Trust
BCM BOX 7892  London WC1N 3XX
Tel: 020 7222 6822
email via website
www.het.org.uk
www.thinkequal.com

## Home Business Alliance
Werrington Business Centre  86 Papyrus Road  Peterborough  PE4 5BH
Tel: 0871 284 5100
info@homebusiness.org.uk
www.homebusiness.org.uk

## Home Office Public Enquiries Unit
Direct Communications Unit  2 Marsham Street  London SW1P 4DF
Tel: 020 7035 4848
public.enquiries@homeoffice.gsi.gov.uk
www.homeoffice.gov.uk

## Home-Start
8 - 10 West Walk  Leicester LE1 7NA
Free info line: 0800 068 63 68
Tel: 0116 258 7900
info@home-start.org.uk
www.home-start.org.uk
Offers support to parents with at least one child under 5, who are finding it difficult to cope

## Homeless International
Queens House  16 Queens Rd  Coventry CV1 3EG
Tel: 02476 632802
info@homeless-international.org
www.homeless-international.org
Supports community-led housing and infrastructure related developments in Asia, Africa and Latin America

## Homeless Link
Gateway House  Milverton Street,  London SE11 4AP
Tel: 020 7840 4430
Email via website
www.homeless.org.uk

Umbrella organisation for organisations working with homeless people

## Homeopathic Association (British)
29 Park St West  Luton LU1 3BE
Tel: 01582 408675
info@britishhomeopathic.org
www.britishhomeopathic.org

## Homeopaths (Society of)
Tel: 0845 450 6611
Info@Homeopathy-Soh.Org
www.homeopathy-soh.org
Professional association

## Homework High
www.channel4learning.com/apps/ homeworkhigh/
Channel 4's website where teachers answer questions. Also contains a searchable bank of questions already asked & their answers

## Homeworking
admin@homeworking.org
www.homeworking.com
A web site with free information for those wishing to work from home

## Honour Network (The)
Karma Nirvana  PO Box 148   Leeds LS13 9DB
Helpline: 0800 5999 247
Tel: 0113 218 0114
Email via website
www.karmanirvana.org.uk/honour-network
To support victims and survivors of forced marriage and honour based violence. Also seeks to increase the reporting of victims and also survivors many of which are disowned by their families

## Hope UK
25f Copperfield St  London SE1 0EN
Tel: 020 7928 0848
enquiries@hopeuk.org
www.hopeuk.org
Drug education charity specialising in work with children & young people

## Horse Society (British)
Abbey Park
Stareton
Kenilworth
Warwickshire  CV8 2XZ
Tel: 0844 848 1666
email via website
www.bhs.org.uk

**Horses and Ponies Protection Association** see HAPPA

**Horses (International League for the Protection of)** now see World Horse Welfare

**Horticultural Society (Royal)** see Royal Horticultural Society

**Hospices** see Help the Hospices

**Hospital and Community Friends** now see Attend

**Hospital Broadcasting Association**
secretary@hbauk.com
www.hbauk.co.uk

**Hostelling International**
2nd Floor, Gate House  Fretherne Road
Welwyn Garden City AL8 6RD
Tel: 01707 324170
info@hihostels.com
www.hihostels.com

**Hostelling International (N. Ireland)**
22-32 Donegall Rd  Belfast BT12 5JN
Tel: 028 9032 4733
info@hini.org.uk
www.hini.org.uk

**Hostelling (Internet Guide to)**
www.hostels.com
List of youth hostels worldwide

**House of Commons Information Office**
Norman Shaw North  London SW1A 2TT
Tel: 020 7219 4272
hcinfo@parliament.uk
www.parliament.uk/mps-lords-and-offices/
offices/commons/hcio/

**House of Lords**
London SW1A 0PW
Tel: 020 7219 3107
hlinfo@parliament.uk
www.parliament.uk/business/lords/

**Housing (Chartered Institute of)**
Octavia House  Westwood Business Park
Westwood Way  Coventry CV4 8JP
Tel: 024 7685 1700
customer.services@cih.org
www.cih.org
The professional body for people working in
the field of social housing

**Housing (Confederation of Co-operative)**
Fairgate House  205 Kings Road  Tyseley
Birmingham B11 2AA
Tel: 0121 449 9588
info@cch.coop
www.cch.coop

**Housing Federation (National)**
Lion Court  25 Procter Street  London WC1V
6NY
Tel: 020 7067 1010
info@housing.org.uk
www.housing.org.uk
Representative organisation for registered
social landlords (mainly housing
associations)

**Housing Justice**
22 - 25 Finsbury Square  London  EC2A 1DX
Tel: 020 7920 6600
info@housingjustice.org.uk
www.housingjustice.org.uk
Takes practical action to prevent, and
campaigns against homelessness

**Housing Ombudsman Service**
81 Aldwych  London WC2B 4HN
Tel: 0300 111 3000
Minicom: 020 7404 7092
info@housing-ombudsman.org.uk
www.housing-ombudsman.org.uk
The Ombudsman Service is free for users.
People with speech or hearing problems can
contact the service via typetalk

**Housing Policy (Centre for)**
University of York  Heslington  York YO10
5DD
Tel: 01904 321480
chp@york.ac.uk
www.york.ac.uk/inst/chp/
Research institute

**HousingCare.org** Options for older people
EAC  3rd Floor  89 Albert Embankment
London SE1 7TP
Tel: 0800 377 7070
Tel: 020 7820 1343
enquiries@eac.org.uk
www.housingcare.org
Aims to help older people make decisions
about where to live, and any support or care
they need

**Howard League for Penal Reform**
1 Ardleigh Rd  London N1 4HS
Tel: 020 7249 7373
info@howardleague.org
www.howardleague.org
Works for humane, effective and efficient
reform of the penal system

**Howtocomplain.com**
PO Box 1290  Salisbury SP1 1YN
enquiries@howtocomplain.com
complaints@howtocomplain.com
www.howtocomplain.com
Independent British website aimed at
making complaints work for everyone

**Hull Truck Theatre**
50 Ferensway  Hull HU2 8LB
Box Office: 01482 323638
Information: 01482 224800
boxoffice@hulltruck.co.uk
admin@hulltruck.co.uk
www.hulltruck.co.uk

## Human Fertilisation & Embryology Authority

21 Bloomsbury Street  London WC1B 3HF
Tel: 020 7291 8200
admin@hfea.gov.uk
www.hfea.gov.uk
A statutory body that regulates infertility treatments including IVF, the use of donated sperm or eggs, and human embryo research. October 2010: To be abolished and its functions transferred to other regulators

## Human Genetics Commission

Dept of Health  605, Wellington House  133-155 Waterloo Rd  London SE1 8UG
Tel: 020 7972 4351
hgc@dh.gsi.gov.uk
www.hgc.gov.uk
Advisory body on new developments in human genetics and how they impact on individual lives. October 2010: Human Genetics Commission will be disbanded and replaced with a Committee of Experts within the Department of Health

## Human Rights (British Institute of)

King's College London  7th Floor  Melbourne House  46 Aldwych  London WC2B 4LL
Tel: 020 7848 1818
gcreaven@bihr.org.uk
www.bihr.org.uk

## Human Rights Commission (N. Ireland)

Temple Court  39 North St  Belfast BT1 1NA
Tel: 028 9024 3987
Email via website
www.nihrc.org
Aims to protect and promote the human rights in law, policy and practice.

## Human Rights Education Association

www.hrea.org
International non-governmental organisation that supports human rights learning

## Human Rights (European Court of)

Council of Europe  67075 Strasbourg-Cedex France
Tel: 0033 3 88 41 20 18
www.echr.coe.int

## Human Rights Policy (International Council on)

Rue Ferdinand-Hodler 17  CH-1207 Geneva Switzerland
Tel: 00 41 22 775 3300
ichrp@ichrp.org
www.ichrp.org
Researches into issues that present dilemmas for human rights organisations

## Human Rights Society

Mariners Hard  High Street  Nr Holt  Norfolk NR25 7RX
Tel: 01263 740990
To oppose legalisation of euthanasia. Provides information on pain relief and hospice care

## Human Rights Watch

2nd Floor  2-12 Pentoville Rd  London N1 9HF
Tel: 020 7713 1995
Email via website
www.hrw.org

## Human Scale Education

96 Carlingcott  Bath BA2 8AW
Tel: 01972 510709
info@hse.clara.net
www.hse.clara.net
Helps large schools find ways to work in smaller units and support parents and teachers wishing to set up their own schools

## Human Writes

4 Lacey Grove  Wetherby  West Yorkshire LS22 6RL
humanwritesuk@yahoo.co.uk
www.humanwrites.org
Support through letter writing to those on death row

## Humane Research Trust

29 Bramhall Lane South  Bramhall Stockport SK7 2DN
Tel: 0161 439 8041
info@humaneresearch.org.uk
www.humaneresearch.org.uk
Works to fund and promote medical research which does not involve animals

## Humane Slaughter Association

The Old School  Brewhouse Hill Wheathampstead  Herts AL4 8AN
Tel: 01582 831 919
info@hsa.org.uk
www.hsa.org.uk
Charity exclusively concerned with the welfare of animals during marketing, transport and slaughter

## Humanist Association (British)

1 Gower St  London WC1E 6HD
Tel: 020 7079 3580
info@humanism.org.uk
www.humanism.org.uk
A non-religious approach to life based on reason & common humanity

## Hunt Saboteurs Association

BM HSA, London, WC1N 3XX
Tel: 0845 4500727
info@huntsabs.org.uk
www.huntsabs.org.uk

**Huntington's Disease Association**
Neurosupport Centre  Norton Street
Liverpool L3 8LR
Tel: 0151 298 3298
info@hda.org.uk
www.hda.org.uk

**Hurricane Center (National)**
www.nhc.noaa.gov
US website

**Hydrology** see CEH

**Hyperactive Children's Support Group**
71 Whyke Lane  Chichester  W Sussex
PO19 7PD
Tel: 01243 539966
hacsg@hacsg.org.uk
www.hacsg.org.uk
Provides information, ideas & literature for
parents, carers & professionals. Focuses on
non medication

**Hypermobility Syndrome Association**
49 Orchard Crescent  Oreston  Plymouth
PL9 7NF
Tel: 0845 345 4465
email via website
www.hypermobility.org

**Hypnotherapists (Online National
Register of)** UK Confederation of
Hypnotherapy Organisations
Suite 404  Albany House  324-326 Regent
Street  London W1B 3HH
Tel: 0800 952 0560
petermatthews@manageyourstress.co.uk
www.ukcho.co.uk
Aims to ensure that hypnotherapists are safe
and competent to practise and adhere to
national standards of ethics and training

# I

**IAAF** see Athletics Federations
(International Association of)

**IASO** see Obesity (International Association
for the Study of)

**IATEFL** International Association of
Teachers of English as a Foreign Language)
Darwin College  University of Kent
Canterbury CT2 7NY
Tel: 01227 824430
generalenquiries@iatefl.org
www.iatefl.org
Educational charity supporting EFL teachers
worldwide

**IBS Helpline**
Helpline: 0114 272 3253

For help with problems related to
Inflammatory Bowel Disease (IBD) and
Irritable Bowel Syndrome

**Ice Hockey UK**
Email via website
www.icehockeyuk.co.uk
National governing body for ice hockey

**Ice Skating Association UK Ltd
(National)**
Grains Building  High Cross Street  Hockley
Nottingham NG1 3AX
Tel: 0115 988 8060
email via website
www.iceskating.org.uk
Body overseeing amateur ice skating in UK

**ICON** Institute of Conservation
1st Floor Downstream Building  1 London
Bridge  London SE1 9BG
Tel: 020 7785 3807
email via website
www.icon.org.uk
For conservators and restorers

**ICSTIS** now see Phonepay Plus

**ICVA** see Voluntary Agencies (International
Council of)

**IDTA** International Dance Teachers
Association
76 Bennett Rd  Brighton BN2 5JL
Tel: 01273 685652
email via website
www.idta.co.uk
An awarding body delivering qualifications
in dance

**IFST** Institute of Food Science &
Technology
5 Cambridge Court  210 Shepherds Bush Rd
London W6 7NJ
Tel: 020 7603 6316
info@ifst.org
www.ifst.org
Professional qualifying body for food
scientists and technologists and educational
charity

**ILO** see International Labour Organization

**Imaginate**
45a George Street  Edinburgh  ES2 2HT
Tel: 0131 225 8050
info@imaginate.org.uk
www.imaginate.org.uk
Promoting and developing performing arts
for children and young people in Scotland

**IMF** see International Monetary Fund

## Immigrants (Joint Council for the Welfare of)

115 Old St  London EC1V 9RT
Tel: 020 7251 8708
info@jcwi.org.uk
www.jcwi.org.uk

**Immigration** see also UK Border Agency

## Immigration Advisory Service

County House  190 Great Dover St  London SE1 4YB
Telephone advice service: 0844 974 4000
Tel: 0844 974 4000
www.iasuk.org

## Immigration Aid Unit (Greater Manchester)

1 Delaunays Road  Crumpsall Green Manchester M8 4QS
Tel: 0161 740 7722
email via website
www.gmiau.org

## Immigration & Asylum Tribunals Service

PO Box 6987  Leicester LE1 6ZX
Tel: 0845 6000 877
Text phone: 0845 606 0766
customer.service@tribunals.gsi.gov.uk
www.tribunals.gov.uk/ImmigrationAsylum
Hears appeals against asylum and immigration decisions

## Immigration Law Practitioners Association

Lindsey House  40-42 Charterhouse St. London EC1M 6JN
Tel: 020 7251 8383
info@ilpa.org.uk
www.ilpa.org.uk

## Immigration Services Commissioner (Office of the)

5th Floor  Counting House  53 Tooley St London SE1 2QN
Tel: 0845 000 0046
Tel: 020 7211 1500
info@oisc.gov.uk
www.oisc.gov.uk
Independent body committed to the elimination of unscrupulous administration advisers and the fair investigation of complaints. October 2010: Future under consideration - including possible merger.

## Imperial Society of Teachers of Dancing see ISTD

## Imperial War Museum HMS Belfast

Morgan's Lane  Tooley Street  London SE1 2JH
Tel: 020 7940 6300
hmsbelfast@iwm.org.uk
http://hmsbelfast.iwm.org.uk
www.iwm.org.uk

## & Churchill Museum and Cabinet War Rooms

Clive Steps  King Charles Street   London SW1A 2AQ
Tel: 020 7930 6961
cwr@iwm.org.uk
http://cwr.iwm.org.uk
www.iwm.org.uk

## Imperial War Museum Collections

http://collections.iwm.org.uk
www.iwm.org.uk
Collection covering all aspects of twentieth and twenty-first century conflict involving Britain and the Commonwealth

## & Duxford

Cambridgeshire CB22 4QR
Tel: 01223 835000
School visit booking line: 020 7416 5313.
duxford@iwm.org.uk
http://duxford.iwm.org.uk
www.iwm.org.uk

## & London

Lambeth Road  London SE1 6HZ
Tel: 020 7416 5320
School visit booking line: 020 7416 5313
mail@iwm.org.uk
http://london.iwm.org.uk
www.iwm.org.uk

## & North

The Quays  Trafford Wharf Road  Trafford Park  Manchester M17 1TZ
Tel: 0161 836 4000
School visit booking line: 0161 836 4064
iwmnorth@iwm.org.uk
http://north.iwm.org.uk
www.iwm.org.uk

**Impotence Association** see Sexual Dysfunction Association

## Include

60 Queens Rd  Reading RG1 4BS
Tel: 0118 902 1000
www.include.org.uk
Projects for children excluded from or not attending school and post 16 'hard to help'.

**Inclusion** see Centre for Economic & Social Inclusion

## Inclusion (National Development Team for) NDTi

Montreux House   18a James Street West Bath BA1 2BT
Tel: 01225 789135
office@ndti.org.uk
www.ndti.org.uk
A not-for-profit organisation concerned with promoting inclusion and equality for people who risk exclusion and who need support to lead a full life

**Inclusive Education (Alliance for)**
336 Brixton Road  London SW9 7AA
Tel: 020 7737 6030
info@allfie.org.uk
www.allfie.org.uk
Campaigning to end segregation in
education

**Inclusive Education (Centre for Studies on)**
New Redland Building  Coldharbour Lane
Frenchay  Bristol BS16 1QU
Tel: 0117 328 4007
admin@csie.org.uk
www.csie.org.uk
Working for inclusive education for all
children and a gradual end to all segregated
education, based on human rights
arguments.

**Incontinence** see Bladder and Bowel
Foundation, ERIC

**Independent Advice Centres** see Advice
UK

**Independent Financial Adviser Promotion Ltd**
2nd Floor  117 Farringdon Rd  London EC1R
3BX
Member Hotline on 0330 303 0025
contact@ifap.org.uk
www.unbiased.co.uk
Promotes the value and accessibility of
independent financial advice to the public

**Independent Living Alternatives**
Trafalgar House  Grenville Place  London
NW7 3SA
Tel: 020 8906 9265
PAServices@ILAnet.co.uk
www.ilanet.co.uk/
Promotes independent living for people with
disabilities

**Independent Midwives Association** see
Midwives Association (Independent)

**Independent News Collective** see INK

**Independent Police Complaints Commission**
90 High Holborn  London WC1V 6BH
Tel: 08453 002 002
enquiries@ipcc.gsi.gov.uk
www.ipcc.gov.uk

**Independent Safeguarding Authority**
0300 123 1111
info@vbs-info.org.uk
To help prevent unsuitable people from
working with children and vulnerable adults.
October 2010: the Vetting and Barring
Scheme is under review and likely to
change.

**Independent Schools Council**
St Vincent House  30 Orange Street  London
WC2H 7HH
Tel: 020 7766 7070
email via website
www.isc.co.uk
Umbrella body representing 1,280
independent schools educating more than
500,000 children in the UK and Ireland

**Independent Television Commission** now
see OFCOM

**Independent Television News** see ITN

**Index on Censorship**
www.indexoncensorship.org
Defends free expression

**Indexers (Society of)**
Woodbourn Business Centre  10 Jessell
Street  Sheffield  S9 3HY
Tel: 0114 244 9561or 0845 872 6807
info@indexers.org.uk
www.indexers.org.uk

**Indian Census**
www.censusindia.net

**Indian Volunteers for Community Service**
now see Volunteers For Rural India

**Indigenous Tribal Peoples of the Tropical
Forests (International Alliance of)**
its@international-alliance.org
www.international-alliance.org

**Individual Rights in Europe (Advice on)**
3rd Floor  17 Red Lion Square  London
WC1R 4QH
Advice Line: 020 7831 3850
Tel: 020 7831 4276
info@airecentre.org
www.airecentre.org

**Indonesia Human Rights Campaign** see
TAPOL

**Industrial Injuries Advisory Council**
2nd Floor  Caxton House  Tothill Street
Lonon SW1H 9NA
Tel: 020 7449 5618
iiac@dwp.gsi.gov.uk
www.iiac.org.uk

**Infant Deaths (Foundation for the Study of)**
11 Belgrave Road  London SW1V 1RB
Helpline: 0808 802 6868
Tel: 020 7802 3200
Fundraising: 020 7802 3201
office@fsid.org.uk
www.fsid.org.uk
Funds research into sudden infant death,
supports bereaving parents & disseminates
baby safety information

**Infertility** see also Fertility Friends, Human Fertilisation & Embryology Authority

**Infertility Counselling Association (British)** (BICA)
111 Harley Street  London WIG 6AW
Tel: 01372 451626
info@bica.net
www.bica.net
Professional association for infertility counsellors and counselling in the UK

**Infertility Network UK**
43 St Leonards Rd  Bexhill on Sea TN40 1JA
Tel:  0800 008 7464

admin@infertilitynetworkuk.com
www.infertilitynetworkuk.com
For those experiencing problems of infertility

**Inform**
Houghton St  London WC2A 2AE
Tel: 020 7955 7654
inform@lse.ac.uk
www.inform.ac
Help and information on new religious movements & cults

**Information and Advice Centres (Federation of)** now see Advice UK

**Information Commissioner's Office**
Wycliffe House  Water Lane  Wilmslow SK9 5AF
Helpline: 0303 123 1113.
Tel: 0303 123 1113
email via website
www.ico.gov.uk
Enforces the Data Protection Act 1998 and The Freedom of Information Act 2000

**Information Management (Association for)** Aslib
Wagon Lane  Howard House  Bingley BD16 1WA
Tel: 01274 777700
gcoult@aslib.com
www.aslib.com
Actively promotes best practice in the management of information resources

**InfoSearcher.com**
www.infosearcher.com
Web site run by a former American school librarian for professionals working to integrate ICT into the curriculum

**Injuries** see Safety/Accidents/Injury theme

**INK** Independent News Collective
F24 Acton Business Centre  School Road London NW10 6TD
Tel: 020 8453 1144
gateway@ink.uk.com
www.ink.uk.com

Association of UK's alternative press with over 70 member publications

**Inland Revenue**  see HM Revenue and Customs

**Inland Revenue Education Service** now see HMRC Education Zone

**Inland Waterways Association**
Island House  Moor Road  Chesham HP5 1WA
Tel: 01494 783 453
iwa@waterways.org.uk
www.waterways.org.uk
Campaigns to conserve & develop inland waterways

**Innovation in Mathematics Teaching (Centre for)**
Rolle Building  University of Plymouth  Drake Circus  Plymouth PL4 8AA
Tel: 01752 585346
www.cimt.plymouth.ac.uk
Aims to enhance the teaching and learning

**INQUEST**
89-93 Fonthill Rd  London N4 3JH
Tel: 020 7263 1111
inquest@inquest.org.uk
www.inquest.org.uk
Helps the families & friends of those who die in custody, special hospitals etc or other controversial circumstances. General advice on coroners inquest system.

**Inside Out Trust**
Hilton House  55-57a High St  Hurstpierpoint West Sussex BN6 9TT
Tel: 01273 833050
info@iotrust.plus.com
www.inside-out.org.uk
Runs projects in prisons to benefit the community and to give prisoners skills

**Institute for Optimum Nutrition** see Optimum Nutrition (Institute for)

**Institute of Contemporary Arts**
12 Carlton House Terrace  London SW1Y 5AH
Tel: 020 7930 0493
Box office: 020 7930 3647
email via website
www.ica.org.uk

**Institute of Directors** see Directors (Institute of)

**Institute of Race Relations** see Race Relations (Institute of)

**Instituto Cervantes** see Spanish Institute

**Insurance Ombudsman** see Financial Ombudsman Service

## Integrated Education (N. Ireland Council for)

Aldersgate House  13-19 University Road
Belfast BT7 1NA
Tel: 028 9023 6200
info@nicie.org.uk
www.nicie.org.uk

## Intellect

Russell Square House  10-12 Russell Square
London WC1B 5EE
Tel: 020 7331 2000
info@intellectuk.org
www.intellectuk.org
UK trade association for information
technology, telecommunications and
electronics companies

## Intellectual Property Office

Concept House  Cardiff Rd  Newport  S
Wales NP10 8QQ
Tel: 0300 300 2000
information@ipo.gov.uk
www.ipo.gov.uk
Executive agency of DTI which stimulates
innovation and competitiveness via patents,
trade marks, copyrights etc.

## Inter Faith Network for the UK

8a Lower Grosvenor Place  London SW1W
0EN
Tel: 020 7931 7766
ifnet@interfaith.org.uk
www.interfaith.org.uk
Promotes mutual respect and understanding
between different faith communities in this
country

## Interact Worldwide

Finsgate  5-7 Cranwood Street  London
EC1V 9LH
Tel: 0300 777 8500
programmes@interactworldwide.org
www.interactworldwide.org
Advancing the rights of all people to exercise
free and informed reproductive health choice
and to have access to confidential sexual
and reproductive health services including
family planning

## Intercountry Adoption Helpline

First Floor  71-73 High Street  Barnet  Herts
EN5 5UR
Advice Line: 0870 516 8742
Tel: 020 8449 2562
Email via website
www.icacentre.org.uk

## Interights

Lancaster House  33 Islington High Street
London N1 9LH
Tel: 020 7278 3230
ir@interights.org
www.interights.org

Expert advice and assistance to those
defending human rights through the law

## Intermediate Technology see Practical Action

## Intermix

9 Dunster Gardens  London NW6 7NG
Tel: 07961 982 398
contact@intermix.org.uk
www.intermix.org.uk
Organisation for the benefit of mixed-race
families, individuals and anyone who feels
they have a multiracial identity

## International Affairs (Royal Institute of)

Chatham House  10 St James's Sq  London
SW1Y 4LE
Tel: 020 7957 5700
contact@chathamhouse.org.uk
www.chathamhouse.org.uk
Brings together people of all nationalities
from government, politics, business, the
academic world and the media

## International Baccalaureate Organization

Route des Morillons 15  Grand-Saconnex,
Genève
  CH-1218  Switzerland
Tel: 00 41 22 791 7740
ibhq@ibo.org
www.ibo.org

## International Criminal Court

www.icc-cpi.int
An independent, permanent court that tries
persons accused of the most serious crimes
of international concern, namely genocide,
crimes against humanity and war crimes.
It will not act if a case is investigated or
prosecuted by a national judicial system.

## International Dance Teachers Association see IDTA

## International Development (Department for)

1 Palace St  London SW1E 5HE
Tel: 0845 300 4100
Tel: 020 7023 0000 (Switchboard)
enquiry@dfid.gov.uk
www.dfid.gov.uk
UK Government department responsible for
promoting development and the reduction
of poverty

## International Labour Organization ILO

4 route des Morillons  CH-1211  Geneva 22
Switzerland
Tel: 00 41 22 799 6111
ilo@ilo.org
www.ilo.org
UN agency which promotes fundamental
principles and rights at work

**International Monetary Fund**
www.imf.org

**International Olympic Committee** IOC
Château de Vidy  Case postale 356  1001
Lausanne
  Switzerland
Tel: 00 41 21 621 6111
www.olympic.org

**International Registry of Organ Donation
and Transplantation** see Organ Donation
and Transplantation (International Registry
of)

**International Service**
Hunter House  57 Goodramgate  York YO1
7FX
Tel: 01904 647799
email via website
www.internationalservice.org.uk
2 year placements for experienced
professionals with development projects in
Latin America, West Africa and Palestine

**International Union for Conservation of
Nature** see IUCN

**Internet** see also ipl2, Nobel Internet
Archive, Nominet, People's Network,
SmartParent, Topmarks, Wired Safety, Wise
up to the net

**Internet Watch Foundation**
East View  5 Coles Ln  Oakington  Cambs
CB24 3BA
Tel: 01223 237700
information@iwf.org.uk.
www.iwf.org.uk
To hinder potentially illegal material on the
internet

**Interpol**
General Secretariat  200 quai Charles de
Gaulle  69006 Lyon  France
Email via website
www.interpol.int

**Investment Ombudsman** see Financial
Ombudsman Service

**Involuntary Tranquilliser Addiction
(Council for)** see Tranquilliser Addiction
(Council for Involuntary)

**IOC** see International Olympic Committee

**IOSH** see Occupational Safety & Health
(Institution of)

**IOTF** see Obesity (International Association
for the Study of) & Obesity TaskForce
(International)

**ipl2**
www.ipl.org
US website. A searchable, annotated

subject directory of more than 8,500 internet
resources selected & evaluated by librarians
for their usefulness to users of public
libraries

**IPSEA** Independent Parental Special
Education Advice
Hunters Court  Debden Road  Saffron
Walden  CB11 4AA
Advice Line: 0800 0184016
Tel: 01799 582030
www.ipsea.org.uk
Advises parents of children with special
educational needs of the obligations of LEAs

**Ironbridge Gorge Museum**
The IRONBRIDGE GORGE MUSEUM
TRUST  Coach Road  Coalbrookdale
Telford, TF8 7DQ
Tel: 01952 884391
Education: 01952 433970
Visitor Information Centre: 01952 433424
Email via website
www.ironbridge.org.uk

**ISCIS** now see Independent Schools
Council

**Islamic Education** see UK Islamic
Education Waqf

**Islamic Human Rights Commission**
PO Box 598  Wembley HA9 7XH
Tel: 020 89044222
info@ihrc.org
www.ihrc.org

**Islamic Relief**
19 Rea St South  Digbeth  Birmingham  B5
6LB
Tel: 0121 605 5555
Email via website
www.islamic-relief.com
Brings relief & development aid to the
world's poorest people

**ISSUE** now see Infertility Network UK

**ISTD** Imperial Society of Teachers of
Dancing
22/26 Paul St  London EC2A 4QE
Tel: 020 7377 1577
www.istd.org
Teaching and examining body

**It's not your fault**
www.itsnotyourfault.org
For children and teenagers whose parents
are getting divorced

**Italian Cultural Institute**
39 Belgrave Sq  London SW1X 8NX
Tel: 020 7235 1461
icilondon@esteri.it
www.icilondon.esteri.it/IIC_Londra

**ITC** see OFCOM

**ITDG** see Practical Action

**ITN** Independent Television News
200 Gray's Inn Rd London WC1X 8XZ
Tel: 020 7833 3000
www.itn.co.uk

**IUCN** International Union for Conservation of Nature
mail@iucn.org
www.iucn.org
Conservation of Nature and Natural Resources (International Union for)

**IVS** International Voluntary Service
Thorn House 5 Rose Street Edinburgh EH2 2PR
Tel: 0131 243 2745
info@ivsgb.org
www.ivsgb.org

**IXIA**
Unit 114 Custard Factory Gibb Street Birmingham B9 4AA
Tel: 0121 753 5301
info@ixia-info.com
www.ixia-info.com
National organisation for public art development in England

**Iyengar Yoga Institute** see Yoga (Iyengar Institute)

# J

**Jane Tomlinson Appeal**
PO BOX 314 Rothwell Leeds LS26 1BY
Tel: 0113 812 9100
info@janetomlinsonappeal.com
www.janetomlinsonappeal.com
Jane Tomlinson undertook feats of sporting endurance to raise money for charity and to show that people with a terminal prognosis can still lead an active and fruitful life

**JANET** Education & Research Networking Association (UK)
Lumen House Library Ave Harwell Science and Innovation Campus Didcot Oxon OX11 0SG
Tel: 01235 822 200
Service Desk: 0300 300 2212
service@ja.net
www.ja.net
A company operating and developing JANET information networks for use in higher education institutions

**Japan Foundation London Language Centre**
6th Floor Russell Square House 10-12 Russell Square London WC1B 5EH
Tel: 020 7436 6698

info.language@jpf.org.uk
www.jpf.org.uk
A support centre for teachers of Japanese

**Jeans for Genes**
c/o GFM Holdings PO Box 5 Colchester CO2 8GE
Freephone: 0800 980 4800
Tel: 020 7199 3300
Email via website
www.jeansforgenes.com
Helps children with genetic disorders

**Jewish Israel Appeal (United)** see UJIA

**Jewish Lads' & Girls' Brigade (JLGB)**
including Hand-in-Hand Young Volunteering Project
3 Beechcroft Rd South Woodford London E18 1LA
Tel: 020 8989 8990
Getinvolved@JLGB.org
www3.jlgb.org

**Jewish Museum**
Raymond Burton House 129-131 Albert St Camden Town
London NW1 7NB
Tel: 020 7284 7384
admin@jewishmuseum.org.uk
www.jewishmuseum.org.uk

**Jewish Women (League of)**
6 Bloomsbury Sq London WC1A 2LP
Tel: 020 7242 8300
office@theljw.org
www.theljw.org
Volunteers who provide welfare care for all people

**Jews (Board of Deputies of British)** see British Jews ( Board of Deputies of)

**Jobcentre Plus**
www.jobcentreplus.gov.uk
Helps people without jobs to find work & employers to fill their vacancies. (Executive Agency of the Dept. of Work & Pensions)

**Jodrell Bank Observatory**
Jodrell Bank Observatory The University of Manchester Macclesfield Cheshire SK11 9DL
Tel: 01477 571321
www.jb.man.ac.uk

**Joint Nature Conservation Committee,**
Monkstone House, City Road Peterborough PE1 1JY
01733 562626
comment@jncc.gov.uk
www.jncc.gov.uk
Advises Government on UK and international nature conservation.

**Joseph Rowntree Foundation**
The Homestead 40 Water End York YO30 6WP

Tel: 01904 629241
info@jrf.org.uk
www.jrf.org.uk
Researches underlying causes of poverty and supports research into housing, social care & social policy

**Journeys**
120-122  Broadway  Roath  Cardiff CF24 1NJ
Tel: 029 2069 2891
email via website
http://www.journeysonline.org.uk/

**Journeywoman.com**
www.journeywoman.com
US site for women travellers

**Ju-Jitsu** see also World Ju-Jitsu Federation (Ireland)

**Ju-Jitsu Association GB National Governing Body (British)**
5 Avenue Parade  Accrington   Lancashire BB5 6PN
Tel: 01254 396806
chairman@bjjagb.com
www.bjjagb.com

**Jubilee Debt Campaign**
The Grayston Centre  28 Charles Square London  N1 6HT
Tel: 020 7324 4722
info@jubileedebtcampaign.org.uk
www.jubileedebtcampaign.org.uk
Aiming to stop poor countries paying money to the rich world and cancellation of unpayable poor country debts

**Jubilee Sailing Trust**
12 Hazel Road  Woolston  Southampton SO19 7GA
Tel: 023 8044 9108
info@jst.org.uk
www.jst.org.uk
Adventure tallship sailing holidays for able bodied & disabled

**Judo Association (British)**
Suite B, Loughborough Tech Park  Epinal Way  Loughborough LE11 3GE
Tel: 01509 631670
bja@britishjudo.org.uk
www.britishjudo.org.uk

**Judo Scotland**
EICA: Ratho,  South Platt Hill  Ratho Newbridge EH28 8AA
Tel: 0131 333 2981
info@judoscotland.com
www.judoscotland.com

**Junk Mail** see Fax Preference Service, Mailing Preference Service

**Just for Kids** (JfK)
402 Harrow Road  London  W9 2HU
Tel: 020 7266 7159
info@justforkidslaw.org
www.justforkidslaw.org
Runs a number of programmes aimed at providing support, advocacy and assistance to young people with a variety of needs.

**Justgiving**
First Floor  30 Eastbourne Terrace  London W2 6LA
Tel: 0845 021 2110
Email via website
www.justgiving.com
Fundraising website

**JUSTICE**
59 Carter Lane  London EC4V 5AQ
Tel: 020 7329 5100
admin@justice.org.uk
www.justice.org.uk
All-party law reform and human rights charity

**Justice (Ministry of)**
102 Petty France  London SW1H 9AJ
Tel: 020 3334 3555
general.queries@justice.gsi.gov.uk
www.justice.gov.uk

# K

**Karate and Martial Art Schools (National Association of)**
PO Box 262  Herne Bay  Kent CT6 9AW
Tel: 01227 370055
info@nakmas.org.uk
www.nakmas.org.uk
National Governing Body for Traditional and Modern Martial Arts

**Karate Board (N. Ireland)**
89 Brooke Drive  Belfast BT11 9NJ
Tel: 028 9061 6453 (Chairman/President)
obrunton@aol.com
www.irishkarate.com
www.learnkarate.net

**Karate England**
PO Box 490  Northwich CW9 9AU
Tel: 07931 545924
admin@karateengland.org.uk
www.karateengland.org.uk

**Karate Governing Body Ltd (Welsh)**
105 Queens Drive  Llantwit Fardre Pontypridd  CF38 2NY
Tel: 01443 203733
wkgb@sky.com
www.wkgb.org.uk

## Keep Britain Tidy
Elizabeth House  The Pier  Wigan WN3 4EX
Tel: 01942 612621
email via website
www.keepbritaintidy.org
Environmental charity and the anti-litter
campaign for England. Also runs programmes
such as Eco-Schools, Blue Flag and Quality
Coast Awards for beaches, and the Green
Flag for parks to demonstrate practical action

## Keep Fit Association
1 Grove House  Foundry Lane  Horsham
West Sussex RH13 5PL
Tel: 01403 266000
kfa@emdp.org
www.keepfit.org.uk

## Kennel Club
1-5 Clarges St  Piccadilly  London W1J 8AB
Tel: 0844 463 3980
Email via website
www.thekennelclub.org.uk
To promote in every way the general
improvement of all dogs

## Kew Gardens see Royal Botanic Gardens, Kew

## Kick It Out
PO Box 29544  London  EC2A 4WR
Freephone: 0800 169 9414 (Hotline for
reporting racist abuse and incidents only)
Tel: 020 7684 4884 (General enquiries)
info@kickitout.org
www.kickitout.org
Football's anti-racism campaign

## Kickboxing and Karate Association (World)
63 Gravelly Ln  Erdington  Birmingham B23
6LX
Tel: 0121 382 2995
email via website
www.wkakickboxing.com

## Kid Info School Subjects
www.kidinfo.com/school_subjects.html
US homework and research site

## Kidney Patient Association (British)
3 The Windmills  St Mary's Close  Turk Street
  Alton
  GU34 1EF
Tel: 01420 541424
info@britishkidney-pa.co.uk
www.britishkidney-pa.co.uk
Financial help, advice & literature for kidney
patients & their families

## Kidney Research UK
Nene Hall
  Lynch Wood Park  Peterborough  PE2 6FZ
Tel: 0845 070 7601
enquiries@kidneyresearchuk.org
www.kidneyresearchuk.org

## Kids' Clubs Network now see 4 Children

## Kids Company
1 Kenbury Street  London  SE5 9BS
Tel: 0845 644 6838
Tel: 0207 274 8378
info@kidsco.org.uk
www.kidsco.org.uk
To deliver emotional and practical support
within structures which are directly accessible
by children - and not dependent on a carer

## Kids for Kids
PO Box 456  Dorking  Surrey RH4 2WS
Tel: 07957 206440
contact@kidsforkids.org.uk
www.kidsforkids.org.uk
Helps children struggling to survive in remote
villages in Darfur, Sudan

## Kids in museums
Downstream Building  One London Bridge
London  SE1 9BG
Tel: 020 7022 1888
getintouch@kidsinmuseums.org.uk
www.kidsinmuseums.org.uk
Guiding museums and galleries across the
country to make family visits engaging and
enjoyable.

## Kidscape
2 Grosvenor Gardens  London SW1W 0DH
Helpline: 08451 205 204
General Enquiries: 020 7730 3300
webinfo@kidscape.org.uk
www.kidscape.org.uk
Helpline for parents/carers of bullied children.
Assertiveness training for bullied young
people. Free resources and literature on
bullying and child safety. Child Safety Training
Programme

## Kilvert (Alice) see Tampon Alert (Alice Kilvert)

## King's Fund
11 - 13 Cavendish Square  London W1G
0AN
Tel: 020 7307 2400
enquiry@kingsfund.org.uk
www.kingsfund.org.uk
An independent charitable foundation
working for better health, especially in
London

## Kite Society of Great Britain
PO Box 2274  Gt Horkesley  Colchester CO6
4AY
Tel: 01206 271489
info@thekitesociety.org.uk
www.thekitesociety.org.uk

**Kiva** Loans that change Lives
www.kiva.org
Helps people out of poverty by direct lending from individuals to selected entrepreneurs in the developing world. Once the money is repaid it can be withdrawn or lent again

**Know Cannabis**
www.knowcannabis.org.uk
Website which can help you assess your cannabis use, its impact on your life and how to make changes if you want to

**Kodaly** see BKA

**Kurdish Human Rights Project**
11 Guilford Street  London WC1N 1DH
Tel: 020 7405 3835
khrp@khrp.org
www.khrp.org

# L

**La Leche League**
PO Box 29  West Bridgford  Nottingham NG2 7NP
Helpline: 0845 120 2918
Tel: 0845 456 1855 (General enquiries)
enquiries@laleche.org.uk
www.laleche.org.uk
Breastfeeding support & information

**Labour Behind the Label**
THE CLEAN CLOTHES CAMPAIGN  10-12 Picton Street  Bristol BS6 5QA
Tel: 0117 944 1700
Email via website
www.labourbehindthelabel.org
Campaigns for better conditions for garment workers around the world and for fair trade

**Labour Party**
Eldon House  Regent Centre  Newcastle Upon Tyne  NE3 3PW
Tel: 08705 900 200
Email via website
www2.labour.org.uk

**Labour Research Department**
78 Blackfriars Rd  London SE1 8HF
Tel: 020 7928 3649
info@lrd.org.uk
www.lrd.org.uk

**Labour Women's Network**
11 Well House Road  LEEDS LS8 4BS
contact@lwn.org.uk
http://labourwomensnetwork.org.uk
Provides advice, information and support for women in the Labour Party seeking public office

**Lacrosse Association (English)**
The Belle Vue Centre
 Pink Bank Lane  Longsight  Manchester M12 5GL
Tel: 0161 227 3626
info@englishlacrosse.co.uk
www.englishlacrosse.co.uk

**Ladies' Golf Association (English)** now see Women's Golf Association (English)

**Ladies' Golf Union**
The Scores  St Andrews KY16 9AT
Tel: 01334 475811
Email via website
www.lgu.org
Governing body of ladies' golf

**Lake District (Friends of the)**
Murley Moss  Oxenholme Rd  Kendal LA9 7SS
Tel: 01539 720788
info@fld.org.uk
www.fld.org.uk
A regional conservation charity dedicated to the protection and enhancement of the landscape and countryside of Cumbria and the Lake District

**Lake District National Park Authority**
Murley Moss  Oxenholme Rd  Kendal LA9 7RL
Tel: 01539 724555
hq@lakedistrict.gov.uk
www.lakedistrict.gov.uk

**Lake District Weather Line**
Tel: 0844 846 2444
www.lakedistrict.gov.uk/weatherline
Provides a weather forecast for the day. The next day's forecast is available after 5.15pm

**Land Registry**
Tel: 0844 892 1111
customersupport@landregistry.gsi.gov.uk
www1.landregistry.gov.uk
Register of ownership of land in England and Wales.  October 2010: body retained but will be substantially changed and private investment will be considered

**Land Yachts** see Sand & Land Yacht Clubs (British Federation of)

**Landlife**
National Wildflower Centre  Court Hey Park Liverpool L16 3NA
Tel: 0151 737 1819
info@landlife.org.uk
www.landlife.org.uk
Environmental charity growing and selling wildflower seeds and plants, promoting new wildflower landscapes

**Landmark Trust**
Shottesbrooke  Maidenhead  Berks SL6 3SW
Tel: 01628 825920

Tel: 01628 825925
info@landmarktrust.org.uk
www.landmarktrust.org.uk
Charity which restores buildings of historic & architectural importance, then secures their future by letting them for holidays

**Landmine Action**
5th Floor  Epworth House  25 City Road  London  EC1Y 1AA
Tel: 020 7256 9500
info@landmineaction.org
www.landmineaction.org
Umbrella organisation campaigning for the elimination of landmines

**Landmines** see also HALO Trust, Mines Advisory Group

**Landmines (International Campaign to Ban)**
www.icbl.org
Key umbrella organisation for anti-landmine groups worldwide

**Landscape Institute**
Charles Darwin House  12 Roger Street  London WC1N 2JU
Tel: 020 7685 2640
www.landscapeinstitute.org.uk
Professional body in UK for landscape architects and designers, planners and managers

**Language Awareness (Association for)**
www.languageawareness.org

**Language Learning (Association for)**
University of Leicester  University Road  Leicester LE1 7RH
Tel: 0116 229 7453
info@all-languages.org.uk
www.all-languages.org.uk
Association for teachers of modern foreign languages

**Language Teaching & Research (Centre for Information on)** now see CILT

**Language Teaching & Research (Scottish Centre for Information on)**
Scottish CILT
Room C317, Crawfurd Building  University of Strathclyde  76 Southbrae Drive  Jordanhill  Glasgow G13 1PP
tel : 0141 950 3308/3369
scilt@strath.ac.uk
www.strath.ac.uk/scilt

**Laogai Research Foundation**
laogai@laogai.org
www.laogai.org
Washington DC based organisation exposing human rights abuses in China

**Lattitude Global Volunteering**
42 Queen's Road  Reading  Berkshire  RG1 4BB
Tel: 0118 959 4914
volunteer@lattitude.org.uk
www.lattitude.org.uk
International voluntary projects for young people on a gap year

**Lavender Trust** at Breast Cancer Care
Breast Cancer Care Helpline: 0808 800 6000
www.breastcancercare.org.uk/about-us/lavender-trust
Raises money specifically to fund Breast Cancer Care's support and information services for younger women

**Law Centres Federation**
22 Tudor Street   London EC4Y 0AY
Tel 020 7842 0720
info@lawcentres.org.uk
www.lawcentres.org.uk
Co-ordinating body for community Law Centres

**Law Commission**
Steel House  11 Tothill Street  London SW1H 9LJ
Tel: 020 3334 0200
chief.executive@lawcommission.gsi.gov.uk
www.lawcom.gov.uk

**Law Society Consumer Complaints Service** now see Legal Complaints Service

**Law Society of England & Wales**
113 Chancery Lane  London WC2A 1PL
Tel: 020 7242 1222
Email via website
www.lawsociety.org.uk
Professional body for solicitors in England and Wales.

**Law Society of Scotland**
26 Drumsheugh Gardens  Edinburgh EH3 7YR
Tel: 0131 226 7411
lawscot@lawscot.org.uk
www.lawscot.org.uk

**Lawn Tennis Association**
The National Tennis Centre  100 Priory Lane  Roehampton  London SW15 5JQ
Tel: 020 8487 7000
Info@LTA.org.uk
www.lta.org.uk
Governing body

**League Against Cruel Sports** see Cruel Sports Ltd (League Against)

**League for the Exchange of Commonwealth Teachers**  see Exchange of Commonwealth Teachers (League for the)

## Leap Confronting Conflict

Unit 7, Wells House  5 - 7 Wells Terrace
Finsbury Park  London, N4 3JU
Tel: 020 7561 3700
info@leapconfrontingconflict.org.uk
www.leaplinx.com
Provides opportunities for young people and adults to explore creative approaches to conflicts in their lives

## Learn To Sign

10th Floor, Coventry Point  Market Way
Coventry, CV1 1EA
Tel: 02476 550936
Textphone: 02476 550393
bda@bda.org.uk
http://bda.org.uk/Learn_to_Sign-i-19.html
British Sign Language for the deaf

## learndirect

Tel: 0800 101 901
www.learndirect.co.uk
Provides adults with free advice on learning and career opportunities

## learndirect Scotland

Freepost SCO5775  PO Box 25249
Glasgow G3 8XN
Helpline: 0808 100 9000
info@learndirectscotland.com
www.learndirectscotland.com

**Learning and Skills Council** now see Skills Funding Agency and Young People's Learning Agency

## Learning and Skills Development Agency Northern Ireland LSDA Northern Ireland

2nd Floor Alfred House  19-21 Alfred Street
Belfast BT2 8ED
Tel: 02890 447700
www.lsdani.org.uk
Improvement and staff development programmes that support specific government initiatives

## Learning and Skills Improvement Service LSIS

Friars House  Manor House Drive  Coventry
West Midlands  CV1 2TE
Tel: 024 7662 7900 (Switchboard)
Tel: 024 7662 7953 (Services and support enquiries)
enquiries@lsis.org.uk
www.lsis.org.uk
Formed from CEL and QIA to develop FE provision

## Learning and Teaching Scotland

The Optima  58 Robertson Street  Glasgow G2 8DU
Tel: 0870 0100 297 (Customer Services)
Tel: 0141 282 5000 (Glasgow)
enquiries@LTScotland.org.uk
www.ltscotland.org.uk
Advice, guidance, products and services relating to the pre-school and school curriculum

## Learning (Campaign for)

19 Buckingham St  London WC2N 6EF
Tel: 020 7930 1111
www.campaign-for-learning.org.uk/cfl/index.asp
Charity working to stimulate learning that will sustain people for life

## Learning Disabilities (British Institute of)

Campion House  Green St  Kidderminster DY10 1JL
Tel: 01562 723010
enquiries@bild.org.uk
www.bild.org.uk

## Learning Disabilities (The Foundation for People with)

Tel:  020 7803 1100
fpld@fpld.org.uk
www.learningdisabilities.org.uk
Aims to improve the quality of life for people with learning disabilities. Part of the Mental Health Foundation

## Learning (Institute for)

First Floor  49-51 East Road  London N1 6AH
Tel: 0844 815 3202
enquiries@ifl.ac.uk
www.ifl.ac.uk
Professional body for teachers, trainers, tutors, student teachers and assessors in the further education and skills sector

## Learning Outside the Classroom

Council for Learning Outside the Classroom  6 Breams Buildings  London  EC4A 1QL
enquiries@lotc.org.uk
www.lotc.org.uk

## Learning Through Action Centre

High Close School  Wiltshire Road  Wokingham
Berkshire RG40 1TT
Tel: 0870 770 7985
Email via website
www.learning-through-action.org.uk
Workshops for children and young people, their parents and carers on social and health issues

## Learning Zone

www.bbc.co.uk/learningzone
BBC education website

## Left 'n' Write

5 Charles St  Worcester WR1 2AQ
Tel: 01905 25798
info@leftshoponline.co.uk
www.leftshoponline.co.uk
Provides information and resources for left handed people, courses for teachers on needs of left handed children

**Legal Action Group**
242 Pentonville Rd  London N1 9UN
Tel: 020 7833 2931
lag@lag.org.uk
www.lag.org.uk
Working with lawyers and advisers to promote equal access to justice through publications, training and policy work

**Legal Complaints Service**
Victoria Court  8 Dormer Place  Royal Leamington Spa CV32 5AE
Helpline: 0845 608 6565 & 0845 601 1682 (Minicom)
Tel: 01926 820082
enquiries@legalcomplaints.org.uk
www.legalcomplaints.org.uk
Deals with complaints about solicitors and regulates their work

**Legal Services Commission**
4 Abbey Orchard Street  London SW1P 2BS
Tel: 020 7783 7000
www.legalservices.gov.uk
Public body managing the Legal Aid Scheme in England and Wales. October 2010: LSC will be abolished in its present form and reconstituted as an Executive Agency of the Ministry of Justice

**Legal Services Ombudsman**
3rd Floor  Sunlight House  Quay Street Manchester M3 3JZ
Helpline: 0845 601 0794
Tel: 0161 839 7262
lso@olso.gsi.gov.uk
www.olso.org
Oversees the handling of complaints about lawyers in England and Wales. October 2010: Both the body and its functions to be abolished by 2011

**legislation.gov.uk**
www.legislation.gov.uk/
Branch of the National Archive which publishes all UK legislation. Provides online access and regulates Crown Copyright

**LEPRA**
28 Middleborough  Colchester  Essex CO1 1TG
Tel: 01206 216700
lepra@leprahealthinaction.org
www.lepra.org.uk
Medical charity aiming to eradicate leprosy and other diseases of poverty

**Lesbian and Gay Switchboard (London)**
PO Box 7324  London N1 9QS
Helpline: 020 7837 7324
Tel: 020 7837 6768 (Admin)
admin@llgs.org.uk
www.llgs.org.uk

Switchboard aims to operate a 24 hour service offering support, information and referrals to callers on any issue relating to lesbian, gay or bisexual life

**Lesbian Information Service**
PO Box 8  Todmorden  Lancs OL14 5TZ
jan@lesbianinformationservice.org
www.lesbianinformationservice.org
Research publications concerned with needs of lesbians and gays and can be downloaded from website

**Lesbians & Gays (Families & Friends of)**
FFLAG
PO Box 395  Little Stoke  Bristol  BS34 9AP
Helpline: 0845 6520311
info@fflag.org.uk
www.fflag.org.uk
A national voluntary organisation for parents of gay sons and lesbian daughters. It provides information and support through confidential helplines, groups and publications

**Let's Face It**
72 Victoria Ave  Westgate-on-Sea Kent CT8 8BH
Tel: 01843 833 724
chrisletsfaceit@aol.com
www.lets-face-it.org.uk
For people with facial disfigurement ie cancer, accidents, congenital acne

**Letslink UK**
12 Southcote Rd  London N19 5BJ
Tel: 020 7607 7852
admin@letslinkuk.net
www.letslink.org
Community development - local exchange of goods & services

**Leukaemia** see also Children with Leukaemia, CLICSargent

**Leukaemia and Lymphoma Research**
43 Great Ormond Street  London  WC1N 3JJ
Tel: 020 7405 0101
info@beatbloodcancers.org
www.beatbloodcancers.org

**LGA** see Local Government Association

**Liberal Democrat Trade Unionists (Association of)**
30 Leigh Rd  Layton  London E10 6JH
http://www.libdems.org.uk/

**Liberal Democrats**
4 Cowley St  London SW1P 3NB
Tel: 020 7222 7999
info@libdems.org.uk
www.libdems.org.uk

**Liberty** National Council for Civil Liberties
21 Tabard St  London SE1 4LA
Tel: 020 7403 3888 or 0203 145 0460
email via website
www.liberty-human-rights.org.uk

**Libraries for Life for Londoners**
31 Milton Park  London N6 5QB
Tel: 020 7607 2665
mail@librarylondon.org
www.librarylondon.org
Campaigning for a comprehensive, high
quality library service for all Londoners

**Library Association** see CILIP

**Library Association (Scottish)** see CILIPS

**Library Campaign**
22 Upper Woburn Place  London WC1H 0TB
Tel: 0845 450 5946
librarycam@aol.com
www.librarycampaign.com
Supporting friends and users of public libraries

**Libri Trust**
56 Brookfield  5 Highgate West Hill  London
N6 6AT
enquiries@libri-forums.org
www.rwevans.co.uk/libri
Charity for libraries

**Lidos**
www.lidos.org.uk
A guide to lidos and open air pools in the UK

**Life**
1 Mill Street  Leamington Spa  Warwickshire
CV31 1ES
National Pregnancy Help Hotline: Tel: 0800
915 4600
Tel: 01926 421587
info@lifecharity.org.uk
www.lifecharity.org.uk
Provides pregnancy and abortion counselling
and support

**Life (Centre for)**
Times Sq  Scotswood Rd  Newcastle Upon
Tyne NE1 4EP
Tel: 0191 243 8223
Email via website
www.life.org.uk
Visitor centre for life sciences

**Lifeguard Skills**
www.lifeguardskills.co.uk
Practical tips on water safety

**Lifelong Learning**
www.lifelonglearning.co.uk
Includes advice about financing study

**Lifesavers** The Royal Life Saving Society UK
River House  High Street  Broom
Warwickshire B50 4HN
Tel: 01789 773994

lifesavers@rlss.org.uk
www.lifesavers.org.uk
Dedicated to the prevention of unnecessary
loss of life, transforming bystanders into
lifesavers

**Lifetracks**
c/o YouthNet  First Floor  50 Featherstone
Street  London EC1Y 8RT
Tel: 020 7250 5700
email via website
www.lifetracks.com
Aims to be the first place all young people turn
to when they're making decisions about their
work, study or training

**Liftshare.com Ltd**
Fairfields  High Street  Attleborough  Norfolk
NR17 2BT
Tel: 01953 451 166
info@liftshare.com
www.liftshare.com
UK wide & web based car share scheme
provider

**Light Rail Transit Authority**
c/o 138 Radnor Avenue  Welling DA16 2BY
Tel: 01179 517785
office@lrta.org
www.lrta.org

**likeitis.org**
www.likeitis.org
Gives young people access to information
about all aspects of sex education and
teenage life

**Lilith Research and Development**
Unit 2.03 Canterbury Court  1-3 Brixton Road
London SW9 6DE
Tel: 020 7735 2062
www.eaves4women.co.uk/Lilith_Research_
And_Development/Lilith_Research_And%20_
Development.php
Research, campaigning and development
project that works on all issues of violence
against women

**Lilleshall** see Sports Centre (Lilleshall
National)

**Limbless Association**
Jubilee House  3 The Drive  Warley Hil
Brentwood  CM13 3FR
Tel: 01277 725 182  or  01277 725 184 or
01277 725 186
enquiries.limblessassociation@yahoo.co.uk
www.limbless-association.org
The charities consortium of users of
disability equipment

**Linguists (Chartered Institute of)**
Saxon House  48 Southwark St  London SE1
1UN
Tel: 020 7940 3100

info@iol.org.uk
www.iol.org.uk
Professional association and examining board for linguists, interpreters, translators, educationists and other professionals for whom a foreign language is a requirement for their daily jobs

**LINK**  Scottish Environment LINK
2 Grosvenor House  Shore Rd  Perth PH2 8BD
Tel: 01738 630804
Email via website
www.scotlink.org
Umbrella organisation providing forum and network for voluntary environmental groups

**Linnean Society of London**
Burlington House  Piccadilly  London W1J 0BF
Tel: 020 7434 4479
info@linnean.org
www.linnean.org
For the study of natural history

**Listening Books**
12 Lant St  London SE1 1QH
Tel: 020 7407 9417
info@listening-books.org.uk
www.listening-books.org.uk
Audio books postal library service for people unable to read in the usual way

**Literacy Association (National)**
87 Grange Road  Ramsgate  Kent CT11 9QB
Tel: 01843 239952
wendy@nla.org.uk
www.nla.org.uk

**Literacy Association (UK)**
4th Floor  Attenborough Building  University of Leicester  LE1 7RH
Tel: 0116 229 7450
admin@ukla.org
www.ukla.org
For teachers, advisers and researchers into literacy education

**Literacy in Primary Education (Centre for)**
Webber St  London SE1 8QW
Tel: 020 7401 3382/3
Tel: 0207 633 0840
info@clpe.co.uk
www.clpe.co.uk

**Literacy Trust (National)**
68 South Lambeth Road  London SW8 1RL
Tel: 020 7587 1842
contact@literacytrust.org.uk
www.literacytrust.org.uk
Works in partnership to enhance literacy standards in the UK

**Live Music Now!**
10 Stratford Place  London W1C 1BA
Tel: 020 7493 3443
email via website
www.livemusicnow.org
Takes live music to those who don't have easy access & offers performance opportunities to young professional musicians

**Live Theatre Company**
27 Broad Chare  Quayside  Newcastle upon Tyne NE1 3DQ
Box Office: 0191 232 1232
Tel: 0191 261 2694 (Admin)
www.live.org.uk

**Liver Trust (British)**
2 Southampton Road  Ringwood  Hampshire BH24 1HY
Helpline: 0800 652 7330
Tel: 01425 481 320
info@britishlivertrust.org.uk
www.britishlivertrust.org.uk
National charity supporting and helping with liver disease

**Living Earth Foundation**
5 Great James Steet  London WC1N 3DB
Tel: 020 7440 9750
info@livingearth.org.uk
www.livingearth.org.uk
Non-membership organisation. International, national and local environmental and community education programmes

**Living Streets**
4th Floor Universal House  88-94 Wentworth Street  London E1 7SA
Tel: 020 7377 4900
info@ livingstreets.org.uk
www.livingstreets.org.uk
Campaigns to achieve safe, pleasant, vibrant & healthy streets for all. Organises Walk to School campaign

**Living Wills** see Dignity in Dying

**Local Authorities (Convention of Scottish)**
Rosebery House  9 Haymarket Terrace Edinburgh EH12 5XZ
Tel: 0131 474 9200
carol@cosla.gov.uk
www.cosla.gov.uk

**Local Economic Strategies (Centre for)**
Express Networks  1 George Leigh St Manchester M4 5DL
Tel: 0161 236 7036
info@cles.org.uk
www.cles.org.uk

## Local Economy Policy Unit
London South Bank University  103 Borough Rd  London SE1 0AA
Tel: 020 7815 7154
lepu@lsbu.ac.uk
www1.lsbu.ac.uk/lepu
Centre for action on local economic development and urban regeneration

## Local Government Association LGA
Local Government House  Smith Sq  London SW1P 3HZ
Tel: 020 7664 3000
info@local.gov.uk
www.lga.gov.uk
For local authorities in England & Wales

## Local Government Information Unit
22 Upper Woburn Place  London WC1H 0TB
Tel: 020 7554 2800
info@lgiu.org.uk
https://member.lgiu.org.uk/Pages/default.aspx

## Local Government Ombudsman (England)
PO Box 4771  Coventry  CV4 0EH
Tel: 0300 061 0614
Tel: 0845 602 1983
advice@lgo.org.uk,
www.lgo.org.uk
Investigates complaints made about maladministration by local authorities in England

## Local History (British Association for)
PO Box 6549  Somersal Herbert  Ashbourne DE6 5WH
Tel: 01283 585947
info@balh.co.uk
www.balh.co.uk

## Logistics and Transport in the UK (Chartered Institute of)
Logistics & Transport Centre  Earlstrees Court  Earlstrees Rd  Corby  Northants NN17 4AX
Tel: 01536 740104
membership@ciltuk.org.uk
www.ciltuk.org.uk

## London Charity Orchestra
info@lco.org.uk
www.londoncharityorchestra.co.uk
Professional musicians, music students and experienced amateurs who help charitable causes

## London Children's Ballet
73 St Charles Square  London W10 6EJ
Tel: 020 8969 1555
info@londonchildrensballet.com
www.londonchildrensballet.com

## London Citizens
112 Cavell Street  London  E1 2JA
Tel: 020 7043 9881
josephine.mukanjira@citizensuk.org.uk
www.londoncitizens.org.uk
Alliance of active citizens and community leaders organising for change

## London Drug & Alcohol Network
c/o DrugScope  Prince Consort House Suite 204  109/111 Farringdon Road  London EC1R 3BW
Tel: 020 7520 7566 or 020 7520 7565
info@ldan.org.uk
www.ldan.org.uk

## London Environment Centre now see Gree Mark

## London Green Belt Council
Tel: 07794 592 924
info@londongreenbeltcouncil.org.uk
http://londongreenbeltcouncil.org.uk

## London Hazards Centre
Hampstead Town Hall Centre  213 Haverstock Hill  London NW3 4QP
Tel: 020 7794 5999
mail@lhc.org.uk
www.lhc.org.uk
Resource centre for Londoners fighting health & safety hazards in the workplace & community

## London Library
14 St James's Square  London SW1Y 4LG
Tel: 020 7930 7705
enquiries@londonlibrary.co.uk
www.londonlibrary.co.uk
Subscription library

## London (Museum of)
150 London Wall  London EC2Y 5HN
Tel: 020 7001 9844
info@museumoflondon.org.uk
www.museumoflondon.org.uk

## London Schools Arts Service
25 King's Terrace  London NW1 0JP
Tel: 020 7387 8882
email via website
www.lonsas.org.uk
Arts projects & partnerships in schools, colleges and education settings

## London Symphony Orchestra LSO
6th Floor  Barbican Centre, Silk Street London EC2Y 8DS
Tel: 020 7588 1116
admin@lso.co.uk
www.lso.co.uk

## London theatres: online
www.officiallondontheatre.co.uk

**London Tourist Board** see Visit London

**London Travel Information**
4th Floor  Zone Y4  14 Pier Walk  North Greenwich  London SE10 0ES
Tel: 0843 222 1234
Tel: 020 7222 5600
enquire@tfl.gov.uk
www.tfl.gov.uk

**London Youth** Federation of London Youth Clubs
47-49 Pitfield Street  London N1 6DA
Tel: 020 7549 8800
hello@londonyouth.org.uk
www.londonyouth.org.uk

**London Zoo**
Zoological Soc. of London  Regents Park London NW1 4RY
Tel: 020 7722 3333
Email via website
www.zsl.org

**London's Transport Museum**
Covent Garden Piazza  London WC2E 7BB
Main switchboard: 020 7379 6344
Tel: 020 7565 7298 (School visits service)
24 hour information: 020 7565 7299
Email via website
www.ltmuseum.co.uk

**Lone Parents** see also Big Brothers & Sisters, Families Need Fathers, Friends United Network, Gingerbread, HELP, One Plus

**Lone Twin Network**
P O Box 5653  Birmingham  B29 7JY
info@lonetwinnetwork.org.uk
www.lonetwinnetwork.org.uk
Offers a network of contacts and support to anyone whose twin has died

**Long Distance Walkers Association**
www.ldwa.org.uk

**Lord Dowding Fund for Humane Research**
Millbank Tower  Millbank  London SW1P 4QP
Tel: 020 7630 3340
email via website
www.ldf.org.uk
Funds and sponsors non-animal research

**Lord's Day Observance Society** now see Day One Christian Ministries

**Lorna Young Foundation**
47 Lea Lane  Netherton  Huddersfield HD4 7DP
projectmanager@lyf.org.uk
www.lyfe.ac
Internationally, the LYF supports smallholder producers in developing countries to build their commercial capacity, shorten supply chains; and create local brands and markets

**Lost Doggies UK**
enquiries@lost-doggies.com
www.lost-doggies.com
Website to report lost or found dogs and to help those wanting to give a home to a rescue dog

**Lottery** see Big Lottery Fund

**Low Pay Commission**
1st Floor  Kingsgate House  66-74 Victoria Street  London SW1E 6SW
Tel: 020 7215 8459
lpc@lowpay.gov.uk
www.lowpay.gov.uk
Independent statutory public body advising the Government on all aspects of the minimum wage

**Lowry** Centre for performing & visual arts
Pier 8, Salford Quays  Manchester M50 3AZ
Tel: 0843 208 6000
Groups: 0843 208 6003
info@thelowry.com
www.thelowry.com

**LSO** see London Symphony Orchestra (LSO)

**Lucy Faithfull Foundation** Working to Protect Children
Bordesley Hall  The Holloway, Alvechurch Birmingham B48 7QA  or Nightingale House 46-48 East Street  Epsom KT17 1HB
Tel: 01527 591922
Tel: 01372 847160
bordesley@lucyfaithfull.org

**Lung Foundation (British)**
73-75 Goswell Road  London EC1V 7ER
Helpline: 08458 50 50 20
Tel: 020 7688 5555
Email via website
www.lunguk.org
Funds research into lung diseases, produces information literature & has support groups

**Lupus UK**
St James House  Eastern Road  Romford Essex RM1 3NH
Tel: 01708 731251
headoffice@lupusuk.org.uk
www.lupusuk.org.uk

# M

## Macmillan Cancer Support
89 Albert Embankment  London SE1 7UQ
Helpline: Ask Macmillan: 0808 808 0000
Tel: 020 7840 7840
email via website
www.macmillan.org.uk

## Mafan Association UK
Rochester House  5 Aldershot Road  Fleet
Hampshire GU51 3NG
Tel: 01252 810472
marfan@tinyonline.co.uk
www.marfan-association.org.uk
Supports sufferers from disorders of the
connective tissue

## Magistrates Association
28 Fitzroy Sq.  London W1T 6DD
Tel: 020 7387 2353
information@magistrates-association.org.uk
www.magistrates-association.org.uk

## Magna: science adventure centre
Sheffield Rd  Templeborough  Rotherham
Yorkshire S60 1DX
Tel: 01709 720002
info@magnatrust.co.uk
www.visitmagna.co.uk

## Mailing Preference Service
DMA House  70 Margaret St  London W1W
8SS
Tel: 020 7291 3310
mps@dma.org.uk
www.mpsonline.org.uk
Allows consumers to remove their names
from mailing lists

## Makaton Vocabulary Development
**Project** MVDP
Manor House  46 London Road  Blackwater
Camberley  Surrey GU17 0AA
Tel: 01276 606760
info@makaton.org
www.makaton.org
Language programme for children and
adults with communication and learning
disabilities

## Make My Vote Count
6 Chancel St  London SE1 0UU
Tel: 020 7928 2076
malcolm@makevotescount.org.uk
www.makemyvotecount.org.uk
Campaigns on changing the way we elect
our MPs

## Making Music National Federation of
Music Societies
2-4 Great Eastern Street  London EC2A
3NW
Tel: 020 7422 8280
info@makingmusic.org.uk
www.makingmusic.org.uk

## Malaria No More UK
33 Ransomes Dock  35-37 Parkgate Road
London SW11 4NP
Tel: 020 7801 3840
info@malarianomore.org.uk
http://malarianomore.org.uk/
Part of a global effort to put an end to the
suffering and death caused by malaria

## MALE (for male victims)
Confidential Helpline: 0808 801 0327
info@mensadviceline.org.uk
www.mensadviceline.org.uk
Advice and support for men in abusive
relationships

## Management (Institute of) see Chartered
Management Institute

## Manchester Museum
University of Manchester  Oxford Rd
Manchester M13 9PL
Tel: 0161 275 2634
museum@manchester.ac.uk
www.museum.manchester.ac.uk

## Manic Depression Fellowship see MDF
The Bipolar Organisation

## ManKind Initiative
Flook House  Belvedere Road  Taunton
Somerset TA1 1BT
Helpline: 01823 334 244
admin@mankind.org.uk
www.mankind.org.uk
Exists to remove discrimination between
men and women

## Mankind UK
P.O.Box 124  Newhaven  East Sussex  BN9
9TQ
Tel: 01273 510447
admin@mankindcounselling.org.uk
www.mankindcounselling.org.uk
Support and resource service for men
who have been sexually abused, sexually
assaulted and/or raped.

## Mapping see Ordnance Survey

## Marathon (Virgin London)
Tel: 020 7902 0200
www.virginlondonmarathon.com

## Marfan Friends World
www.marfan-friends-world.org.uk
Forum for sufferers from disorders of the
connective tissue

## Margaret Pyke Family Planning Centre
73 Charlotte St  London W1T 4PL
Tel: 020 7530 3600 (switchboard)
Tel: 020 7530 3650 appointments
www.margaretpyke.org

Provides advice and treatment on contraception, family planning, HRT, plus pregnancy testing

**Marie Curie Cancer Care**
89 Albert Embankment  London SE1 7TP
Tel: 020 7599 7777
email via website
www.mariecurie.org.uk
Free practical nursing care at home and specialist care at 10 centres. Conducts research into the causes and treatment of cancer

**Marie Stopes International**
Helpline: 0845 300 8090 (24 hours)
Tel: 020 7636 6200
services@mariestopes.org.uk
www.mariestopes.org.uk
Counselling and help with women's sexual health, termination of pregnancy, contraception, sterilisation, vasectomy

**Marine Conservation Society**
Unit 3, Wolf Business Park  Alton Road Ross-on-Wye HR9 5NB
Tel: 01989 566017
email via website
www.mcsuk.org
The UK charity dedicated to the protection of the marine environment and its wildlife

**Marine Leisure Association (MLA)**
Marine House  Thorpe Lea Road Egham
Surrey TW20 8BF
Tel: 0845 366 5499
 info@marineleisure.co.uk
www.marineleisure.co.uk
Learning to sail. Practical and theory courses. Beginners to advanced MCA and RYA qualifications

**Marine Life Rescue** see Divers Marine Life Rescue (British)

**Marine Life Study Society (British)**
Glaucus House  14 Corbyn Cres  Shoreham-by-Sea BN43 6PQ
Tel:  01273 465433
glaucus@hotmail.com
www.glaucus.org.uk

**Marine Society and Sea Cadets**
202 Lambeth Rd  London SE1 7JW
Tel: 020 7654 7000
info@ms-sc.org
www.ms-sc.org

**Marine Stewardship Council**
3rd Floor  Mount Barrow House  6-20 Elizabeth Street  London SW1W 9RB
Tel: 020 7811 3300

Email via website
www.msc.org
Promotes responsible fishing practices

**Maritime & Coastguard Agency**
Spring Place  105 Commercial Rd Southampton SO15 1EG
Tel: 023 8032 9329
Email via website
www.mcga.gov.uk

**Maritime Museum (National)**
Greenwich  London SE10 9NF
Tel: 020 8858 4422
Info Line: 020 8312 6565
Bookings: 020 8312 6608
comments@nmm.ac.uk
www.nmm.ac.uk

**Maritime Trust** see Cutty Sark Trust

**Martial Arts** see thematic guide - Sport & Leisure

**Martial Association (Amateur)**
169 Cotswold Crescent  Walshaw Park  Bury BL8 1QL
Tel: 0161 763 5599
www.amauk.co.uk
National association of martial arts and kickboxing

**Martin Luther King Center**
information@thekingcenter.org
www.thekingcenter.org
Set up in 1968 as a memorial to Dr Martin Luther King Jnr to further his philosophy of non-violence in human relations

**Marx Memorial Library**
37A Clerkenwell Green  London EC1R 0DU
Tel: 020 7253 1485
info@marx-memorial-library.org
www.marx-memorial-library.org
Collection of books about politics, economics and social sciences with a left-wing emphasis

**Mary's Meals**
Craig Lodge  Dalmally  Argyll  PA33 1AR
Tel: 01838 200605
info@marysmeals.org
www.marysmeals.org
An international movement to set up school feeding projects in communities where poverty and hunger prevent children from gaining an education.

**Marylebone Cricket Club** see MCC

**MATCH**  Mothers Apart from Their Children
BM Box No. 6334  London  WC1N 3XX
enquries@matchmothers.org
www.matchmothers.org
For mothers living apart from their children, and those mothers who have little or no contact with their children

**Maternal & Childhealth Advocacy International (MCAI)**
83 Derby Road  Nottingham NG1 5BB
Tel: 0115 950 6662
office@mcai.org.uk
www.mcai.org.uk
Medical aid to children worldwide

**Maternity Services (Association for Improvements in the)** see AIMS

**Mathematical Association**
259 London Rd  Leicester LE2 3BE
Tel: 0116 221 0013
office@m-a.org.uk
www.m-a.org.uk
Long established professional subject association devoted to the needs of classroom mathematics teachers & lecturers

**Mathematics** see also Basic Skills Agency, Innovation in Mathematics Teaching (Centre for), Smile Mathematics, Teachers of Mathematics (Association of)

**Mathematics (Centre for the Popularisation of)**
http://www.popmath.org.uk/centre/index.html

**MAYC** Supporting Youth Work in the Methodist Church
www.mayc.info

**MCC** Marylebone Cricket Club
Lord's Cricket Ground  St John's Wood
London NW8 8QN
Tel: 020 7616 8500
reception@mcc.org.uk
www.lords.org
Guardian of the laws of cricket

**MDF The Bipolar Organisation**
Castle Works  21 St. George's Road  London SE1 6ES
Tel: 020 7793 2600
mdf@mdf.org.uk
www.mdf.org.uk
Provides support for all affected by manic depression

**ME** see also Young People with ME (Association of)

**ME (Action for)**
PO Box 2778  Bristol BS1 9DJ
Tel: 0845 123 2380
Tel: 0117 927 9551
admin@afme.org.uk
www.afme.org.uk
Information and campaigning about ME

**ME Association**
7 Apollo Office Court  Radclive Road  Gawcott  Bucks MK18 4DF
Helpline: 0844 576 5326
Tel: 01280 827070

meconnect@meassociation.org.uk
www.meassociation.org.uk
Organises support groups and provides information

**Meat & Livestock Commission** now see Agriculture and Horticulture Development Board

**Mechanics Centre Ltd.**
Mechanics Institute  103 Princess St  Manchester M1 6DD
Tel: 0161 236 9336
info@mechanicsinstitue.co.uk
Conference/function centre

**Medau** Movement for life
1 Grove House  Foundry Lane  Horsham  West Sussex RH13 5PL
Tel: 01403 266000
medau@emdp.org
www.medau.org.uk
Dance based workout

**Médecins sans Frontières (UK)**
67-74 Saffron Hill  London EC1N 8QX
Tel: 020 7404 6600
office-ldn@london.msf.org
www.msf.org.uk/Default.aspx
International medical aid organisation

**Media Center (Independent)**
www.indymedia.org
Grassroots, non-corporate coverage of world news

**Media for Development**
3rd Floor  Willow House  72-74 Paul Street  London EC2A 4NA
Tel: 020 7033 2170
jonathanw@mediafordevelopment.org.uk
www.mediafordevelopment.org.uk
A media consultancy specialising in the design & implementation of public education campaigns in the developing world and the UK

**Media Trust**
Riverwalk House  157-161 Millbank  London SW1P 4RR
Tel: 020 7217 3717
info@mediatrust.org
www.mediatrust.org
Charity building partnerships between the media & the voluntary sector

**Mediation** see also Family Mediation Scotland

**MediaWise Trust**
University of the West of England  Canon Kitson  Oldbury Court Road  Bristol BS16 2JP
Tel: 0117 93 99 333
info@mediawise.org.uk
www.mediawise.org.uk
Registered charity providing advice, information and training on media matters

## Medical Accidents (Action Against)
44 High Street  Croydon  Surrey CR0 1YB
Helpline: 0845 1232352
www.avma.org.uk
National charity which provides independent advice and support to anyone who has suffered a medical accident

## Medical Advisory Service
info@medicaladvisoryservice.org.uk
www.medicaladvisoryservice.org.uk
Various helplines on different medical matters

## Medical Advisory Services for Travellers Abroad Ltd.
Moorfield Rd  Yeadon  Leeds LS19 7BN
www.masta-travel-health.com

## Medical Aid for Palestinians
33a Islington Park St  London N1 1QB
Tel: 020 7226 4114
info@map-uk.org
www.map-uk.org

## Medical Conditions at School
c/o Asthma UK  Summit House  70 Wilson Street  London EC2A 2DB
Tel: 08456 03 81 43
info@asthma.org.uk
www.medicalconditionsatschool.org.uk
Information to help schools and school healthcare professionals support all pupils with medical conditions

## Medical Emergency Relief International see MERLIN

## Medical Foundation for the Care of Victims of Torture
111 Isledon Road  London N7 7JW
Tel: 020 7697 7777
email via website
www.torturecare.org.uk
Provides help for victims, documentary evidence of torture, training for professionals and education for the public

## Medical Helpline (General)
Helpline: 020 8994 9874
Covers all general medical queries

## Medical Herbalists (National Institute of)
Elm House  54 Mary Arches Street  Exeter EX4 3BA
Tel: 01392 426022
info@nimh.org.uk
www.nimh.org.uk

## Medical Progress (Europeans for) now see Safer Medicines Campaign

## Medical Research Charities (Association of)
61 Gray's Inn Rd  London WC1X 8TL
Tel: 020 7269 8820
Email via website
www.amrc.org.uk

AMRC is a membership organisation that works to advance medical research in the UK and, in particular, aims to improve the effectiveness of the charitable sector in medical research

## Medical Research Council (MRC)
20 Park Crescent  London W1B 1AL
Tel: 020 7636 5422
corporate@headoffice.mrc.ac.uk
www.mrc.ac.uk

## Medical Trust (Britain-Nepal)
130 Vale Rd  Tonbridge  Kent TN9 1SP
Tel: 01732 360 284
info@britainnepalmedicaltrust.org.uk
www.britainnepalmedicaltrust.org.uk
Works on projects within Nepal's own developing health programme

## MedicAlert Foundation
1 Bridge Wharf  156 Caledonian Rd  London N1 9UU
Tel: 0800 581 420
info@medicalert.org.uk
www.medicalert.org.uk
Emergency identification system for people with hidden medical conditions and allergies

## Medicines & Healthcare Products Regulatory Agency
151 Buckingham Palace Road,  Victoria London, SW1W 9SZ
Tel: 020 3080 6000.
info@mhra.gsi.gov.uk
www.mhra.gov.uk
Ensures that all medicines & healthcare products on the UK market meet appropriate standards of safety, quality and efficacy

## Meet A Mum Association
Helpline: 0845 120 3746 (7pm - 10pm Weekdays Only)
www.mama.co.uk
UK registered charity which aims to provide friendship and support to all mothers and mothers-to-be, especially those feeling lonely or isolated after the birth of baby or moving to a new area

## Men's Health Helpline
Helpline: 020 8995 4448

## Men's Morris & Sword Dance Clubs (National Association of)
www.themorrisring.org.uk/

## Mencap
123 Golden Lane  London EC1Y 0RT
Learning Disability Helpline: 0808 808 1111 or mencap Direct: 0300 333 1111
Tel: 020 7454 0454
Typetalk: 18001 0808 808 1111
Text: 07717 989 029
help@mencap.org.uk
www.mencap.org.uk

### & Cymru
31 Lambourne Crescent  Cardiff Business Park  Llanishen  Cardiff    CF14 5GF
helpline.wales@mencap.org.uk

### & Ireland
Segal House  4 Annadale Avenue  Belfast BT7 3JH
Tel: 028 9069 1351
mencapni@mencap.org.uk
www.mencap.org.uk

### Meningitis Research Foundation
Midland Way  Thornbury  Bristol BS35 2BS
Helpline: 080 8800 33 44
Tel: 01454 281 811
info@meningitis.org
www.meningitis.org
Funds scientific research into meningitis & septicaemia, raises awareness of the diseases and supports those affected

### Meningitis Trust
Fern House  Bath Rd  Stroud GL5 3TJ
Freephone: 0800 028 1828
Tel: 01453 768000
info@meningitis-trust.org
www.meningitis-trust.org
Working towards a world that is free from meningitis where those affected by the disease receive quality care and support

### Menopause see Daisy Network

### Mental Health Act Commission now see Care Quality Commission
www.

### Mental Health Foundation
9th Floor, Sea Containers House  20 Upper Ground  London SE1 9QB
Tel: 020 7803 1100
mhf@mhf.org.uk
www.mentalhealth.org.uk
Covers all aspects of mental illness & learning disabilities

### Mental Health (Scottish Association for)
Cumbrae House  15 Carlton Court  Glasgow G5 9JP
SAMH Information Service: 0800 917 34 66
Tel: 0141 568 7000
enquire@samh.org.uk
www.samh.org.uk

### Mental Welfare Commission for Scotland
91 Haymarket Terrace  Edinburgh  EH12 5HE
Freephone: 0800 389 6809
Tel: 0131 313 8777
enquiries@mwcscot.org.uk
www.mwcscot.org.uk
Protects the rights and interests of people with a mental illness or learning disability in Scotland

### Mentoring and Befriending Foundation
First Floor  Charles House  Albert St  Eccles  Manchester M30 0PW
Tel: 0161 787 8600
info@mandbf.org.uk
www.mandbf.org.uk
Provides assistance and support for the development of mentoring

### Mercy Corps
40 Sciennes  Edinburgh EH9 1NJ
Tel: 0131 662 5160
email via website
www.mercycorps.org.uk
To alleviate suffering, poverty and oppression by helping people all over the world

### MERLIN
12th Floor  207 Old Street  London EC1V 9NR
Tel: 020 7014 1600
email via website
www.merlin.org.uk
Provides emergency healthcare to people affected by wars, epidemics and natural disasters

### Mermaids
BM Mermaids  London  WC1N 3XX
Information line: 0208 1234819
mermaids@freeuk.com
www.mermaidsuk.org.uk
Family and individual support for teenagers and children with gender identity issues

### Message Home Helpline (over 18) see also Missing People and Runaway Helpline (under 18)
Freefone: 0800 700 740
messagehome@missingpeople.org.uk
www.missingpeople.org.uk/areyoumissing/message-home/
Helps missing people who feel unable to make direct contact with the people they have left behind, by forwarding a message on their behalf. They will only pass on the message and will not tell the family any other information

### Met Office
FitzRoy Road  Exeter   Devon EX1 3PB
Tel: 0870 900 0100
Tel: 01392 885680
enquiries@metoffice.gov.uk  education@metoffice.gov.uk
www.metoffice.gov.uk
www.metoffice.gov.uk/education
UK's national weather service

### Metabolic Diseases see Climb

### Meteorological Organization (World)
7 bis, avenue de la Paix, Case Postale 2300  CH 1211 Geneva 2   Switzerland
Tel: 00 41 22 730 8111

wmo@wmo.int
www.wmo.int

**Meteorological Society (Royal)**
104 Oxford Rd  Reading RG1 7LL
Tel: 01189 568500
chiefexec@rmets.org
www.rmets.org

**Meteorology** see Met Office

**Methodist Association of Youth Clubs** see MAYC

**Methodist Church**
25 Marylebone Road   London NW1 5JR
Tel: 020 7486 5502
helpdesk@methodistchurch.org.uk
www.methodistchurch.org.uk

**Metropolitan Police**
New Scotland Yard  Broadway  London SW1H 0BG
Tel: 0300 123 1212
Email via website
www.met.police.uk

**Michael Palin Centre** see Stammering Children (Michael Palin Centre for)

**Midi Music Company**
77 Watson's St  Deptford  London SE8 4AU
Tel: 020 8694 6093
theteam@themidimusiccompany.co.uk
www.themidimusiccompany.co.uk
Uses arts to bring groups of young disadvantaged people together. Provides a range of music and midi technology activities

**Midwives Association (Independent)**
PO Box 539  Abingdon  OX14 9DF
Tel: 0845 4600105
information@independentmidwives.org.uk
www.independentmidwives.org.uk
Working outside the NHS to give individualised care to women

**Migraine Action Association**
4th Floor  27 East Street  Leicester LE1 6NB
Tel: 01162758317
Email via website
www.migraine.org.uk
www.migraineadventure.org.uk

**Migraine Trust**
55-56 Russell Square  London WC1B 4HP
Tel: 020 7462 6601
info@migrainetrust.org
www.migrainetrust.org
Patient support and medical research charity providing information and support

**Migration Policy Group**
205 Rue Belliard, Box 1  1040 Brussels  Belgium
Tel: 32 2 230 59 30
info@migpolgroup.com
www.migpolgroup.com

Independent organisation committed to policy development on mobility, migration, diversity, equality and anti-discrimination

**Millennium Seed Bank**
Royal Botanic Gardens, Kew  Wakehurst Place
Ardingly  Haywards Heath  W. Sussex RH17 6TN
Tel: 020 8332 5655
info@kew.org
www.kew.org
Aims to safeguard over 24,000 plant species worldwide & to secure the future of UK native flowering plants

**MIND** (National Association for Mental Health)
15-19 Broadway  London E15 4BQ
Helpline: 08457 660163
Tel: 020 8519 2122
contact@mind.org.uk
www.mind.org.uk
Leading mental health charity in England and Wales

**Mine Action Service (UN)**
www.mineaction.org
Supports planning & co-ordination of global mine action programmes, issues, best practice & technologies

**Mines** see also HALO Trust, Landmines

**Mines Advisory Group** MAG
68 Sackville Street  Manchester M1 3NJ
Tel: 0161 236 4311
info@maginternational.org
www.maginternational.org
Mine clearance & awareness programmes

**Mining Museum (Scottish)**
Lady Victoria Colliery  Newtongrange
Midlothian EH22 4QN
Tel: 0131 663 7519
enquiries@scottishminingmuseum.com
www.scottishminingmuseum.com

**Ministry of Defence** see Defence (Ministry of)

**Minority Rights Group International**
54 Commercial Street  London E1 6LT
Tel: 020 7422 4200
minority.rights@mrgmail.org
www.minorityrights.org
Working to secure the rights of ethnic, linguistic and religious minorities and indigenous peoples worldwide

**Miracles**
PO Box 3003  Littlehampton  West Sussex BN16 1SY
Tel: 01903 775673
miracles@fastnet.co.uk
www.miraclesthecharity.org
Crisis funding to alleviate situations of dire and multiple distress; positive thinking; a listening ear, and practical support for those with nowhere else to turn.

## Miscarriage Association
c/o Clayton Hospital  Northgate  Wakefield
WF1 3JS
Tel: 01924 200 799
Tel: 01924 200795 (admin)
info@miscarriageassociation.org.uk
www.miscarriageassociation.org.uk
Provides support and information on pregnancy
loss

## Missing Children website
www.missingkids.co.uk

## Missing Persons Helpline (National)
284 Upper Richmond Road West  London
SW14 7JE
Helpline: 0500 700 700 (24hr confidential
freefone service)
Tel: 020 8392 4590
info@missingpeople.org.uk
www.missingpeople.org.uk/

## Mobilise
Nat. HQ  Ashwellthorpe  Norwich NR16 1EX
Tel: 01508 489449
enquiries@mobilise.info
www.mobilise.info
To improve independence of disabled people
through better mobility.

## Mobility Information Service
20 Burton Close  Dawley  Telford TF4 2BX
Tel: 01743 340269
mis@nmcuk.freeserve.co.uk
www.mis.org.uk
Service for the disabled

## MoD see Defence (Ministry of)

## Monetary Justice (Christian Council for)
21 Bousfield Rd  London SE14 5TP
Tel: 020 7207 0509
info@ccmj.org
www.ccmj.org
Campaigning for democratic control of the
monetary system

## Money Claim Online
customerservice.mcol@hmcourts-service.gsi.
gov.uk
www.hmcourts-service.gov.uk
Electronic service can be used by individuals,
solicitors, businesses and government
departments to sue for money owing, subject
to conditions

## Moneysavingexpert.com
www.moneysavingexpert.com
Tips on how to save money and get the best
deals

## Mongabay.com
www.mongabay.com
Environmental science and conservation news
sites

## Moniack Mhor Ltd. now see Arvon
Foundation

## Monopolies and Mergers Commission now
see Competition Commission

## MontageWorld now see British Council
Global web-based programme of curriculum
projects, which encourages international
communication between young people

## Montessori Centre International
18 Balderton St  London W1K 6TG
Tel: 020 7493 8300
centre@montessori.org.uk
www.montessori.org.uk
Training college for those wishing to train in the
Montessori method of teaching young children

## Monuments see Public Monuments &
Sculpture Association

## Morris Federation
pres@morrisfed.org.uk
www.morrisfed.org
Association of self-governing Morris clubs

## Mosac
c/o West Greenwich Community & Arts Centre
141 Greenwich High Road  London SE10 8JA
Helpline: 0800 980 1958
Email via website
www.mosac.org.uk
Supports all non-abusing parents and carers
whose children have been sexually abused,
providing advocacy, information and advice,
befriending, counselling, play therapy and
support groups following alleged child sexual
abuse

## Most Wanted
Crimestoppers: 0800 555 111
http://wanted.crimestoppers-uk.org
Website aimed at tracking Britain's most
wanted crime suspects

## Mothers see also Full Time Mothers, MATCH

## Mothers Union
Mary Sumner House  24 Tufton St  London
SW1P 3RB
Tel: 020 7222 5533
mu@themothersunion.org
www.themothersunion.org

## Motor Manufacturers & Traders Ltd.
## (Society of)
Forbes House  Halkin St  London SW1X 7DS
Tel: 020 7235 7000
Email via website
www.smmt.co.uk
Encouraging and promoting in the UK and
abroad, the interests of the motor industry

## Motor Neurone Disease Association
PO Box 246  Northampton NN1 2PR
Helpline: 08457 626262

Tel: 01604 250505
enquiries@mndassociation.org
www.mndassociation.org
Provides support and advice to people affected
by Motor Neurone Disease and funds research

**Motorvations Project**
13-14 Maldon Road  Romford  Essex  RM7 0JB
Tel: 01708 723733
Motorvations@mail.com
www.haveringmotorvations.com
To engage young people in motor vehicle and
related activities  to enable them to break the
cycle of social exclusion

**Mountain Leader Training England**
Siabod Cottage  Capel Curig  Conwy LL24
0ES
Tel: 01690 720314
info@mlte.org
www.mlte.org
Administers the training programme and
qualifications for leaders of groups hill walking
and rock climbing in mountainous country

**Mountaineering Council (British)**
The Old Church  177-179 Burton Rd
Manchester M20 2BB
Tel: 0161 445 6111
office@thebmc.co.uk
www.thebmc.co.uk
Governing body for sport of mountaineering in
Britain

**Mountaineering Council of Scotland**
The Old Granary  West Mill St  Perth PH1 5QP
Tel: 01738 493942
info@mcofs.org.uk
www.mcofs.org.uk
Representative body for mountaineers and
walkers

**Mousetrap Theatre Projects**
23-24 Henrietta Street  Covent Garden  London
WC2E 8ND
Tel: 020 7836 4388
info@mousetrap.org.uk
www.mousetrap.org.uk
Charity dedicated to creating theatre access
and education programme for young people
with limited resources or support

**Mouth Cancer Foundation**
Helpline: 01924 950 950
info@mouthcancerfoundation.org
www.mouthcancerfoundation.org

**Movie Review Query Engine**
info@mrqe.com
www.mrqe.com
Allows access to reviews of over 30,000 film
titles

**MRC** see Medical Research Council

**MS** see Multiple Sclerosis

**Multimap**
www.multimap.com
Street map of any postcode address in UK,
London tube map, information

**Multiple Births** see also Twins & Multiple
Births Association

**Multiple Births Foundation**
Hammersmith House Level 4  Queen
Charlotte's and Chelsea Hospital  Du Cane Rd
London W12 0HS
Tel: 020 3313 3519
mbf@imperial.nhs.uk
www.multiplebirths.org.uk

**Multiple Sclerosis Society**
MS National Centre  372 Edgware Rd  London
NW2 6ND
Helpline: 0808 800 8000
Tel: 020 8438 0700
Email via website
www.mssociety.org.uk

**Multiple Sclerosis Therapy Centres
(Federation of)**
PO Box 126  Whitchurch SY14 7WL
Tel: 0845 3670977
info@msntc.org.uk
www.msntc.org.uk

**Multiple Sclerosis Trust**
Spirella Building  Bridge Road  Letchworth
Garden City  Herts SG6 4ET
Free Phone Information Service: 0800 032
38 39
Tel: 01462 476700
info@mstrust.org.uk
www.mstrust.org.uk

**Mumsnet**
contactus@mumsnet.com
www.mumsnet.com
Product reviews and parenting advice given
by parents

**Murder** see SAMM

**Muscular Dystrophy Campaign**
61 Southwark Street  London SE1 0HL
Tel: 0800 652 6352 (freephone)
Tel: 020 7803 4800
info@muscular-dystrophy.org
www.muscular-dystrophy.org
Provides support and information

**Musculoskeletal Medicine (British Institute
of)**
PO Box 1116  Bushey  Herts WD23 9BY
Tel: 020 8421 9910
deena@bimm.org.uk
www.bimm.org.uk

**Museum Net**
www.museums.co.uk
Search for museums throughout the UK by
keyword or name

**Museums (International Council of)** ICOM
Secretariat
> Maison de l'UNESCO 1, rue Miollis 75732
> Paris Cedex 15
> Tel: 00 33 1 47 34 05 00
> secretariat@icom.museum
> http://icom.museum

**Museums, Libraries & Archives Council**
> 14 Bennetts Hill Birmingham B2 5RS
> Tel: 0121 345 7300
> info@mla.gov.uk
> www.mla.gov.uk
> October 2010: the body will be abolished and
> its functions transferred

**Music and the Deaf**
> 7 Northumberland St Huddersfield HD1 1RL
> Tel: 01484 483115
> Textphone: 01484 483 117
> email via website
> www.matd.org.uk
> Helping deaf people access music and the
> performing arts through workshops, schools
> projects & signed theatre performances

**Music Council (National)**
> 60/62 Clapham Rd London SW9 0JJ
> Tel: 020 7422 8297
> info@nationalmusiccouncil.org.uk
> www.nationalmusiccouncil.org.uk

**Music Educators (National Association of)**
NAME
> www.name.org.uk
> Supports its members in development of
> highest quality music education accessible
> to all

**Music for Youth**
> 3rd Floor, South Wing Somerset House
> Strand London WC2R 1LA
> Tel: 020 7759 1830
> mfy@mfy.org.uk
> www.mfy.org.uk
> Organises the National Festival of Music
> for Youth, Regional Festivals and the
> Schools Proms and promotes performance
> opportunities for young people.

**Music Information Centre (British)** now see
Sound and Music

**Music Publishers Association**
> 6th Floor British Music House 26 Berners
> Street London W1T 3LR
> Tel: 020 7580 0126
> info@mpaonline.org.uk
> www.mpaonline.org.uk
> Trade Association supporting UK based music
> publishers

**Music (Royal Academy of)** see Royal
Academy of Music

**Music Societies (National Federation Of)**
see Making Music

**Music Therapy (British Society for)**
> 24-27 White Lion Street London N1 9PD
> Tel: 020 7837 6100
> info@bsmt.org
> www.bsmt.org
> Aims to promote use and development of
> music therapy

**Musicians (Incorporated Society of)**
> 10 Stratford Place London W1C 1AA
> Tel: 020 7629 4413
> membership@ism.org
> www.ism.org
> Professional body for musicians

**Musicians Union**
> 33 Palfrey Place London SW8 1PE
> Tel: 020 7582 5566
> info@theMU.org
> www.musiciansunion.org.uk
> Trade Union for professional musicians

**Muslim Schools UK (Association of)**
> PO Box 14109 Birmingham B6 9BN
> Tel: 0844 482 0407
> email via website
> www.ams-uk.org
> Supports & develops excellence in full-time
> Muslim schools & acts as a voice for Islamic
> education with government bodies & the
> media. Gives advice to new Muslim schools

**Muslim Welfare House**
> 233 Seven Sisters Rd Finsbury Park London
> N4 2DA
> Tel: 020 7263 3071
> info@mwht.org.uk
> www.mwht.org.uk
> Provides marriage counselling, courses in
> English for Speakers of Other Languages, IT,
> crafts, careers, business advice, out of school
> care for children for whole community

**Muslim Women's Helpline**
> Helplines: 020 8904 8193
> Provides a confidential telephone counselling
> service, support and advice

**My Supermarket**
> www.mysupermarket.co.uk
> Supermarket price comparison website

**Myalgic Encephalomyelitis** see also ME
(Action for), ME Association, Young People
with ME (Association of)

**MyBnk** My money, our future
> MyBnk @ Unit 4 Huguenot Place, Heneage
> Street, London, E1 5LN
> Tel: 020 7377 8770

info@mybnk.org
www.mybnk.org
Provides young people with the skills to manage their money effectively.

**Mycological Society (British)**
City View House  5 Union Street,  Ardwick, Manchester,  M12 4JD
Tel: 0161 277 7638 / 7639
admin@britmycolsoc.info
www.britmycolsoc.org.uk
Promotes study of fungi in all its aspects

# N

**NAACE** National Association of Advisers for Computers in Education
PO Box 6511  Nottingham NG11 8TN
Tel: 0870 240 0480
office@naace.co.uk
www.naace.co.uk
Advancing education through ICT

**NAAR** see Racism (National Assembly Against)

**NABSS** National Association of Black Supplementary Schools
PO Box 59330  London NW8 1DY
Tel: 07958 348 558
info@nabss.org.uk
Central resource for parents, helpers and members of the Afrikan/Caribbean community to find help with their children's education in their locality

**Nacro** The Crime Reduction Charity
Park Place  10-12 Lawn Lane  London SW8 1UD
Tel: 020 7840 7200
Email via website
www.nacro.org.uk/
Runs crime reduction projects including housing, training, prison projects and youth work

**NAME** see Music Educators (National Association of)

**NAN (National Advocacy Network)** see ARX Advocacy Resource Exchange

**NAPS** see Premenstrual Syndrome (National Association for)

**Narcolepsy Association UK (UKAN)**
PO Box 13842  Penicuik EH26 8WX
Tel: 0845 4500 394
info@narcolepsy.org.uk
www.narcolepsy.org.uk
Narcolepsy causes excessive daytime sleepiness and attacks of paralysis

**Narcotics Anonymous UK**
Helpline: 0300 999 1212
ukso@ukna.org
www.ukna.org
A fellowship of recovering addicts who meet regularly to help each other stay clean

**NATE** see Teaching of English (National Association for the)

**National Advocacy Network** see ARX Advocacy Resource Exchange

**National Archives**
Kew  Richmond TW9 4DU
Tel: 020 8876 3444
email via website
www.nationalarchives.gov.uk
UK national archives with records from 11th century to today. Visits are available for schools and further education

**National Archives of Scotland (NAS)**
HM General Register House  2 Princes St Edinburgh EH1 3YY
Tel: 0131 535 1314
enquiries@nas.gov.uk
www.nas.gov.uk

**National Childbirth Trust** NCT
Alexandra House  Oldham Terrace  London W3 6NH
Tel: 0300 3300 770
email via website
www.nct.org.uk
Information & support for all pregnant women & parents of young children

**National Churches Trust**
31 Newbury Street  London EC1A 7HU
Tel: 0207 600 6090
info@nationalchurchestrust.org
www.nationalchurchestrust.org

**National Debtline**
Tricorn House  51-53 Hagley Road  Edgbaston Birmingham B16 8TP
Helpline: 0808 808 4000
Email via website
www.nationaldebtline.co.uk
National telephone helpline for people with debt problems in England, Wales & Scotland. Free, confidential, independent

**National Energy Action**
St Andrew's House  90-92 Pilgrim St Newcastle-upon-Tyne NE1 6SG
Tel: 0191 261 5677
info@nea.org.uk
www.nea.org.uk
Develops and promotes energy efficiency to tackle the heating and insulation problems of low income households

### National Extension College
Michael Young Centre  Purbeck Rd  Cambridge CB2 8HN
Customer Relations: 0800 389 2839
Tel: 01223 400200
info@nec.ac.uk
www.nec.ac.uk
Specialises in distance learning courses, training materials, open learning packs, open and distance learning consultancy services

### National Forest Company
Enterprise Glade  Bath Yard  Moira Swadlincote  Derbyshire  DE12 6BA.
01283 55121
enquiries@nationalforest.org
www.nationalforest.org
A project, blending new and maturing woodland,  transforming 200 square miles of central England

### National Foundation for Educational Research see NFER

### National Gallery
Trafalgar Square   London WC2N 5DN
Tel: 020 7747 2885
Education: 020 7747 2424
information@ng-london.org.uk
www.nationalgallery.org.uk

### National Gallery of Scotland
The Mound  Edinburgh EH2 2EL
Tel: 0131 624 6200
Education: 0131 624 6410
enquiries@nationalgalleries.org
www.nationalgalleries.org

### National Institute for Health and Clinical Excellence NICE
MidCity Place  71 High Holborn  London WC1V 6NA
Tel: 0845 003 7780
nice@nice.org.uk
www.nice.org.uk

### National Libraries (Friends of the)
c/o Dept of Manuscripts  The British Library  96 Euston Rd  London NW1 2DB
Tel: 020 7412 7559
secretary@fnlmail.org.uk
www.friendsofnationallibraries.org.uk
Gives grants to libraries, record offices etc for rare books and manuscripts and archival acquisitions

### National Library of Scotland
George IV Bridge  Edinburgh EH1 1EW
Tel: 0131 623 3700
enquiries@nls.uk
www.nls.uk

### National Library of Wales
Aberystwyth  Ceredigion SY23 3BU
Tel: 01970 632 800

Email via website
www.llgc.org.uk

### National Media Museum
Bradford   West Yorkshire BD1 1NQ
Tel: 0844 856 3797(General & Box Office)
Groups & schools: 0844 856 3799
www.nationalmediamuseum.org.uk

### National Museum and Gallery Cardiff
Cathays Park  Cardiff CF10 3NP
Tel: 029 2039 7951
Email via website
www.museumwales.ac.uk

### National Museum of Labour History see People's History Museum

### National Opera Studio
The Clore Building  2 Chapel Yard  Wandsworth High Street   London SW18 4HZ
Tel: 020 8874 8811
info@nationaloperastudio.org.uk
www.nationaloperastudio.org.uk

### National Parks (Campaign for)
6-7 Barnard Mews  London SW11 1QU
Tel: 020 7924 4077
info@cnp.org.uk
www.cnp.org.uk
Campaigning environmental charity

### National Portrait Gallery
St Martin's Place  London WC2H 0HE
Tel: 020 7306 0055
www.npg.org.uk

### National Society for the Prevention of Cruelty to Children see NSPCC

### National Theatre
South Bank  London SE1 9PX
Tel: 020 7452 3000 (Box Office)
Tel: 020 7452 3400 (Info Desk)
info@nationaltheatre.org.uk
www.nationaltheatre.org.uk

### National Tidal and Sea Level Facility
Proudman Oceanographic Laboratory  Joseph Proudman Building  6 Brownlow Street Liverpool   L3 5DA
Tel: 0151 795 4800
Email via website
www.pol.ac.uk/ntslf/
Tidal predictions for selected UK and Irish ports

### National Trust
PO Box 39  Warrington WA5 7WD
Tel: 0844 800 1895
Minicom: 0844 800 4410
enquiries@nationaltrust.org.uk
www.nationaltrust.org.uk

### National Trust for Ireland  see An Taisce

### National Trust for Scotland
Wemyss House  28 Charlotte Sq  Edinburgh EH2 4ET

Tel: 0844 493 2100
information@nts.org.uk
www.nts.org.uk
Conservation charity that protects and
promotes Scotland's natural and cultural
heritage

**National Trust Holiday Cottages**
PO Box 536  Melksham SN12 8SX
Tel: 0844 8002070 (Booking Line)
cottages@nationaltrust.org.uk
www.nationaltrustcottages.co.uk

**National Trust Volunteering**
National Trust Central Volunteering Team  Heelis
Kemble Drive  Swindon  SN2 2NA
Tel: 01793 817632
volunteers@nationaltrust.org.uk
www.nationaltrust.org.uk/main/w-trust/w-
volunteering.htm

**National Trust Working Holidays**
Tel: 01793 817 637 (Working Holidays Team)
working.holidays@nationaltrust.org.uk
www.nationaltrust.org.uk/main/w-trust/w-
volunteering/w-workingholidays.htm
Working holidays in beautiful locations
undertaking countryside conservation (min.
age 18)

**National Union of Students** see NUS

**National Youth Ballet**
The Old Dairy  Wintersell Farm  Dwelly Lane
Edenbridge TN8 6QD
info@nyb.org.uk
www.nyb.org.uk
An amateur ballet company for young people
of 8-18 years

**Natural Death Centre**
In The Hill House  Watley Lane  Twyford
Winchester  SO21 1QX
Tel: 01962 712 690
contact@naturaldeath.org.uk
www.naturaldeath.org.uk
Info on green, inexpensive, DIY & woodland
funerals and living wills

**Natural England**
Northminster House  Peterborough  PE1 1UA
Tel: 0845 600 3078
enquiries@naturalengland.org.uk
www.naturalengland.gov.uk
Working for people, places and nature now and
in the future. October 2010: Organisation will be
retained but will be substantially changed.

**Natural Environment Research Council**
Polaris House  North Star Ave  Swindon SN2
1EU
Tel: 01793 411500
www.nerc.ac.uk

**Natural Heritage (Scottish)**
Great Glen House  Leachkin Road  Inverness

IV3 8NW
Tel: 01463 725000
enquiries@snh.gov.uk
www.snh.gov.uk
Concerned with all environmental issues in
Scotland

**Natural History Museum**
Cromwell Road  South Kensington  London
SW7 5BD
Tel: 020 7942 5000
Tel: 020 7942 5555 (Group Bookings)
email via website www.nhm.ac.uk

**Natural Voice**
Tel: 01923 444440
admin@naturalvoice.net
www.naturalvoice.net
Umbrella organisation for local singing groups
that aim to recreate the sense that singing is
natural and open to all

**Naturewatch** Campaigning Against Animal
Cruelty
14 Hewlett Road  Cheltenham GL52 6AA
Tel: 01242 252871
info@naturewatch.org
www.naturewatch.org
Campaigns for vital changes in the law to help
stop animal abuse

**Navigation (Royal Institute of)**
1 Kensington Gore  London SW7 2AT
Tel: 020 7591 3130
info@rin.org.uk
www.rin.org.uk
To unite in one body those interested in the
science and art of navigation

**Navy (US)**
www.navy.mil
Official information site

**NAWE** see Writers in Education (National
Association of )

**NBCS** National Blind Children's Society
Bradbury House  Market Street  Highbridge
Somerset  TA9 3BW
Freephone: 0800 781 1444 (Family Support and
Information)
Tel: 01278 764764
enquiries@nbcs.org.uk
www.nbcs.org.uk

**NCB** see Children's Bureau (National)

**NCDL** see Dogs Trust

**NCDT** see Drama Training (National Council
for)

**NCF** see Sports Coach UK

**NCH (National Children's Homes)** now see
Action for Children

**NCT** see National Childbirth Trust

**NDT** see People with Learning Disabilities (National Development Team for)

**need2know**
www.need2know.co.uk
Advice on Relationships, Student Life, Money Troubles, Travel and Leisure, plus a wide range of tips and resources

**Neonatal Death** see Stillbirth & Neonatal Death Society

**NESTA** see Science, Technology & the Arts (National Endowment for)

**Net House Prices**
www.nethouseprices.com
Access to the latest house prices for England, Scotland and Wales

**Netball Association (All England)** AENA
Netball House  9 Paynes Park  Hitchin SG5 1EH
Tel: 01462 442344
info@englandnetball.co.uk
www.englandnetball.co.uk

**Netdoctor**
www.netdoctor.co.uk
Online health advice

**Network '81**
1-7 Woodfield Terrace  Stansted  Essex CM24 8AJ
Helpline: 0845 077 4055
Tel: (admin) 0845 077 4056
info@network81.org
www.network81.org
For parents of children with special educational needs

**Neurofibromatosis Association**
Quayside House  38 High Street  Kingston on Thames  Surrey KT1 1HL
Helpline 0845 602 4173
Tel: 020 8439 1234
info@nfauk.org
www.nfauk.org
Provides help, support and advice to those affected, their families and the professionals working with them

**New Bridge**
27a Medway Street  London SW1P 2BD
Tel: 020 7976 0779
info@newbridgefoundation.org.uk
www.newbridgefoundation.org.uk
Befriending service for prisoners (prison visiting and writing) & resettlement service

**New Economics Foundation**
3 Jonathan St  London SE11 5NH
Tel: 020 7820 6300
info@neweconomics.org
www.neweconomics.org
NEF works to put people and the environment at the centre of economic thinking

**New Internationalist**
www.newint.org
New Internationalist Publications is a communications co-operative. It exists to report on issues of world poverty and inequality. Publishes New Internationalist magazine, films, books and other materials

**New Music (Society for the Promotion of)** now see Sound and Music

**New Opportunities Fund** now see Big Lottery Fund

**Newlife Foundation for Disabled Children**
Newlife Centre  Hemlock Way  Cannock Staffordshire, WS11 7GF
Tel: 01543 462 777
info@newlifecharity.co.uk
www.newlifecharity.co.uk

**Newspaper Library (British Library)**
http://newspapers.bl.uk/blcs/
UK National Newspaper Archive. Only available to over 18 years with proof of I.D.

**NFER** National Foundation for Educational Research
The Mere  Upton Park  Slough SL1 2DQ
Tel: 01753 574123
enquiries@nfer.ac.uk
www.nfer.ac.uk
Independent educational research body

**NHS Careers**
Tel: 0345 60 60 655
Email via website
www.nhscareers.nhs.uk/

**NHS Confederation**
29 Bressenden place  London SW1E 5DD
Tel: 020 7074 3200
enquiries@nhsconfed.org
www.nhsconfed.org
Dedicated to improving health policy and practice

**NHS Direct**
Helpline: 0845 4647
www.nhsdirect.nhs.uk
Helpline provides direct contact with a trained nurse

**NHS Health Scotland**
Woodburn House  54 Canaan Ln  Edinburgh EH10 4SG
Tel: 0131 536 5500
Textphone: 0131 536 5503
nhs.healthscotland-generalenquiries@nhs.net
www.healthscotland.com

**NHS Support Federation**
info@nhscampaign.org.uk
www.nhscampaign.org
A campaign by NHS staff and the public to ensure the survival of a comprehensive and adequately funded NHS

**NIACE** Adult Continuing Education (National Institute of)

    20 Princess Rd West  Leicester LE1 6TP

    Tel: 0116 204 4200/1

    enquiries@niace.org.uk

    www.niace.org.uk

**Nicaragua Solidarity Campaign**

    86 Durham Road  London N7 7DT

    Tel: 020 7561 4836

    nsc@nicaraguasc.org.uk

    www.nicaraguasc.org.uk

**Nil by Mouth**

    c/o SCVO  3rd Floor, Centrum Offices  38 Queen Street  Glasgow G1 3DX

    Tel: 0141 225 8008

    mail@nilbymouth.org

    www.nilbymouth.org

    Campaign against sectarianism in Scotland

**NIPPA** now see Early Years

**No candidate deserves my vote**

    8 Belmont Court  Belmont Hill  St Albans AL1 1RB

    Tel: 01727 847370

    admin@nocandidate.org.uk

    www.nocandidate.org.uk

    Political party whose presence on a ballot paper allows voters to abstain positively

**No Panic**

    93 Brands Farm Way  Telford  Shropshire England TF3 2JQ

    Helpline: Freephone 0808 808 0545

    Tel: 01952 590005

    ceo@nopanic.org.uk

    www.nopanic.org.uk

    Help on panic attacks, phobias & obsessive/compulsive disorders

**No Sweat**

    5 Caledonian Road  London N1 9DX

    Tel: 07904 431959

    admin@nosweat.org.uk

    www.nosweat.org.uk

    Campaigning against sweatshop bosses, in solidarity with workers, worldwide

**NOAH** National Organization for Albinism and Hypopigmentation

    www.albinism.org

    Volunteer self-help organisation for research and education. It does not diagnose, treat or provide genetic counselling

**Nobel Internet Archive**

    www.almaz.com/nobel/peace/

    List of prizewinners

**NODA** National Operatic & Dramatic Association

    58-60 Lincoln Rd  Peterborough PE1 2RZ

    Tel: 01733 865 790

    info@noda.org.uk

    www.noda.org.uk

**Noise Abatement Society**

    Suite 2  26 Brunswick Terrace  Brighton East Sussex  BN3 1HJ

    Tel: 01273 823850

    info@noise-abatement.org

    www.noiseabatementsociety.com

**Nominet UK**

    nominet@nominet.org.uk

    www.nominet.org.uk

    National registry of all Internet Domain Names ending in .uk

**Non-smokers** see also Cleanair, QUIT

**NORCAP - Supporting Adults Affected by Adoption**

    112 Church Rd  Wheatley  Oxon OX33 1LU

    Tel: 01865 875000

    enquiries@norcap.org.uk

    www.norcap.org.uk

**North of England Open Air Museum** see Beamish

**Northern Ballet**

    Quarry Hill  Leeds  LS2 7PA

    Tel: 0113 220 8000

    info@northernballet.com

    http://northernballet.com

    Professional touring ballet company with the most widespread touring programme of any UK company

**Northern Broadsides**

    Dean Clough  Halifax HX3 5AX

    Tel: 01422 369704

    www.northern-broadsides.co.uk

    National touring theatre company presenting classic texts

**Northern Ireland Environment Link**

    89 Loopland Drive  Belfast  BT6 9DW

    Tel: 02890 455770

    iona@nienvironmentlink.org

    www.nienvironmentlink.org

**Northern Ireland Executive**

    Stormont Castle  Stormont Estate  Belfast BT4 3TT

    Tel: 028 9052 8400

    www.northernireland.gov.uk

**Northern Ireland Office**

    Stormont House  Stormont Estate  Belfast Northern Ireland  BT4 3SH

    Tel: 028 9052 0700

    Email via website

    www.nio.gov.uk

**Northern Ireland Ombudsman**

    Progressive House  33 Wellington Pl.  Belfast BT1 6HN  OR write to: The Ombudsman Freepost BEL1478  Belfast BT1 6BR

Helpline: 0800 343424
Tel: 028 9023 3821
ombudsman@ni-ombudsman.org.uk
www.ni-ombudsman.org.uk

**Northern Stage**
Barras Bridge  Newcastle upon Tyne NE1 7RH
Tel: 0191 230 5151 (Box Office)
info@northernstage.co.uk
www.northernstage.co.uk
Producing theatre company

**Norwood** Children and Families First
Broadway House  80-82 The Broadway
Stanmore  Middlesex  HA7 4HB
Tel: 020 8954 4555
Tel: 020 8954 4555
info@norwood.org.uk
www.norwood.org.uk
Services to children and their families facing
social difficulties and children and adults with
learning disabilities

**NSPCC** National Society for the Prevention of
Cruelty to Children
Weston House  42 Curtain Rd  London EC2A
3NH
Helpline: 0808 800 5000
Tel: 020 7825 2500
Textphone:  0800 056 0566
Childline: 0800 1111
info@nspcc.org.uk
www.nspcc.org.uk

**NSPCC Asian Child Protection**
Tel: 0800 096 7719
Counselling, information and advice on child
protection matters for the Asian community

**Nuclear Disarmament** see CND

**Nuclear Tourist**
www.nucleartourist.com
Independent website on nuclear power &
nuclear power stations

**Nursing & Midwifery Council**
23 Portland Place  London W1B 1PZ
Tel: 020 7333 9333
communications@nmc-uk.org
www.nmc-uk.org

**NUS** National Union of Students
4th Floor  184-192 Drummond Street  London
NW1 3HP
Tel: 0207 380 6600
Text phone: 0207 380 6600
www.nus.org.uk

**& Wales**
13 Lambourne Crescent  Cardiff Business Park
Llanishen CF14 5GF
Tel: 029 2068 0070
office@nus-wales.org.uk

**& Ireland**
42 Dublin Road  Belfast  BT2 7HN
Tel: 028 9024 4641
Textphone: 028 9032 4878
info@nistudents.org

**& Scotland**
29 Forth Street  Edinburgh  EH1 3LE
Tel: 0131 556 6598
mail@nus-scotland.org.uk

**Nutrition Foundation (British)**
High Holborn House  52-54 High Holborn
London WC1V 6RQ
Tel: 020 7404 6504
postbox@nutrition.org.uk
www.nutrition.org.uk

**Nutrition Society**
10 Cambridge Court  210 Shepherds Bush
Road  London  W6 7NJ
Tel: 0207 602 0228
office@nutsoc.org.uk
www.nutritionsociety.org
Aims to advance the scientific study of nutrition
and its application to the maintenance of
human and animal health

**NWR** see Women's Register (National)

**NYAS** see Youth Advocacy Service (National)

**OASIS** Overseas Adoption Support and
Information Service
Helpline: 0870 241 7069
email via website
www.adoptionoverseas.org
For people who want to adopt children from
orphanages abroad

**Obesity** see also International Association for
the Study of Obesity

**Obesity Forum (National)**
First Floor  6a Gordon Road  Nottingham  NG2
5LN
Tel: 0115 846 2109
info@nof.uk.com
Raises awareness of the growing impact of
obesity and being overweight on patients and
our National Health Service

**Obesity (International Association for
the Study of) & Obesity TaskForce
(International)** IASO & IOTF
28 Portland Place  London     W1B 1LY
Tel: 020 7467 9610
enquiries@iaso.org
www.iaso.org
Works with WHO to alert the world to the
growing problem of obesity

### Occupational Hygiene Society (British)
5-6 Melbourne Business Court  Millennium Way
Pride Park  Derby  DE24 8LZ
Tel: 01332 298101
admin@bohs.org
www.bohs.org

### Occupational Safety & Health (Institution of) IOSH
The Grange  Highfield Drive  Wigston  Leics
LE18 1NN
Tel: 0116 257 3100
Email via website
www.iosh.co.uk
Professional body

### OCD Action
Suite 506-509  Davina House  137-149 Goswell
Road  London EC1V 7ET
Helpline: 0845 390 6232
Tel: 020 7253 5272 (Office)
Tel: 020 7253 2664
support@ocdaction.org.uk
www.ocdaction.org.uk
Promoting recovery from obsessive compulsive
disorders

### Ocean Mammal Institute
PO Box 14422  Reading  PA 19612  USA
Tel: 00 1 610 670 7386
operations@oceanmammalinst.org
www.oceanmammalinst.com

### Ocean Youth Trust
www.oyt.org.uk
Offshore sail training

### OCR/Oxford Cambridge and RSA Examinations
1 Hills Road  Cambridge CB1 2EU
Tel: 01223 553311
info@cambridgeassessment.org.uk
www.cambridgeassessment.org.uk

### ODL QC see Open & Distance Learning Quality Council

### OFCOM
Riverside House  2A Southwark Bridge Rd
London SE1 9HA
Tel: 020 7981 3040
Switchboard: 0300 123 3000 or 020 7981 3000
www.ofcom.org.uk/
Regulator of UK communication
Industries encompassing television, radio,
telecommunications & wireless communication
services. October 2010: Ofcom will absorb the
postal regulator Postcomm. several Ofcom
duties will be removed or modified

### Offenders see UNLOCK, Nacro, SACRO

### Office for National Statistics ONS
Room 1.101  Government Buildings  Cardiff
Road  Newport  South Wales NP10 8XG
Tel: 0845 601 3034

info@statistics.gov.uk
www.statistics.gov.uk/default.asp

### Office of Government Commerce
Rosebery Court  St Andrew's Business Park
Norwich  NR7 0HS
Tel: 0845 000 4999
ServiceDesk@ogc.gsi.gov.uk
www.ogc.gov.uk
Government agency with wide-ranging
programme to modernise government
purchasing and deliver value for money
improvements.

### Office of the Public Guardian
PO Box 15118  Birmingham B16 6GX
Tel: 0300 456 0300
customerservices@publicguardian.gsi.gov.uk
www.publicguardian.gov.uk
Supports and promotes decision making for
those who lack capacity or would like to plan
for their future

### Official Residences of the Queen now see
The British Monarchy (The official website of)

### OFGEM see Gas & Electricity Markets (Office of)

### Ofqual Office of Qualifications and
Examinations Regulation
Spring Place  Coventry Business Park  Herald
Avenue  Coventry  CV5 6UB
Helpline: 0300 303 3346
0300 303 3344
Textphone: 0300 303 3345
info@ofqual.gov.uk
/www.ofqual.gov.uk
Regulates general and vocational qualifications
in England and vocational qualifications in
Northern Ireland.

### OFSTED Office for Standards in Education
Royal Exchange Buildings  St. Ann's Square
Manchester M2 7LA
tel: 0300 123 4234 about education or adult
skills
enquiries@ofsted.gov.uk
www.ofsted.gov.uk
Inspection of schools, local education
authorities, teacher training institutions and
youth work and registration of early years
childcare

### OFWAT see Water Services (Office of)

### Old Bailey, London (Proceedings of) 1674 to 1834
www.oldbaileyonline.org
Accounts of over 100,000 criminal trials held at
London's central criminal court

### Olympic Association (British)
60 Charlotte Street  London W1T 2NU
Tel: 0207 842 5700

boa@boa.org.uk
www.olympics.org.uk

**Olympic Committee (International)** see
International Olympic Committee

**Ombudsman** Public Services Ombudsman
for Wales
1 Ffordd yr Hen Gae  Pencoed CF35 5LJ
Tel: 01656 641 150
ask@ombudsman-wales.org.uk
www.ombudsman-wales.org.uk

**Ombudsman Association (British & Irish)**
BIOA
PO Box 308  Twickenham  London TW1 9BE
Tel: 020 8894 9272
secretary@bioa.org.uk
www.bioa.org.uk
The website lists the ombudsmen and other
complaint-handling bodies

**ONE International**
www.one.org
Aims to raise awareness about, and spark
response to the crises swamping Africa:
unpayable Debts, uncontrolled spread of AIDS,
and unfair Trade rules which keep Africans poor

**One Parent Families** see Big Brothers &
Sisters, Families Need Fathers, Friends United
Network, Gingerbread, HELP, One Plus

**One World Action**
Bradley's Close  74-77 White Lion St.  London
N1 9PF
Tel: 020 7833 4075
info@oneworldaction.org
www.oneworldaction.org
Works to combat poverty and to promote
democracy and human rights in Africa, Asia
and Central America

**Onekind**
10 Queensferry St  Edinburgh EH2 4PG
Tel: 0131 225 6039
email via website
www.onekind.org
Campaigns against all animal abuse

**Online National Register of
Hypnotherapists** see Hypnotherapists (Online
National Register of)

**ONS** see Office for National Statistics

**Open College of the Arts**
Michael Young Arts Centre  Redbrook Business
Park  Wilthorpe Rd  Barnsley S75 1JN
Freephone: 0800 731 2116
enquiries@oca-uk.com
www.oca-uk.com
Providing high quality arts courses by distance
learning

**Open & Distance Learning Quality Council**
44 Bedford Row,  London WC1R 4LL

Tel: 020 7447 2543
info@odlqc.org.uk
www.odlqc.org.uk
Accreditation of open and distance learning
providers

**Open Spaces Society**
25 A Bell St  Henley-on-Thames RG9 2BA
Tel: 01491 573535
hq@oss.org.uk
www.oss.org.uk
Preserves commons & protects footpaths and
public open spaces

**Open University**
PO Box 197  Milton Keynes  MK7 6BJ
Tel: 0845 300 6090
general-enquiries@open.ac.uk
www.open.ac.uk

**& East of England**
Cintra House  12 Hills Rd  Cambridge CB2 1PF
Tel: 01223 364721
east-of-england@open.ac.uk
www.open.ac.uk

**& East Midlands**
Clarendon Park  Clumber Ave  Sherwood Rise
Nottingham NG5 1AH
Tel: 0115 962 5451
east-midlands@open.ac.uk
www.open.ac.uk

**& Ireland**
110 Victoria Street  Belfast  BT1 3GN
Tel: 028 9024 5025
ireland@open.ac.uk
www.open.ac.uk

**& London**
1-11 Hawley Crescent  Camden Town  London
NW1 8NP
Tel: 020 7485 6597
london@open.ac.uk
www.open.ac.uk

**& North**
Abbots Hill  Baltic Business Quarter  Gateshead
NE8 3DF
Tel: 0191 477 6100
north@open.ac.uk
www.open.ac.uk

**& North West**
351 Altrincham Rd  Sharston  Manchester M22
4UN
Tel: 0161 998 7272
north-west@open.ac.uk
www.open.ac.uk

**& West Midlands**
66 High Street  Harborne  Birmingham B17
9NB
Tel: 0121 426 1661
west-midlands@open.ac.uk
www.open.ac.uk

**& Scotland**
10 Drumsheugh Gardens  Edinburgh EH3 7QJ
Tel: 0131 226 3851
scotland@open.ac.uk
www.open.ac.uk

**& South**
Foxcombe Hall  Boars Hill  Oxford OX1 5HR
Tel: 01865 327000
Minicom: 01865 486202
south@open.ac.uk
www.open.ac.uk

**& South East**
St James's House  150 London Road  East
Grinstead RH19 1HG
Tel: 01342 327821
south-east@open.ac.uk
www.open.ac.uk

**& South West**
4 Portwall Lane  Bristol BS1 6ND
Tel: 0117 929 9641
south-west@open.ac.uk
www.open.ac.uk

**& Wales**
18 Custom House Street  Cardiff CF10 1AP
Tel: 029 2047 1019
wales@open.ac.uk
www.open.ac.uk

**& Yorkshire**
2 Trevelyan Square  Boar Lane  Leeds LS1 6ED
Tel: 0113 2444431
yorkshire@open.ac.uk
www.open.ac.uk

**Open-City**
44-46 Scrutton Street  London EC2A 4HH
Tel: 020 3006 7008
admin@open-city.org.uk
www.open-city.org.uk
Architectural education charity

**Opera** see English National Opera, NODA,
Royal Opera, Scottish Opera, Welsh National
Opera, Youth Opera (British)

**Operation Black Vote**
18a Victoria Park Sq  Bethnal Green
  London E2 9PB
Tel: 020 8983 5430/5426/5471
info@obv.org.uk
www.obv.org.uk
To raise the profile of the democratic rights of
the black community in the UK

**Operation Smile UK**
Unit 15, The Coda Centre   189 Munster Road
London SW6 6AW
Tel: 0844 581 1110
Tel: 020 7386 9386
info@operationsmile.org.uk
www.operationsmile.org.uk

Medical charity providing reconstructive surgery
to young people with facial disfigurements in
developing countries

**Opportunity International UK**
Angel Court  81 St Clements  Oxford OX4 1AW
Tel: 01865 725304
info@opportunity.org.uk
www.opportunity.org.uk
A charity working to create income-raising
opportunities with the world's poor people

**Opportunity Now**
137 Shepherdess Walk  London N1 7RQ
Tel: 0207 566 8650
onweb@bitc.org.uk
www.opportunitynow.org.uk
Business-led campaign for recruitment,
retention and development of women
employees

**Optimum Nutrition (Institute for)**
Avalon House  72 Lower Mortlake Road
Richmond  Surrey TW9 2JY
Tel: 020 8614 7800
ionreception@ion.ac.uk
www.ion.ac.uk
Educational trust for the study, research &
practice of nutritional therapy

**Oral History Society**
PO Box 464  Berkhamsted  Hertfordshire  HP4
2UR
Tel: 01422 879097
rob.perks@bl.uk
www.ohs.org.uk

**Orangutan Foundation**
7 Kent Terrace  London NW1 4RP
Tel: 020 7724 2912
email via website
www.orangutan.org.uk

**Orchestras (Association of British)**
20 Rupert Street  London W1D 6DF
Tel: 020 7287 0333
info@abo.org.uk
www.abo.org.uk

**Orchid Cancer Appeal**
St Bartholomew's Hospital  London  EC1A 7BE
Tel: 0207 601 7167
info@orchid-cancer.org.uk
www.orchid-cancer.org.uk
Dedicated to funding research into diagnosis,
prevention and treatment of prostate and
testicular cancer as well as promoting
awareness of these previously neglected
diseases.

**Ordnance Survey**
Romsey Rd  Southampton SO16 4GU
Helpline: 08456 050505
customerservices@ordnancesurvey.co.uk

www.ordnancesurvey.co.uk
National mapping organisation

**Organ Donation**
NHS Blood and Transplant  Organ Donation
and Transplantation Directorate  Fox Den Rd
Stoke Gifford  Bristol BS34 8RR
Tel: 0300 123 2323 (to register as an organ
donor)
Tel: 0117 975 7575
enquiries@nhsbt.nhs.uk
www.uktransplant.org.uk

**Organ Donation and Transplantation
(International Registry of)** IRODAT
www.tpm.org/secciones/irodat.swf
A complete database that provides the annual
values of the donation and transplantation
activity from the countries that dispose of them

**Orienteering Federation (British)**
8a Stancliffe House  Whitworth Road  Darley
Dale  Matlock  DE4 2HJ
Tel: 01629 734 042
info@britishorienteering.org.uk
www.britishorienteering.org.uk

**Ornithology (British Trust for)**
The Nunnery  Thetford  Norfolk IP24 2PU
Tel: 01842 750050
info@bto.org
www.bto.org

**Osteopathic Council (General)**
176 Tower Bridge Rd  London SE1 3LU
Tel: 020 7357 6655
contactus@osteopathy.org.uk
www.osteopathy.org.uk
Statutory regulatory body for osteopaths

**Osteoporosis Society (National)**
Camerton  Bath BA2 0PJ
Helpline: 0845 450 0230
Tel: 01761 471 771 / 0845 130 3076
info@nos.org.uk
www.nos.org.uk

**Our Dynamic Earth**
112 Holyrood Rd  Edinburgh EH8 8AS
Tel: 0131 550 7800
Email via website
www.dynamicearth.co.uk
Interactive visitor attraction showing the story
of the Earth

**Out of Joint**
7 Thane Works   London N7 7NU
Tel: 020 7609 0207
ojo@outofjoint.co.uk
www.outofjoint.co.uk
Theatre company touring primarily new work
nationally and internationally

**Outdoor Learning (Institute for)**
Warwick Mill Business Centre  Warwick Bridge
Carlisle  CA4 8RR

Tel: 01228 564 580
institute@outdoor-learning.org
www.outdoor-learning.org
Learning through outdoor experience

**Outward Bound Trust**
Hackthorpe Hall  Hackthorpe  Penrith  Cumbria
CA10 2HX
Tel: 01931 740000
enquiries@outwardbound.org.uk
www.theoutwardboundtrust.org.uk
Inspiring young people through challenging
outdoor experiences

**Overeaters Anonymous**
483 Green Lanes  London  N13 4BS
Nat. Helpline: 07000 784985
general@oagb.org.uk
www.oagb.org.uk

**Overseas Adoption Support and
Information Service** see OASIS

**Overseas Development Institute**
111 Westminster Bridge Rd  London SE1 7JD
Tel: 020 7922 0300
odi@odi.org.uk
www.odi.org.uk
Independent think-tank on international
development and humanitarian issues

**Oxfam**
Oxfam House  John Smith Drive  Oxford OX4
2JY
Tel: 0300 200 1300
Email via website
www.oxfam.org.uk

**Oxfam International**
www.oxfam.org/en

# P

**PACE** Project for Advocacy, Counselling and
Education
34 Hartham Rd  London N7 9JL
Tel: 020 7700 1323
info@pacehealth.org.uk
www.pacehealth.org.uk
Lesbian and gay counselling, groups,
advocacy, employment, HIV prevention and
youthwork services and family therapy

**Pain Relief Foundation**
Clinical Sciences Centre  University Hospital
Aintree  Lower Lane  Fazakerley  Liverpool L9
7AL
Tel: 0151 529 5820
secretary@painrelieffoundation.org.uk
www.painrelieffoundation.org.uk
Researches the causes & treatment of chronic
pain

## Pain Society (British)
Churchill House 35 Red Lion Square London
WC1R 4SG
Tel: 020 7269 7840
info@britishpainsociety.org
www.britishpainsociety.org

## Pain Support
www.painsupport.co.uk

## Palliative Care (National Council for)
The Fitzpatrick Building 188-194 York Way
London N7 9AS
Tel: 020 7697 1520
enquiries@ncpc.org.uk
www.ncpc.org.uk
Umbrella body

## Panos Institute
9 White Lion St London N1 9PD
Tel: 020 7278 1111
info@panos.org.uk
www.panos.org.uk
Non-profit institute providing information
on global issues with a developing country
perspective

## Paperboy
www.thepaperboy.com
Web site with links to more than 5,000
newspapers worldwide

## Papworth Trust
Bernard Sunley Centre Papworth Everard
Cambridge
CB23 3RG
Freephone 0800 952 5000
Tel: 01480 357200
info@papworth.org.uk
www.papworth.org.uk
Helps disabled people progress to greater
independence

## PAPYRUS (Prevention of Suicides)
Lodge House Thompson Park Ormerod Road
Burnley Lancashire BB11 2RU
HOPELineUK 0800 068 41 41
Tel: 01282 432555
admin@papyrus-uk.org
www.papyrus-uk.org
Founded by parents who have lost a young
person through suicide & wish to reduce such
tragedies in the future

## Parachute Association (British)
5 Wharf Way Glen Parva Leicester LE2 9TF
Tel: 0116 2785271
skydive@bpa.org.uk
www.bpa.org.uk
Governing body of sport parachuting
(skydiving) in UK

## Paralympic Association (British)
60 Charlotte Street, London W1T 2NU
Tel: 020 7842 5789

info@paralympics.org.uk
www.paralympics.org.uk
Organisation responsible for GB Team
competing at Paralympic Games

## Parent Teacher Associations (National Confederation of)
39 Shipbourne Road Tonbridge Kent TN10
3DS
Tel: 01732 375460
email via website
www.ncpta.org.uk
Encourages formation of PTAs and
involvement of parents in their children's
education

## Parenting UK
Unit 431 Highgate Studios 53-79 Highgate
Road London NW5 1TL
Tel: 020 7284 8370
ppark@parentinguk.org
www.parentinguk.org
The national organisation for people working
with parents

## Parentline Plus
520 Highgate Studios 53-79 Highgate Road,
Kentish Town London, NW5 1TL
National Helpline: 0808 800 2222
Tel: 020 7284 5500
Textphone: 0800 783 6783
Email via website
www.parentlineplus.org.uk
National telephone helpline for anyone in
a parenting role. Parenting courses and
professional training

## Parents & Abducted Children Together
PACT
22 The Vineyard Richmond Surrey TW10
6AN
Tel: 07506 448 116
support@pact-online.org
www.pact-online.org
To fight parental child abduction across
borders and to locate and retrieve missing
children

## Parents for Children now see TACT The Adolescent and Children's Trust

## Parents for Inclusion
336 Brixton Road London SW9 7AA
Helpline: 0800 652 3145
Tel: 020 7738 3888
info@parentsforinclusion.org
www.parentsforinclusion.org
Supports parents of disabled children who
want to be included in mainstream school &
society as a whole

## Parkinson's Disease Society
215 Vauxhall Bridge Road London SW1V 1EJ
Helpline: 080 8800 0303

Tel: 020 7931 8080
hello@parkinsons.org.uk
www.parkinsons.org.uk

## Parliament
www.parliament.uk/
UK parliament website - includes all aspects
of Westminster

## Parliamentary and Health Service Ombudsman
Millbank Tower  Millbank  London SW1P 4QP
Helpline: 0345 015 4033
phso.enquiries@ombudsman.org.uk
www.ombudsman.org.uk
Carries out independent investigations
into complaints about UK government
departments and their agencies, and the NHS
in England

## Parliamentary Education Unit
Houses of Parliament  London SW1A 2TT
Tel: 020 7219 4496
education@parliament.uk
www.parliament.uk
Information about the work of parliament for
students & teachers

## Parliaments (Websites of National)
www.ipu.org/english/parlweb.htm
Portal opening to worldwide parliaments

## Partially Sighted Society
7-9 Bennetthorpe  Doncaster  DN2 6AA
Tel: 0844 477 4966
Fax: 0844 477 4969
info@partsight.org.uk
www.partsight.org.uk
Help visually impaired people make the best
use of their remaining vision

## Passenger Focus
FREEPOST (RRRE-ETTC-LEET)
 PO Box 4257  Manchester M60 3AR
Tel: 0300 123 2350
info@passengerfocus.org.uk
www.passengerfocus.org.uk
Official, independent watchdog for rail
passengers. October 2010: body retained but
subject to substantial change

## Passenger Transport UK (Confederation of) CPT
Drury House  34-43 Russell Street  London
WC2B 5HA
Tel: 020 7240 3131
www.cpt-uk.org
National trade association for bus, coach &
light rail operators

## Passion for Jazz
www.apassion4jazz.net
History of Jazz music origins, styles and
musicians featuring timeline, photos, festivals,
glossary, guitar & piano chords, scales &
online lessons.

## Passport Office London
Globe House  89 Eccleston Square  London
SW1V 1PN
Passport Adviceline: 0300 222 0000
Typetalk: 18001 0300 222 0000
www.direct.gov.uk/en/TravelAndTransport/
Passports/index.htm
You will need to visit a Regional Passport
Office if you need a passport urgently and
want to apply in person using the Fast Track
one-week or Premium one-day service. You
must make an appointment by calling the
passport advice line

## & Belfast
Hampton House  47-53 High Street  Belfast
BT1 2QS
Tel: 0300 222 0000 (Adviceline)

## & Glasgow
3 Northgate  96 Milton Street  Cowcaddens
Glasgow G4 0BT
Tel: 0300 222 0000 (Adviceline)

## & Liverpool
101 Old Hall Street  Liverpool L3 9BD
Tel: 0300 222 0000 (Adviceline)

## & Newport
Olympia House  Upper Dock Street  Newport
Gwent NP20 1XA
Tel: 0300 222 0000 (Adviceline)

## & Peterborough
Aragon Court  Northminster Road
Peterborough PE1 1QG
Tel: 0300 222 0000 (Adviceline)

## & Durham
Millburngate House  Durham DH97 1PA
Tel: 0300 222 0000 (Adviceline)

## Pastoral Care in Education (National Association for)
PO Box 4997  Coventry, CV4 0FD
Tel: 07531 453 670
Email Via website
www.napce.org.uk

## Patent Office (European)
www.epo.org

## Patient Safety Agency (National)
4-8 Maple Street  London W1T 5HD
Tel: 020 7927 9500
enquiries@npsa.nhs.uk
www.npsa.nhs.uk
Improving the safety and quality of care in the
NHS

## Patient UK
www.patient.co.uk
Medical website

## Patients Association
PO Box 935  Harrow  Middlesex  HA1 3YJ
Helpline: 0845 608 4455
Tel: 020 8423 9111 (Admin)
mailbox@patients-association.com
www.patients-association.com
Represents the needs & wishes of patients in the NHS

## Paul D'Auria Cancer Support Centre
3rd Floor  Woburn House  155 Falcon Road
London SW11 2PD
Tel: 020 7924 3924
email via website
www.pauldauriacentre.org.uk
Providers of information and support, complementary therapies and educational programmes

## Paul Mellon Centre for Studies in British Art see Studies in British Art (Paul Mellon Centre for)

## Pax Christi
Christian Peace Education Centre  St Joseph's
Watford Way  Hendon  London NW4 4TY
Tel: 020 8203 4884
info@paxchristi.org.uk
www.paxchristi.org.uk
International workcamps, peace education, campaigning on arms trade and nuclear disarmament issues

## Payplan
Kempton House  Dysart Road  Grantham
NG31 7LE
Freephone: 0800 280 2816
Email via website
www.payplan.com
A not-for-profit organisation which works closely with charities who are involved in assisting individuals who have unmanageable debts

## PDSA People's Dispensary for Sick Animals
Whitechapel Way  Priorslee  Telford TF2 9PQ
Helpline: 0800 7312502
Tel: 01952 290999
Email via website
www.pdsa.org.uk
Free veterinary services for sick & injured animals of needy owners

## Peace Alliance
1st Floor  Heron House  Hale Wharf  Ferry
Lane  Tottenham Hale  N17 9NF
Will be moving - address unknown at time of going to press
Tel: 020 8808 9439
info@peacealliance.org.uk
www.peacealliance.org.uk
A national crime reduction charity working to reduce crime and the fear of crime in the community

## Peace Brigades International UK Section
Development House  56-64 Leonard Street
London EC2A 4LT
Tel: 020 7065 0775
Email via website
www.peacebrigades.org
Humanitarian organisation working for non-violent transformation of conflict & to raise awareness of human rights

## Peace & Freedom (Women's International League for) WILPF
1 rue de Varembe  Case Postale 28  1211
Geneva 20  Switzerland
Tel: 00 41 22 919 7080
infoquest@wilpf.ch
www.wilpfinternational.org

## Peace Pledge Union
1 Peace Passage  London N7 0BT
Tel: 020 7424 9444
email via website
www.ppu.org.uk
www.learnpeace.org.uk
Provides a wide range of teaching and study resources on peace and war

## Pedestrians see Living Streets

## PEN see English PEN

## Penal Reform see also Howard League for Penal Reform

## Penal Reform International
60-62 Commercial Street  London E1 6LT
Tel: 020 7247 6515
info@penalreform.org
www.penalreform.org
Works for penal reform and against the death penalty

## Pensioners Convention (National)
19-23 Ironmonger Row  London EC1V 3QN
Tel: 020 7553 6510
info@npcuk.org
www.npcuk.org
Campaigns for better pensions, health services and other services for older people

## Pensions Ombudsman
11 Belgrave Rd  London SW1V 1RB
Tel: 020 7630 2200
enquiries@pensions–ombudsman.org.uk
www.pensions-ombudsman.org.uk
Investigates and decides complaints and disputes concerning occupational & personal pension schemes. October 2010: Merged with the Pension Protection Fund Ombudsman

## People and Planet
51 Union St  Oxford OX4 1JP
Tel: 01865 245678
people@peopleandplanet.org
www.peopleandplanet.org

Network of UK students campaigning on issues of world poverty, human rights and the environment

**People First**
Unit 3.46 Canterbury Court  Kennington Park Business Centre  1-3 Brixton Road  London SW9 6DE
Tel: 020 7820 6655
general@peoplefirstltd.com
www.peoplefirstltd.com
Run for and by people with learning difficulties to help them speak up for themselves

**People for the Ethical Treatment of Animals** see PETA Europe Ltd

**People with Learning Disabilities (National Development Team for)** now see Inclusion (National Development Team for) NDTi

**People's Dispensary for Sick Animals** see PDSA

**People's History Museum**
Left Bank
  Spinningfields  Manchester  M3 3ER
Tel: 0161 838 9190
info@phm.org.uk
www.phm.org.uk

**People's Network**
www.peoplesnetwork.gov.uk
Access to a wide range of software and digital content, in public libraries already  with a trained and supportive staff

**People's Trust for Endangered Species**
15 Cloisters House  8 Battersea Park Road London  SW8 4BG
Tel: 020 7498 4533
enquiries@ptes.org
www.ptes.org
Ensures a future for endangered species throughout the world

**Peoples Close to Nature (Friends of)** see Friends of Peoples Close to Nature

**Performing Arts and Technology** see BRIT School for Performing Arts and Technology

**Performing Arts Medicine (British Association for)**
4th Floor, Totara Park House  34-36 Gray's Inn Road  London WC1X 8HR
Tel: 020 7404 5888
Tel: 020 7404 8444 (Clinic)
enquiries@bapam.org.uk
www.bapam.org.uk
Diagnosis and treatment for medical problems encountered by performers of all kinds

**Performing Rights Society**
Copyright House  29-33 Berners St  London W1T 3AB
Tel: 020 7580 5544

Email via website
www.prsformusic.com

**Permaculture Association (Britain)**
BCM Permaculture Assoc   London WC1N 3XX
Tel: 0845 458 1805
Email via website
www.permaculture.org.uk
Provides information about courses, groups and projects concerned with a sustainable life style

**Personal Finance Education Group** pfeg
Fifth Floor  14 Bonhill Street  London EC2A 4BX
Tel: 020 7330 9470
Tel: 0845 241 0925
info@pfeg.org
www.pfeg.org
Helps schools to teach personal finance

**Personal Injury Lawyers (Association of)** APIL
11 Castle Quay  Nottingham NG7 1FW
Tel: 0115 958 0585
Email via website
www.apil.org.uk
Dedicated to improving the service provided to victims of accidents and clinical negligence

**Personal Investment Authority Ombudsman** see Financial Ombudsman Service

**Personnel & Development (Chartered Institute of)**
151 The Broadway  London SW19 1JQ
Tel: 020 8612 6200
email via website
www.cipd.co.uk
Professional body

**Pesticide Action Network UK**
54-64 Leonard Street  Development House London EC2A 4LT
Tel: 020 7065 0905
Email via website
www.pan-uk.org
Independent health and ecological charity working to eliminate the hazards of pesticides

**Pet Advisory Committee**
198 High Holborn  London WC1V 7BD
Tel: 020 7025 2341
www.petadvisory.org.uk
Makes recommendations to central and local government to encourage responsible pet ownership in society

**Pet Behaviour Counsellors (Association of)**
PO Box 46  Worcester WR8 9YS
Tel: 01386 751151
info@apbc.org.uk
www.apbc.org.uk

## Pet Care Trust
Bedford Business Centre  170 Mile Rd  Bedford
MK42 9TW
Tel: 01234 273933
Email via website
www.petcare.org.uk
Association promoting responsible pet
ownership and professionalism in the trade

## Pet Health Council
4th Floor,  6 Catherine Street  London, WC2B
5JJ
Tel: 0207 379 6545
enquiries@pethealthcouncil.co.uk
www.pethealthcouncil.co.uk
Promotes health & welfare of pet animals

## Pet Month (National)
3 Crossfield Chambers  Gladbeck Way  Enfield
EN2 7HF
Tel: 020 8370 3688
info@nationalpetmonth.org.uk
www.nationalpetmonth.org.uk
Encourages responsible pet ownership via
National Pet Week annually - first week in May

## PETA EUROPE Ltd People for the Ethical
Treatment of Animals
PO Box 36678  London SE1 1YE
Tel: 020 7357 9229
info@peta.org.uk
www.peta.org.uk
Campaigns against all forms of animal abuse

## PetLog Database (National)
The Kennel Club
4A Alton House  Gatehouse Way  Aylesbury
Bucks HP19 8XU
Tel: 0844 463 3999
Minicom: 01296 337 517
petlogadmin@thekennelclub.org.uk
www.petlog.org.uk
The National Pet Identification Scheme using
microchips

## Pets as Therapy
3a Grange Farm Cottages  Wycombe Rd
Saunderton  Princes Risborough HP27 9NS
Tel: 01844 345 445
reception@petsastherapy.org
www.petsastherapy.org
Provides therapeutic visits to hospitals,
hospices, nursing and care homes, special
needs schools etc by volunteers with their own
friendly temperament tested and vaccinated
dogs and cats

## Phab Physically Disabled & Able Bodied
(England)
Summit House  50 Wandle Rd  Croydon CRO
1DF
Tel: 020 8667 9443
info@phab.org.uk
www.phab.org.uk
Brings together people with & without physical
disabilities

## Pharmaceutical Society (Royal)
1 Lambeth High St  London SE1 7JN
Tel: 020 7735 9141
enquiries@rpsgb.org
www.rpsgb.org
Professional, regulatory and statutory body
of Britain's practising pharmacists

## Philip Lawrence Awards Network PLAnet
c/o Catch 22  Churchill House  142-146 Old
Street  London E1V 9BW
Tel: 020 7336 4800
philiplawrenceawards@catch-22.org.uk
www.philiplawrenceawards.net
Award scheme which acclaims and
rewards outstanding achievements in good
citizenship by young people of 11-20 years

## Phonebrain
www.phonebrain.org.uk/
Interactive website providing a young person's
guide to the real cost of premium phone lines

## Phonepay Plus formerly Independent
Committee for the Supervision of Standards
of Telephone Information Services
4th Floor  Clove Building  4 Maguire Street
London SE1 2NQ
Free Helpline: 0800 500212
Tel: 020 7940 7474
Tel: 020 7940 7440 (press office)
www.phonepayplus.org.uk
Regulates products or services - such as
competitions, TV voting, helplines, adult
entertainment, downloads, new alerts or
interactive games - that are charged to users'
phone bills or pre-pay accounts.

## Photographic Society of Great Britain
(Royal)
Fenton House  122 Wells Road  Bath BA2 3AH
Tel: 01225 325733
reception@rps.org
www.rps.org

## photoLondon
www.photolondon.org.uk

## Physical Education (Association for)
Room 117
Bredon  University of Worcester  Henwick
Grove  Worcester WR2 6AJ
Tel: 01905 855 584
enquiries@afpe.org.uk
www.afpe.org.uk
Professional association for teachers of
physical education

**Physical Recreation (Central Council of)**
4th Floor  Burwood House  14-16 Caxton
Street  London SW1H 0QT
Tel: 020 7976 3900
info@ccpr.org.uk
www.ccpr.org.uk
Umbrella organisation to which all sport &
recreation governing bodies in the UK are
affiliated

**Physically Disabled & Able Bodied
(England)** see Phab

**Physics (Institute of)**
76 Portland Place  London W1B 1NT
Tel: 020 7470 4800
physics@iop.org
www.iop.org

**Physiotherapy (Chartered Society of)**
14 Bedford Row  London WC1R 4ED
Tel: 020 7306 6666
Email via website
www.csp.org.uk
Professional, educational and trade union
body for chartered physiotherapists, students
and assistants

**Pilates Foundation**
PO Box 58235  London N1 5UY
Tel: 020 7033 0078
admin@pilatesfoundation.com
www.pilatesfoundation.com
Promotes & develops body awareness

**Pipedown**
1 The Row  Berwick St James  Salisbury SP3
4TP
Tel: 01722 790622
Tel: 07971 518976
Email via website
www.pipedown.info
Campaigns for the right to freedom from piped
music in public places

**Pituitary Foundation**
PO Box 1944  Bristol BS99 2UB
Tel: 0845 450 0375 (Support and Information
HelpLine)
Tel: 0845 450 0376
Email via website
www.pituitary.org.uk
Provides information and support to sufferers
of pituitary disorders and their relatives, friends
and carers

**Placement Survival Guide**
www.placementsurvivalguide.com
Skills for life for 14-19 years, comprising work
experience, community involvement and
personal challenge

**Plaid Cymru - The Party of Wales**
Ty Gwynfor
Marine chambers  Anson Court  Atlantic Wharf
Caerdydd CF10 4AL
Tel: 029 20 472272
post@plaidcymru.org
www.plaidcymru.org

**Plain English Campaign**
PO Box 3  New Mills  High Peak SK22 4QP
Tel: 01663 744409
info@plainenglish.co.uk
www.plainenglish.co.uk
Campaigning for clarity of official
communications, edits documents & does
training in plain English

**Plan International UK**
Finsgate  5-7 Cranwood Street  London
EC1V 9LH
Tel: 0300 777 9777
mail@plan-international.org.uk
www.plan-uk.org
Humanitarian child-focused organisation
working with families and their communities to
meet the needs of children around the world

**Planned Parenthood Federation
(International)** IPPF
4 Newhams Row  London SE1 3UZ
Tel: 020 7939 8200
info@ippf.org
www.ippf.org
Global network of family planning associations
in 182 countries

**PlanningAlerts.com**
www.planningalerts.com
Searches many local authority planning
websites and emails details of applications
near you to enable shared scrutiny of what is
being built (and knocked down)

**Plantlife**
14 Rollestone Street  Salisbury  Wiltshire SP1
1DX
Tel: 01722 342730
enquiries@plantlife.org.uk
www.plantlife.org.uk
The UK's leading plant conservation charity

**Platform** see GFS Platform for Young
Women

**Play** see also thematic guide - Children &
Young People

**Play England**
8 Wakley St  London EC1V 7QE
Tel: 020 7843 6300
email via website
www.playengland.org.uk
Aims for all children and young people in
England to have regular access to and
opportunity for free, inclusive, local play
provision and play space

**Play Wales**
Baltic House  Mount Stuart Sq  Cardiff CF10 5FH
Tel: 029 2048 6050
mail@playwales.org.uk
www.playwales.org.uk
Aims to influence the policy of all organisations that have an interest in children's play

**Playbus Association (National)**
Brunswick Court  Brunswick Square  Bristol BS2 8PE
Tel: 0117 916 6580
playbus@playbus.org.uk
www.playbus.org.uk
Promotes effective use of community work on converted vehicles throughout the UK

**PLAYLINK**
72 Albert Palace Mansions  Lurline Gardens London SW11 4DQ
Tel/: 020 7720 2452
info@playlink.org
www.playlink.org
Works to improve opportunities for children's free play in quality environments

**Plus**
Email via website
www.plusgroups.org.uk
Voluntary social activities organisation for 18-36 year olds

**PMS** see Premenstrual Syndrome (National Association for)

**Pod Charitable Trust**
Mount Hall  Llanfair Caereinion  Welshpool SY21 0BH
Tel: 01938 810374
Email via website
www.podcharity.org.uk
Entertainment for children in hospital

**Podiatrists** see Chiropodists & Podiatrists

**Poetry Library**
Level 5  Royal Festival Hall  London SE1 8XX
Tel: 020 7921 0943/0664
Email via website
www.poetrylibrary.org.uk
www.poetrymagazines.org.uk
Premises not accessible till June

**Poetry Society**
22 Betterton St  London WC2H 9BX
Tel: 020 7420 9880
info@poetrysociety.org.uk
www.poetrysociety.org.uk

**Police** see also Black Police Association (National), Independent Police Complaints Commission, INQUEST, Metropolitan Police

**Police Federation of England & Wales**
Federation House  Highbury Drive

Leatherhead  Surrey KT22 7UY
Tel: 01372 352000
gensec@polfed.org
www.polfed.org

**Police Federation (Scottish)**
5 Woodside Place  Glasgow G3 7QF
Tel: 0141 332 5234
gensec@spf.org.uk
www.spf.org.uk

**Police National Legal Database**
www.askthe.police.uk/content
Access to the Police National Database with an a-z of frequently asked questions including 'How old do I have to be to carry an air weapon?' 'How much alcohol can I drink and not be over the limit?' 'What is domestic violence?'

**Policy on Ageing (Centre for)**
25-31 Ironmonger Row  London EC1V 3QP
Tel: 020 7553 6500
cpa@cpa.org.uk
www.cpa.org.uk
Policy formation, library and information services on all aspects of aging and later life

**Policy Studies (Centre for)**
57 Tufton St  London SW1P 3QL
Tel: 020 7222 4488
tim@cps.org.uk
www.cps.org.uk
Centre-right independent think tank

**Policy Studies Institute**
50 Hanson Street  London W1W 6UP
Tel: 020 7911 7500
admin@policystudiesinstitute.org.uk
www.psi.org.uk
Non-politically affiliated independent research institute concerned with government policy

**Polio Fellowship (British)**
Eagle Office Centre  The Runway  South Ruislip HA4 6SE
Freephone: 0800 0180586
info@britishpolio.org.uk
www.britishpolio.org.uk

**Political Studies Association**
Department of Politics  University of Newcastle Newcastle-upon-Tyne NE1 7RU
Tel: 0191 222 8021
psa@ncl.ac.uk
www.psa.ac.uk
The learned society for political scientists in British universities

**Polka Theatre** World-class theatre for children
240 The Broadway  Wimbledon  London SW19 1SB
Box Office: 020 8543 4888
www.polkatheatre.com

## Pony Club
Stoneleigh Park  Kenilworth  Warwicks CV8 2RW
Tel: 024 7669 8300
enquiries@pcuk.org
www.pcuk.org
International youth organisation for those interested in ponies & riding

## Pool Association (English)
Email via website
www.epa.org.uk

## Popular Astronomy (Society for)
www.popastro.com/
Aims to help beginners, and those who like a less technical approach, to learn about astronomy

## Population Concern see Interact Worldwide

## Population Services International PSI
www.psi.org
Non-profit organisation which deploys commercial marketing strategies to promote health products, services etc to low income people

## Population Statistics
www.world-gazetteer.com
World population statistics

## Port of London Authority
London River House  Royal Pier Road Gravesend   Kent DA12 2BG
Tel: 01474 562200
Email via website
www.pla.co.uk

## Portman Group
4th Floor,  20 Conduit Street,  London,  W1S 2XW
Tel: 020 7290 1460
info@portmangroup.org.uk
www.portmangroup.org.uk
Funded by the drinks industry to promote responsible drinking

## Positively UK
347-349 City Road  London EC1V 1LR
Tel: 020 7713 0444
info@positivelyuk.org
www.positivelywomen.org.uk
Provides free and strictly confidential practical and peer support for women with HIV and AIDS

## Post Natal Illness
www.pni.org.uk
Community site and forum offering support and information

## Post Office
Tel: 08457 223344
Minicom: 08457 22 33 55
Email via website
www.postoffice.co.uk
These are central contact details for the Post Office Group, which consists of Post Office Counters, Royal Mail & Parcel Force. October 2010: future under review. Government plans to transfer Royal Mail Holdings to the private sector over time.

## Post-Adoption Centre
5 Torriano Mews  Torriano Avenue  London NW5 2RZ
Advice Line: 020 7284 5879
Tel: 020 7284 0555
advice@postadoptioncentre.org.uk
www.postadoptioncentre.org.uk
Offers support, counselling, family work & advice to anyone involved in adoption

## Post-natal illness (Association for)
145 Dawes Rd  Fulham  London SW6 7EB
Helpline: 020 7386 0868
Email via website
www.apni.org

## Postcodes
www.royalmail.com
Find postcodes online, or find addresses if you only have the postcode and other useful information about postal services

## Postcomm (Postal Services Commission)
Hercules House  6 Hercules Road  London SE1 7DB
Tel: 020 7593 2100
info@psc.gov.uk
www.psc.gov.uk
October 2010: Will be merged with Ofcom

## Postwatch now see Consumer Focus

## Poverty (UK Coalition Against)
1-27 Bridport Street  Liverpool L3 5QF
Tel: 0151 475 7067
www.ukcap.org

## Practical Action
The Schumacher Centre for Technology & Development  Bourton Hall  Bourton on Dunsmore  Rugby CV23 9QZ
Tel: 01926 634400
practicalaction@practicalaction.org.uk
www.practicalaction.org
Specialises in helping people to use technology for practical answers to poverty

## Pre-School Learning Alliance
The Fitzpatrick Building  188 York Way  London N7 9AD
Tel: 020 7697 2500
info@pre-school.org.uk
www.pre-school.org.uk
Educational charity providing support, information & training for people working with under 5s & their families

**Pre-School Play Association (Scottish)**
SPPA
> 21-23 Granville Street  Glasgow G3 7EE
> Tel: 0141 221 4148
> info@sppa.org.uk
> www.sppa.org.uk
> Works to improve pre-school provision

**Pre-School Playgroups Association (Wales)**
Cymdeithas Clychoedd Chwarae Cyn-ysgol Cymru
> Unit 1 The Lofts  9 Hunter Street  Cardiff Bay
> Cardiff CF10 5GX
> Tel: 029 2045 1242
> cardiffoffice@walesppa.org
> www.walesppa.org
> Works to improve pre-school provision in Wales

**Premenstrual Syndrome (National Association for)**  NAPS
> 41 Old Rd  East Peckham  Kent TN12 5AP
> Tel: 0844 8157311
> contact@pms.org.uk
> www.pms.org.uk
> Information, advice & support for PMS sufferers & their families

**Preservation Trusts (UK Association of)**
> 9th Floor  Alhambra House  27-31 Charing Cross Road  London WC2H 0AU
> Tel: 020 7930 1629
> director.apt@ahfund.org.uk
> www.ukapt.org.uk
> Representative body for building preservation trusts in UK, offering support and advice

**Press and Broadcasting Freedom (Campaign for)**
> 2nd Floor, Vi & Garner Smith House  23 Orford Rd  London E17 9NL
> Tel: 020 8521 5932
> freepress@cpbf.org.uk
> www.cpbf.org.uk
> Campaigns for a diverse, democratic & accountable media

**Press Association**
> 292 Vauxhall Bridge Rd  London SW1V 1AE
> Tel: 0870 1203200
> Email via website
> www.pressassociation.com
> UK National news agency

**Press Complaints Commission**
> Halton House  20-23 Holborn  London  EC1N 2JD
> Helpline: 0845 600 2757
> Tel: 020 7831 0022
> complaints@pcc.org.uk
> www.pcc.org.uk
> Investigates written complaints concerning the editorial content of newspapers & magazines in the UK

**Prevention of Accidents (Royal Society for the)**  see RoSPA

**Prevention of Cruelty to Animals** see RSPCA

**Prevention of Cruelty to Animals (Scottish Society for the)**
> Kingseat Road  Halbeath  Dunfermline KY11 8RY
> Tel: 03000 999 999
> Tel: 03000 999 999
> Email via website
> www.scottishspca.org

**Prevention of Cruelty to Children** see CHILDREN 1ST, NSPCC Asian Child Protection, NSPCC

**Primary Education (Association for the Study of)**
> The Swallow Barn  The Brandon Court Station Road  Long Marston  Herts HP23 4RA
> mary@swallowbarn.fsnet.co.uk
> www.aspe-uk.eu

**Primary Education (National Association for)**
> Moulton College Management Centre, Moulton,  Northampton  NN3 7RR
> Tel 01604 647646
> nationaloffice@nape.co.uk
> www.nape.org.uk
> NAPE is an independent voice in the world of education seeking to represent and raise the profile of the primary phase of education

**Primary School Science** see SCIcentre

**Primate Protection League (International)**
> Gilmore House  166 Gilmore Rd  London SE13 5AE
> Tel: 020 8297 2129
> enquiries@ippl-uk.org
> www.ippl.org.uk
> Dedicated to the rescue of monkeys and apes

**Prince's Trust (Head Office)**
> 18 Park Sq East  London NW1 4LH
> Freephone: 0800 842 842
> Tel: 020 7543 1234
> Textphone: 020 7543 1374
> webinfops@princes-trust.org.uk
> www.princes-trust.org.uk
> Practical solutions to help young people get their lives working

**Princess Royal Trust for Carers** see Carers (The Princess Royal Trust For)

**Prison Advice & Care Trust (PACT)**
> Park Place  12 Lawn Lane  Vauxhall  London SW8 1UD
> Tel: 020 7735 9535
> info@prisonadvice.org.uk
> www.prisonadvice.org.uk

Works with prisoners who have mental health needs and support prisoners' families

**Prison Reform Trust**
15 Northburgh St  London EC1V 0JR
Tel: 020 7251 5070
prt@prisonreformtrust.org.uk
www.prisonreformtrust.org.uk
Wide range of publications on penal issues and information and advice to prisoners and their families & campaign for reform

**Prison Service NI**
Prison Service Headquarters  Dundonald House  Upper Newtownards Road  Belfast BT4 3SU
Tel: 028 9052 5065
info@niprisonservice.gov.uk
www.niprisonservice.gov.uk/

**Prison Studies (International Centre for)**
King's College, London School of Law
Tel: 020 7848 1922
icps@kcl.ac.uk
www.kcl.ac.uk/schools/law/research/icps
Seeks to assist governments & other relevant agencies to develop appropriate policies on prisons & the use of imprisonment

**Prison Visitors (National Association of Official)**
info@naopv.com
www.naopv.com

**Prisoners Abroad**
89-93 Fonthill Rd  Finsbury Park  London N4 3JH
Family freephone 0808 172 0098
Tel: 020 7561 6820
info@prisonersabroad.org.uk
www.prisonersabroad.org.uk
Charity providing practical support to British Citizens imprisoned abroad

**Prisoners' Advice Service**
PO Box 46199  London EC1M 4XA
Tel: 0207 2533323
advice@prisonersadvice.org.uk
www.prisonersadvice.org.uk
Advice on prisoners' rights in England & Wales

**Prisoners' Families (Action for)**
Unit 21, Carlson Court  116 Putney Bridge Road  London SW15 2NQ
Tel: 020 8812 3600
info@actionpf.org.uk
www.prisonersfamilies.org.uk
Info on local support services and lobby on behalf of prisoners' families

**Prisoners' Families and Friends Service**
20 Trinity St  London SE1 1DB
Freephone for prisoners' families and friends: 0808 808 3444
Tel: 020 7403 4091 (Admin)

info@pffs.org.uk
www.pffs.org.uk

**Prisoners of Conscience Appeal Fund**
PO Box 61044  London SE1 1UP
Tel: 020 7407 6644
info@prisonersofconscience.org
www.prisonersofconscience.org
Helps those persecuted for conscientiously-held beliefs, provided they have not used or advocated violence

**Prisons and Probation Ombudsman for England and Wales**
Ashley House  2 Monck St  London SW1P 2BQ
Tel: 020 7035 2876 or 0845 010 7938
mail@ppo.gsi.gov.uk
www.ppo.gov.uk

**Privacy International**
265 Strand  London WC2R 1BH
Tel: 020 8123 7933
privacyint@privacy.org
www.privacyinternational.org
Human rights group formed as a watchdog on surveillance by governments & corporations

**Probation Service (National)**
1st Floor  Abell House  John Islip Street London SW1P 4LH
www.probation.homeoffice.gov.uk

**Professional Footballers Association**
Tel: 0161 236 0575
info@thepfa.co.uk
www.givemefootball.com
The union for professional footballers

**Professional Golfers' Association**
Centenary House
  The Belfry
  Sutton Coldfield  West Midlands B76 9PT
Tel: 01675 470 333
email via website
www.pga.info

**Professional Music Therapists (Association of)**
24-27 White Lion Street  London N1 9PD
Tel: 020 7837 6100
APMToffice@aol.com
www.apmt.org
Assists music therapists in professional matters and maintains standards of training and practice

**Professional Theatre for Children and Young People (Association of)** now see Theatre for Children and Young People (International Association of)

**Project Gutenberg**
www.promo.net/pg/
American website providing texts of literature which is out of copyright

**Project Trust**
The Hebridean Centre  Isle of Coll  Argyll PA78 6TE  Scotland
Tel: 01879 230444
info@projecttrust.org.uk
www.projecttrust.org.uk
Gap year placements abroad, teaching or social projects

**Promotion of New Music** see New Music (Society for the Promotion of)

**Proofreaders** see Editors and Proofreaders (Society for)

**Prostate Cancer Helpline**
Helpline: 0800 074 8383

**Protection of Animals (World Society for)** see WSPA

**Protection of Birds** see RSPB

**Protection of Horses (International League for the)**  now see World Horse Welfare

**Protection of Rural Wales (Campaign for the)**  Ymgyrch Diogelu Cymru Wledig
Ty Gwyn  31 High St  Welshpool  Powys SY21 7YD
Tel: 01938 552 525 / 556 212
info@cprwmail.org.uk
www.cprw.org.uk

**Psoriasis Association**
Dick Coles House  2 Queensbridge Northampton  NN4 7BF
Tel: 01604 251620
Local rate: 0845 676 0076
mail@psoriasis-association.org.uk
www.psoriasis-association.org.uk
Help & support for sufferers

**Psychiatrists (Royal College of)**
National Headquarters  17 Belgrave Square London SW1X 8PG
Tel: 020 7235 2351
reception@rcpsych.ac.uk
www.rcpsych.ac.uk

**Psychical Research (Society for)**  SPR
49 Marloes Rd  London W8 6LA
Tel: 020 7937 8984
Email via website
www.spr.ac.uk
For anyone interested in the paranormal, have a library, publish a journal and fund university research into paranormal phenomena

**Psychological Society (British)**
St Andrews House  48 Princess Rd East Leicester LE1 7DR
Tel: 0116 254 9568
enquiries@bps.org.uk
www.bps.org.uk
Professional and regulatory body of psychologists

**Psychotherapists (British Association of)**
37 Mapesbury Rd  London NW2 4HJ
Tel: 020 8452 9823
admin@bap-psychotherapy.org
www.bap-psychotherapy.org

**Psychotherapy** see thematic guide - Counselling & Mental Health

**Psychotherapy (UK Council for)**
2nd Floor  Edward House  2 Wakley Street London EC1V 7LT
Tel: 020 7014 9955
info@ukcp.org.uk
www.psychotherapy.org.uk
Umbrella body and voluntary regulatory organisation. Promotes psychotherapy for public benefit & provides a register of suitably trained psychotherapists

**Public Art Forum** now see IXIA

**Public Concern at Work**
3rd Floor, Bank Chambers  6 - 10 Borough High Street  London SE1 9QQ
Tel: 020 7404 6609
whistle@pcaw.co.uk
www.pcaw.co.uk
Leading authority on whistleblowing in the workplace offering advice/services to employees and organisations

**Public Management and Policy Association**
3 Robert St  London WC2N 6RL
Tel: 0207 543 5679
info.pmpa@cipfa.org
www.cipfa.org.uk/pmpa/
Networking organisation for workers in central & local government

**Public Monuments & Sculpture Association**
70 Cowcross Street  London EC1M 6EJ
Tel: 020 7490 5001
pmsa@btconnect.com
www.pmsa.org.uk
For the promotion and protection of public monuments and sculpture in UK. Website contains details of National Recording Project which is surveying all public monuments & sculpture in the UK

**Public Policy Research (Institute for)**
30-32 Southampton St  London WC2E 7RA
Tel: 020 7470 6100
info@ippr.org
www.ippr.org
Progressive research think-tank

**Public Record Office** now see National Archives

**Public Sector Information (Office of)** now see legislation.gov.uk/

**Public Service Excellence (Association for)**
2nd Floor, Washbrook House  Lancastrian Office Centre  32 Talbot Rd  Old Trafford  Manchester

M32 0FP
Tel: 0161 772 1810
enquiries@apse.org.uk
www.apse.org.uk
Advises local councils on best practice in delivery of public services

**Public Services Ombudsman (Scottish)**
Freepost EH641 Edinburgh EH3 0BR
Tel: 0800 377 7330
Email via website
www.spso.org.uk
Investigates complaints about maladministration and service failure in public services in Scotland

**Public Whip**
www.publicwhip.org.uk/
A searchable site providing the complete voting record of every MP

**PWSA (UK)** Prader-Willi Syndrome Association UK
125a London Road Derby DE1 2QQ
Tel: 01332 365 676
admin@pwsa.co.uk
www.pwsa.co.uk
Supports those affected by this chromosomal disorder

**Pyramid**
pyramid@continyou.org.uk
www.continyou.org.uk/children_and_families/pyramid/home
Helps primary-school children build self-esteem and confidence

# Q

**QCA** see Qualifications and Curriculum Authority

**Quaker Voluntary Action**
1 Holt Lane Holmfirth West Yorkshire HD9 3BW
Tel: 01484 687139
mail@qva.org.uk
www.qva.org.uk
Volunteer projects in the UK and abroad

**Quakers in Britain**
Friends House 173-177 Euston Rd London NW1 2BJ
Tel: 020 7663 1000
enquiries@quaker.org.uk
www.quaker.org.uk

**Qualifications and Curriculum Development Authority** QCDA
53-55 Butts Road Earlsdon Park Coventry CV1 3BH
Tel: 0300 303 3010
Enqiry line: 0300 303 3011
info@qcda.gov.uk

www.qcda.gov.uk
Promotes quality & coherence in education & training and is a guardian of standards. October 2010 to be abolished and some functions transferred to the Department for Education

**Qualifications Authority (Scottish)** see Scottish Qualifications Authority (SQA)

**Quality in Study Support and Extended Services**
www.canterbury.ac.uk/education/quality-in-study-support
Provides consultancy, professional development and an accredited recognition scheme for study support

**Questionpoint**
http://questionpoint.org
US library service with live reference staff

**Quilters' Guild of the British Isles**
St Anthony's Hall York YO1 7PW
Tel: 01904 613 242
info@quiltersguild.org.uk
www.quiltersguild.org.uk

**QUIT** National Society of Non Smokers
63 St.Marys Ave London EC3A 8AA
Quit line: 0800 002200
Tel: 0207 469 0400
info@quit.org.uk
www.quit.org.uk
Helping smokers to quit

# R

**Rabbit Council (British)**
Purefoy House 7 Kirkgate Newark Notts NG24 1AD
Tel: 01636 676042
info@thebrc.org
www.thebrc.org
Governing body for exhibition rabbit fancying

**RAC**
www.rac.co.uk

**Race Equality Foundation**
Unit 35 Kings Exchange Tileyard Road London N7 9AH
Tel: 0207 619 6220

**Race Relations (Institute of)**
2-6 Leeke St London WC1X 9HS
Tel: 020 7837 0041
Tel: 020 7833 2010
info@irr.org.uk
www.irr.org.uk

**Racial Equality (Commission for)** now see Equality and Human Rights Commission

**Racism** see also thematic guide Race

**Racism and Fascism (Campaign Against)**
CARF
BM Box 8784  London WC1N 3XX
Tel: 020 7837 1450
info@carf.org.uk
www.carf.org.uk

**Racism in Europe (Youth Against)**
PO Box 858  London E11 1YG
Tel: 020 8558 7947
yrehq@yahoo.co.uk
www.yre.org.uk

**Racism (National Assembly Against)** NAAR
28 Commercial St  London E1 6LS
Tel: 020 7247 9907
info@naar.org.uk
www.naar.org.uk

**RAD** see Royal Academy of Dance

**RADA** Royal Academy of Dramatic Art
62-64 Gower St  London WC1E 6ED
Tel: 020 7636 7076
enquiries@rada.ac.uk
www.rada.org
Vocational training for actors and theatre
technicians

**RADAR** Royal Association for Disability &
Rehabilitation
12 City Forum  250 City Road  London EC1V
8AF
Tel: 020 7250 3222
Tel: 020 7250 4119 (Minicom)
radar@radar.org.uk
www.radar.org.uk
Umbrella organisation of 500 member groups,
campaigning for disabled people's right to
social inclusion

**Radio** see also BBC

**Radio Authority** now see OFCOM

**Radio Communications Agency** now see
OFCOM

**Radio Society of GB**
3 Abbey Court  Fraser Road  Priory Business
Park  Bedford MK44 3WH
Tel: 01234 832 700
postmaster@rsgb.org.uk
www.rsgb.org
Supports and promotes amateur (or ham)
radio

**Radiological Protection Board** see Health
Protection Agency Centre for Radiation etc

**Rail Enquiries (National)**
www.nationalrail.co.uk
Rail timetables, fares etc for all national rail
services in UK

**Rail Europe**
34 Tower View  Kings Hill  West Malling  Kent
ME19 4ED

General Reservations: 08448 484 064
www.raileurope.co.uk
Information for travellers and rail fans. Gives
links to national timetables

**Rail Regulation (Office of)**
1 Kemble Street  London  WC2B 4AN
Tel: 020 7282 2000
contact.cct@orr.gsi.gov.uk
www.rail-reg.gov.uk

**Railfuture**
www.railfuture.org.uk
Independent campaign for a better passenger
and freight rail network

**Railway Children**
1st Floor  1 The Commons  Sandbach
Cheshire CW11 1EG
Tel: 01270 757596
enquiries@railwaychildren.org.uk
www.railwaychildren.org.uk
Helps runaway and abandoned children in the
UK & internationally

**Railway Crime (Partners Against)** now
see Trackoff

**Railway Museum (National)**
Leeman Road  York YO26 4XJ
Tel: 0844 815 3139
Education: 01904 686230
nrm@nrm.org.uk
www.nrm.org.uk

**Railways** see also Community Rail
Partnerships (Association of), Rail
Europe, Heritage Railway Association,
Passenger Focus, Passenger Transport
UK (Confederation of), Sustrans, Trainline,
Transport 2000, WalesRails

**Rainer** now seeCatch22

**Rainforest** see also thematic guide
Environment & Countryside

**Rainforest Concern**
8 Clanricarde Gardens  London W2 4NA
Tel: 020 7229 2093
info@rainforestconcern.org
www.rainforestconcern.org
Conservation & protection of rainforests in
Central and South America & Asia

**Rainforest Foundation**
Imperial Works  Perren Street  London  NW5
3ED
Tel: 020 7485 0193
info@rainforestuk.com
www.rainforestfoundationuk.org
Protects the world's rainforests and their
inhabitants

**Raleigh International**
Raleigh  3rd Floor  207 Waterloo Road
London SE1 8XD

200

Tel: 020 7183 1270
info@raleigh.org.uk
www.raleighinternational.org
Youth development charity running
community, environmental and adventure
projects in developing countries

## Rambert Dance Company

94 Chiswick High Rd  London W4 1SH
Tel: 020 8630 0600
rdc@rambert.org.uk
www.rambert.org.uk
Contemporary dance with education and
community units

## Ramblers' Association

2nd Floor  Camelford House  87-90 Albert
Embankment  London SE1 7TW
Tel: 020 7339 8500
ramblers@ramblers.org.uk
www.ramblers.org.uk
Britain's biggest charity working on behalf
of walkers

## Ramblers' Association Scotland

Kingfisher House  Auld Mart Business Park
Milnathort  Kinross KY13 9DA
Tel: 01577 861222
scotland@ramblers.org.uk
www.ramblers.org.uk/scotland

## Ramblers' Association Wales Cymdeithas
y Cerddwyr

3 Coopers Yard  Curran Road  Cardiff CF10
5NB
Tel: 029 2064 4308
cerddwyr@ramblers.org.uk
www.ramblers.org.uk/wales

## Rape see Crossroads Women's Centre,
Mankind UK, Roofie Foundation, Women
Against Rape

## Rape Crisis

Rape Crisis (England & Wales)
  BCM Box 4444  London  WC1N 3XX
National Freephone Helpline: 0808 802 9999
info@rapecrisis.org.uk
www.rapecrisis.co.uk
Gives contact information about rape crisis
centres throughout the UK

## Rare Breeds Survival Trust

Stoneleigh Park, Nr Kenilworth  Warwick
CV8 2LG
Tel: 024 7669 6551
email via website
www.rbst.org.uk
Works to conserve endangered breeds of
British farm livestock

## Rathbone

4th Floor  Churchgate House  56 Oxford St
Manchester M1 6EU
Free Phone: 0800 731 5321

Tel: 0161 236 5358
Email via website
www.rathboneuk.org
Charity helping people with special
educational and training needs. Helpline
advises parents on special education
procedures

## Raw Material Music and Media

2 Robert St  London SW9 0DJ
Tel: 020 7737 6103 (Brixton)
info@raw-material.org
www.raw-material.org
A music and media education facility,
primarily for young people

## Raynaud's & Scleroderma Association

112 Crewe Rd  Alsager  Cheshire ST7 2JA
Tel: 01270 872776
Tel: 0800 9172494
info@raynauds.org.uk
www.raynauds.org.uk
Offers support to sufferers of both
conditions and raises funds for research and
welfare

## RDA see Riding for the Disabled
Association

## Re-Cycle

www.re-cycle.org
Collects secondhand bicycles to send to
Africa, some help health/AIDS workers
reach remote villages and even provide an
ambulance service

## REACH

89 Albert Embankment  London SE1 7TP
Tel: 020 7582 6543
email via website
www.reachskills.org.uk
Job placement for managerial and
professional people available to offer
part-time services as unpaid volunteers to
voluntary organisations

## REACT Rapid Effective Assistance for
Children with potentially Terminal illness

St Luke's House  270 Sandycombe Rd  Kew,
Surrey  TW9 3NP
Tel: 020 8940 2575
Email via website
www.reactcharity.org
Helps families facing the financial burden of
caring for a potentially terminally ill child

## Reading see also BookCrossing, Book
Power, BOOKTRUST, Listening Books,
Literacy Association (UK), People's
Network, Volunteer Reading Help

## Reading Agency

60 Farringdon Road  London  EC1R 3GA
Tel:  0871 750 1207
info@readingagency.org.uk

www.readingagency.org.uk
A charity aiming to inspire a reading nation by working with readers, writers, libraries and their partners

**Real Ale (Campaign for)** see CAMRA

**Real Education (Campaign for)**
18 Westlands Grove  York YO31 1EF
Tel: 01904 424134
cred@cre.org.uk
www.cre.org.uk
For higher standards and more choice in state schools

**Reclaim the Streets**
www.rts.gn.apc.org
Direct action on social & environmental issues

**Recording Services (Association of Professional)** APRS
PO Box 22  Totnes TQ9 7YZ
Tel: 01803 868600
email via website
www2.aprs.co.uk
Representing audio professionals

**Recycle for London**
Helpline: 0845 600 0323
www.recycleforlondon.com

**Recycle more**
Valpak Ltd   Stratford Business Park  Banbury Road
  Stratford-Upon-Avon  CV37 7GW
Tel: 08450 682 572
recycle-more@valpak.co.uk
www.recycle-more.co.uk
Encourages homes, businesses and schools to recycle more waste

**Recycle now campaign**
Helpline: 0845 600 0323
Email via website
www.recyclenow.com

**Recycling** see also Aluminium Packaging Recycling Organisation, bikerecycling.net, Computer Aid International, Freecycle, Furniture Recycling Network, Garden Organic, Save A Cup, Steel Can Recycling Information Bureau, Waste Watch, WRAP

**Recycling Appeal**
31-37 Etna Road  Falkirk  FK2 9EG
Tel: 08451 30 20 10
info@recyclingappeal.com
www.recyclingappeal.com
Collects mobile phones, PDAs and printer cartridges for reuse and recycling, raising funds and helping the environment.

**Red Cross (British)**
44 Moorfields  London EC2Y 9AL
Tel: 0844 871 1111

Tel: 0844 412 2804
information@redcross.org.uk
www.redcross.org.uk

**Red Cross (International Committee of the)**
19 Avenue de la Paix  CH-1202  Geneva
Tel: 00 41 22 734 6001
info@irc.org
www.icrc.org

**Red List of Endangered Species**
www.iucnredlist.org
The World Conservation Union assesses the threat to species

**Red Ribbon International** see AIDS Trust (National)

**REDRESS**
3rd Floor  87 Vauxhall Walk  London SE11 5HJ
Tel: 020 7793 1777
info@redress.org
www.redress.org
Seeking reparation for torture survivors

**Redundant Technology Initiative**
Access Space  1 Sidney Street  Sheffield S1 4RG
Tel: 0114 249 5522
www.lowtech.org
The Access Space is an open access centre where people can come to work artistically with redundant technology

**Redwings Horse Sanctuary**
Hapton  Norwich NR15 1SP
Tel: 01508 481000
info@redwings.co.uk
www.redwings.org.uk
To provide and promote the welfare, care and protection of horses, ponies, donkeys and mules

**Reflexology Association (British)**
Monks Orchard  Whitbourne  Worcester WR6 5RB
Tel: 01886 821207
bayly@britreflex.co.uk
www.britreflex.co.uk
Representative body for reflexology practitioners and students

**Reform Judaism (Movement for)**
The Sternberg Centre for Judaism  80 East End Rd  London N3 2SY
Tel: 020 8349 5640
Email via website
www.reformjudaism.org.uk

**Refuge**
4th Floor  International House  1 St Katharine's Way  London  E1W 1UN
24 hr national domestic violence helpline: 0808 2000 247 run in partnership between Women's

**Aid and Refuge**
Tel: 020 7395 7700
info@refuge.org.uk
www.refuge.org.uk
www.womensaid.org.uk
Provides safe accommodation for women
& children experiencing domestic violence.
Support, advice and referrals

**Refugee Agency (United Nations)** see
UNHCR

**Refugee Council**
240-250 Ferndale Road  Brixton  London SW9
8BB
Tel: 020 7346 6700
email via website
www.refugeecouncil.org.uk
Promotes refugees' rights in the UK and abroad
and advocate on their behalf

**Refugees & Exiles (European Council on)**
Secretariat  Rue Royale 146, 2nd Floor  1000
Brussels  Belgium
Tel: +32 (0)2 234 3800
ecre@ecre.org
www.ecre.org
Umbrella organisation of over 70 agencies
working in 30 countries to assist refugees

**Refugees (Student Action for)** STAR
Oxford House  Derbyshire Street  London E2
6HG
Tel: 020 7729 8880
email via website
www.star-network.org.uk
Network of university based students and
young people aged 16-25 supporting refugees
locally and nationally

**Refugees (US Committee for)**
www.refugees.org

**Register Office for Northern Ireland
(General)**
Oxford House  49-55 Chichester St  Belfast
BT1 4HL
Tel: 028 9151 3101
GRO_NISRA@dfpni.gov.uk
www.groni.gov.uk

**Register Office for Scotland (General)**
New Register House  3 West Register Street
Edinburgh EH1 3YT
Tel: 0131 334 0380
Email via website
www.gro-scotland.gov.uk
Responsible for registration of births, marriages,
deaths, divorces & adoptions, censuses of
population

**Relate**
Tel: 0300 100 1234
www.relate.org.uk
Supports family life. Provides counselling &
therapy for couples with relationship problems

**Relationships Scotland**
18 York Place  Edinburgh EH1 3EP
Tel: 0845 1192020
email via website
www.relationships-scotland.org.uk
Helps separating and divorcing parents,
children, young people and families.

**Relatives & Residents Association**
24 The Ivories  6-18 Northampton Street
London N1 2HY
Tel: 020 7359 8136
Tel: 020 7359 8148 (Admin)
info@relres.org
www.relres.org
Promotes the well being of older people in
homes and long stay hospitals

**Release** National drugs and legal helpline
124-128 City Road  London EC1V 2NJ
Advice Line: 0845 4500215
Tel: 020 7324 2989
ask@release.org.uk
www.release.org.uk

**Religious Education (Professional Council
for)** PCfRE
1020 Bristol Rd  Selly Oak  Birmingham B29
6LB
Tel: 0121 472 4242
admin@retoday.org.uk
www.retoday.org.uk
Publications and courses for teachers for
religious education

**Religious Society of Friends** see Quakers
in Britain

**REMAP**
D9 Chaucer Business Park  Kemsing
Sevenoaks TN15 6YU
Tel: 0845 1300 456
email via website
www.remap.org.uk
UK-wide charity with panels of local voluntary
engineers who help disabled people by making
specialist equipment for free

**Remploy**
18c Meridian East  Meridian Business Park
Leicester     LE19 1WZ
0845 155 2700
Minicom: 0845 155 0532
info@remploy.co.uk
www.remploy.co.uk
Provides employment services and
employment to people with disabilities and
complex barriers to work.

**RenewableUK**
Greencoat House  Francis Street  London
SW1P 1DH
Tel: 020 7901 3000
info@renewable-uk.com
www.bwea.com
Professional body for the UK wind industry

**REonline**
www.reonline.org.uk

**Reporters sans Frontières**
47 Rue Vivienne  75002 Paris
Tel: 00 33 1 44 83 84 84
rsf@rsf.org
www.rsf.org
Defends jailed journalists and press freedom
throughout the world

**Research Into Ageing** see Ageing (Research
Into)

**Resolution**
PO Box 302  Orpington BR6 8QX  DX 154460
Petts Wood 3
Tel: 01689 820272
info@resolution.org.uk
www.resolution.org.uk

**ReSolv** The Society for the Prevention of
Solvent & Volatile Substance Abuse
30A High St  Stone  Staffs ST15 8AW
Tel: 01785 817885
office@re-solv.org
www.re-solv.org
Aims to prevent solvent & volatile substance
abuse

**Resource Information Service** now see
Homeless Link

**RESPECT**
1st Floor Downstream Building  1 London
Bridge  London SE1 9BG
Tel: 0845 122 8609
Tel: 020 7022 1801
info@respect.uk.net
www.respect.uk.net
Promoting, supporting, delivering and
developing effective interventions with
perpetrators to end violence and abuse in
intimate partner and close family relationships

**Respect for Animals**
PO Box 6500  Nottingham NG4 3GB
Tel: 0115 952 5440
info@respectforanimals.org
www.respectforanimals.co.uk
Campaign against the international fur trade

**Restless Development**
7 Tufton Street  London SW1P 3QB
Tel: 020 7976 8070
info@restlessdevelopment.org
www.restlessdevelopment.org

An international development charity that
recruits and trains young adults  as volunteer
Peer Educators, to lead programmes that
address urgent health and environmental issues
in Africa and Asia

**Restricted Growth Association**
PO Box 15755  SOLIHULL  B93 3FY
RGA Office & Helpline: 0300 111 1970
office@restrictedgrowth.co.uk
www.restrictedgrowth.co.uk
Support and information for people with
restricted growth, families, professionals and
other interested parties

**Rethink**  Severe Mental Illness
89 Albert Embankment  London SE1 7TP
Tel: 0845 456 0455
info@rethink.org
www.rethink.org
Exists to improve the lives of everyone affected
by schizophrenia and other severe mental
illnesses

**reunite**  International Child Abduction Centre
PO Box 7124  Leicester LE1 7XX
Adviceline: 0116 255 6234
Tel: 0116 255 5345 (Admin)
reunite@dircon.co.uk
www.reunite.org
Information & support for parents who fear
or have experienced the abduction of a child

**Revision** see Bitesize: BBC revision web
site

**RIBA** see Architects (Royal Institute of British)

**Ricability**
Unit G03  The Wenlock Business Centre  50-52
Wharf Road  London N1 7EU
Tel: 020 7427 2460 (voice)
Textphone: 020 7427 2469
mail@ricability.org.uk
www.ricability.org.uk
Provides consumer information for elderly and
disabled consumers about useful products and
services

**RICS** see Chartered Surveyors (Royal Institute
of)

**Riding for the Disabled Association** RDA
Norfolk House  1A Tournament Court  Edgehill
Drive  Warwicks CV34 6LG
Tel: 0845 658 1082
Email via website
www.rda.org.uk

**Rifle Association (National)**
National Rifle Association  Bisley   Brookwood
Surrey GU24 0PB
Tel: 01483 797777
Email via website
www.nra.org.uk

## Rights of Women
52-54 Featherstone St  London EC1Y 8RT
Tel: 020 7251 6577
Tel: 020 7251 6575 (Admin)
info@row.org.uk
www.rightsofwomen.org.uk
Research into the law affecting women & free
legal advice line for women

## Rising Tide
info@risingtide.org.uk
www.risingtide.org.uk
UK coalition of groups committed to a
grassroots approach to fighting climate change

## RNIB see Blind (Royal National Institute of the)

## RNIB National Library Service
PO Box 173  Peterborough  PE2 6WS
Helpline: 0303 123 9999
Tel: 0303 123 9999
library@rnib.org.uk
www.rnib.org.uk
Provides a range of services for visually
impaired people and promotes access to
mainstream library and information services NB
Scheduled to become part of RNIB in January
2007 but details unavailable at time of going
to press

## RNID For deaf & hard of hearing people
19-23 Featherstone St  London EC1Y 8SL
Information Line: 0808 808 0123 (voice) 0808
808 9000 (text)
Tel: 020 7296 8000 (voice) & 020 7296
8001(text)
informationline@rnid.org.uk
www.rnid.org.uk

## Road Haulage Association
Roadway House  35 Monument Hill  Weybridge
Surrey KT13 8RN
Tel: 01932 841515
www.rha.uk.net

## Road Runners Club
www.roadrunnersclub.org.uk
Represents road runners nationwide

## RoadPeace UK National Charity for Road Crash Victims
Shakespeare Business Centre  245a Cold
Harbour Lane  Brixton  London SW9 8RR
Helpline: 0845 4500355
Tel: 020 7733 1603
info@roadpeace.org
www.roadpeace.org
For bereaved & injured road traffic victims.
Provides help and support for road crash
victims

## Roller Hockey Association of England Ltd. (National)
www.nrha.co.uk

## Roller Skating see Artistic Roller Skating (Federation of)

## Rona Sailing Project
Universal Marina  Crableck Lane  Sarisbury
Green  Southampton SO31 7ZN
Tel: 01489 885098
ann@ronatrust.com
www.ronasailingproject.org
Provides voyages for underprivileged and
disadvantaged youngsters aged 14-25 years
and for young people and adults with special
needs

## Roofie Foundation
1 Prime Parkway  Prime Enterprise Park  Derby
DE1 3QB
Helpline: 0800 783 2980
Tel: 01723 367251
email via website
www.roofie.com
Helpline for people who have been drug raped
or sexually abused through drink spiking

## Room to Read World Change Starts with Educated Children
www.roomtoread.org
Seeks to transform the lives of millions of
children in developing countries by focusing
on literacy and gender equality in education

## RoSPA Royal Society for the Prevention of Accidents
RoSPA House  Edgbaston Park  353 Bristol Rd
Birmingham B5 7ST
Tel: 0121 248 2000
help@rospa.co.uk
www.rospa.com

## Roundhouse
Chalk Farm Rd  London NW1 8EH
Tel: 0844 482 8008
Tel: 020 7424 9991
info@roundhouse.org.uk
www.roundhouse.org.uk
Performing arts venue

## Rowing see British Rowing

## Rowntree see Joseph Rowntree Foundation

## Roy Castle Lung Cancer Foundation
4-6 Enterprise Way  Wavertree Technology Park
Liverpool  L13 1FB
Tel: 0151 254 7200
foundation@roycastle.org
www.roycastle.org
The only charity in the world wholly dedicated
to defeating lung cancer, the biggest cancer
killer in the world

**Royal Academy of Arts**
Burlington House  Piccadilly  London W1J 0BD
Tel: 020 7300 8000
Education: 020 7300 5995
Bookings: 0844 209 0051
www.royalacademy.org.uk

**Royal Academy of Dance**
36 Battersea Sq  London SW11 3RA
Tel: 020 7326 8000
info@rad.org.uk
www.rad.org.uk
Exists to promote knowledge, understanding
and practice of dance internationally

**Royal Academy of Dramatic Art** see RADA

**Royal Academy of Music**
Marylebone Rd  London NW1 5HT
Tel: 020 7873 7373
go@ram.ac.uk
www.ram.ac.uk
Britain's senior music conservatoire, training
performers and composers. Part of the
University of London

**Royal Air Force**
Email via website
www.raf.mod.uk

**Royal Airforce Museum Cosford**
Shifnal  Shropshire  TF11 8UP
01902 376 200
cosford@rafmuseum.org

**& London**
Grahame Park Way  London  NW9 5LL
020 8205 2266
london@rafmuseum.org

**Royal Armouries Museum**
Armouries Drive  Leeds LS10 1LT
Tel: 0113 220 1999
enquiries@armouries.org.uk
www.royalarmouries.org

**Royal Ballet**
Royal Opera House  Covent Garden  London
WC2E 9DD
Tel: 020 7240 1200 (Admin)
Tel: 020 7304 4000 (Box Office & Info)
Email via website
www.roh.org.uk

**Royal Botanic Garden Edinburgh**
20a Inverleith Row  Edinburgh  EH3 5LR
Tel: 0131 552 7171
Email via website
www.rbge.org.uk

**Royal Botanic Gardens, Kew**
Richmond  Surrey TW9 3AB
Tel: 020 8332 5000
Tel: 020 8332 5655 (24-hour visitor information
line)

info@kew.org
www.kew.org
Saving plants for life

**Royal College of Veterinary Surgeons**
Belgravia House  62-64 Horseferry Rd  London
SW1P 2AF
Tel: 020 7222 2001
admin@rcvs.org.uk
www.rcvs.org.uk

**Royal Geographical Society** with The
Institute of British Geographers
1 Kensington Gore  London SW7 2AR
Tel: 020 7591 3000
Email via website
www.rgs.org

**Royal Horticultural Society**
80 Vincent Sq  London SW1P 2PE
Tel: 0845 260 5000
Email via website
www.rhs.org.uk

**Royal Institution & Michael Faraday
Museum**
21 Albemarle Street  London W1S 4BS
Tel: 020 7409 2992
ri@ri.ac.uk
www.rigb.org
For cutting edge scientific research & public
understanding of science

**Royal Mail** see Post Office

**Royal Mint (British)**
Freepost NAT23496  PO Box 500  Llantrisant
Pontyclun CF72 8YT
Tel: 01443 222111
Email via website
www.royalmint.com

**Royal Museum of Scotland** contact Scotland
(Museum of)

**Royal National Lifeboat Institution**
West Quay Road  Poole  Dorset BH15 1HZ
Tel: 0845 045 6999
email via website
www.rnli.org.uk
A charity that saves lives at sea and provides
sea safety and educational resources

**Royal Naval Museum**
HM Naval Base (PP66)  Portsmouth       PO1
3NH
023 9272 7562
email via website
www.royalnavalmuseum.org

**Royal Navy**
www.royalnavy.mod.uk

## Royal Observatory Greenwich
c/o National Maritime Museum  Park Row
Greenwich  London SE10 9NF
Tel: 020 8858 4422
www.nmm.ac.uk

## Royal Opera
Royal Opera House  Covent Garden  London
WC2E 9DD
Tel: 020 7240 1200 (Admin)
Tel: 020 7304 4000 (Box Office & Info)
email via website
www.roh.org.uk

## Royal Parks
The Old Police House  Hyde Park  London  W2
2UH
Tel: 020 7298 2000
hq@royalparks.gsi.gov.uk
www.royalparks.org.uk
Locations and history

## Royal Scottish Academy
The Mound  Edinburgh EH2 2EL
Tel: 0131 225 6671
Email via website
www.royalscottishacademy.org
Promotes living artists in Scotland through
its annual and student shows, scholarships,
awards and other exhibitions

## Royal Shakespeare Theatre see RSC

## Royal Society
6-9 Carlton House Terrace  London SW1Y 5AG
Tel: 020 7451 2500
Email via website
http://royalsociety.org/
The society has three roles: as the UK academy
of science, as a learned society and as a
funding agency

## Royal Society of Medicine RSM
1 Wimpole Street  London W1G 0AE
Tel: 020 7290 2900
sections@rsm.ac.uk
www.rsm.ac.uk
Educational activities and opportunities for
doctors, dentists, veterinary surgeons and allied
professions

## RSA  Royal Society for the Encouragement of Arts, Manufactures and Commerce
8 John Adam St  London WC2N 6EZ
Tel: 020 7930 5115
general@rsa.org.uk
www.thersa.org

## RSA Exams see OCR/Oxford Cambridge and RSA Examinations

## RSC Royal Shakespeare Company
The Courtyard Theatre   Southern Lane
Stratford-upon-Avon  Warwickshire CV37 6BB
Tel: 0844 800 1110 (General and tickets)
Tel: 0844 800 1113 (School tickets)
Other Education enquiries: 01789 272520
Email via website
www.rsc.org.uk

## RSM see Royal Society of Medicine

## RSPB Royal Society for the Protection of Birds
The Lodge  Potton Road  Sandy  Bedfordshire
SG19 2DL
Tel: 01767 680551
Email via website
www.rspb.org.uk

## RSPCA Royal Society for the Prevention of Cruelty to Animals
Headquarters  Wilberforce Way  Southwater
Horsham  W Sussex RH13 9RS
Cruelty Advice Line: 0300 1234 999 (24 hrs)
Tel: 0300 1234 555
www.rspca.org.uk

## RSSPCC see CHILDREN 1ST

## RSVP/CSV
237 Pentonville Rd  London N1 9NJ
Tel: 020 7643 1385
rsvpinfo@csv.org.uk
www.csv-rsvp.org.uk
Enables people aged 50+ to become actively
involved in voluntary work of their choice

## RTPI see Town Planning Institute (Royal)

## Rugby see also Scrum.com

## Rugby Football League
Red Hall  Red Hall Lane  Leeds LS17 8NB
Tel: 08444 777113
Tel: 0870 990 1313 (Ticket enquiries)
enquiries@rfl.uk.com
www.rfl.uk.com

## Rugby Football Union
Rugby House  Twickenham Stadium  200
Whitton Road
 Twickenham  Middlesex TW2 7BA
Tel: 0871 222 2120
enquiries@therfu.com
www.rfu.com

## Rugby Football Union for Women
Rugby House  Twickenham Stadium  200
Whitton Road  Twickenham  Middlesex TW2
7BA
Tel: 0871 222 2120
enquiries@therfu.com
www.rfu.com
Co-ordinating body for women's rugby in the
UK

## Rugby Football Union (Irish)
10/12 Lansdowne Rd  Dublin 4  Ireland
Tel: 00 353 1 6473 800
info@irishrugby.ie
www.irishrugby.ie

## Rugby Museum
World Rugby Museum  Twickenham Stadium
Rugby Road  Twickenham  Middlesex TW1
1DZ
Tel: 020 8892 8877
Email via website
www.rfu.com/microsites/museum

## Runaway Helpline (under 18)
Missing People  284 Upper Richmond Road
West  London SW14 7JE
Helpline: 0808 800 70 70
Tel: 020 8392 4590
Freefone 0500 700 700
runaway@missingpeople.org.uk
info@missingpeople.org.uk
www.runawayhelpline.org.uk
24hr national freecall helpline for those who
are away from home to leave a confidential
message for their family or carer and to seek
help and advice. For over 18s see Message
Home Helpline

## Runnymede Trust
7 Plough Yard  Shoreditch  London EC2A 3LP
Tel: 020 7377 9222
info@runnymedetrust.org
www.runnymedetrust.org
Conducts research & policy analysis in racial
equality and cultural diversity

**Rural affairs** see CLA, Communities in Rural
England (Action with), Cottage and Rural
Enterprises Ltd (CARE), Countryside Alliance,
CPRE: Campaign to Protect Rural England,
Environment, Food & Rural Affairs (Department
for), Natural England, Protection of Rural
Wales (Campaign for the)

## Rural Communities (Commission for)
John Dower House  Crescent Place
Cheltenham GL50 3RA
Tel: 01242 521381
info@ruralcommunities.gov.uk
www.ruralcommunities.gov.uk
Advises the Government on rural issues in
England. October 2010: This body will be
abolished and its concerns reflected in general
Government policy.

## Rural Research (Centre for)
Department of Geography  University of
Worcester  Henwick Road  Worcester WR2 6AJ
Tel: 01905 855185
crr@worc.ac.uk
www.worc.ac.uk/crr
An academic research unit specialising
in economic, social, agricultural and
environmental change in the countryside

## Rural Scotland (Association for the Protection of) APRS
Gladstone's Land (3rd Floor)  483 Lawnmarket
Edinburgh EH1 2NT

Tel: 0131 225 7012
info@ruralscotland.org
www.ruralscotland.btik.com
Scotland's countryside champion

## Ruskin College
Walton St  Oxford OX1 2HE
Tel: 01865 554331
enquiries@ruskin.ac.uk
www.ruskin.ac.uk
To enable mature students with little or no
qualifications to study

## RYA Sailability
RYA House  Ensign Way  Hamble
Southampton SO31 4YA
Tel: 02380 604 100
Email via website
www.rya.org.uk/programmes/ryasailability
UK development charity for disabled sailing

# S

### S4C
Parc Ty Glas  Llanishen  Cardiff CF14 5DU
Tel: 0870 600 4141
Email via website
www.s4c.co.uk
Welsh fourth TV channel

**SACRO** Safeguarding Communities -
Reducing Offending in Scotland
29 Albany Street  Edinburgh  EH1 3QN
Tel: 0131 624 7270
info@national.sacro.org.uk
www.sacro.org.uk
Services to reduce conflict and offending, to
make communities safer

**SAD** see Seasonal Affective Disorder
Association

### SADS
www.sads.org.uk
Information for the family and relatives of
a young person who has died of Sudden
Arrhythmic Death Syndrome - SADS
sometimes called sudden adult death
syndrome

### Safer Medicines Campaign
PO Box 62720  London   SW2 9FQ
Tel: 020 8265 2880
info@safermedicines.org
www.curedisease.net
Scientists and medical professionals who
question the value of testing human drugs on
animals

### Saferworld
The Grayston Centre  28 Charles Square
London N1 6HT
Tel: 020 7324 4646

general@saferworld.org.uk
www.saferworld.co.uk
Independent foreign affairs think tank working
for prevention of armed conflict

**Safety Council Awards (British)**
Email via website
www.britsafe.org

**Safety Council (British)**
70 Chancellors Rd  London W6 9RS
Tel: 020 8741 1231
mail@britsafe.org
www.britsafe.org
Corporate membership organisation that
provides health, safety and environmental
training, auditing, information and publications

**Sailing** see also Cirdan Sailing Trust,
Ellen MacArthur Trust, Historical Maritime
Society, Jubilee Sailing Trust, Marine Leisure
Association, Ocean Youth Trust, Rona
Sailing Project, RYA Sailability, Sea Ranger
Association, Tall Ships Youth Trust

**Saint John Ambulance**
St John Ambulance  27 St. John's Lane
London EC1M 4BU
Tel: 08700 10 49 50
National Helpline: 0870 010 4950
Email via website
www.sja.org.uk

**Salvation Army**
101 Newington Causeway  London SE1 6BN
Tel: 020 7367 4500
Email via website
www2.salvationarmy.org.uk

**SALVO** Architectural Salvage Listings
www.salvo.co.uk

**Samaritans**
PO Box 9090  Stirling  FK8 2SA
Nat. Helpline: 08457 909090 & 08457 90 91 92
(minicom)
jo@samaritans.org
www.samaritans.org
For local branches see phone book.
Samaritans offer 24 hour emotional support to
anyone in distress

**SAMM** Support After Murder & Manslaughter
Helpline: 0845 872 3440
support@samm.org.uk
www.samm.org.uk
Offers support and understanding to families
bereaved through murder and manslaughter

**Sand & Land Yacht Clubs (British Federation of)**
www.bfslyc.org.uk

**SANDS** see Stillbirth & Neonatal Death
Society

**SANE**
1st Floor  Cityside House  40 Adler St  London
E1 1EE
Saneline: 0845 767 8000
Tel: 020 7375 1002
info@sane.org.uk
www.sane.org.uk
National helpline providing information and
support for anyone affected by mental illness
and campaigns for better services for mental
health problems

**Sargent Cancer Care for Children** now see
CLICSargent

**Save our Building Societies**
8 Belmont Court  Belmont Hill  St Albans
Herts AL1 1RB
Tel: 01727 847370
info@sobs.org.uk
www.sobs.org.uk
Campaign to prevent building societies
changing to banks. Champions any mutual
organisation under threat

**Save our Waterways**
campaign@saveourwaterways.org
www.saveourwaterways.org
Campaigns on behalf of all waterways users
and those who live beside the waterways

**Save the Children (UK)**
1 St John's Lane  London EC1M 4AR
Tel: 0207 012 6400
supporter.care@savethechildren.org.uk
www.savethechildren.org.uk
Emergency relief runs alongside long-term
development & prevention work

**Saving Faces**
Facial Surgery Research Foundation  St
Bartholomew's Hospital  West Smithfield
London EC1A 7BE
Tel: 020 7601 7582
Email via website
www.savingfaces.co.uk
Raises awareness about facial disfigurement
through art. Fundraising charity for research
into the causes of facial cancers and other
conditions leading to disfigurement

**Schizophrenia** see also Rethink Severe
Mental Illness

**School Councils UK**
Tel: 0845 4569428
email via website
www.schoolcouncils.org
Charity training teachers & pupils to set up
effective structures for pupil involvement

**School Curriculum & Assessment Authority**
see Qualifications and Curriculum Authority
(QCA)

## School Food Trust
3rd Floor
2 St Paul's Place
125 Norfolk St
Sheffield
S1 2JF
0114 2742318
info@sft.gsi.gov.uk
www.schoolfoodtrust.org.uk
Has the remit of transforming school food and
food skills. October 2010: the body will no
longer have government funding. As of April
2011 it will continue as a charity.

## School Governors (National Association of)
Ground Floor
36 Great Charles Street Birmingham
B3 3JY
Tel: 0121 237 3780
governorhq@nga.org.uk
www.nga.org.uk
By school governors for governors

## School Journey Association
48 Cavendish Rd London SW12 0DH
Tel: 020 8675 6636
Tel: 0208 673 4849
thesja@btconnect.com
www.sjatours.org
Educational tours for school groups and young
people

## School Librarianship (International Association of) IASL
iasl@iasl-online.org
www.iasl-online.org
Provides an international forum for those
interested in promoting school library
programmes worldwide

## School Library Association
Unit 2 Lotmead Business Village Wanborough
Swindon SN4 0UY
Tel: 01793 791787
info@sla.org.uk
www.sla.org.uk
Committed to promotion and development of
libraries and information literacy in schools

## Schools Adjudicator (Office of the)
Mowden Hall Staindrop Road Darlington DL3
9BG
Tel: 01325 735303
OSA.TEAM@osa.gsi.gov.uk
www.schoolsadjudicator.gov.uk
Decides on schools organisation issues &
admission arrangements which can't be
resolved locally

## Schools Health Education Unit
3 Manaton Court Manaton Close Matford
Exeter EX2 8PF
Tel: 01392 667272
sheu@sheu.org.uk
www.sheu.org.uk

## Schools Music Association of Great Britain
Brook House 24 Royston Street Potton,
Bedfordshire SG19 2LP
info@schoolsmusic.org.uk
www.schoolsmusic.org.uk
SMA provides a vital link between school music
teachers and the education policy makers

## Schumacher see also Practical Action

## Schumacher UK
Create Environment Centre Smeaton Rd
Bristol BS1 6XN
Tel: 0117 903 1081
admin@schumacher.org.uk
www.schumacher.org.uk
Promotes human scale sustainable
development "as though people matter" in the
UK and abroad

## SCIAF Scottish Catholic International Aid Fund
19 Park Circus Glasgow G3 6BE
Tel: 0141 354 5555
sciaf@sciaf.org.uk
www.sciaf.org.uk

## SCIcentre The National Centre for Initial Teacher Training in Primary School Science
School of Education University of Leicester 21
University Road Leicester LE1 7RF
Tel: 0116 252 3659
iab6@le.ac.uk
www.le.ac.uk/se/centres/sci/SCIcentre.html
Produces resources to help with the training
of student teachers in the teaching of
science

## Science and Industry in Manchester (Museum of)
Liverpool Road Castlefield Manchester M3
4FP
Tel: 0161 832 2244
email via website
www.mosi.org.uk

## Science Association (British)
Wellcome Wolfson Building 165 Queen's
Gate London SW7 5HD
Tel: 0870 770 7101
email via website
www.britishscienceassociation.org
Nationwide organisation dedicated to
public engagement with science through
programmes and membership

## Science Centre (Glasgow)
50 Pacific Quay Glasgow G51 1EA
Tel: 0141 420 5000
Email via website
www.glasgowsciencecentre.org

This is a visitor attraction with a focus on science

**Science Education (Association for)**
College Lane  Hatfield  Herts AL10 9AA
Tel: 01707 283000
info@ase.org.uk
www.ase.org.uk
The subject association for teachers, technicians and others involved in science education

**Science Education (Centre for)**
Centre for Science Education  Sheffield Hallam University  City Campus  Howard St Sheffield S1 1WB
Tel: 0114 225 4870
n.a.fuller@shu.ac.uk
www.shu.ac.uk/research/cse/

**Science in the Public Interest (Center for)**
cspi@cspinet.org
www.cspinet.org
US organisation that focuses on food and alcohol & on reducing the carnage caused by alcoholic beverages

**Science Museum**
Exhibition Road  London SW7 2DD
Tel: 0870 870 4868 (Switchboard)
Education Bookings: 020 7942 4777
Email via website
www.sciencemuseum.org.uk

**Science, Technology & the Arts (National Endowment for)** NESTA
1 Plough Place  London  EC4A 1DE
Tel: 020 7438 2500
information@nesta.org.uk
www.nesta.org.uk
Promotes talent, innovation and creativity. October 2010: moved from the public to the voluntary sector to become a charitable company (subject to approval by the Charity Commission)

**Scientific Exploration Society**
Expedition Base  Motcombe  Nr Shaftesbury Dorset SP7 9PB
Tel: 01747 853353
Email via website
www.ses-explore.org
Expeditions for ordinary people to do extraordinary things for conservation and the environment

**Scientists for Global Responsibility**
Ingles Manor  Castle Hill Avenue  Folkestone Kent  CT20 2RD
Tel: 01303 851965
info@sgr.org.uk
www.sgr.org.uk/
Promotes ethical science and technology

**Scoliosis Association (UK)**
4 Ivebury Court  325 Latimer Rd  London W10 6RA
Helpline: 020 8964 1166
Tel: 020 8964 5343
info@sauk.org.uk.
www.sauk.org.uk
Links sufferers from curvature of the spine

**Scope**
6 Market Rd  London N7 9PW
Helpline: 0808 800 3333
Office tel: 020 7619 7100
response@scope.org.uk
www.scope.org.uk
Disability organisation whose focus is people with cerebral palsy

**Scotland (Museum of)**
Chambers St  Edinburgh EH1 1JF
Tel: 0131 225 7534
info@nms.ac.uk
www.nms.ac.uk

**Scotland Office**
Dover House  Whitehall  London SW1A 2AU
Tel: 020 7270 6754
Email via website
www.scotlandoffice.gov.uk

**Scots Language Resource Centre**
A K Bell Library  York Place  Perth PH2 8EP
Tel: 01738 440199
info@scotslanguage.com
www.scotslanguage.com

**Scottish Arts Council** see Arts Council (Scottish)

**Scottish Athletics Ltd**
Caledonia House  South Gyle  Edinburgh EH12 9DQ
Tel: 0131 539 7320
admin@scottishathletics.org.uk
www.scottishathletics.org.uk
Governing body for athletics in Scotland

**Scottish Awards Agency** now see Student Awards Agency for Scotland

**Scottish Ballet**
Tramway 25 Albert Drive  Glasgow G41 2PE
Tel: 0141 331 2931
email via website
www.scottishballet.co.uk
Scotland's National Dance Company

**Scottish Cultural Resources Access Network** now see SCRAN

**Scottish Cycle Union** now see Scottish Cycling

**Scottish Cycling**
Caledonia House  South Gyle  Edinburgh EH12 9DQ
Tel: 0131 317 9704

info@scottishcycling.org.uk
http://new.britishcycling.org.uk/scotland

**Scottish Government**
Office of 1st Minister  St Andrew's House
Regent Road  Edinburgh EH1 3DG
Tel: 08457 741 741
ceu@scotland.gsi.gov.uk
www.scotland.gov.uk

**Scottish National Disability Information Service** see UPDATE

**Scottish National Gallery of Modern Art**
75 Belford Rd  Edinburgh EH4 3DR
Tel: 0131 624 6200
gmainfo@nationalgalleries.org
www.nationalgalleries.org
Includes the Dean Gallery

**Scottish National Party** see SNP

**Scottish National Portrait Gallery**
Tel: 0131 624 6200
pginfo@nationalgalleries.org
www.nationalgalleries.org

**Scottish Opera**
39 Elmbank Crescent  Glasgow  G2 4PT
Tel: 0141 248 4567
information@scottishopera.org.uk
www.scottishopera.org.uk

**Scottish Parliament**
The Scottish Parliament  Edinburgh EH99 1SP
Tel: 0131 348 5000
Tel: 0800 092 7500
Textphone: 0800 092 7100
sp.info@scottish.parliament.uk
www.scottish.parliament.uk

**Scottish Qualifications Authority** SQA
Ironmills Road  Dalkeith  Midlothian  EH22 1LE
Tel: 0845 279 1000
customer@sqa.org.uk
www.sqa.org.uk
Main body in Scotland, responsible for all qualifications except degrees and some professional qualifications

**Scottish Society for the Prevention of Cruelty to Animals** see Prevention of Cruelty to Animals (Scottish Society for the)

**Scottish Tourist Board** now see Visit Scotland

**Scottish Youth Theatre**
105 Brunswick Street  Glasgow G1 1TF
Tel: 0141 552 3988
info@scottishyouththeatre.org
www.scottishyouththeatre.org

**Scout Association**
Gilwell Park  Bury Rd  Chingford  London E4 7QW
Helpline: 0845 3001818 (Scout Info Centre)
Tel: 020 8433 7100

info.centre@scout.org.uk
www.scouts.org.uk

**SCRAN**
John Sinclair House  16 Bernard Terrace
Edinburgh  EH8 9NX
Tel: 0131 662 1456
Email via website
www.scran.ac.uk
An educational resource for worldwide culture & human history

**Scrum.com**
www.scrum.com
Rugby website

**Sea Fish Industry Authority**
18 Logie Mill  Logie Green Rd  Edinburgh EH7 4HS
Tel: 0131 558 3331
Email via website
www.seafish.org

**Sea Ranger Association**
'Lord Amory'  631 Manchester Road  Dollar Bay  London  E14 3NU
info@searangers.org.uk
www.searangers.org.uk
For girls aged 10-21, all forms of boating

**Sealed Knot Ltd.**
Email via website
www.thesealedknot.org.uk
Charity teaching about the 17th century by re-enacting civil war battles

**Searchlight Magazine**
PO Box 1576  Ilford  Essex IG5 0NG
Tel: 020 7681 8660
editors@searchlightmagazine.com
www.searchlightmagazine.com
Anti racism and fascism monthly magazine

**Seasonal Affective Disorder Association** SAD
PO Box 989  Steyning  West Sussex  BN44 3HG
www.sada.org.uk
Advises sufferers. Informs public & health professions

**SEBDA** Social, Emotional & Behavioural Difficulties Association
Room 211  The Triangle  Exchange Square  Manchester M4 3TR
Tel: 0161 240 2418
admin@sebda.org
www.sebda.org

**Secular Society (National)**
25 Red Lion Square  London WC1R 4RL
Tel: 020 7404 3126
enquiries@secularism.org.uk
www.secularism.org.uk

Fights religious privilege & upholds the rights of those without religion. Works for separation of Church and State

**SeeAbility**
SeeAbility House  Hook Rd  Epsom  Surrey KT19 8SQ
Tel: 01372 755 000
enquiries@seeability.org
www.seeability.org
SeeAbility if the operating name of the Royal School for the Blind

**Self Unlimited**
14 Nursery Court  Kibworth Business Park Harborough Road  Kibworth  Leicester LE8 0EX
Tel: 0116 279 3225
info@selfunlimited.co.uk
www.selfunlimited.co.uk
Maintains a network of support services for people with learning disabilities across the country. Assisting people to live as independently as possible and to realise their full potential

**Self-Injury Guidance & Network Support** see FirstSigns

**Sense** National Deaf-Blind & Rubella Association
101 Pentonville Road  London N1 9LG
Tel: 0845 127 0060(voice)
Tel: 0845 127 0062 (text)
info@sense.org.uk
www.sense.org.uk
National organisation for the deaf blind and all involved with them

**SEPA** see Environment Protection Agency (Scottish)

**Serene** now see Cry-sis

**Serious Fraud Office**
Elm House  10-16 Elm St  London WC1X OBJ
Tel; 020 7239 7388 (Report a fraud)
Tel: 020 7239 7272
Email via website
www.sfo.gov.uk

**Seriously Ill for Medical Research**
www.simr.org.uk
A pressure group of patients who are seriously ill and wish research to continue into their conditions, free from the pressure exerted by anti-vivisection groups

**Seven Stories** The Centre for Children's Books
30 Lime Street  Newcastle upon Tyne  NE1 2PQ
Tel: 0845 2710777
info@sevenstories.org.uk
www.sevenstories.org.uk

Exhibitions, activities and events based on children's books

**Sex Education Forum**
National Children's Bureau  8 Wakley St London EC1V 7QE
Tel: 020 7843 1901
sexedforum@ncb.org.uk
www.ncb.org.uk/sef
Information and support for teachers and other professionals

**Sexual Abuse** see Survivors of Sexual Abuse

**Sexual Advice Association**
Tel: 0207 486 7262
info@sexualadviceassociation.co.uk
www.sda.uk.net
Provides advice & information on male and female sexual problems

**Sexwise** now see RU Thinking

**SFA** see Football Association (Scottish)

**SFL** see Football League (Scottish)

**Shakespeare** see also Folger Shakespeare Library, RSC

**Shakespeare Association (British)**
Email via website
www.britishshakespeare.ws

**Shakespeare at the Tobacco Factory**
The Tobacco Factory  Raleigh Rd  Bristol BS3 1TF
Tel: 0117 963 3054
Box Office: 0117 902 0344
office@sattf.org.uk
www.sattf.org.uk

**Shakespeare Birthplace Trust**
The Shakespeare Centre  Henley St  Stratford-upon-Avon CV37 6QW
Tel: 01789 204016
Tel: 01789 201806 (School groups & lifelong learning)
info@shakespeare.org.uk
www.shakespeare.org.uk
Lectures, workshops, day schools, courses & library with archive of Royal Shakespeare Company

**Shakespeare Schools Festival**
32-36 Loman Street  Southwark London, SE1 0EH
Tel: 0207 922 7755
enquiries@ssf.uk.com
www.ssf.uk.com

**Shakespeare's Globe Theatre**
21 New Globe Walk  Bankside  London SE1 9DT
Tel: 020 7902 1400
info@shakespearesglobe.com
www.shakespeares-globe.org

**Shared Experience Theatre**
13 Riverside House  27/29 Vauxhall Grove
London SW8 1SY
Tel: 020 7587 1596
admin@sharedexperience.org.uk
www.sharedexperience.org.uk

**Shared Interest Society Ltd**
2 Cathedral Square  The Groat Market
Newcastle-upon-Tyne NE1 1EH
Tel: 0191 233 9100
info@shared-interest.com
www.shared-interest.com
Ethical investment – finance for fair trade

**Shared Parenting Information Group** SPIG
www.spig.clara.net
To encourage and promote the continuation
of parenting by both parents after family
breakdown.

**ShareGift**
17 Carlton House Terrace  London SW1Y 5AH
Telephone: 020 7930 3737
help@sharegift.org.uk
www.sharegift.org.uk
Charity share donation scheme exists to make
it easy to give any number of shares to charity

**Shark Alliance**
info@sharkalliance.org
www.sharkalliance.org
Restoring and conserving shark populations by
improving shark conservation policies

**Shelter**
88 Old St  London EC1V 9HU
Shelterline: 0808 800 4444
Tel: 0300 330 0516
info@shelter.org.uk
www.shelter.org.uk
Housing charity

**Shelter Cymru**
25 Walter Road  Swansea SA1 5NN
Helpline: 0845 075 5005
Tel: 01792 469400
Email via website
www.sheltercymru.org.uk

**Shelter (Scotland)**
4th Floor, Scotiabank House  6 South Charlotte
Street  Edinburgh EH2 4AW
Helpline: 0808 800 4444
Tel: 0300 330 0516
info@shelter.org.uk
www.shelter.org.uk
Helps people find and keep a home and
campaigns for decent housing for all

**Shiatsu Society (UK)**
PO Box 4580  Rugby  CV21 9EL
Tel: 0845 130 4560
Email via website
www.shiatsusociety.org

Complementary therapy based on oriental
medicine

**Shine a Light**
info@shinealight.org
www.shinealight.org
Helping young homeless people via grassroots
organisations in Latin America

**Shingles Support Society**
41 North Rd  London N7 9DP
Helpline: 0845 1232305
info@herpes.org.uk
www.herpes.org.uk
Enclose sae for information on all aspects of
herpes virus infections

**Shoplifting** see Crisis Counselling for Alleged
Shoplifters

**Shopmobility (National Federation of)**
PO Box 6641  Christchurch  BH23 9DQ
Tel: 08456 442446
info@shopmobilityuk.org
www.shopmobilityuk.org
Shopmobility schemes provide wheelchairs &
scooters for use in over 260 shopping areas

**Short Persons Support**
www.shortsupport.org

**Show Jumping Association (British)**
National Agricultural Centre  Stoneleigh Park
Kenilworth CV8 2LR
Tel: 024 7669 8800
email via website
www.britishshowjumping.co.uk

**Show Racism the Red Card**
PO Box 141  Whitley Bay  Tyne & Wear NE26 3YH
Tel: 0191 257 8519
info@theredcard.org
www.srtrc.org
Against racism in football

**Sibs**
Meadowfield  Oxenhope  West Yorkshire
BD22 9JD
Tel: 01535 645453
Email via website
www.sibs.org.uk
For brothers and sisters of people with
special needs

**Sick Children (Action for)**
32b Buxton Rd,  High Lane  Stockport SK6
8BH
Helpline: 0800 0744 519
Tel: 01663 763 004
Email via website
www.actionforsickchildren.org
Aims to improve standards in children's
healthcare

**Sickle Cell Society**
54 Station Rd  London NW10 4UA
Tel: 020 8961 7795

info@sicklecellsociety.org
www.sicklecellsociety.org
Provides info, counselling & care for people with sickle cell disorder

## Sight Savers International
Grosvenor Hall  Bolnore Rd  Haywards Heath RH16 4BX
Tel: 01444 446600
info@sightsavers.org
www.sightsavers.org
Projects to prevent & cure blindness in the developing world and train incurably blind people

## Signature
Mersey House  Mandale Business Park Belmont  Durham DH1 1TH
Tel: 0191 383 1155
Tel: 0191 383 7915 (Textphone Answerphone)
durham@signature.org.uk
www.signature.org.uk
Promotes communication between deaf & hearing people. National examination board of British Sign Language

## Signed Performances in Theatre see SPIT

## Sikh Organisations UK (Network of)
Suite 405  Highland House  165 The Broadway  Wimbledon  London SW19 1NE
Tel: 020 8544 8037
sikhmessenger@aol.com
www.nsouk.co.uk
Addresses issues of common concern and organises celebration of Sikh activities

## Simon Community
St. Joseph's House  129 Malden Road  London NW5 4HS
Tel: 020 7485 6639
Tel: 020 7482 0447
info@simoncommunity.org.uk
www.simoncommunity.org.uk
Provides caring & campaigns for London's street homeless

## Simon Jones Memorial Campaign
Community Base  113 Queens Road  Brighton BN1 3XG.
action@simonjones.org.uk
www.simonjones.org.uk
Campaigns against the dangers of casualisation of the workforce, following the death of Simon Jones in 1998

## Simon Wiesenthal Centre
Email via website
www.wiesenthal.com
International Jewish human rights organisation dedicated to preserving the memory of the Holocaust

## Simple Free Law Advisor
Email via website
www.sfla.co.uk

## Siobhan Dowd Trust
c/o DFB  31 Beaumont Street  Oxford OX1 2NP
Email via website
www.siobhandowdtrust.com/
Bringing books and reading to disadvantaged young people in the UK through the legacy of an award winning writer

## Ski Club of Great Britain
The White House  57-63 Church Rd Wimbledon  London SW19 5SB
Tel: 0845 4580 780
skiers@skiclub.co.uk
www.skiclub.co.uk

## Skill: National Bureau for Students with Disabilities
Unit 3, Floor 3  Radisson Court  219 Long Lane London SE1 4PR
Helpline: 0800 328 5050 & 18001 0800 328 5050 (Text)
Tel: 020 7450 0620
skill@skill.org.uk
www.skill.org.uk
Promoting equality in post-16 education, work-based learning and transition to employment

## Skills for Care
West Gate  6 Grace Street  Leeds  LS1 2RP
Tel: 0113 245 1716
info@skillsforcare.org.uk
www.skillsforcare.org.uk
Aiming to modernise adult social care in England, by ensuring qualifications and standards continually adapt to meet the changing needs of people who use care services

## Skills for Justice
Centre Court  Atlas Way  Sheffield  S4 7QQ
Tel:  0114 261 1499
info@skillsforjustice.com
www.skillsforjustice.com
Works with employers to raise skills across the Justice Sector

## Skills Funding Agency
Cheylesmore House  Quinton Road  Coventry CV1 2WT
Learner Support helpline: 0800 121 8989
Tel: 0845 377 5000
info@skillsfundingagency.bis.gov.uk
http://skillsfundingagency.bis.gov.uk

## Skillshare International
126 New Walk  Leicester LE1 7JA
Tel: 0116 254 1862
info@skillshare.org
www.skillshare.org
Development agency working in Africa and Asia

**Sky** British Sky Broadcasting
www.sky.com

**Skylight Circus Arts**
email via website
www.skylightcircusarts.com
Circus skills workshops and projects for young
people, can lead to performances

**Slavery** see Anti-Slavery International

**Sleep Council**
Freephone leaflet line: 0800 018 7923
Tel: 0845 058 4595
info@sleepcouncil.org.uk
www.sleepcouncil.org.uk
Promotes the benefits to health of a good
night's sleep. Non-profit organisation funded by
bed manufacturers & retailers.

**Slivers of Time**
www.sliversoftime.com
Social enterprise running online marketplaces
where anyone can sell spare hours, on their
own terms, to multiple employers.

**Slow Food**
6 Neal's Yard  Covent Garden  London WC2H
9DP
Tel: 020 7099 1132
info@slowfood.org.uk
www.slowfood.org.uk
To save & protect small-scale quality specialist
food production from industrial standardisation
& to list & protect threatened varieties of
foodstuffs

**Small Animal Veterinary Association
(British)**
Woodrow House  1 Telford Way  Waterwells
Business Park  Quedgeley  Gloucester GL2
2AB
Tel: 01452 726700
administration@bsava.com
www.bsava.com

**Small Businesses (Federation of)**
Head Office  Sir Frank Whittle Way  Blackpool
Business Park  Blackpool FY4 2FE
Tel: 01253 336000
membership@fsb.org.uk
www.fsb.org.uk

**Smallpeice Trust**
Holly House  74 Upper Holly Walk  Leamington
Spa  Warwickshire CV32 4JL
Tel: 01926 333200
info@smallpeicetrust.org.uk
www.smallpeicetrust.org.uk
Engineering awareness courses for students
13 - 18 years old

**SmartParent**
www.parentsmart.com
Gives advice to parents on safe use of the
internet

**Smith Institute**
4th Floor  Somerset House  South Wing  Strand
London WC2R 1LA
Tel: 020 7845 5845
info@smith-institute.org.uk
www.smith-institute.org.uk
Independent think-tank undertaking research/
education in issues arising from interaction of
equality and enterprise

**Smokefree (NHS)**
Helpline: 0800 0224332
http://smokefree.nhs.uk/

**Snow and Ice Data Center (National)**
http://nsidc.org/
Support scientific research that informs the
world about our planet and our climate systems

**SNP** Scottish National Party
3 Jackson's Entry  Edinburgh EH8 8PJ
Tel: 0800 633 5432
snp.hq@snp.org
www.snp.org

**SOCA (Serious Organised Crime Agency)**
PO Box 8000  London SE11 5EN
Tel: 0370 496 7622
www.soca.gov.uk
October 2010: Functions will be merged into
the new National Crime Agency

**Social Care Association**
350 West Barnes lane  Motspur Park
Motspur Park  KT3 6NB
Tel: 020 8949 5837
www.socialcaring.co.uk
Professional membership association for all
staff in the social care service

**Social Democratic & Labour Party**
121 Ormeau Rd  Belfast BT7 1SH
Tel: 028 9024 7700
info@sdlp.ie
www.sdlp.ie

**Social & Economic Research (Institute for)**
University of Essex  Wivenhoe Park  Colchester
CO4 3SQ
Tel: 01206 872957
iser@essex.ac.uk
www.iser.essex.ac.uk
Production and analysis of longitudinal data –
evidence tracking changes in the lives of the
same individuals over time

**Social Entrepreneurs (School for)**
18 Victoria Park Sq  London E2 9PF
Tel: 020 8981 0300
email via website
www.sse.org.uk

Provides socially aware independent people in the public sector and business with the training to make their ideas a reality

## Social Issues Research Centre
28 St Clements  Oxford OX4 1AB
Tel: 01865 262255
group@sirc.org
www.sirc.org
Independent, non-profit organisation conducting research on social & lifestyle issues

## Social Market Foundation
11 Tufton St  London SW1P 3QB
Tel: 020 7222 7060
enquiries@smf.co.uk
www.smf.co.uk
Social policy think tank

## Social Sciences (Association for the Teaching of the) ATSS
Old Hall Lane  Manchester M13 0XT
Tel: 0161 248 9375
atss@btconnect.com
www.atss.org.uk

## Social Security (Department of) see Work & Pensions (Department for)

## Social Workers (British Association of)
16 Kent St  Birmingham B5 6RD
Tel: 0121 622 3911
info@basw.co.uk
www.basw.co.uk

## Socialism see also Christian Socialist Movement

## Socialist Health Association
22 Blair Road   Manchester  M16 8NS
Tel: 0161 286 1926
admin@sochealth.co.uk
www.sochealth.co.uk

## Socialist Labour Party
PO Box 112  Leigh  WN7 4WS
Tel: 01942 603335
info@socialist-labour-party.org.uk
www.socialist-labour-party.org.uk
Aims to end capitalism & replace it with socialism

## Soil Association
Soth Plaza  Malborough Street  Bristol  BS1 3NX
Tel: 0117 314 5000
www.soilassociation.org
Campaigning for organic food and farming and sustainable forestry

## Solar Energy Society UK-ISES
PO Box 489  Abingdon OX14 4WY
Tel: 0776 016 3559
info@uk-ises.org
www.uk-ises.org

## Solicitors Family Law Association see Resolution

## Solicitors for the Elderly
Room 17  Conbar House  Mead Lane  Hertford SG13 7AD
admin@solicitorsfortheelderly.com
www.solicitorsfortheelderly.com
National association committed to providing high quality legal services for older people, their family and carers

## Solidar
Rue de Commerce 22  B-1000   Brussels Belgium
Tel: 00 322 500 1020
email via website
www.solidar.org
Lobbying for trade union rights, development and humanitarian aid

## Solo Clubs (National Federation of)
PO Box 2278  Nuneaton  CV11 5PA
Tel: 0247 673 6499
national@federation-solo-clubs.co.uk
www.federation-solo-clubs.co.uk

## Songwriters, Composers and Authors (British Academy of)
26 Berners St  London W1T 3LR
email via website
www.basca.org.uk
Membership organisation for music writers of all genres

## Sonic Arts Network now see Sound and Music

## Sorted In 10
www.sortedin10.co.uk
Practical information and advice on erectile difficulties

## SOS Children
Terrington House  13-15 Hills Road  Cambridge CB2 1NL
Tel: 01223 365589
info@soschildren.org
www.soschildren.org
A child welfare organisation providing families for orphaned and abandoned children in 131 countries

## Sound and Music
Somerset House  3rd Floor, South Wing  Strand London WC2R 1LA
Tel: 020 7759 1800
info@soundandmusic.org
www.soundandmusic.org
UK's landmark agency for new music and sound

## Sound Seekers see Deaf (Commonwealth Society for the)

## Sound Sense
info@soundsense.org
www.soundsense.org
Offers comprehensive advice and information on all aspects of community music and music and disability

## SoundJunction
www.soundjunction.org
Interactive site about exploring, discovering and creating music. Produced by the Associated Board of the Royal Schools of Music

## Southern Africa (Action for)
231 Vauxhall Bridge Road  London  SW1V 1EH
Tel: 020 3263 2001
actsa@actsa.org
www.actsa.org
Campaigns for peace, democracy and development in Southern Africa

## SOVA Supporting Others Through Volunteer Action
1st Floor  Chichester House  37 Brixton Rd London SW9 6DZ
Tel: 020 7793 0404
email via website
www.sova.org.uk
Recruits & supports volunteers working with offenders and socially excluded people

## Space Agency (European)
www.esa.int

## Space Agency (UK)
Polaris House  North Star Avenue  Swindon Wiltshire  SN2 1SZ
Tel: 020 7215 5000
email via website
www.ukspaceagency.bis.gov.uk
At the heart of the UK efforts to explore and benefit from space

## Space Centre (National)
Exploration Drive  Leicester LE4 5NS
Tel: 0116 2610261
info@spacecentre.co.uk
www.spacecentre.co.uk

## Spanish Embassy Education Office
Resources Centre  20 Peel St  London  W8 7PD
Tel: 020 7727 2462
www.mec.es/sgci/uk

## Spanish Institute Instituto Cervantes
102 Eaton Sq  London SW1W 9AN  & 326 Deansgate  Manchester M3 4FN
Tel: 020 7235 0353 (London)
Tel: 0161 661 4200 (Manchester)
cenlon@cervantes.es
www.cervantes.es
Spanish courses, lectures, cultural activities and library

## Sparks
Heron House  10 Dean Farrar Street  London SW1H 0DX
Tel: 020 7799 2111
www.sparks.org.uk
Funds pioneering research that has a practical and positive impact on the lives of babies and children

## Spartacus Educational
www.spartacus.schoolnet.co.uk
History website

## Spatial Literacy
www.spatial-literacy.org
Teaching, research and outreach activities in higher education and a portal to guide best practice across a range of public sector geographic information system activities

## Speakers Clubs (Association of)
national.secretary@the-asc.org.uk
www.the-asc.org.uk

## Speaking up now see Voiceability

## Special Educational Advice (Independent Panel for) see IPSEA

## Special Educational Needs & Disability Tribunal  SENDIST
Mowden Hall  Staindrop Road  Darlington DL3 9BG
Tel: 01325 392760
sendistenquiries@tribunals.gsi.gov.uk
www.sendist.gov.uk

## Special Educational Needs (National Association for)
NASEN House  4/5 Amber Business Village Amber Close  Amington  Tamworth  Staffs B77 4RP
Tel: 01827 311500
welcome@nasen.org.uk
www.nasen.org.uk

## Special Needs Education (European Agency for Development in)
Østre Stationsvej 33  DK-5500 Odense C Denmark
Tel: 00 45 64 41 00 20
secretariat@european-agency.org
www.european-agency.org

## Special Olympics GB
Tel: 020 7247 8891
info@sogb.org.uk
www.specialolympicsgb.org
For people with learning disabilities

## Specialist Schools and Academies Trust
16th Floor  Millbank Tower  21-24 Millbank London SW1P 4QP
Tel: 020 7802 2300
info@ssatrust.org.uk
www.ssatrust.org.uk

To promote an educational culture emphasising the specialisms of science, technology, maths and computing, languages, humanities, arts, music, sport, engineering, business and enterprise, vocational

**Speech** see also Afasic, Cued Speech Association UK, Stammering Association (British), Stammering Children (Michael Palin Centre for)

**Speech and Language Therapists (Royal College of)**
2 White Hart Yard  London SE1 1NX
Tel: 020 7378 1200
info@rcslt.org
www.rcslt.org
Professional body for UK speech and language therapists. Sets standards of practice. Provides careers information to the public

**Spelling Society (English)**
enquiries@spellingsociety.org
www.spellingsociety.org

**Spina Bifida** see ASBAH

**Spinal Injuries Association**
SIA House  2 Trueman Place  Oldbrook Milton Keynes MK6 2HH
Tel: 08456 786633
sia@spinal.co.uk
www.spinal.co.uk
Represents spinal cord injured people regardless of how the impairment occurred

**Spinal Injury Research, Rehabilitation & Reintegration (Association for)**
ASPIRE National Training Centre  Wood Lane  Stanmore HA7 4AP
Tel: 020 8954 5759
info@aspire.org.uk
www.aspire.org.uk
Services those with spinal cord injury and the wider disabled community

**SPIT** Signed Performances in Theatre
email via website
www.spit.org.uk
Promotes BSL interpreted performances of mainstream theatre

**Sport England**
3rd Floor Victoria House  Bloomsbury Square  London WC1B 4SE
Tel: 08458 508508
info@sportengland.org
www.sportengland.org
To lead the development of sport in England. October 2010: To merge with UK Sport

**Sport Northern Ireland**
House of Sport  2a Upper Malone Rd Belfast BT9 5LA
Tel: 028 90 381 222
info@sportni.net
www.sportni.net

**Sport Wales**
Sophia Gardens  Cardiff CF11 9SW
Tel: 0845 045 0904
info@sportwales.co.uk
www.sportwales.org.uk/

**Sports Aid Foundation** now see SportsAid

**Sports Association for People with Learning Disabilities (UK)**
1st Floor, 12 City Forum  250 City Road London EC1V 2PU
Tel: 020 7490 3057
info@uksportsassociation.org
www.uksportsassociation.org
Co-ordinates and develops sporting opportunities

**Sports Centre (Lilleshall National)**
Tel: 01952 603003
email via website
www.lilleshallnsc.co.uk
Sports and conference centre run on behalf of Sport England

**Sports Coach UK** National Coaching Foundation
114 Cardigan Rd  Headingley  Leeds LS6 3BJ
Tel: 0113 274 4802
email via website
www.sportscoachuk.org
To help develop sports coaching

**Sports Council (Northern Ireland)** now see Sport Northern Ireland

**Sports Council UK** see UK Sport

**Sports Leaders UK**
23-25 Linford Forum  Rockingham Drive Linford Wood  Milton Keynes MK14 6LY
Tel: 01908 689180
contact@sportsleaders.org
www.sportsleaders.org
Funds and administers the Sports Leader awards

**SportsAid**
Tel: 020 7273 1975
mail@sportsaid.org.uk
www.sportsaid.org.uk
Charity assisting sports people who need help with training

**sportscotland**
Doges  Templeton on the Green  62 Templeton Street  Glasgow G40 1DA
Tel: 0141 534 6500
sportscotland@sportscotland.org.uk
www.sportscotland.org.uk

**sportscotland Avalanche Information Service**
www.sais.gov.uk
Daily forecasts on web of avalanche and climbing conditions in 5 main Scottish climbing areas from mid December - mid April

**SPPA** see Pre-School Play Association (Scottish)

**SPR** see Psychical Research (Society for)

**SQA** see Scottish Qualifications Authority

**Squatters (Advisory Service for)**
Angel Alley  84b Whitechapel High Street London E1 7QX
Tel: 020 3216 0099
advice@squatter.org.uk
www.squatter.org.uk

**SSPCA** see Prevention of Cruelty to Animals (Scottish Society for the)

**Stakeholder Forum**
3 Bloomsbury Place  London  WC1A  2QL
Tel: 0207 580 6912
info@stakeholderforum.org
www.stakeholderforum.org
Concerned with sustainable development

**Stammering Association (British)**
15 Old Ford Rd  London E2 9PJ
Helpline:
0845 603 2001
Tel: 020 8983 1003
mail@stammering.org
www.stammering.org

**Stammering Children (Michael Palin Centre for)** The Association for Research into Stammering in Childhood
Finsbury Health Centre  Pine St  London EC1R OLP
Tel: 020 7530 4238
email via website
www.stammeringcentre.org
Provides a specialist advice and assessment service for children from all over the UK

**STAR** see Refugees (Student Action for)

**State Education (Campaign for)**
98 Erlanger Road  London SE14 5TH
Tel: 07932 149942
contact@campaignforstateeducation.org.uk
www.campaignforstateeducation.org.uk
Campaigns for the best in state education for all children

**Statewatch**
PO Box 1516  London N16 0EW
Tel: 020 8802 1882
office@statewatch.org
www.statewatch.org

Monitors the state and civil liberties in the UK and the EU

**Statistics** see also Australian Bureau of Statistics, Databank, Education Statistics (USA National Center for), General Register Office, Indian Census, Office for National Statistics, National Archives, Office for National Statistics, Population Statistics, Register Office for N. Ireland, Register Office for Scotland, Worldometers

**Statistics New Zealand**
info@stats.govt.nz
www.stats.govt.nz

**Steel Can Recycling Information Bureau**
Trostre Works  Llanelli  Carmarthenshire SA14 9SD
Tel: 01554 712632
nicola.bennett@ tatasteel.com
www.cspr.co.uk

**Steiner Waldorf Education (European Council for)** ECSWE
Kidbrooke Park  Forest Row  East Sussex RH18 5JA
Tel: 01342 822115
office@steinerwaldorf.org
www.steinerwaldorf.org.uk
Represents over 600 European Steiner schools. 31 schools in UK & Ireland form the Steiner Waldorf Schools Fellowship UK

**Stephen Lawrence Charitable Trust**
39 Brookmill Road  London SE8 4HU
Tel: 020 8100 2800
information@stephenlawrence.org.uk
www.stephenlawrence.org.uk/
Established in memory of Stephen Lawrence to provide young black people with opportunities to study architecture and associated arts

**Stillbirth & Neonatal Death Society**
SANDS
28 Portland Place  London W1B 1LY
National Helpline: 020 7436 5881
Tel: 020 7436 7940
support@uk-sands.org
www.uk-sands.org

**Stock Exchange (London)**
10 Paternoster Square  London EC4M 7LS
Tel: 020 7797 1000
www.londonstockexchange.com

**Stonewall**
Tower Building  York Road  London SE1 7NX
Tel: 08000 50 20 20
info@stonewall.org.uk
www.stonewall.org.uk
Equality and justice for lesbians, gay men and bisexuals

## Stop Climate Chaos Coalition
c/o Oxfam  232-242 Vauxhall Bridge Road
London SW1V 1AU
Tel: 020 7802 9989
admin@stopclimatechaos.org
www.stopclimatechaos.org/icount
The UK's largest group of people dedicated to
action on climate change and limiting its impact
on the world's poorest communities

## Stop Climate Chaos Scotland
c/o RSPB Scotland  25 Ravelston Terrace
Edinburgh  EH4 3TP
Tel: 0131 311 6512
info@stopclimatechaosscotland.org

## Storytelling (Society for)
c/o The Morgan Library  Aston St  Wem
Shropshire SY4 5AU
Tel: 0753 457 8386
admin@sfs.org.uk
www.sfs.org.uk

## Stress Management Association
(International) ISMA UK
PO Box 491  Bradley  Stoke  Bristol BS34 9AH
Tel: 01179 697284
info@isma.org.uk
www.isma.org.uk
Promotes sound knowledge and best practice

## Stroke Association
Stroke House  240 City Road  London EC1V
2PR
Helpline: 0303 303 3100
Tel: 020 7566 0300
info@stroke.org.uk
www.stroke.org.uk
Helps stroke sufferers and their families to fight
stroke which is the third biggest killer and most
serious disabler in the UK

**Strokes** see also Different Strokes

## Student Awards Agency for Scotland
Gyleview House  3 Redheughs Rigg  Edinburgh
EH12 9HH
Tel: 0845 111 1711
Email via website
www.saas.gov.uk
Processes applications from Scottish students
for higher education courses throughout the UK

## Student Drama Festival (National)
Woolyard  54 Bermondsey Street  London SE1
3UD
Tel: 020 7036 9027
info@nsdf.org.uk
www.nsdf.org.uk
Britain's premier festival of the finest student
theatre. An annual event 1-7 April 2006

## Student Loans Company Ltd
100 Bothwell St  Glasgow G2 7JD
See website for regional student finance

enquiry telephone numbers
Tel: 0141 306 2000 (Admin)
www.slc.co.uk
Administers the Government's student loans
schemes for undergraduates in the UK.
October 2010: future under review

**Students** see also thematic guide - Education

**Students in Europe** see ESIB - The National
Unions of Students in Europe

**Students Partnership Worldwide** now see
Restless Development

## Studies in British Art (Paul Mellon Centre for)
16 Bedford Sq  London  WC1B 3JA
Tel: 020 7580 0311
info@paul-mellon-centre.ac.uk
www.paul-mellon-centre.ac.uk

**Study Support** see Quality in Study Support
and Extended Services

## Sub Aqua Club (British)
Telford's Quay  South Pier Road  Ellesmere Port
CH65 4FL
Tel: 0151 350 6200
info@bsac.com
www.bsac.com

**Substance abuse** see thematic guide for
Drugs and substance abuse & for Alcohol

**Suicide** see Hopeline UK, PAPYRUS
(Prevention of Suicides), Survivors of
Bereavement by Suicide

## Sundial Society (British)
email via website
www.sundialsoc.org.uk
Concerned with art & science of gnomonics

## Sunsmart Campaign
www.sunsmart.com.au
Australian website providing sun protection
advice

## Supervision of Solicitors (Office for the)
now see Law Society Consumer Complaints
Service

**Support After Murder & Manslaughter** see
SAMM

## Support Dogs
21 Jessops Riverside  Brightside Lane
Sheffield S9 2RX
Tel: 0114 261 7800
supportdogs@btconnect.com
www.support-dogs.org.uk
Trains dogs for people with epilepsy, physical
disabilities and other specific medical
conditions

## Surf Life Saving Association of GB
1st Floor  19 Southernhay West  Exeter EX1
1PJ

Tel: 01392 218007
mail@slsgb.org.uk
www.surflifesaving.org.uk
Teaching, sport & patrolling of surf beaches

**Surfers Against Sewage**
Unit 2 Wheal Kitty Workshops  St Agnes
Cornwall TR5 0RD
Tel: 01872 553001
email via website
www.sas.org.uk
Campaigns for cessation of marine sewage and
toxic waste discharge

**Surfing Association (British)**
International Surfing Centre  Fistral Beach
Newquay  Cornwall TR7 1HY
Tel: 01637 876474
info@britsurf.co.uk
www.britsurf.co.uk

**Surgerydoor.co.uk**
www.surgerydoor.co.uk
UK health website

**Surname Profiler**
www.nationaltrustnames.org.uk
Maps the distribution of surnames in Great
Britain, both current and historic, showing
patterns of population movement, social
mobility, regional economic development and
cultural identity

**Survival International**
6 Charterhouse Buildings  London EC1M 7ET
Tel: 020 7687 8700
info@survivalinternational.org
www.survivalinternational.org
Supports tribal peoples and helps them protect
their lives, lands and human rights

**Survivors of Bereavement by Suicide**
The Flamsteed Centre  Albert Street  Ilkeston
Derby  DE7 5GU
National Helpline: 0844 561 6855
Tel: 0115 944 1117
sobs.admin@care4free.net
www.uk-sobs.org.uk

**Sustain** The Alliance for Better Food &
Farming
94 White Lion St  London N1 9PF
Tel: 020 7837 1228
sustain@sustainweb.org
www.sustainweb.org
102 national organisations promoting good
food and farming policy

**SustainAbility**
20-22 Bedford Row  London WC1R 4EB
Tel: 020 7269 6900
email via website
www.sustainability.com
Specialises in business strategy & sustainable
development

**Sustrans**
2 Cathedral Square  College Green  Bristol BS1
5DD
Infoline: 0845 113 0065
Tel: 0117 926 8893
info@sustrans.org.uk
www.sustrans.org.uk
Sustainable transport charity developing the
national cycle network and safe routes to
schools

**& Cymru**
123 Bute Street   Cardiff  CF10 5AE
Tel: 029 2065 0602
sustranscymru@sustrans.org.uk
www.sustrans.org.uk

**& Northern Ireland**
Ground Floor  Premier Business Centres  20
Adelaide Street  Belfast    BT2 8GD
Tel: 028 9043 4569
belfast@sustrans.org.uk
www.sustrans.org.uk

**& Scotland**
Glenorchy House  20 Union Street  Edinburgh
EH1 3LR
Tel: 0131 539 8122
scotland@sustrans.org.uk
www.sustrans.org.uk

**Suzuki Institute (British)**
Unit 1.01  The Lightbox  111 Power Road
Chiswick  London W4 5PY
Tel: 020 3176 4170
info@britishsuzuki.com
www.britishsuzuki.com
Charity promoting the Suzuki method of music
education

**Suzy Lamplugh Trust**
National Centre for Personal Safety  218 Strand
London WC2R 1AT
Tel: 020 7091 0014
info@suzylamplugh.org
www.suzylamplugh.org
The UK's leading authority on personal safety.
We provide training, confidence and lots of
personal safety resources including alarms

**Swimming** see also Lifeguard Skills,
Lifesavers, Surf Life Saving Association of GB

**Swimming**
email via website
www.swimming.org
Also gives access to British Swimming,
Amateur Swimming Association and the
Institute of Swimming

### Swimming Clubs for the Handicapped (National Association of)

The Willows  Mayles Lane  Wickham  Hants PO17 5ND
Tel: 01329 833689
naschswim-willows@yahoo.co.uk
www.nasch.org.uk

# T

### Table Tennis Association (English)

Queensbury House  Havelock Rd  Hastings TN34 1HF
Tel: 01424 456217
admin@etta.co.uk
www.englishtabletennis.org.uk

### Tacade Advisory Council for Alcohol & Drug Education

Old Exchange Buildings  6 St Ann's Passage Manchester M2 6AD
Tel: 0161 836 6850
ho@tacade.co.uk
www.tacade.com
Consultancy, training service, publications, projects concerned with citizenship, sexual health & relationships, drugs & alcohol education & other health related issues

### TACT

The Courtyard,  303 Hither Green Lane  Hither Green  London, SE13 6TJ
Tel: 0800 232 1157
Tel: 020 8695 8142
enquiries@tactcare.org.uk
www.tactcare.org.uk
Finds new families for adoption & fostering of children with special needs

### TAG Telecommunications Action Group

info@deaftag.org.uk
www.deaftag.org.uk
Promotes access to electronic communications, including telecommunications and broadcasting for deaf and hard of hearing people

### Tai Chi Finder

www.taichifinder.co.uk
Locates classes and organisations

### Tai Chi Union for GB

5 Corrunna Dr  Horsham  West Sussex  RH13 5HG
email via website
www.taichiunion.com

### Talk Adoption

5 Blantyre Street  Manchester M15 4JJ
Helpline: 0800 0568 578
Tel: 0161 839 4932
information@afteradoption.org.uk
www.afteradoption.org.uk
Telephone helpline for any young person who has any issues about adoption

### Talking Newspaper Association

National Recording Centre  Heathfield  East Sussex TN21 8DB
Tel: 01435 866102
info@tnauk.org.uk
www.tnauk.org.uk
Subscription service supplying, in alternative format, newspapers and magazines to blind, visually impaired and disabled people.

### Tall Person's Club (GB & Ireland)

Unit 36  88-90 Hatton Garden  London EC1N 8PN
Tel: 07000 825512
admin@tallclub.co.uk
www.tallclub.co.uk
Promotes interest of tall people and gives practical, medical and social information. Subsection - 'Little Big Ones'  for tall children and their parents

### Tall Ships Youth Trust

2A The Hard  Portsmouth PO1 3PT
Tel: 023 9283 2055
info@tallships.org
www.tallships.org
A personal development experience on board the Tall Ships "Stavros S. Niarchos" and "Prince William"

### Tampon Alert (Alice Kilvert)

16 Blinco Rd  Urmston   Manchester M41 9NF
Tel: 0161 748 3123
enquiries@tamponalert.org.uk
www.tamponalert.org.uk
Provides information about tampon related toxic shock syndrome and support for those affected

### Tandem Club

secretary@tandem-club.org.uk
www.tandem-club.org.uk
To promote and help tandem riding

### TAPOL The Indonesia Human Rights Campaign

111 Northwood Rd  Thornton Heath  Surrey CR7 8HW
Tel: 020 8771 2904
tapol@gn.apc.org
www.tapol.org
Campaigns to expose human rights violations in Indonesia, East Timor, West Papua and Aceh

### Taskforce for the Rural Poor (International)

12 Eastleigh Ave  Harrow  Middlesex HA2 0UF
Tel: 020 8864 4740
an_singh2002@yahoo.co.uk
www.ivcs.org.uk/intaf

Network of development workers, researchers and organisations working for the rural poor in the Third World

**Tate Britain**
Millbank  London SW1P 4RG
Tel: 020 7887 8888
visiting.britain@tate.org.uk
www.tate.org.uk

**Tate Liverpool**
Albert Dock  Liverpool, L3 4BB
Tel: 0151 702 7400
visiting.liverpool@tate.org.uk
www.tate.org.uk/liverpool
One of the largest galleries of modern art outside London

**Tate Modern**
Bankside  London SE1 9TG
Tel: 020 7887 8888
visiting.modern@tate.org.uk
www.tate.org.uk/modern

**Tate St Ives**
Porthmeor Beach  St Ives  Cornwall TR26 1TG
Tel:  01736 796226
visiting.stives@tate.org.uk
www.tate.org.uk/stives

**Tax** see also Conscience, HMCR Education Service, HM Revenue and Customs

**TaxAid**
Room 304  Linton House  164-180 Union St Southwark  London SE1 0LH
Advice Line: 0845 120 3779
email via website
www.taxaid.org.uk
Charity providing free tax advice to people in financial need

**Tea Council Ltd.**
9 The Courtyard  Gowan Ave  London SW6 6RH
Tel: 020 7371 7787
info@teacouncil.co.uk
www.tea.co.uk

**Teacher Support Network**
Support lines: England - 08000 562 561
Wales - 08000 855 088
Scotland - 0800 564 2270
email via website
www.teachersupport.info
Counselling, support and services for trainees, working teachers and retired teachers, plus free and confidential 24hr telephone support line

**Teacher Training in Primary School Science** see SCIcentre

**TeacherNet**
email via website
www.teachernet.gov.uk
Teaching information site

**Teachers of Mathematics (Association of)**
7 Prime Industrial Park  Shaftesbury St  Derby DE23 8YB
Tel: 01332 346599
admin@atm.org.uk
www.atm.org.uk

**Teaching Council for England (General)**
Victoria Square House  Victoria Square Birmingham B2 4AJ
Tel: 0370 001 0308
info@gtce.org.uk
www.gtce.org.uk
Aim is to work in the public interest to help improve standards of teaching and learning. October 2010: The body is expected to close by 31 March 2012. Government to announce plans for tackling underperforming teachers late in 2010.

**Teaching Council for Wales (General)**
4th Floor  Southgate House  Wood St  Cardiff CF10 1EW
Tel: 029 20 550350
information@gtcw.org.uk
www.gtcw.org.uk

**Teaching English & Other Community Languages to Adults (National Association for)**
South Birmingham College  Room HA205, Hall Green Campus  Cole Bank Road  Hall Green Birmingham  B28 8ES
Tel: 0121 688 8121
co-ordinator@natecla.fsnet.co.uk
www.natecla.org.uk

**Teaching of Drama (National Association for)** NATD
www.natd.eu

**Teaching of English (National Association for the)** NATE
50 Broadfield Rd  Sheffield S8 0XJ
Tel: 0114 255 5419
info@nate.org.uk
www.nate.org.uk

**Tearfund**
100 Church Rd  Teddington  Middlesex TW11 8QE
Tel: 0845 355 8355
enquiry@tearfund.org
www.tearfund.org
Evangelical Christian relief and development charity

**Technology Colleges Trust** now see Specialist Schools and Academies Trust

**Technology Means Business**
Filden House  14 Weywood Lane  Farnham Surrey GU9 9DP
Tel: 01784 473005
www.tmb.org.uk

Industry standard accreditation for providers of ICT advice to small & medium sized enterprises

**Teenage Cancer Trust**
3rd Floor  93 Newman Street  London  W1T 3EZ
Tel: 020 7612 0370
email via website
www.teenagecancertrust.org

**Telecommunications Action Group** see TAG

**Telephone Directories On Web**
www.infobel.com/teldir
Telephone directories of various types for most countries of the world, including UK

**Telephone Preference Service**
DMA House  70 Margaret St  London W1W 8SS
Tel: 020 7291 3300
Resgistration Line: 0845 070 0707
tps@dma.org.uk
www.tpsonline.org.uk
Opt-out facility to avoid cold-call phone sales

**Telephone Standards** see Phonepay Plus

**Telescope (Bradford Robotic)**
www.telescope.org/
Concerned with astronomical education and observation

**Television** see also thematic guide - Media

**Telework Association**
Tel: 0800 616008
email via website
www.telework.org.uk
Encourages take up of telework - providing information and advice to employers and employees

**Temperance League (British National)** see BNTL-Freeway

**Tenant Participation Advisory Service for England**
5th Floor  Trafford House  Chester Rd  Manchester M32 0RS
Tel: 0161 868 3500
info@tpas.org.uk
www.tpas.org.uk
Non-profit organisation providing information, advice, training on all aspects of involving tenants in their housing management

**Tenovus** Your Cancer Charity
9th Floo,. Gleider House  Ty Glas Road  Llanishen  Cardiff CF14 5BD
Freephone cancer support line: 0808 808 10 10
Tel: 029 2076 8850
post@tenovus.org.uk
www.tenovus.org.uk

**Terrence Higgins Trust**
314-320 Gray's Inn Rd  London WC1X 8DP
Helpline: 0845 1221 1200

Tel: 020 7812 1600
info@tht.org.uk
www.tht.org.uk
Inform, advise and help about AIDS and HIV infection

**Thalidomide Society (UK)**
Tel: 01462 438212
info@thalsoc.demon.co.uk
www.thalidomidesociety.co.uk
User-led organisation offering support, information and advice to people affected by Thalidomide and similarly disabled

**The British Monarchy (The official website of)**
email via website
www.royal.gov.uk

**The Deep**
Tower Street  Hull HU1 4DP
Tel: 01482 381000
info@thedeep.co.uk
www.thedeep.co.uk
Aquarium telling the story of the world's oceans

**The Sikh Way**
Sikh Education Council  27 Gloucester Street  London WC1N 3XX
Tel: 07870 138 616
Email via website
www.thesikhway.com
To raise cultural awareness of Sikh people through workshops and educational activities

**The White Ribbon Alliance**
2nd Floor, 138 Portobello Road  London  W11 2DZ
Tel: 0207 965 6060
info-uk@whiteribbonalliance.org
www.whiteribbonalliance.org
Aims to ensure that pregnancy and childbirth are safe for all women and newborns in every country around the world.

**Theatre** see also thematic guide - Arts, Dance & Music. Refer also to the Dance, Drama, Music & Performing Arts Schools section

**Theatre Council (Independent)**
12 The Leathermarket  Weston St  London SE1 3ER
Tel: 020 7403 1727
admin@itc-arts.org
www.itc-arts.org
Management association for performing arts organisations

**Théâtre de Complicité**
14 Anglers Lane  London NW5 3DG
Tel: 020 7485 7700
email@complicite.org
www.complicite.org

## Theatre for Children and Young People (International Association of)
www.assitej-international.org
Networking, training, advocacy, regular magazine 'Theatre First' and website

## Theatre Network (The Amateur)
PO Box 536
Norwich MLO
Norfolk NR6 7JZ  Norwich MLO  Norfolk NR6 JZ
email via website
http://amdram.co.uk

## Theatrenet
www.theatrenet.com
News, events and links

## Theatres Trust
22 Charing Cross Rd  London WC2H 0QL
Tel: 020 7836 8591
info@theatrestrust.org.uk
www.theatrestrust.org.uk
Protecting our theatres and making them better. October 2010 no longer a public body with funding from government but continuing as a charitable trust.

## Thesite Your guide to the real world
www.thesite.org
Aims to be the first place all young adults turn to when they need support and guidance through life. Provides factsheets and articles on all the key issues facing young people including: sex and relationships; drinking and drugs; work and study; housing, legal and finances; and health and wellbeing

## TheyWorkForYou.com
team@theyworkforyou.com
www.theyworkforyou.com
Not for profit organisation to help keep tabs on MPs

## Third Age Trust University of the Third Age National Office
Old Municipal Buildings  19 East Street
Bromley  BR1 1QE
Tel: 020 8466 6139
email via website
www.u3a.org.uk
Self-help learning organisation

## Third World First now see People and Planet

## Thrive
The Geoffrey Udall Centre  Beech Hill  Reading RG7 2AT
Tel: 0118 988 5688
email via website
www.carryongardening.org.uk
www.thrive.org.uk
Gardening & horticulture charity

## Tibet see also Free Tibet Campaign

## Tibet Society UK
Unit 9  139 Fonthill Road  Finsbury Park
London N4 3HF
Tel: 020 7272 1414
info@tibetsociety.com
www.tibetsociety.com

## Tibetan Nuns Project
www.tibetan-nuns-project-uk.co.uk
Helps to support 3 nunneries in NW India through sponsorship and fundraising in the UK

## Time for God
North Bank  28 Pages Lane  Muswell Hill
London N10 1PP
Tel: 020 8883 1504
office@timeforgod.org
www.timeforgod.org
Christian organisation arranging volunteering opportunities for 18-25 year olds in the UK, Europe and worldwide

## Tinnitus Association (British)
Ground Floor Unit 5  Acorn Business Park
Woodseats Close  Sheffield S8 0TB
Enquiry Line: 0800 018 0527
Tel: 0114 250 9922
Minicom: 0114 258 5694
info@tinnitus.org.uk
www.tinnitus.org.uk

## Tisserand Aromatherapy Institute
Newtown Road  Hove   Sussex BN3 7BA
Tel: 01273 325 666
sales@tisserand.com
www.tisserand.com
Training institute is based in South Kensington, London. Provides training in holistic aromatherapy

## Toc H
The Coach House  The Firs  High Street
Whitchurch  Bucks HP22 4JU
Tel: 01296 640055
accounts@toch.org.uk
www.toch.org.uk
Short-term residential volunteering opportunities

## Tommy's, the baby charity
Nicholas House  3 Laurence Pountney Hill
London EC4R 0BB
Tel: 0207 398 3400
mailbox@tommys.org
www.tommys.org
Funds medical research on causes and prevention of miscarriage, stillbirth, premature birth and pregnancy health.

## Tools for Self Reliance
Ringwood Road  Netley Marsh  Southampton SO40 7GY
Tel: 023 8086 9697
info@tfsr.org

www.tfsr.org
Volunteers throughout the UK collect and refurbish handtools for grassroots development projects in Africa

**Topmarks**
contact@topmarks.co.uk
www.topmarks.co.uk
Free website to help teachers, parents and pupils to use the internet effectively for learning

**Torture** see Amnesty International, Medical Foundation for the Care of Victims of Torture, REDRESS

**Torture (Association for the Prevention of)**
Route de Ferney 10  Case postale 2267  CH-1211  Geneva 2
Tel: 00 41 22 919 2170
apt@apt.ch
www.apt.ch
Independent non-governmental organisation committed to working internationally to tackle the global problem of torture and ill-treatment

**Torture (The World Organisation Against)**
PO Box 21  8, rue du Vieux-Billard  CH-1211 Geneva 8
Tel: 00 41 22 809 4939
omct@omct.org
www.omct.org

**Tour de France**
www.letour.fr
This official website is multilingual

**Tour Operators (Association of Independent)**
133A St Margaret's Rd  Twickenham  Middlesex TW1 1RG
Tel: 020 8744 9280
info@aito.com
www.aito.co.uk
Represents around 160 specialist tour operators

**Tourism Concern**
Stapleton House  277-281 Holloway Rd London N7 8HN
Tel: 020 7133 3800
email via website
www.tourismconcern.org.uk
Campaigning for fairly traded and ethical tourism.

**Tourism for All**
c/o Vitalise  Shap Road Industrial Estate Kendal  Cumbria L9 6NZ
Tel: 0845 124 9971
info@tourismforall.org.uk
www.tourismforall.org.uk
Advises people with special needs about holidays

**Tourism Offices Worldwide Directory**
www.towd.com
Provides information about tourist offices in most countries of the world

**Town & Country Planning Association**
17 Carlton House Terrace  London SW1Y 5AS
Tel: 020 7930 8903
tcpa@tcpa.org.uk
www.tcpa.org.uk
Registered charity providing independent comment on planning and environmental policy in the UK and Europe

**Town Planning Institute (Royal)** RTPI
41 Botolph Ln  London EC3R 8DL
Tel: 020 7929 9494
www.rtpi.org.uk
Chartered professional body for Town Planning in the UK

**Trackoff**
If you see someone behaving in an unsafe way on the railway or putting other people in danger, report it.
Call free on 0800 40 50 40
email via website
www.trackoff.org/
Britain's rail industry initiative to help educate children and teenagers about safe conduct on the railway

**Trade Union** see also European Trade Union Confederation, Friedrich Ebert Foundation, Liberal Democrat Trade Unionists (Association of), People's Centre, Simon Jones Memorial Campaign, Solidar

**Trade Union Rights (International Centre for)**
UCATT House  177 Abbeville Rd  London SW4 9RL
Tel: 020 7498 4700
ictur@ictur.org
www.ictur.org

**Trade Unions Confederation (International)** ITUC
Boulevard du Roi Albert II, 5, Bte 1  1210 Brussels  Belgium
Tel: 00 32 2 224 0211
info@ituc-csi.org
www.ituc-csi.org

**Trades Union Congress**
Congress House  Great Russell St  London WC1B 3LS
Tel: 020 7636 4030
email via website
www.tuc.org.uk

**Trading Standards Institute**
www.tradingstandards.gov.uk
A one stop shop for consumer protection
information

**Traffic Statistics (Global)** from UK Road
Safety Ltd
www.uk-roadsafety.co.uk/Rs_Documents/
accident_count.htm
Live updating road safety statistics

**Traffic Victims** see Roadpeace

**Traidcraft**
Kingsway Team Valley Trading Estate
Gateshead NE11 0NE
Tel: 0191 491 0591
email via website
www.traidcraft.co.uk
Fighting poverty through fair trade with the
developing world. Mail order catalogue
available free

**Training & Development Agency for
Schools** TDA
Tel: 0845 600 0991 (For English speakers)
0845 6000 992 (For Welsh speakers)
Minicom 0117 915 8161
www.tda.gov.uk
October 2010: Under review

**Training Standards Council** now see Adult
Learning Inspectorate

**Trainline**
www.thetrainline.com
Website providing information about train times
and tickets for routes on mainland UK and a
booking service

**Tranquillisers, Antidepressants and
Painkillers (Council for Information on)**
The JDI Centre 3-11 Mersey View Waterloo
Liverpool L22 6QA
Helpline: 0151 932 0102
Tel: 0151 474 9626
cita@citap.org.uk
www.citawithdrawal.org.uk
National helpline, support and information
service

**Transform Drug Policy Foundation**
Easton Business Centre Felix Rd Bristol BS5
0HE
Tel: 0117 941 5810
info@tdpf.org.uk
www.tdpf.org.uk
Advocates an effective system of regulation and
control of drugs at national & international levels

**Transforming Conflict**
National Centre for Restorative Justice in Youth
Settings Mortimer Hill Mortimer Berkshire
RG7 3PW
Tel: 0118 933 1520
info@transformingconflict.org

www.transformingconflict.org
Citizenship and human rights education

**Transparency International**
International Secretariat Alt Moabit 96 10559
Berlin Germany
Tel: 49-30-3438 20-0
ti@transparency.org
www.transparency.org
Fights bribery & corruption worldwide. Collects
and makes available information about
corruption and anti-corruption measures

**Transport (Department for)**
Great Minster House 76 Marsham St London
SW1P 4DR
Tel: 0300 330 3000
FAX9643@dft.gsi.gov.uk
www.dft.gov.uk

**Transport & Environment (European
Federation for)**
Rue d'Edinbourg, 26 1050 Brussels Belgium
Tel: +32 (0)2 893 0841
info@transportenvironment.org
www.transportenvironment.org
Co-ordinates European groups on transport
related environmental campaigning

**Transport for London**
London Travel 24hr Info Line: 0843 222 1234
email via website
www.tfl.gov.uk

**Transport Safety (Parliamentary Advisory
Council for)**
Clutha House 10 Storey's Gate London SW1P
3AY
Tel: 020 7222 7732
admin@pacts.org.uk
www.pacts.org.uk
Registered charity advising parliament on air,
rail and road safety issues

**Travel advice** see Foreign and
Commonwealth Office Travel Advice

**Travel and Tourism (Institute of)**
PO Box 217 Ware Herts SG12 8WY
Tel: 0844 4995 653
enquiries@itt.co.uk
www.itt.co.uk

**Travel Warnings (US State Department)**
www.travel.state.gov

**Travellers** see Education of Travelling
Communities (European Federation for the),
Foreign and Commonwealth Office Travel
Advice, Friends, Families and Travellers,
Medical Advisory Services for Travellers
Abroad Ltd.

## Treasury

Correspondence and Enquiries Unit  1 Horse Guards Rd  London SW1A 2HQ
Tel: 020 7270 4558
public.enquiries@hm-treasury.gov.uk
www.hm-treasury.gov.uk

## Tree Council

71 Newcomen Street  London SE1 1YT
Tel: 020 7407 9992
info@treecouncil.org.uk
www.treecouncil.org.uk
Promotes improvement of environment through planting and conservation of trees.

## Treloar Trust

Upper Froyle  Alton  Hampshire GU34 4JX
Tel: 01420 526526
info@treloar.org.uk
www.treloar.org.uk
Provides residential education, care & independence training for young people aged 7-25 with severe physical disabilities

## Triathlon Association (British)

PO Box 25  Loughborough  Leicestershire LE11 3WX
Tel: 01509 226161
info@britishtriathlon.org
www.britishtriathlon.org

## Triumph over Phobia (TOP UK)

PO Box 3760  Bath BA2 3WY
Tel: 0845 6009601
info@topuk.org
www.topuk.org
Network of self-help groups for phobia and obsessive compulsive disorder sufferers

## TRóCAIRE

Maynooth  Co. Kildare  Ireland
Tel: +353 1 6293333
email via website
www.trocaire.org
Irish Catholic agency for world development

## Tropical Diseases (Hospital for)

Mortimer Market Building  Capper Street  Tottenham Court Road  London WC1E 6JB
Tel: 020 7388 9600 (Travel clinic)
email via website
www.thehtd.org
Travel health advice

## Tuberous Sclerosis Association

PO Box 12979  Barnt Green  Birmingham  B45 5AN
Tel: 0121 445 6970
email via website
www.tuberous-sclerosis.org

## Turning Point

Standon House  21 Mansell Street  E1 8AA
Tel: 020 7481 7600
info@turning-point.co.uk
www.turning-point.co.uk
Drug, alcohol-related & mental health problems & learning disabilities

## Twentieth Century Society

70 Cowcross St   London EC1M 6EJ
Tel: 020 7250 3857
caseworker@c20society.org.uk
www.c20society.org.uk
Exists to safeguard the heritage of architecture & design in Britain from 1914 onwards

## Twins & Multiple Births Association (TAMBA)

2 The Willows  Gardner Rd  Guildford  Surrey GU1 4PG
Twinline: 0800 138 0509
Tel: 01483 304 442
enquiries@tamba.org.uk
www.tamba.org.uk
Information and support for families with twins, triplets and more and for professionals involved with their care

# U

**U3A** see Third Age Trust

## UCAS

Rosehill  New Barn Lane  Cheltenham GL52 3LZ
Tel: 0871 468 0 468
enquiries@ucas.ac.uk
www.ucas.com
Handles all applications for entry to UK universities and other higher education institutions

## UEFA

Route de Geneve 46  Case postale  CH-1260 Nyon 2  Switzerland
Tel: 00 41 (0)848 00 2727
www.uefa.com

## UK Border Agency

www.ind.homeoffice.gov.uk
Responsible for securing the United Kingdom borders and controlling migration in the United Kingdom

## UK Climate projections

http://ukcp09.defra.gov.uk/
Information on observed and future climate change, based on the latest scientific understanding

## UK Film Council
10 Little Portland St  London W1W 7JG
Tel: 020 7861 7861
info@ukfilmcouncil.org.uk
www.ukfilmcouncil.org.uk
Invests public money in film and co-funds a
number of other organisations. October 2010:
the Film Council was one of the organisations
scheduled to close as a result of government
cuts.

## UK Islamic Education Waqf UKIEW
17 Brendon Road  Nottingham  NG8 1HW
Tel: 0115 8602048
info@ukiew.org
www.ukiew.org
Subsidises fees for children of families in
financial need to attend Islamic schools which
are members of Association of Muslim Schools
of UK

## UK New Citizen
Tel: 07946 808976
info@uknewcitizen.org
www.uknewcitizen.org
Promotes the social integration of refugees,
immigrants and their descendants through
citizenship and a sense of democracy

## UK Parents Lounge
www.ukparents.co.uk
Online magazine and forum for parents

## UK Sport
40 Bernard St  London WC1N 1ST
Tel: 020 7211 5100
info@uksport.gov.uk
www.uksport.gov.uk
Governing body for whole of UK for elite
athletics. October 2010: To merge with Sport
England

## UK Theatre Web
www.uktw.co.uk
Database of information on people, plays,
venues, performances etc. and extensive
archive

## UK Youth
Avon Tyrrell  Bransgore  Hampshire  BH23 8EE
Tel: 01425 672347
info@ukyouth.org
www.ukyouth.org
Helps young people to develop skills and
interests

## UKAEA
www.ukaea.org.uk
Statutory body responsible for the
decommissioning of nuclear power stations
and for the UK's input into the European Fusion
Research Programme. October 2010: future
under review

## UKERNA see JANET

## UN High Commissioner for Human Rights (Office of the)
www.ohchr.org

## Unborn Children (Society for the Protection of)
3 Whitacre Mews  Stannary Street  London
SE11 4AB
Tel: 020 7091 7091
information@spuc.org.uk
www.spuc.org.uk
Defending human life, through education and
political lobbying, from conception until natural
death

## Uncaged Campaigns
5th Floor, Alliance House  9 Leopold Street
Sheffield S1 2GY
Tel: 0114 272 2220
info@uncaged.co.uk
www.uncaged.co.uk
Pressure group campaigning to abolish animal
experiments and for animal rights

## Undercurrents
Old Exchange  Pier Street  Swansea SA1 1RY
Tel: 01792 455900
info@undercurrents.org
www.undercurrents.org
Video support and training and archive materials
for the use of social and environmental groups

## Understanding Animal Research
25 Shaftesbury Avenue  London W1D 7EG
Tel: 020 7287 2818
Email via website
www.understandinganimalresearch.org.uk
Information about the use of animals in medical
research

## UNESCO United Nations Educational, Scientific & Cultural Organisation
UK Permanent Delegation to UNESCO (Paris)  1
rue Miollis  75732 Paris
Tel: 00 331 45 68 1000
Email via website
www.unesco.org

## UNHCR The UN Refugee Agency
Strand Bridge House  138 - 142 Strand  London
WC2R 1HH
Tel: 020 7759 8090
gbrloea@unhcr.org
www.unhcr.org.uk

## Uni4me
www.aimhigher.ac.uk/uni4me/home/
Answers questions about what it is like to be a
university student. Web site developed by all the
universities in Greater Manchester

## UNICEF UK
2 Kingfisher House  Woodbrook Crescent
Billericay  CM12 0EQ

Tel: 0844 801 2414
Email via website
www.unicef.org.uk
United Nations children's fund

**Unicorn Theatre for Children**
147 Tooley Street  More London  Southwark
London SE1 2HZ
Tel: 020 7645 0500
admin@unicorntheatre.com
www.unicorntheatre.com

**Union Cycliste Internationale** see Cycling
Union (International)

**Unistats**
http://unistats.direct.gov.uk/
Brings information about universities and their
courses together in one place

**Unite**
35 King Street  Covent Garden  London WC2E
8JG
Tel: 020 7420 8900
email via website
www.unitetheunion.org
Unite was formed by a merger between two of
Britain's' leading unions, the T&G and Amicus.

**Unite Against Fascism**
www.uaf.org.uk
New national campaign against the extreme
right

**United Nations Association of the UK**
3 Whitehall Court  London SW1A 2EL
Tel: 020 7766 3444
Email via website
www.una-uk.org
Membership organisation, campaigning and
educating to turn the ideals of the UN into a
reality

**United Nations Development Programme**
(UNDP)
www.undp.org
The UN's global development network

**United Nations Educational, Scientific &
Cultural Organisation** see UNESCO

**United Nations Environment Programme**
unepinfo@unep.org
www.unep.org

**United Nations High Commissioner for
Refugees** see UNHCR

**United Nations Volunteers**
information@unvolunteers.org
www.unvolunteers.org
Volunteer arm cf the United Nations

**United Reformed Church**
86 Tavistock Place  London WC1H 9RT
Tel: 020 7916 2020
urc@urc.org.uk
www.urc.org.uk

**Universities and Colleges Sport (British)**
20-24 Kings Bench Street  London  SE1 0QX
Tel: 020 7633 5080
info@bucs.org.uk
www.bucs.org.uk
Organises inter-university championships and
GB team for World University Championships

**University of the First Age**
St Paul's Cottages  59-60 Water Street  The
Jewellery Quarter  Birmingham  B3 1EP
Tel: 0121 212 9838
ufa@ufa.org.uk
www.ufa.org.uk
National educational charity working in
partnership to develop the confidence and
achievement of young people

**University of the Third Age Trust** see Third
Age Trust

**UNLOCK** National Association of Ex-
Offenders
35A High St  Snodland  Kent ME6 5AG
Tel: 01634 247350
enquiries@unlock.org.uk
www.unlock.org.uk
Works with statutory and voluntary agencies in
the criminal justice system to reduce crime

**Unlock Democracy** incorporating Charter 88
6 Cynthia Street  Islington  London N1 9JF
Tel: 020 7278 4443
info@unlockdemocracy.org.uk
www.unlockdemocracy.org.uk
Campaigns for a modern democracy and
human rights

**UPDATE** Scotland's National Disability
Information Service
Hays Community Business Centre  4 Hay
Avenue  Edinburgh  EH16 4AQ
Tel: 0131 669 1600
info@update.org.uk
www.update.org.uk

**Urban Saints**
Kestin House  45 Crescent Rd  Luton LU2 0AH
Tel: 01582 589 850
email@urbansaints.org
www.urbansaints.org
Christian youth organisation with weekly groups
and summer holidays

**US Department of State**
www.state.gov

**US Educational Advisory Service** see
Fulbright Commission

**USA President**
The White House  1600 Pennsylvania Avenue NW  Washington DC 20500
Tel: 001 202 456 1414
email via website
www.whitehouse.gov

# V

**Values Education for Life (The Collegiate Centre for)**
College House  Albion Place  Hockley Hill Birmingham B18 5AQ
Tel: 0121 523 0222
info@vefl.org.uk
http://birmingham.schooljotter.com/valueseducation
Works with disadvantaged youngsters

**Vatican**
www.vatican.va
Website giving information on many aspects of the Vatican in many European languages

**Vatican Museums & Sistine Chapel**
www.christusrex.org/www1/vaticano/0-Musei.html
Information on various Vatican museums including opening dates and times

**Vegan Society**
21 Hylton Street  Hockley  Birmingham  B18 6HJ
Tel: 0121 523 1730
info@vegansociety.com
www.vegansociety.com
Advocating lifestyle free from animal products

**Vegetarian Society**
Parkdale  Dunham Rd  Altrincham  Cheshire WA14 4QG
Tel: 0161 925 2000
info@vegsoc.org
www.vegsoc.org

**Vegetarian & Vegan Foundation**
8 York Court  Wilder St  Bristol BS2 8QH
Tel: 0117 970 5190
info@vegetarian.org.uk
www.vegetarian.org.uk
Provides free information on becoming vegetarian/vegan. Researches health & nutrition issues relating to diet.

**Vegetarians International Voice for Animals**
see Viva!

**Venice in Peril Fund**
Unit 4, Hurlingham Studios  Ranelagh Gardens London SW6 3PA
Tel: 020 7736 6891
info@veniceinperil.org
www.veniceinperil.org
British charity for restoration and preservation of Venice

**Venuemasters**
Tel: 0114 249 3090
Email via website
www.venuemasters.co.uk
Offers free venue finding service for meeting and accommodation facilities at UK academic venues

**Victim Support**
Supportline: 0845 303 0900
supportline@victimsupport.org.uk
www.victimsupport.org
National charity providing help and information to people affected by crime

**Victorian Society**
1 Priory Gardens  London W4 1TT
Tel: 020 8994 1019
admin@victoriansociety.org.uk
www.victoriansociety.org.uk
Organises events and publishes books on restoring your Victorian house

**Video Standards Council**
Kinetic Business Centre  Theobald St Borehamwood  Herts WD6 4PJ
Tel: 020 8387 4020
vsc@videostandards.org.uk
www.videostandards.org.uk
Advises shops on legality of video sales and rental

**Vision Aid Overseas**
12 The Bell Centre  Newton Rd  Manor Royal Crawley  W Sussex RH10 2FZ
Tel: 01293 535016
info@vao.org.uk
www.vao.org.uk
Provides spectacles and training in eye care in developing countries.

**Visit England**
1 Palace Street  London SW1E 5HX
Tel: 020 7578 1400
email via website
www.enjoyengland.com
National organisation for marketing England overseas and in the UK

**Visit London**
Tel: 08701 566 366
email via website
www.visitlondon.com
The official tourism organisation for London

**Visit Scotland**
Ocean Point 1  94 Ocean Drive  Edinburgh EH6 6JH
Tel: 0845 225 5121
info@visitscotland.com
www.visitscotland.com

**Visit Wales**
www.visitwales.com

**VisitBritain**
1 Palace Street  London SW1E 5HX
Tel: 020 7578 1000
email via website
www.visitbritain.com
National organisation for marketing Britain overseas and in the UK

**Visual Arts & Galleries Association**
The Old Village School  Witcham  Ely CB6 2LQ
Tel: 01353 776356
admin@vaga.co.uk
www.vaga.co.uk
Network & voice for the visual arts world

**Vitiligo Society**
125 Kennington Road  London SE11 6SF
Freephone: 0800 018 2631
www.vitiligosociety.org.uk/
Promotes and funds research projects

**Viva!** Vegetarians International Voice for Animals
8 York Court  Wilder St  Bristol BS2 8QH
Tel: 0117 944 1000
info@viva.org.uk
www.viva.org.uk
Campaigning organisation working to end factory farming and educate people on vegetarian and vegan diets

**Vivisection** see also Anti-Vivisection Society (National), Humane Research Trust, PETA EUROPE Ltd, Respect for Animals, Uncaged Campaigns, Viva!

**Vivisection (British Union for the Abolition of)** BUAV
16A Crane Grove  London N7 8NN
Tel: 020 7700 4888
info@buav.org
www.buav.org
Campaigns peacefully to end all animal experiments

**Voice**
320 City Road  London EC1V 2NZ
Helpline: 0808 800 5792
Tel: 020 7833 5792
info@voiceyp.org
www.voiceyp.org
Working and campaigning for children and young people in public care

**Voice for Choice**
www.vfc.org.uk
Campaigning for abortion on request throughout the UK

**Voice of the Listener and Viewer**
PO Box 401  Gravesend  Kent DA12 9FY
Tel: 01474 338711 or 01474 338716
info@vlv.org.uk
www.vlv.org.uk
Represents the citizen and consumer on all broadcasting issues and works for quality and diversity

**VoiceAbility**
Email via website
www.voiceability.org
Gives a voice to vulnerable people and supports them to take control of their lives

**Voices Foundation** Transforming children through singing
34 Grosvenor Gardens  London SW1W 0DH
Tel: 020 7730 6677
vf@voices.org.uk
www.voices.org.uk
Music education

**Voices in the Wilderness UK**
5 Caledonian Road  King's Cross  London N1 9DX
Tel: 0845 458 2564
voicesuk@fastmail.fm
www.voicesuk.org
Working in solidarity with ordinary families in Iraq

**Volleyball Association (English)**
SportPark  Loughborough University  3 Oakwood Drive  Loughborough LE11 3QF
Tel: 01509 227722
info@volleyballengland.org
www.volleyballengland.org

**Volleyball Association (Scottish)**
48 The Pleasance  Edinburgh EH8 9TJ
Tel: 0131 556 4633
www.scottishvolleyball.org

**Voluntary Action (Wales Council for)** WCVA
Baltic House  Mount Stuart Square  Cardiff CF10 5FH
Helpdesk: 0800 2888 329
Minicom: 0808 1804 080
help@wcva.org.uk
www.wcva.org.uk
Voice of the voluntary sector

**Voluntary Agencies (International Council of)** ICVA
26-28 avenue Guiseppe Motta  Geneva 1202 Switzerland
Tel: 00 41 22 950 96 00

secretariat@icva.ch
www.icva.ch
Advocacy network of non-governmental organisations

## Voluntary and Community Action (National Association for)
The Tower  2 Furnival Square  Sheffield  S1 4QL
Tel: 0114 2786636
navca@navca.org.uk
www.navca.org.uk
The England-wide organisation which provides services to local councils for voluntary service

## Voluntary Arts Network VAN
121 Cathedral Road  Pontcanna  Cardiff CF11 9PH
Tel: 029 20 395395
info@voluntaryarts.org
www.voluntaryarts.org
To help people, irrespective of age, participate in the arts

## Voluntary Euthanasia Society see Dignity in Dying

## Voluntary Organisations (National Council for) (NCVO)
Regent's Wharf  8 All Saints St  London N1 9RL
Helpline: 0800 2798 798
Tel: 020 7713 6161
Minicom: 0800 0188111
ncvo@ncvo-vol.org.uk
www.ncvo-vol.org.uk
Umbrella body

## Voluntary Organisations (Scottish Council for)
Mansfield Traquair Centre  15 Mansfield Place Edinburgh EH3 6BB
Helpline: 0800 1690022
Tel: 0131 556 3882
enquiries@scvo.org.uk
www.scvo.org.uk
Umbrella body for all voluntary organisations in Scotland

## Voluntary Youth Services (National Council for)
3rd Floor  Lancaster House  33 Islington High Street  London N1 9LH
Tel: 020 7278 1041
mail@ncvys.org.uk
www.ncvys.org.uk
Represents voluntary organisations working with young people and volunteers

## Volunteer Action for Peace
16 Overhill Road  East Dulwich  London SE22 0PH
Tel: 0844 20 90 927
action@vap.org.uk

www.vap.org.uk
UK based charity organisation which works towards creating and preserving international peace, justice and human solidarity for people and their communities

## Volunteer Development Scotland
Jubilee House  Forthside Way  Stirling FK8 1QZ
Tel: 01786 479593
vds@vds.org.uk
www.vds.org.uk
Support organisations in Scotland who involve volunteers

## Volunteer Now
129 Ormeau Road  Belfast  BT7 1SH
Tel: 028 9023 6100
info@volunteernow.co.uk
www.volunteernow.co.uk
Promotes and develops volunteering in Northern Ireland

## Volunteer Reading Help
14-15 Perseverance Works  38 Kingsland Rd London E2 8DD
Tel: 020 7729 4087
info@vrh.org.uk
www.vrh.org.uk
Supports volunteers to help primary school children

## Volunteering England
Regent's Wharf  8 All Saints St  London N1 9RL
Tel: 020 7520 8900
volunteering@volunteeringengland.org.uk
www.volunteering.org.uk
Promotes volunteering as a force for change for volunteers and the community as a whole

## Volunteers For Rural India
12 Eastleigh Avenue  South Harrow HA2 0UF
Tel: 020 8864 4740
enquiries@vri-online.org.uk
www.vri-online.org.uk
DRIVE scheme - opportunity to live in rural India

## VSO
Carlton House  27A Carlton Drive  Putney London SW15 2BS
Tel: 020 8780 7500
enquiry@vso.org.uk
www.vso.org.uk
International development charity that works through volunteers

# W

**W.I.** see Women's Institutes (National Federation of)

**Wales Environment Link**
27 Pier Street  Aberystwyth  SY23 2LN
Tel: 01970 611621
Email via website
www.waleslink.org

**Wales Office**
Gwydyr House  Whitehall  London SW1A 2NP
Tel: 020 7270 0534
wales.office@walesoffice.gsi.gov.uk
www.walesoffice.gov.uk

**WalesRails**
www.walesrails.co.uk
Independent survey of railways & the attractions they serve

**Walk to School** see Living Streets

**Walking** see also Backpackers Club, Byways & Bridleways Trust, Long Distance Walkers Association

**Walking Federation (British)**
Ground Floor  5 Windsor Square  Silver Street Reading RG1 2TH
info@bwf-ivv.org.uk
www.bwf-ivv.org.uk

**Walkit**
www.walkit.com
The urban walking route planner

**WalkScotland**
www.walkscotland.com
Scottish outdoor & countryside news updated weekly

**WAMT** see Women and Manual Trades

**War on Want**
Development House  44-48 Shepherdess Walk London N1 7JP
Tel: 020 7324 5040
mailroom@waronwant.org
www.waronwant.org
Campaign against world poverty

**War Resisters League**
339 Lafayette St  New York NY 10012
Tel: 001 212 228 0450
wrl@warresisters.org
www.warresisters.org

**Waste Watch**
56-64 Leonard Street  London EC2A 4LT
Tel: 020 7549 0300
info@wastewatch.org.uk
www.wastewatch.org.uk
Deals with methods of reduction, reuse and recycling of waste.

**WATCh?** What About The Children?
Ebrington  Grove Lane  Uxbridge  UB8 3RG
Tel: 0845 602 7145
enquiries@whataboutthechildren.org.uk
www.whataboutthechildren.org.uk
Information, research & education on the emotional needs of children under 3

**Water Aid**
47-49 Durham Street  London SE11 5JD
Tel: 020 7793 4594
Tel: 020 7793 4500
Email via website
www.wateraid.org
Sustainable provision of safe water, sanitation and hygiene education to the world's poorest

**Water Services (Office of)** OFWAT
Centre City Tower  7 Hill St  Birmingham B5 4UA
Tel: 0121 644 7500
enquiries@ofwat.gsi.gov.uk
www.ofwat.gov.uk
October 2010: The organisation will be retained but reviewed by June 2011

**Water Ski & Wakeboard (British)**
Unit 3 The Forum  Hanworth Lane  Chertsey Surrey KT16 9JX
Tel: 01932 560 007
Email via website
www.britishwaterski.org.uk
Governing body

**Waterway Recovery Group**
Island House  Moor Road  Chesham HP5 1WA
Tel: 01494 783 453
enquiries@wrg.org.uk
www.wrg.org.uk
Restores derelict canals

**Waterways (British)**
64 Clarendon Road  Watford WD17 1DA
Tel: 01923 201120
enquiries.hq@britishwaterways.co.uk
www.britishwaterways.co.uk
Manages canals and navigable rivers in UK. October 2010 Government announced its intention to transfer British Waterways' functions into a new charitable body, similar to National Trust, by April 2012

**Waterways Museum (National)**
South Pier Road  Ellesmere Port  Cheshire CH65 4FW
Tel: 0151 355 5017
ellesmereport@thewaterwaystrust.org
www.nwm.org.uk

**Weather Centre (BBC Online)**
www.bbc.co.uk/weather

**Weights & Measures Association (British)**
11 Greensleeves Ave  Broadstone  Dorset
BH18 8BJ
bwma@email.com
www.bwmaonline.com
Promotion of traditional weights and measures
and opposition to compulsory metrication

**WellBeing of Women**
27 Sussex Place  Regent's Park  London NW1 4SP
Tel: 020 7772 6400
wellbeingofwomen@rcog.org.uk
www.wellbeingofwomen.org.uk
Medical research charity concerned with
women's reproductive health

**Welsh Assembly Government** Llywodraeth
Cynulliad Cymru
Cathays Park  Cardiff CF10 3NQ
Tel: 0300 0603300 or 0845 010 3300
Tel: Welsh: 0300 0604400 or 0845 010 4400
wag-en@mailuk.custhelp.com
www.wales.gov.uk
For general enquiries

**Welsh Athletics**
Cardiff International Sports Stadium  Leckwith
Road  Cardiff CF11 8AZ
www.welshathletics.org

**Welsh Language Board (Bwrdd yr Iaith
Gymraeg)**
Market Chambers  5/7 St Mary Street  Cardiff
CF10 1AT
Tel: 029 20 878000
Email via website
www.welsh-language-board.org.uk

**Welsh Language Society** see Cymdeithas yr
Iaith Gymraeg

**Welsh National Opera**
Wales Millennium Centre  Bute Place  Cardiff
CF10 5AL
Tel: 029 2063 5000
enquiries@wno.org.uk
www.wno.org.uk

**Welsh Office** see Wales (National Assembly
for)

**Welsh Sports Council** see Sport Wales

**Wessex Cancer Trust**
Bellis House  11 Westwood Rd  Southampton
SO17 1DL
Tel: 023 8067 2200
wct@wessexcancer.org
www.wessexcancer.org
Provides emotional support for anyone whose
life is touched by cancer

**Whale & Dolphin Conservation Society**
Brookfield House  38 St Paul St  Chippenham
Wiltshire SN15 1LY
Tel: 01249 449 500
info@wdcs.org
www.wdcs.org

**What about the Children?** See WATCh?

**Wheelchair Sports Foundation (British)**
see WheelPower

**WheelPower** British Wheelchair Sport
Guttmann Rd  Stoke Mandeville  Bucks HP21
9PP
Tel: 01296 395995
info@wheelpower.org.uk
www.wheelpower.org.uk
To promote and develop sports for both adults
and children

**Wheels for All** see Cycling Projects

**Which?**
Castlemead  Gascoyne Way  Hertford  SG14
1LH
Tel: 01992 822800
which@which.co.uk
www.which.co.uk

**Whizz-Kidz**
Elliot House, 10-12 Allington Street  London
SW1E 5EH
Tel: 020 7233 6600
Email via website
www.whizz-kidz.org.uk
Provides mobility equipment to disabled
children

**Who Cares? Trust**
Kemp House  152-160 City Rd  London EC1V
2NP
Tel: 020 7251 3117
mailbox@thewhocarestrust.org.uk
www.thewhocarestrust.org.uk
Improving education, employment, health,
counselling & information services for young
people in public care

**Wild Flower Society**
Email via website
www.thewildflowersociety.com
Identifies and records wild flowers in Britain

**Wildfowl & Wetlands Trust (WWT)**
Slimbridge  Gloucs GL2 7BT
Tel: 01453 891900
enquiries@wwt.org.uk
www.wwt.org.uk

**Wildlife Aid**
Randalls Farm House  Randalls Rd
Leatherhead  Surrey KT22 OAL
Helpline: 09061 800 132
Tel: 01372 377332 (Admin only)

Email via website
www.wildlifeaid.org.uk
Rescue, rehabilitation, care of sick, injured
and orphaned British wildlife and strong
educational emphasis

## Wildlife and Countryside Link
89 Albert Embankment  London  SE1 7TP
Tel: 020 7820 8600
enquiry@wcl.org.uk
www.wcl.org.uk

## Wildlife Trusts (Royal Society of)
The Kiln  Waterside  Mather Rd  Newark NG24
1WT
Tel: 01636 677711
enquiry@wildlifetrusts.org
www.wildlifetrusts.org
Administers lottery funding to provide grants
to communities for various environmental
projects. The 47 regional Wildlife Trusts are
dedicated to protecting wildlife for the future

## Williams Syndrome Foundation (UK)
161 High Street  Tonbridge  Kent TN9 1BX
Tel: 01732 365152
John.nelson-wsfoundation@btinternet.com
www.williams-syndrome.org.uk
Supports those affected by this  non-
hereditary chromosomal disorder

## Willow Foundation
Willow House  18 Salisbury Square  Hatfield
Hertfordshire AL9 5BE
Tel: 01707 259777
info@willowfoundation.orguk
www.willowfoundation.org.uk
Charity dedicated to improving the quality of
life of seriously ill young people aged 16-40
through the provision of special days

**WILPF** see Peace & Freedom (Women's
International League for)

## Wimbledon
www.wimbledon.com
Official site of the tennis tournament

## Wind Energy Association (European)
EWEA
Rue d'Arlon 80  B-1040 Brussels  Belgium
Tel: 0032 2 213 1811
ewea@ewea.org
www.ewea.org

## Wind Sand & Stars
PO Box 4322  Bath BA1 2BU
Tel: 01225 320 839
office@windsandstars.co.uk
www.windsandstars.co.uk
School journeys and expeditions for young
people to the desert and mountains of Sinai,
Egypt

## Windsurfing Association (UK) UKWA
PO Box 703  Haywards Heath  RH16 9EE
admin@ukwindsurfing.com
www.ukwindsurfing.com
Organises & provides first class national
competition

## Winston Churchill Memorial Trust
South Door  29 Great Smith Street  London
SW1P 3 BL
Tel: 0207 799 1660
office@wcmt.org.uk
www.wcmt.org.uk
Offers Fellowships to acquire knowledge and
experience abroad.

## Winston's Wish
4th Floor  St James's House  St James Square
Cheltenham  Gloucestershire GL50 3PR
Helpline: 0845 2030405
Tel: 01242 515157
info@winstonswish.org.uk
www.winstonswish.org.uk
For grieving children and their families

## Winvisible (Women with visible & invisible disabilities) contact Crossroads Women's Centre
www.allwomencount.net

## Wired Safety
www.wiredsafety.org
Dedicated to helping protect children in
cyberspace

## Wireless for the Blind Fund (British)
10 Albion Place  Maidstone  Kent ME14 5DZ
Tel: 01622 754 757
Email via website
www.blind.org.uk
Provides radio equipment on free permanent
loan to registered blind & partially-sighted
people in need

## Womankind Worldwide
2nd Floor, Development House  56-64 Leonard
Street  London EC2A 4LT
Tel: 020 7549 0360
info@womankind.org.uk
www.womankind.org.uk
Working with women in the developing world
and the UK in the field of human rights

## Women and Manual Trades WAMT
52-54 Featherstone St  London EC1Y 8RT
Tel: 020 7251 9192
info@wamt.org
www.wamt.org
The national organisation for tradeswomen and
women training in skilled craft trades

## Women Entrepreneurs (British Association of)
Tel: 01827 312 812
president@bawe-uk.org
www.bawe-uk.org
British Affiliate to the World Association of Women Entrepreneurs (FCEM) with 40 countries and 80,000 members founded in France 1945

## Women in Prison
347-349 City Road  London  EC1V 1LR
Freephone advice line: 0800 953 0125 (offenders and ex-offenders seeking help only)
Tel: 020 7841 4760
Email via website
www.womeninprison.org.uk
Campaigns on issues affecting women in prison and provides education, support and welfare

## Women in Publishing
info@wipub.org.uk
www.wipub.org.uk
Website of information designed to promote the status of women working in publishing

## Women Into Science & Engineering (WISE)
Weston House  246 High Holborn  London WC1V 7EX
Tel: 020 3206 0408
info@wisecampaign.org.uk
www.wisecampaign.org.uk

## Women living under Muslim laws
www.wluml.org
An international network that provides information, solidarity and support for all women whose lives are shaped, conditioned or governed by laws and customs said to derive from Islam

## Women (National Assembly of)
92 Wansbeck Avenue  Cullercoats  Tyne & Wear NE30 3DJ
Tel: 0191 2520961
naw@sisters.org.uk
www.sisters.org.uk
Campaigning for full social, economic, legal, political & cultural equality for women

## Women of Great Britain (National Council of)
72 Victoria Road  Darlington  Co. Durham DL1 5JG
Tel: 01325 367375
info@ncwgb.org
www.ncwgb.org

## Women Solicitors (Association of)
Email via website
www.womensolicitors.org.uk

## Women Working Worldwide
MMU Manton Building  Rosamond St West Manchester M15 6LL
Tel: 0161 247 1760
contact@women-ww.org
www.women-ww.org
Supports the struggles of women workers throughout the world

## Women's Aid Federation (N. Ireland)
129 University St  Belfast BT7 1HP
24 hr domestic violence helpline: 0800 917 1414
Tel: 028 9024 9041
info@womensaidni.org
www.womensaidni.org
Provides help for women and children experiencing domestic violence in N. Ireland

## Women's Aid Federation of England
PO Box 391  Bristol BS99 7WS
24hr National Domestic Violence Helpline: 0808 2000 247
Tel: 0117 944 4411 (general enquiries only)
info@womensaid.org.uk helpline@womensaid.org.uk
www.womensaid.org.uk
www.thehideout.org.uk

## Women's Aid (Scottish)
2nd Floor  132 Rose Street  Edinburgh EH2 3JD
24 hr Domestic Abuse Helpline: 0800 027 1234
Tel: 0131 226 6606
contact@scottishwomensaid.org.uk
www.scottishwomensaid.org.uk
National office for 40 affiliated Women's Aid groups in Scotland who provide information, refuge and support for women, children and young people experiencing domestic abuse

## Women's Aid (Welsh)
Wales Domestic Abuse Helpline: 0808 8010800
email via website
www.welshwomensaid.org
National umbrella organisation for women's aid groups throughout Wales

## Women's Archive of Wales
South Wales Miners' Library  Hendrefoelan Campus  Gower Road  Swansea SA2 7NB
Tel: 01873 855760
info@womensarchivewales.org
www.womensarchivewales.org
Collecting, preserving and publicising sources for women's history in Wales

## Women's Bowling Federation (English)
www.fedbowls.co.uk

**Women's Clubs (National Association of)**
5 Vernon Rise  King's Cross Rd  London WC1X 9EP
Tel: 020 7837 1434
www.nawc.org.uk
Clubs to promote education, recreation and friendship for the benefit of women

**Women's Cricket** see Cricket Board (England & Wales)

**Women's Engineering Society**
The IET  Michael Faraday House  Six Hills Way Stevenage  Hertfordshire SG1 2AY
Tel: 01483 765506
Email via website
www.wes.org.uk

**Women's Environmental Network**
Ground Floor  20 Club Row  London E2 7EY
Tel: 020 7481 9004
info@wen.org.uk
www.wen.org.uk
Campaigns on issues which link women, the environment and health

**Women's Food & Farming Union**
Cargill plc  Witham St Hughs  Lincoln LN6 9TN
Tel: 0844 3350 342
secretary@wfu.org.uk
www.wfu.org.uk

**Women's Golf Association (English)**
11 Highfield Rd  Edgbaston  Birmingham B15 3EB
Tel: 0121 456 2088
office@englishwomensgolf.org
www.englishwomensgolf.org

**Women's Institutes (National Federation of)**
104 New Kings Rd  London SW6 4LY
Tel: 020 7371 9300
Email via website
www.womens-institute.org.uk

**Women's Library**
London Metropolitan University  25 Old Castle St  London E1 7NT
Tel: 020 7320 2222
moreinfo@thewomenslibrary.ac.uk
www.thewomenslibrary.ac.uk
The most extensive collection of women's history in the UK

**Women's National Commission**
2/J5 Eland House  Bressenden Place  London SW1E 5DU
Tel: 030344 44009
wnc@communities.gsi.gov.uk
www.thewnc.org.uk
Official, independent advisory body giving the views of women to the government. Closed down on 31 December 2010 and its core functions brought into the Government Equalities Office

**Women's Register (National)**
Unit 23 Vulcan House  Vulcan Rd North Norwich NR6 6AQ
Tel: 0845 450 0287
Email via website
www.nwr.org
Coordinates women's groups to enable women to find new friends and widen their horizons

**Women's Resource Centre**
Ground Floor East  33-41 Dallington Street London EC1V 0BB
Tel: 020 7324 3030
Email via website
www.wrc.org.uk
Co-ordinating and support body for non-profit groups working for and with women

**Women's Royal Voluntary Service** see WRVS

**Women's Sports & Fitness Foundation**
Victoria House  Bloomsbury Square  London WC1B 4SE
Tel: 0207 273 1740
www.wsf.org.uk

**Women's Therapy Centre**
10 Manor Gardens  London N7 6JS
Tel: 020 7263 6200
Tel: 020 7263 7860 (General enquiries)
enquiries@womenstherapycentre.co.uk
www.womenstherapycentre.co.uk
Individual and group psychotherapy advice and information, training and education to professionals

**Wood Green Animal Shelters**
601 Lordship Lane  Wood Green  London N22 5LG
Tel: 0844 248 8181
info@woodgreen.org.uk
www.woodgreen.org.uk

**Woodcraft Folk**
Units 9/10  83 Crampton Street  London SE17 3BF
Tel: 020 7703 4173
info@woodcraft.org.uk
www.woodcraft.org.uk
Activities for young people

**Woodland Trust**
Grantham  Lincolnshire NG31 6LL
Tel: 01476 581111
enquiries@woodland-trust.org.uk
www.woodland-trust.org.uk
Protects native woodland heritage

**Woodworking Federation (British)**
Royal London House  22-25 Finsbury Square London EC2A 1DX
Tel: 0844 209 2610
bwf@bwf.org.uk
www.bwf.org.uk

**Work Foundation**
21 Palmer Street  London   SW1H 0AD
Tel: 020 7976 3565
www.theworkfoundation.com
Campaign to make a better working life for
employees

**Work & Pensions (Department for)** Public
Enquiry Office
www.dwp.gov.uk
Government agency responsible for benefit &
pension claims

**Workaholics Anonymous**
www.workaholics-anonymous.org
Self help groups with international coverage

**Workers Educational Association**
4 Luke Street  London EC2A 4XW
Tel: 020 7426 3450
national@wea.org.uk
www.wea.org.uk
Provides education for adults who are not full-
time students

**Working Class Movement Library**
51 The Crescent  Salford M5 4WX
Tel: 0161 736 3601
Email via website
www.wcml.org.uk
NB Access by appointment only

**Working Families**
1-3 Berry St  London EC1V 0AA
Helpline: 0800 013 0313
Tel: 020 7253 7243
advice@workingfamilies.org.uk
www.workingfamilies.org.uk
Information & support & campaigns on issues
of concern for working parents

**Working For A Charity**
NCVO  Regent's Wharf  8 All Saints Street
London N1 9RL
Tel: 020 7520 2512
www.workingforacharity.org.uk
Offers training courses aimed at people wanting
to move into the voluntary sector

**Working Men's College for Women & Men**
44 Crowndale Rd  London NW1 1TR
Tel: 020 7255 4700
info@wmcollege.ac.uk
www.wmcollege.ac.uk
Europe's longest established college for adult
learning

**Working with men**
Unit K308  Tower Bridge Business Complex
100 Clements Road  London SE16 4DG
Tel: 020 7237 5353
info@workingwithmen.org
www.workingwithmen.org

Develop and implement support projects that
benefit the development of men and boys.
Raise awareness of issues impacting upon men
and boys in addition to trying to gain a greater
understanding of the underlying issues behind
male behaviour

**WorkLife Support Limited**
Suite G, Maples Business Centre  144 Liverpool
Road  London N1 1LA
Tel: 0845 873 5680
Email via website
www.worklifesupport.com
Provides employee assistance programmes for
LEAs and schools and also programmes where
staff feedback to management ideas of what
works in a school to improve its atmosphere
and culture

**World AIDS Day**
www.worldaidsday.org
Takes place on 1st December every year

**World Bank**
www.worldbank.org

**World Challenge Expeditions**
17-21 Queens Road  High Wycombe
Buckinghamshire  HP13 6AQ
Tel: 01494 427600
welcome@world-challenge.co.uk
www.world-challenge.co.uk
Provides leadership, teamwork & personal
development training for young people

**World Civil Society Forum**
www.worldcivilsociety.org
Aims to strengthen international co-operation

**World Cup**
www.fifa.com
The official site for the Football World Cup

**World Development Movement**
66 Offley Road  London SW9 0LS
Tel: 020 7820 4900
Email via website
www.wdm.org.uk
Campaigns to tackle the root causes of poverty.

**World Food Programme (United Nations)**
Via C.G.Viola 68  Parco dé Medici  00148 Rome
Italy
Tel: 00 39 06 65131
Email via website
www.wfp.org

**World Health Organisation**
Avenue Appia 20  1211 Geneva 27  Switzerland
Tel: 00 41 22 791 21 11
info@who.int
www.who.int

## World Horse Welfare

Anne Colvin House  Ada Cole Avenue
Snetterton  Norwich NR16 2LR
UK Welfare Hotline: 08000 480180
Tel: 01953 498682
info@worldhorsewelfare.org
www.ilph.org
One of the world's leading equine welfare
charities

## World Jewish Relief

Oscar Joseph House  54 Crewys Road
London NW2 2AD
Tel: 020 8736 1250
info@wjr.org.uk
www.wjr.org.uk
Acts on behalf of the UK Jewish community
to provide emergency and development aid to
those in need throughout the world regardless
of race, religion or ethnic origin

## World Ju-Jitsu Federation (Ireland)

PO Box 142  Ballymena BT43 7YB
Tel: 028 2565 1502
wjjf@jujitsuireland.com
www.jujitsuireland.com

## World Land Trust

FREEPOST  ANG20000  PO Box 27
Halesworth  Suffolk IP19 8ZT
Tel: 0845 054 4422
info@worldlandtrust.org
www.worldlandtrust.org
Purchases and protects critically threatened
wilderness areas

## World Monuments Fund in Britain

2 Grosvenor Gardens  London SW1W 0DH
Tel: 020 7730 5344
enquiries@wmf.org.uk
www.wmf.org.uk
Charity which promotes on-site conservation
of cultural landmarks and supports educational
activities

## World Society for the Protection of Animals
see WSPA

## World Space Week

www.worldspaceweek.org
The Largest Public Space Event on Earth –
celebrated in over 55 Nations every October
4-10

## World Tourism Organization WTO

Capitan Haya 42  28020 Madrid  Spain
Tel: 00 34 91 567 81 00
omt@unwto.org
www.world-tourism.org
Inter-governmental body for the promotion and
development of tourism

## World Trade Organisation WTO

www.wto.org

Administers multilateral trade agreements,
acts as a forum for negotiations, and handles
international trade disputes

## World Travel & Tourism Council

1-2 Queen Victoria Terrace  Sovereign Court
London E1W 3HA
Tel: 0870 727 9882/ 020 7481 8007
enquiries@wttc.org
www.wttc.org

## World Vision UK

Opal Drive  Fox Milne  Milton Keynes MK15
0ZR
Tel: 01908 841000
info@worldvision.org.uk
www.worldvision.org.uk
Humanitarian aid and development agency

## World Wide Fund for Nature see WWF - UK

**Worldometers** World statistics updated in
real time
contact@worldometers.info
www.worldometers.info

## Worldwide Opportunities on Organic Farms
see WWOOF Association (International)

## Worldwide Volunteering

7 North St Workshops  Stoke sub Hamdon
Somerset TA14 6QR
Tel: 01935 825588
wwv@wwv.org.uk
www.wwv.org.uk
Search and match database of 350,000 UK
and worldwide volunteering opportunities for
all ages

**WPPA** see Pre-School Playgroups Association
(Wales)

## WRAP

The Old Academy  21 Horse Fair  Banbury,
OX16 0AH
Resource Efficiency Helpline:  0808 100 2040
Switchboard: 01295 819 900
Envirowise advice line: 0800 585 794
Email via website
www.wrap.org.uk
Works in partnership, helping businesses and
the general public to reduce waste, to use more
recycled material and recycle more things more
often

## Writers' Guild of Great Britain

40 Rosebery Avenue  London EC1R 4RX
Tel: 020 7833 0777
erik@writersguild.org.uk
www.writersguild.org.uk

**Writers in Education (National Association of)** NAWE
PO Box 1 Sheriff Hutton York YO60 7YU
Tel: 01653 618 429
www.nawe.co.uk
Supports development of creative writing

**WriteToThem.com**
Email via website
www.writetothem.com
Allows you to contact your MP even if you don't know their name or your constituency

**WRVS**
Beck Court Cardiff Gate Business Park Cardiff CF23 8RP
Tel: 029 2073 9000
Tel: 0845 601 4670 (to volunteer)
Email via website
www.wrvs.org.uk
Helps people maintain independence and dignity in their homes and communities, particularly in later life

**WSPA** World Society for the Protection of Animals
5th Floor 222 Grays Inn Road London WC1X 8HB
Tel: 0800 316 9966
wspa@wspa.org.uk
www.wspa.org.uk

**WWF-UK**
Panda House Weyside Park Godalming Surrey GU7 1XR
Tel: 01483 426 444
Email via website
www.wwf.org.uk
www.panda.org (international)
Conserves and protects endangered species & habitats, for the benefit of people & nature

**WWOOF Association (International)**
Worldwide Opportunities on Organic Farms
PO Box 2154 Winslow
Buckinghamshire MK18 3WS
Email via website
www.wwoof.org.uk
Helps those who wish to work as volunteers on organic farms (UK & international)

# Y

**Y Care International**
Kemp House 152-160 City Road London EC1V 2NP
Tel: 020 7549 3150
enquiries@ycareinternational.org
www.ycareinternational.org
Working with young people for world development

**Yachting Association (Royal)**
RYA House Ensign Way Hamble Southampton SO31 4YA
Tel: 0845 345 0400
enquiries@rya.org.uk
www.rya.org.uk

**Year Out Group**
Queensfield 28 Kings Road Easterton Wiltshire SN10 4PX
info@yearoutgroup.org
www.yearoutgroup.org

**YHA** see Youth Hostel Association (England & Wales) Ltd

**YMCA (National Council of)** Young Men's Christian Association
640 Forest Rd London E17 3DZ
Tel: 020 8520 5599
enquiries@ymca.org.uk
www.ymca.org.uk
Committed to helping young people, particularly at times of need

**Ymgyrch Diogelu Cymru Wledig** see Protection of Rural Wales (Campaign for the)

**Yoga (British Wheel of)**
25 Jermyn St Sleaford Lincs NG34 7RU
Tel: 01529 306851
office@bwy.org.uk
www.bwy.org.uk

**Yoga (Iyengar Institute)**
223a Randolph Ave Maida Vale London W9 1NL
Tel: 020 7624 3080
office@iyi.org.uk
www.iyi.org.uk

**YOMAG**
www.yomag.net
European e-zine produced by young consumers

**Young Christian Workers**
St Josephs, off St Joseph's Grove Watford Way London NW4 4TY
Tel: 020 8203 6290
info@ycwimpact.com
www.ycwimpact.com

## Young Concert Artists Trust
23 Garrick St  London WC2E 9BN
Tel: 020 7379 8477
info@ycat.co.uk
www.ycat.co.uk
A charity representing outstanding young
musicians selected by annual auditions

## Young Engineers
Chiltlee Manor  Liphook  Hampshire GU30 7AZ
Tel: 01428 727265
Email via website
www.youngeng.org
National network of engineering, electronics
& technology clubs and run engineering
competitions in schools and colleges

## Young Enterprise
Peterley House  Peterley Rd  Oxford OX4 2TZ
Tel: 01865 776845
info@young-enterprise.org.uk
www.young-enterprise.org.uk
Practical enterprise activities for young people
aged 4-25, supported by business and industry
volunteers

## Young Farmers' Clubs (National Federation of)
YFC Centre  10th Street  Stoneleigh Park
Kenilworth  Warwickshire CV8 2LG
Tel: 024 7685 7200
post@nfyfc.org.uk
www.nfyfc.org.uk

## Young Father's Initiative
Unit K401 Tower Bridge Business Complex
100 Clements Road  London  SE16 4DG
Tel: 020 7237 5353
info@workingwithmen.org
www.young-fathers.org.uk
Information and advice about fatherhood

## Young Men's Christian Association see
YMCA (National Council of)

## Young People in Focus
23 New Rd  Brighton BN1 1WZ
Tel: 01273 693311
info@youngpeopleinfocus.org.uk
www.youngpeopleinfocus.org.uk

## Young People with ME (Association of)
10 Vermont Place  Tongwell  Milton Keynes
MK15 8JA
Tel: 08451 232389
info@ayme.org.uk
www.ayme.org.uk
Offers cheerful support for all children and
young people with ME aged 5 to 25. Free
membership to eligible applicants

## Young People's Learning Agency
Cheylesmore House  Quinton Road  Coventry
CV1 2WT
Learner Support helpline: 0800 121 8989
Tel: 0845 337 2000
enquiries@ypla.gov.uk
www.ypla.gov.uk
October 2010: under review

## Young Scot
Rosebery House  9 Haymarket Terrace
Edinburgh EH12 5EZ
InfoLine: 0808 801 0338 or text 'callback' to
07781 484 317
infoline@youngscot.org
www.youngscot.org
Scotland's national youth information &
discount service

## Young Women's Christian Association see
YWCA England & Wales

## YoungMinds
48-50 St John Street  London EC1M 4DG
Parents helpline: 0808 802 5544
Tel: 020 7336 8445
Email via website
www.youngminds.org.uk
National charity committed to improving the
mental health of all children and young people

## Your Life
www.your-life.com
Accurate information related to reproductive
and sexual health.

## Youth Access
1 - 2 Taylors Yard  67 Alderbrook Rd
London SW12 8AD
Tel: 020 8772 9900
admin@youthaccess.org.uk
www.youthaccess.org.uk
Provides referral service to youth
information, advice & counselling services
across the country

## Youth Advocacy Service (National) NYAS
Egerton House  Tower Road  Birkenhead  Wirral
CH41 1FN
Tel: 0800 616101
Tel: 0151 649 8700
help@nyas.net
www.nyas.net
Help and guidance for all young people

## Youth Agency (National)
Eastgate House  19-23 Humberstone Road
Leicester LE5 3GJ
Tel: 0116 242 7350
Email via website
www.nya.org.uk
www.youthinformation.com

Aims to advance youth work to promote young people's development and their voice in public life

**Youth Arts Wales (National)**
245 Western Ave  Cardiff CF5 2YX
Tel: 02920 265 060
nyaw@nyaw.co.uk
www.nyaw.co.uk
Representing the National Youth Brass Band, Chamber Ensemble, Choir, Orchestra and Theatre of Wales and National Youth Dance, Wales

**Youth at Risk**
The Old Warehouse  31 Upper King St  Royston Herts SG8 9AZ
Tel: 01763 241120
Email via website
www.youthatrisk.org.uk
Support and mentors for disadvantaged 15 -19 year olds

**Youth Award Scheme** see ASDAN Educational Limited

**Youth Choir of Great Britain (National)**
Pelaw House  University of Durham  Leazes Road  Durham DH1 1TA
Tel: 0191 3348110
office@nycgb.net
www.nycgb.net
Summer school held from mid-July to September

**Youth Clubs (UK)** see UK Youth

**Youth Council (British)**
CAN Mezzanine London Bridge  1 Downstream Building  1 London Bridge  London SE1 9BG
Tel: 0845 458 1489
email via website
www.byc.org.uk
National voice for young people in the UK

**Youth Council for N. Ireland**
Forestview  Purdy's Lane  Belfast BT8 7AR
Tel: 028 9064 3882
info@ycni.org
www.ycni.org
Advisory body on quality of life for children and young people

**Youth for Christ**
Coombswood Way  Halesowen  West Midlands B62 8BH
Tel: 0121 502 9620
yfc@yfc.co.uk
www.yfc.co.uk
Christian outreach

**Youth Hostel** see also Hostelling (Internet Guide to)

**Youth Hostel Association (England & Wales) Ltd** YHA
Trevelyan House  Dimple Road  Matlock Derbyshire DE4 3YH
Tel: 01629 592600
customerservices@yha.org.uk
www.yha.org.uk
Accommodation and activity provider. All ages, families and groups welcome

**Youth Hostel Association (N. Ireland)** now see Hostelling International (N. Ireland)

**Youth Hostel Federation (International)** now see Hostelling International

**Youth Hostels Association (Scottish)**
7 Glebe Crescent  Stirling FK8 2JA
Tel: 01786 891400
info@syha.org.uk
www.syha.org.uk
Provider of budget accommodation across all of Scotland from rural areas to cities

**Youth in Action**
British Council  10 Spring Gardens  London SW1A 2BN
Tel: 020 7389 4030
youthinaction@britishcouncil.org
www.britishcouncil.org/youthinaction
UK National Agency for the European Commission's YOUTH programme eg youth exchange, voluntary service etc

**Youth Information** The information toolkit for Young People
www.youthinformation.com
Information for young people from the National Youth Agency

**Youth Justice Board for England and Wales**
1 Drummond Gate  London SW1V 2QZ
Tel: 020 3372 8000
enquiries@yjb.gov.uk
www.yjb.gov.uk
October 2010: Youth Justice Board (YJB), will cease to function and its functions will be transferred into the Ministry of Justice.

**Youth Music**
One America St  London SE1 0NE
Tel: 020 7902 1060
info@youthmusic.org.uk
www.youthmusic.org.uk

**Youth Music Theatre (National)**
2-4 Great Eastern St  London EC2A 3NW
Tel: 020 7422 8290
enquiries@nymt.org.uk
www.nymt.org.uk

**Youth Opera (British)**
LSBU  103 Borough Road  London SE1 0AA
Tel: 020 7815 6090
info@byo.org.uk
www.byo.org.uk
An opera training company for young people
aged 20-30 with annual performances in
London

**Youth Orchestra (National of GB)**
Zetland House  5-25 Scrutton Street  London
EC2A 4HJ
Tel: 020 7613 7810
info@nyo.org.uk
www.nyo.org.uk

**Youth Sport Trust**
SportPark  Loughborough University  3
Oakwood Drive  Loughborough LE11 3QF
Tel: 01509 226600
info@youthsporttrust.org
www.youthsporttrust.org
Quality physical education and sport
programmes for all young people

**Youth Theatre** see Scottish Youth Theatre,
Youth Music Theatre (National)

**Youth Theatre of GB (National)**
Woolyard  52 Bermondsey Street  London SE1
3UD
Tel: 020 7281 3863
info@nyt.org.uk
www.nyt.org.uk
Acting, administration, costume making,
lighting and sound, scenery and prop making or
stage management for 14 - 21 year olds

**Youth Theatres (National Association of)**
Arts Centre  Vane Terrace  Darlington DL3 7AX
Tel: 01325 363 330
Email via website
www.nayt.org.uk
Umbrella organisation for youth theatres

**Youthhealthtalk**
info@youthhealthtalk.org
www.youthhealthtalk.org
Young people's real life experiences of health
and lifestyle

**YouthNet UK**
www.youthnet.org
Website directs young people to where they
can obtain information about organisations and
publications

**YWCA England & Wales**
Clarendon House  52 Cornmarket St  Oxford
OX1 3EJ
Tel: 01865 304200
info@ywca.org.uk
www.ywca.org.uk
A force for change for young women to
challenge and overcome discrimination and
disadvantage

**Z**

**Zoo Check** see Born Free Foundation

# Universities & Colleges

The majority of institutions accept applications via UCAS, but some, particularly specialist dance, drama, music and art institutions, require a direct application.

The institutions are arranged in alphabetical order by place name wherever possible.

**UCAS**
(Universities & Colleges Admissions Service)
www.ucas.ac.uk

**Unistats**
unistats.direct.gov.uk

**Aberdeen**
www.abdn.ac.uk/sras

**Abertay**
www.abertay.ac.uk

**Aberystwyth**
www.aber.ac.uk

**Accrington & Rossendale College**
www.accrosshighereducation.co.uk

**American InterContinental University - London**
www.aiulondon.ac.uk

**Anglia Ruskin University**
www.anglia.ac.uk

**Anglo European College of Chiropractic**
www.aecc.ac.uk

**Askham Bryan College**
www.askham-bryan.ac.uk

**Aston**
Birmingham
www.aston.ac.uk

**Bangor**
www.bangor.ac.uk

**Barking and Dagenham College**
www.barkingcollege.ac.uk

**Barony College**
www.barony.ac.uk

**Basingstoke College of Technology**
www.bcot.ac.uk

**Bath**
www.bath.ac.uk

**Bath College (City of )**
www.citybathcoll.ac.uk

**Bath Spa**
www.bathspa.ac.uk

**Bedford College**
www.bedford.ac.uk

**Bedfordshire**
www.beds.ac.uk

**Belfast**
see Queen's University, St. Mary's University College & Stranmillis University College

**Birkbeck**
University of London
www.bbk.ac.uk

**Birmingham**
www.bham.ac.uk

**Birmingham (City College)**
www.citycol.ac.uk

**Birmingham City University**
www.bcu.ac.uk

**Birmingham Metropolitan College**
www.bmetc.ac.uk

**Birmingham, University College**
www.ucb.ac.uk

**Bishop Burton College**
Beverley, East Yorkshire
www.bishopburton.ac.uk

**Bishop Grosseteste College**
Lincoln
www.bishopg.ac.uk

**Blackburn College**
www.blackburn.ac.uk

**Blackpool and The Fylde College**
www.blackpool.ac.uk

**Bolton**
www.bolton.ac.uk

**Bournemouth**
www.bournemouth.ac.uk

**Bournemouth**
The Arts University College at
www.aucb.ac.uk

**BPP University College Of Professional Studies Limited**
London
www.bpplawschool.com

**Bradford**
www.bradford.ac.uk

**Bradford College**
www.bradfordcollege.ac.uk

**Bridgwater College**
www.bridgwater.ac.uk

**Brighton**
www.brighton.ac.uk

**Brighton & Sussex Medical School**
www.bsms.ac.uk

**Bristol**
www.bristol.ac.uk

**Bristol College (City of)**
www.cityofbristol.ac.uk

**Bristol Filton College**
www.filton.ac.uk

**British Institute of Technology & E-commerce**
London
www.bite.ac.uk

**British School of Osteopathy**
www.bso.ac.uk

**Brooklands College**
www.brooklands.ac.uk

**Brooksby Melton College**
www.brooksbymelton.ac.uk

**Brunel University**
www.brunel.ac.uk

**Buckingham**
www.buckingham.ac.uk

**Buckinghamshire New University**
www.bucks.ac.uk

**Cambridge**
www.cam.ac.uk

**Canterbury Christ Church University**
www.canterbury.ac.uk

**Cardiff**
www.cardiff.ac.uk

**Cardiff  see also UWIC**
www.uwic.ac.uk

**Carmarthenshire College**
see Coleg Sir Gar

**Castle College Nottingham**
www.castlecollege.ac.uk

**Central Lancashire**
www.uclan.ac.uk

**Central School of Speech & Drama**
www.cssd.ac.uk

**Chester (University College)**
www.chester.ac.uk

**Chichester**
www.chiuni.ac.uk

**Chichester College**
www.chichester.ac.uk

**City of Westminster College**
www.cwc.ac.uk

**City University**
www.city.ac.uk

**Cleveland College of Art and Design**
www.ccad.ac.uk

**Cliff College**
www.cliffcollege.ac.uk

**Colchester Institute**
www.colchester.ac.uk

**Coleg Llandrillo, Cymru**
www.llandrillo.ac.uk

**Coleg Menai**
www.menai.ac.uk

**Coleg Sir Gar/Carmarthenshire College**
www.colegsirgar.ac.uk

**College of Agriculture, Food and Rural Enterprise**
www.cafre.ac.uk

**Cornwall College**
www.cornwall.ac.uk

**Courtauld Institute of Art**
(University of London)
www.courtauld.ac.uk

**Coventry**
www.coventry.ac.uk

**Coventry (City College)**
www.covcollege.ac.uk

**Craven College**
www.craven-college.ac.uk

**Creative Arts, University for the**
www.ucreative.ac.uk

**Croydon College**
www.croydon.ac.uk

**Cumbria University**
www.cumbria.ac.uk

**Dartington College of Arts**
Now see Falmouth

**Dearne Valley College**
www.dearne-coll.ac.uk

**Derby**
www.derby.ac.uk

**Dewsbury College**
now see Kirklees College

**Doncaster College**
www.don.ac.uk

**Duchy College**
www.duchy.ac.uk

**Dudley College of Technology**
www.dudleycol.ac.uk

**Dundee**
www.dundee.ac.uk

**Durham**
www.dur.ac.uk

**Durham (New College)**
www.newdur.ac.uk

**Ealing, Hammersmith & West London College**
www.wlc.ac.uk

**East Anglia**
www.uea.ac.uk

**East London**
www.uel.ac.uk

**East Riding College**
www.eastridingcollege.ac.uk

**East Surrey College**
(Incorporating Reigate School of Art and Design)
www.esc.ac.uk

**Edge Hill University**
www.edgehill.ac.uk

**Edinburgh**
www.ed.ac.uk

**Edinburgh**
see also Heriot-Watt, Napier, Queen Margaret

**Edinburgh College of Art**
www.eca.ac.uk

**Edinburgh: Queen Margaret University**
www.qmu.ac.uk

**Essex**
www.essex.ac.uk

**European Business School, London**
www.ebslondon.ac.uk

**European School of Economics**
www.eselondon.ac.uk

**European School of Osteopathy**
www.eso.ac.uk

**Exeter**
www.ex.ac.uk

**Exeter College**
www.exe-coll.ac.uk /he

**Falmouth (University College)**
www.falmouth.ac.uk

**Farnborough College of Technology**
www.farn-ct.ac.uk

**Glamorgan, Cardiff and Pontypridd**
www.glam.ac.uk

**Glasgow**
www.gla.ac.uk

**Glasgow Caledonian University**
www.gcal.ac.uk

**Glasgow School of Art**
www.gsa.ac.uk

**Gloucestershire**
www.glos.ac.uk

**Gloucestershire College**
www.gloscol.ac.uk

**Glyndwr University**
formerly North East Wales Institute of Higher Education
www.glyndwr.ac.uk

**Goldsmiths College**
(University of London)
www.goldsmiths.ac.uk

**Gower College Swansea**
www.swancoll.ac.uk

**Greenmount and Enniskillen Colleges**
see College of Agriculture, Food and Rural Enterprise

**Greenwich**
www.gre.ac.uk

**Greenwich School of Management**
www.greenwich-college.ac.uk

**Grimsby Institute of Further and Higher Education**
www.grimsby.ac.uk

**Guildford College of Further and Higher Education**
www.guildford.ac.uk

**Harper Adams University College**
www.harper-adams.ac.uk

**Havering College of Further and Higher Education**
www.havering-college.ac.uk

**Hereford College of Arts**
www.hca.ac.uk

**Heriot-Watt**
www.hw.ac.uk

**Hertfordshire**
www.herts.ac.uk

**Heythrop College**
(University of London)
www.heythrop.ac.uk/

**Highbury College**
www.highbury.ac.uk

**Highlands & Islands**
see UHI Millennium Institute

**Holborn College**
www.holborncollege.ac.uk

**Hopwood Hall College**
www.hopwood.ac.uk/

**Huddersfield**
www.hud.ac.uk

**Huddersfield Technical College**
now see Kirklees College

**Hull**
www.hull.ac.uk

**Hull College**
www.hull-college.ac.uk/HE

**Hull York Medical School**
www.hyms.ac.uk

**ifs School of Finance**
www.ifslearning.ac.uk

**Imperial College**
(University of London)
www.imperial.ac.uk

**Islamic College for Advanced Studies**
www.islamic-college.ac.uk

**Keele**
www.keele.ac.uk

**Kensington College of Business**
www.kensingtoncoll.ac.uk

**Kent**
www.kent.ac.uk

**Kent Institute of Art and Design**
see University College for the Creative Arts

**King Alfred's Winchester**
see Winchester (University College)

**King's College London**
www.kcl.ac.uk

**Kingston**
www.kingston.ac.uk

**Kirklees College**
www.kirkleescollege.ac.uk

**Lakes College West Cumbria**
www.lcwc.ac.uk

**Lampeter**
(University of Wales)
www.lamp.ac.uk

**Lancaster**
www.lancs.ac.uk

**Leeds**
www.leeds.ac.uk

**Leeds City College**
www.leedscitycollege.ac.uk

**Leeds College of Art**
www.leeds-art.ac.uk

**Leeds College of Music**
www.lcm.ac.uk

**Leeds Metropolitan University**
www.leedsmet.ac.uk

**Leeds: Trinity University**
(formerly Leeds Trinity and All Saints)
www.leedstrinity.ac.uk

**Leicester**
www.le.ac.uk

**Leicester College**
www.lec.ac.uk

**Leicester: De Montfort**
www.dmu.ac.uk

**Lincoln**
www.lincoln.ac.uk

**Lincoln College**
www.lincolncollege.ac.uk

**Liverpool**
www.liv.ac.uk

**Liverpool Community College**
www.liv-coll.ac.uk

**Liverpool Hope University College**
www.hope.ac.uk

**Liverpool Institute for Performing Arts**
www.lipa.ac.uk

**Liverpool John Moores University**
www.ljmu.ac.uk

**Llandrillo College**
see Coleg Llandrillo

**London College, UCK**
www.lcuck.ac.uk

**London Electronics College**
www.lec.ac.uk

**London Guildhall University**
see London Metropolitan University

**London Metropolitan University**
www.londonmet.ac.uk

**London: Queen Mary**
(University of London)
www.qmul.ac.uk

**London School of Commerce**
www.lsclondon.co.uk

**London School of Economics and
Political Science**
(University of London)
www.lse.ac.uk

**London School of Science and
Technology**
www.lsst.com

**London South Bank University**
www.lsbu.ac.uk

**Loughborough**
www.lboro.ac.uk

**Loughborough College**
www.loucoll.ac.uk

**Manchester**
www.manchester.ac.uk

**Manchester College, The**
formerly Manchester City College and The
Manchester College of Art and Technology
www.themanchestercollege.ac.uk

**Manchester Metropolitan University**
www.mmu.ac.uk

**Matthew Boulton College of Further and
Higher Education**
Now see Birmingham Metropolitan

**Medway School of Pharmacy**
www.kent.ac.uk

**Menai**
see Coleg Menai

**Mid-Cheshire College**
www.midchesh.ac.uk

**Middlesex**
www.mdx.ac.uk

**Moulton College**
www.moulton.ac.uk

**Mountview Academy of Theatre Arts**
www.mountview.ac.uk

**Myerscough College**
www.myerscough.ac.uk

**Napier**
www.napier.ac.uk

**Nazarene Theological College**
www.nazarene.ac.uk

**Neath Port Talbot College**
www.nptc.ac.uk

**NESCOT**
North East Surrey College of Technology
www.nescot.ac.uk

**New College Telford**
www.nct.ac.uk

**Newcastle**
www.ncl.ac.uk

**Newcastle College**
www.newcastlecollege.co.uk

**Newham College of Further Education**
www.newham.ac.uk

**Newman University College Birmingham**
www.newman.ac.uk

**Newport**
www.newport.ac.uk

**North East Surrey College of Technology**
see NESCOT

**North East Worcestershire College**
www.ne-worcs.ac.uk

**North Glasgow College**
northglasgowcollege.ac.uk

**North Lindsey College**
www.northlindsey.ac.uk

**North London**
see London Metropolitan University

**North Warwickshire and Hinckley College**
www.nwhc.ac.uk

**Northampton**
www.northampton.ac.uk

**Northbrook College Sussex**
www.northbrook.ac.uk

**Northumberland College**
www.northland.ac.uk

**Northumbria**
www.northumbria.ac.uk

**Norwich: City College of Further & Higher Education**
www.ccn.ac.uk

**Norwich University College of the Arts**
www.nuca.ac.uk

**Nottingham**
www.nottingham.ac.uk

**Nottingham (New College)**
www.ncn.ac.uk

**Nottingham Trent University**
www.ntu.ac.uk

**Open University**
www.open.ac.uk

**Oxford**
www.ox.ac.uk

**Oxford and Cherwell Valley College**
www.ocvc.ac.uk/

**Oxford Brookes**
www.brookes.ac.uk

**Paisley**
now see West of Scotland

**Paris (University of London Institute in)**
www.ulip.lon.ac.uk

**Pembrokeshire College**
www.pembrokeshire.ac.uk

**Peninsula College of Medicine and Dentistry**
Universities of Exeter & Plymouth
www.pms.ac.uk

**Peterborough - University Centre**
www.anglia.ac.uk/ucp

**Petroc**
www.petroc.ac.uk

**Plymouth**
www.plymouth.ac.uk

**Plymouth College of Art**
www.plymouthart.ac.uk

**Portsmouth**
www.port.ac.uk

**Queen's University**
Belfast
www.qub.ac.uk

**Ravensbourne**
www.rave.ac.uk

**Reading**
www.reading.ac.uk

**Regents Business School London**
www.rregents.ac.uk

**Richmond, The American International University in London**
www.richmond.ac.uk

**Riverside College Halton**
Widnes
www.riversidecollege.ac.uk

**Robert Gordon**
Aberdeen
www.rgu.ac.uk

**Roehampton**
(University of Surrey)
www.roehampton.ac.uk

**Rose Bruford**
Sidcup
www.bruford.ac.uk

**Rotherham College of Arts and Technology**
www.rotherham.ac.uk

**Royal Academy of Dance**
London
www.rad.org.uk

**Royal Agricultural College**
Gloucester
www.rac.ac.uk

**Royal College of Art**
London (Post graduate only)
www.rca.ac.uk

**Royal Holloway**
London
www.rhul.ac.uk

**Royal Veterinary College**
London
www.rvc.ac.uk

**Royal Welsh College of Music & Drama**
Cardiff
www.rwcmd.ac.uk

**Ruskin College Oxford**
www.ruskin.ac.uk

**SAE Institute**
(School of Audio Engineering) Glasgow, Liverpool & London
www.sae.edu

**Salford**
www.salford.ac.uk

**Salisbury College**
now see Wiltshire College

**Sandwell College**
www.sandwell.ac.uk

**School of Oriental and African Studies**
(University of London)
www.soas.ac.uk

**School of Pharmacy**
(University of London)
www.pharmacy.ac.uk

**Scottish Agricultural College**
(The National College for Food, Land and Environmental Studies)
www.sac.ac.uk

**Sheffield**
www.sheffield.ac.uk

**Sheffield College**
www.sheffcol.ac.uk

**Sheffield Hallam**
www.shu.ac.uk

**Solihull College**
www.solihull.ac.uk

**Somerset College of Arts and Technology**
www.somerset.ac.uk

**South Cheshire College**
www.s-cheshire.ac.uk

**South Downs College**
www.southdowns.ac.uk

**South Essex College**
www.southessex.ac.uk

**South Nottingham College**
www.snc.ac.uk

**South Tyneside College**
www.stc.ac.uk

**Southampton**
www.southampton.ac.uk

**Southampton Solent University**
www.solent.ac.uk

**Southport College**
www.southport-college.ac.uk/

**Sparsholt College Hampshire**
www.sparsholt.ac.uk

**St Andrews**
Fife
www.st-andrews.ac.uk

**St George's University of London**
Formerly St George's Hospital Medical School
www.sgul.ac.uk

**St Helens College**
www.sthelens.ac.uk

**St Martin's College, Lancaster: Ambleside: Carlisle: London**
now see Cumbria University

**St Mary's University College**
Twickenham
www.smuc.ac.uk

**St Mary's University College**
Belfast
www.smucb.ac.uk

**Staffordshire**
www.staffs.ac.uk

**Stamford New College**
www.stamford.ac.uk

**Stephenson College Coalville**
www.stephensoncoll.ac.uk

**Stirling**
www.stir.ac.uk

**Stockport College**
www.stockport.ac.uk

**Stourbridge College**
www.stourbridge.ac.uk

**Stranmillis University College**
Belfast
www.stran.ac.uk

**Stratford upon Avon College**
www.stratford.ac.uk

**Strathclyde**
www.strath.ac.uk

**Suffolk, University Campus**
www.ucs.ac.uk

**Sunderland**
www.sunderland.ac.uk

**Sunderland College (City of)**
www.citysun.ac.uk

**Surrey**
www.surrey.ac.uk

**Sussex**
www.sussex.ac.uk

**Sutton Coldfield College**
now see Birmingham Metropolitan College

**Swansea**
www.swansea.ac.uk

**Swansea Metropolitan University**
formerly Swansea Institute
www.smu.ac.uk

**Swindon College**
www.swindon-college.ac.uk

**Tameside College**
www.tameside.ac.uk

**Teesside**
www.tees.ac.uk

**Thames Valley**
(The University of West London)
www.tvu.ac.uk

**Trinity St David**
Carmarthen
www.trinity-cm.ac.uk

**Truro and Penwith College**
www.trurocollege.ac.uk

**Tyne Metropolitan College**
www.tynemet.ac.uk

**UCP Marjon**
St Mark and St John  (The College of),
Plymouth
www.marjon.ac.uk

**UHI Millennium Institute**
www.uhi.ac.uk

**Ulster**
www.ulster.ac.uk

**University College London**
www.ucl.ac.uk

**University of the Arts London**
Camberwell College of Arts, Central Saint
Martins College of Art and Design, Chelsea
College of Art and Design, London College
of Communication, London College of
Fashion, Wimbledon College of Art
www.arts.ac.uk

**University of Wales Institute, Cardiff**
www.uwic.ac.uk

**UWIC**
(University of Wales Institute Cardiff)
www.uwic.ac.uk

**Uxbridge College**
www.uxbridgecollege.ac.uk

**Wakefield College**
www.wakefield.ac.uk

**Walsall College**
www.walsallcollege.ac.uk

**Warrington Collegiate**
www.warrington.ac.uk

**Warwick**
www.warwick.ac.uk

**Warwickshire College**
www.warwickshire.ac.uk

**West Anglia (College of)**
www.col-westanglia.ac.uk

**West Cheshire College**
www.west-cheshire.ac.uk

**West of England**
Bristol
www.uwe.ac.uk

**West of Scotland**
formerly Paisley University
www.uwc.ac.uk

**West Thames College**
www.west-thames.ac.uk

**Westminster**
www.westminster.ac.uk

**Westminster Kingsway College**
www.westking.ac.uk

**Wigan and Leigh College**
www.wigan-leigh.ac.uk/

**Wiltshire College**
www.wiltshire.ac.uk

**Winchester**
www.winchester.ac.uk

**Wirral Metropolitan College**
www.wmc.ac.uk

**Wolverhampton**
www.wlv.ac.uk

**Worcester**
www.worcester.ac.uk

**Worcester College of Technology**
www.wortech.ac.uk

**Writtle College**
www.writtle.ac.uk

**York**
www.york.ac.uk

**York College**
www.yorkcollege.ac.uk

**York St John University College**
w3.yorksj.ac.uk

**Yorkshire Coast College of Further and Higher Education**
www.yorkshirecoastcollege.ac.uk

# Dance, drama, music & performing arts

The institutions listed offer post-16 vocational training. This is different from the theatre, dance, drama and performing arts degrees offered by many universities.

Some institutions accept applications through UCAS but for the majority application will be direct.

Those listed as DADA are accredited to offer Dance and Drama (DADA) Awards. These cover most of the tuition fees for their courses, which are at National Certificate or National Diploma level. See www.direct.gov.uk for full information.

The National Council for Drama Training (NCDT) is a partnership of employers in theatre, broadcast and media industries, employee representatives and training providers which accredits vocational courses,

The Council for Dance Education and Training (CDET) is the national standards body of the professional dance industry. It accredits programmes of training in vocational dance schools.

There are also prestigious institutions which function outside of other systems and administer their own admissions and funding.

## Academy of Live and Recorded Arts (Alra)
Studio 24
Royal Victoria Patriotic Building
John Archer Way
London SW18 3SX
Tel: 020 8870 6475
info@alra.co.uk
www.alra.co.uk
DADA NCDT. ALRA North opened in September 2010 in Wigan

## Arts Ed London
Cone Ripman House
14 Bath Rd
London W4 1LY
Tel: 020 8987 6666
c.smith@artsed.co.uk
www.artsed.co.uk
CDET DADA NCDT

## Bird College – Dance and Drama Theatre Performance
The Centre
27 Station Rd
Sidcup DA15 7EB
Tel: 020 8300 6004
kerensa.gardner@birdcollege.co.uk
www.birdcollege.co.uk
CDET DADA

## Birmingham School of Acting
G2 - Millennium Point
Curzon Street
Birmingham B4 7XG
Tel: 0121 331 7220
yinka.issac@bcu.ac.uk
www.bsa.uce.ac.uk
NCDT

## Bristol Old Vic Theatre School
2 Downside Road
Clifton
Bristol BS8 2XF
Tel: 0117 973 3535
enquiries@oldvic.ac.uk
www.oldvic.ac.uk
NCDT
Conservatoire for Dance and Drama

## Cambridge Performing Arts at Bodyworks

Bodywork Dance Studios
25-29 Glisson Rd
Cambridge CB1 2HA
Tel: 01223 314461
www.bodywork-dance.co.uk
CDET DADA

## Central School of Ballet

10 Herbal Hill
Clerkenwell Road
London EC1R 5EG
Tel: 020 7837 6332
info@csbschool.co.uk
www.centralschoolofballet.co.uk
Conservatoire for Dance and Drama

## Central School of Speech and Drama

Eton Avenue
London NW3 3HY
Tel: 020 7722 8183
admissions@cssd.ac.uk
www.cssd.ac.uk
NCDT

## Circus Space

Coronet Street
London
N! 6HD
Tel: 020 7729 9522
info@thecircusspace.co.uk
www.thecircusspace.co.uk
slight change to emal

## Conservatoire for Dance and Drama

Tavistock House, Tavistock Square
London
WC1H 0JJ
Tel: 020 7387 5101
info@cdd.ac.uk
www.cdd.ac.uk
Established to protect and promote some of
the best schools offering vocational training
in dance, drama and circus arts. Each of
the Conservatoire's eight schools is a small,
specialist institution with an international
reputation for high quality training: London
Contemporary Dance School: Royal Academy
of Dramatic Art; Bristol Old Vic Theatre School;
Northern School of Contemporary Dance;
Central School of Ballet; Circus Space; London
Academy of Music and Dramatic Art; Rambert
School of Ballet and Contemporary Dance

## Drama Centre

Central St Martins College of Art and Design
Southampton Row
London WC1B 4AP
Tel: 020 7514 7022
info@csm.arts.ac.uk
www.csm.arts.ac.uk
NCDT

## Drama Studio London

Grange Court
1 Grange Rd
London W5 5QN
Tel: 020 8579 3897
admin@dramastudiolondon.co.uk
www.dramastudiolondon.co.uk
DADA NCDT

## East 15 Acting School

Hatfields
Rectory Lane
Loughton
Essex IG10 3RY
Tel: 020 8508 5983
east15@essex.ac.uk
www.east15.ac.uk
NCDT

## Elmhurst School for Dance (in association
with Birmingham Royal Ballet)

249 Bristol Rd
Edgbaston
Birmingham B5 7UH
Tel: 0121 472 6655
enquiries@elmhurstdance.co.uk
www.elmhurstdance.co.uk
CDET DADA

## English National Ballet School

Carlyle Building
Hortensia Road
London SW10 0QS
Tel: 020 7376 7076
info@enbschool.org.uk
www.enbschool.org.uk
CDET, DADA

## Guildford School of Acting

Stag Hill Campus,
Guildford
Surrey GU2 7X
Tel: 01483 560701
gsaenquiries@gsa.surrey.ac.uk
www.conservatoire.org/
DADA NCDT

## Guildhall School of Music & Drama

Silk Street
Barbican
London EC2Y 8DT
Tel: 020 7628 2571
registry@gsmd.ac.uk
www.gsmd.ac.uk
NCDT

**Hammond School**
Hoole Bank
Mannings Lane
Chester CH2 4ES
Tel: 01244 305350
enquiries@thehammondschool.co.uk
www.thehammondschool.co.uk
CDET, DADA

**Italia Conti Academy of Theatre Arts Ltd**
For BA (Hons) Acting: 'Avondale'
72 Landor Road
London, SW9 9PH
For Theatre Arts School: Italia Conti House
23 Goswell Road
London EC1M 7AJ
Tel: 020 7733 3210(BA)
Tel: 020 7608 0047 (Ages 10-16)
admin@italiaconti.com
www.italiaconti.com
CDET DADA  NCDT

**Laban** see Trinity Laban Conservatoire of Music
and Dance

**Laine Theatre Arts**
The Studios
East Street
Epsom
Surrey KT17 1HH
Tel: 01372 724 648
info@laine-theatre-arts.co.uk
www.laine-theatre-arts.co.uk
CDET DADA

**LAMDA** see London Academy of Music &
Dramatic Art

**Leeds College of Music**
3 Quarry Hill
Leeds LS2 7PD
Tel: 0113 222 3400
enquiries@lcm.ac.uk
www.lcm.ac.uk

**Liverpool Institute for Performing Arts**
Mount Street
Liverpool L1 9HF
Tel: 0151 330 3000
Minicom: 0151 330 3055
admissions@lipa.ac.uk
www.lipa.ac.uk
CDET

**Liverpool Theatre School and College**
Performing Arts Centre
19 Aigburth Road
Liverpool L17 4JR
Tel: 0151 728 7800
info@liverpooltheatreschoolandcollege.co.uk
www.liverpooltheatreschoolandcollege.co.uk
CDET DADA

**London Academy of Music & Dramatic Art
(LAMDA)**
155 Talgarth Road
London W14 9DA
Tel: 020 8834 0500
enquiries@lamda.org.uk
www.lamda.org.uk
NCDT
Conservatoire for Dance and Drama

**London Contemporary Dance School**
The Place
17 Dukes Road
London WC1H 9PY
Tel: 020 7121 1000
email via website
www.theplace.org.uk
Conservatoire for Dance and Drama

**London Studio Centre**
42-50 York Way
London N1 9AB
Tel: 020 7837 7741
info@london-studio-centre.co.uk
www.london-studio-centre.co.uk
CDET

**Merseyside Dance and Drama Centre**
The Studios
13-17 Camden Street
Liverpool, L3 8JR
Tel: 0151 207 6197
info@mddcdance.co.uk0
www.mddcdance.co.uk
CDET

**Midlands Academy of Dance and Drama**
Century House, Building B
428 Carlton Hill
Nottingham
NG4 1QA
Helpline:
Tel: 0115 911 0401
admin@maddcollege.supanet.com
www.maddcollege.co.uk
CDET

**Millennium Performing Arts**
29 Thomas Street
Woolwich
London SE18 6HU
Tel: 020 8301 8744
info@md2000.co.uk
www.md2000.co.uk
DADA

## Mountview Academy of Theatre Arts
Ralph Richardson Memorial Studios
Clarendon Road
Wood Green
London N22 6XF
Tel: 020 8881 2201
enquires@mountview.ac.uk
www.mountview.org.uk/
DADA NCDT

## Northern Ballet School
The Dancehouse
10 Oxford Road
Manchester M1 5QA
Tel: 0161 237 1406
enquiries@northernballetschool.co.uk
www.northernballetschool.co.uk
CDET DADA

## Northern School of Contemporary Dance
98 Chapeltown Road
Leeds LS7 4BH
Tel: 0113 219 3000
info@nscd.ac.uk
www.nscd.ac.uk
Conservatoire for Dance and Drama

## Oxford School of Drama
Sansomes Farm Studios
Woodstock
Oxfordshire OX20 1ER
Tel: 01993 812 883
info@oxforddrama.ac.uk
www.oxforddrama.ac.uk
DADA NCDT

## Performers College
Southend Road
Corringham
Essex SS17 8JT
Tel: 01375 672 053
lesley@performerscollege.co.uk
www.performerscollege.co.uk
CDET DADA

## Rambert School of Ballet & Contemporary Dance
Clifton Lodge
St. Margaret's Drive
Twickenham  TW1 1QN
Tel: 0208 892 9960
info@rambertschool.org.uk
www.rambertschool.org.uk
Conservatoire for Dance and Drama

## Rose Bruford College
Lamorbey Park
Burnt Oak Lane
Sidcup
Kent DA15 9DF
Tel: 020 8308 2600
enquiries@bruford.ac.uk
www.bruford.ac.uk
NCDT

## Royal Academy of Dance (Faculty of Education)
36 Battersea Square
London SW11 3RA
Tel: 020 7326 8000
info@rad.org.uk
www.rad.org.uk

## Royal Academy of Dramatic Art (RADA)
62-64 Gower Street
London WC1E 6ED
Tel: 020 7636 7076
enquiries@rada.ac.uk
www.rada.org
NCDT
Conservatoire for Dance and Drama

## Royal Academy of Music
Marylebone Rd
London NW1 5HT
Tel: 020 7873 7373
email via wbsite
www.ram.ac.uk

## Royal Ballet School
Upper School: 46 Floral Street
Covent Garden, London, WC2E 9DA
Lower School: White Lodge
Richmond Park
Richmond
Surrey TW10 5HR
Tel: 020 7836 8899 (Upper School)
Tel: 020 8392 8440 (Lower School)
enquiries@royalballetschool.co.uk
www.royal-ballet-school.org.uk

## Royal College of Music
Prince Consort Rd
London SW7 2BS
Tel: 020 7589 3643
info@rcm.ac.uk
www.rcm.ac.uk

## Royal Northern College of Music
124 Oxford Rd
Manchester M13 9RD
Tel: 0161 907 5200
info@rncm.ac.uk
www.rncm.ac.uk

**Royal Scottish Academy of Music & Drama**
100 Renfrew St
Glasgow G2 3DB
Tel: 0141 332 4101
registry@rsamd.ac.uk
www.rsamd.ac.uk
NCDT

**Royal Welsh College of Music &** Drama
Castle Grounds
Cathays Park
Cardiff CF10 3ER
Tel: 029 2034 2854
admissions@rwcmd.ac.uk
www.rwcmd.ac.uk
NCDT

**SLP College Leeds**
5 Chapel Lane
Garforth
Leeds LS25 1AG
Tel: 01332 868 136
info@slpcollege.co.uk
www.slpcollege.co.uk
CDET, DADA

**Stella Mann College**
10 Linden Road
Bedford MK40 2DA
Tel: 01234 213331
administrator@stellamanncollege.co.uk
www.stellamanncollege.co.uk
CDET DADA

**Tring Park School for the Performing Arts**
Tring
Hertfordshire HP23 5LX
Tel: 01442 824 255
info@tringpark.com
www.tringpark.com
CDET DADA

**Trinity Laban Conservatoire of Music and Dance**
Dance Faculty
Laban
Creekside
London
SE8 3DZ
Tel: 020 8469 9400
email via website
www.laban.org

**&**
Music faculty
King Charles Court
Old Royal Naval College
Greenwich
London SE10 9JF
Tel: 020 8305 4444
email via website
Laban and Trinity College of Music have
merged to form Trinity Laban: the UK's 1st
Conservatoire of Music and Dance.

**Urdang Academy**
The Old Finsbury Town Hall
Rosebery Avenue
London EC1R 4RP
Tel: 0207 713  7710
info@theurdangacademy.com
www.theurdangacademy.com
CDET DADA

**WAC Performing Arts and Media College**
Hampstead Town Hall Centre
213 Haverstock Hill
London NW3 4QP
Tel: 020 7692 5888
info@wac.co.uk
www.wac.co.uk
DADA

# Theatres & touring companies

**London theatres: online**
www.officiallondontheatre.co.uk

**Theatrenet**
www.theatrenet.com

**UK Theatre Web**
www.uktw.co.uk/

**Aberdeen: His Majesty's Theatre**
Rosemount Viaduct
Aberdeen AB25 1GL
Tel: 01224 641122
www.hmtaberdeen.com

**Action Transport**
Whitby Hall
Stanney Lane
Ellesmere Port CH65 9AE
Tel: 0151 357 2120
www.actiontransporttheatre.co.uk

**Arc Theatre**
First Floor
The Malthouse Studios
62-76 Abbey Road
Barking
Essex IG11 7BT
Tel: 020 8594 1095
www.arctheatre.com

**Basingstoke: Anvil, Forge and Haymarket**
Anvil Arts
Churchill Way
Basingstoke RG21 7QR
Tel: 01256 819 797
Box Office: 01256 844244
www.anvilarts.org.uk

**Bath: Theatre Royal**
Sawclose
Bath BA1 1ET
Box Office: 01225 448844
www.theatreroyal.org.uk

**Birmingham Repertory Theatre**
Centenary Sq
Broad St
Birmingham B1 2EP
Box Office: 0121 236 4455
www.birmingham-rep.co.uk

**Blackpool: Grand Theatre**
33 Church Street
Blackpool FY1 1HT
Box Office: 01253 290190
Groups:01253 743232
www.blackpoolgrand.co.uk

**Blackpool: Opera House**
Church Street
Blackpool FY1 1HW
Box Office: 0845 856 1111
www.blackpoollive.co.uk

**Bolton: Octagon Theatre**
Howell Croft South
Bolton BL1 1SB
Box Office: 01204 520661
www.octagonbolton.co.uk

**Bradford: Alhambra Theatre**
Morley Street
Bradford BD7 1AJ
Tel: 01274 432375
Box Office: 01274 432000
www.bradford-theatres.co.uk/alhambra_2.asp

**Bradford: Theatre in the Mill**
Shearbridge Rd
Bradford BD7 1DP
Box Office: 01274 233200
www.brad.ac.uk/admin/theatre

**Bristol Old Vic**
King St
Bristol BS1 4ED
Tel: 0117 949 3993
Box Office: 0117 987 7877
www.bristol-old-vic.co.uk

**Bromley: The Churchill Theatre**
High Street
Bromley
Kent BR1 1HA
Box Office: 0844 871 7627
www.ambassadortickets.com/The-Churchill

**Buxton Opera House**
Water St
Buxton SK17 6XN
Tel: 01298 72050
Box Office: 0845 1272190
www.buxtonoperahouse.org.uk/

**Cambridge Arts Theatre**
6 St Edward's Passage
Cambridge CB2 3PJ
Box Office: 01223 503333
www.cambridgeartstheatre.com

**Canterbury: Marlowe Theatre**
New theatre under construction. Performances
at various venues
Box Office: 01227 787787
www.marlowetheatre.com

**Cardiff: New Theatre**
Park Place
Cardiff CF10 3LN
Box Office: 029  2087 8889
www.newtheatrecardiff.co.uk

**Cardiff: Sherman Theatre**
Senghennydd Rd
Cardiff CF24 4YE
Box Office: 029 2064 6900
www.shermancymru.co.uk

**Clwyd Theatr Cymru**
Mold
Flintshire CH7 1YA
Box Office: 0845 330 3565
www.clwyd-theatr-cymru.co.uk

**Colchester: Mercury Theatre**
Balkerne Gate
Colchester CO1 1PT
Box Office: 01206 573948
www.mercurytheatre.co.uk

**Coventry: Belgrade Theatre**
Belgrade Sq
Coventry CV1 1GS
Box Office: 024 7655 3055
www.belgrade.co.uk

**Darlington: Civic Theatre**
Parkgate
Darlington DL1 1RR
Box Office: 01325 486555
www.darlingtonarts.co.uk

**Derby Theatre**
Eagle Centre
Derby DE1 2NF
Box Office: 01332 255800
www.derbytheatre.co.uk

**Dundee Repertory Theatre**
Tay Sq
Dundee DD1 1PB
Box Office: 01382 223530
www.dundeereptheatre.co.uk

**Edinburgh: FestivalTheatre**
13/29 Nicolson Street
Edinburgh EH8 9FT
Tel: 0131 529 6000
www.eft.co.uk

**Edinburgh: Kings Theatre**
2 Leven Street
Edinburgh EH3 9LQ
Tel: 0131 529 6000
www.eft.co.uk

**Edinburgh Playhouse**
18-22 Greenside Place
Edinburgh EH1 3AA
Tickets: 0844 847 1660
www.edinburghplayhouse.org.uk

**Edinburgh: Royal Lyceum Theatre**
Grindlay St
Edinburgh EH3 9AX
Box Office: 0131 248 4848
Groups: 0131 248 4949
www.lyceum.org.uk

**Edinburgh: Traverse Theatre**
Cambridge St
Edinburgh EH1 2ED
Box Office: 0131 228 1404
www.traverse.co.uk

**English Touring Theatre**
25 Short St
London SE1 8LJ
Tel: 020 7450 1990
www.ett.org.uk

**Exeter: Northcott Theatre**
Stocker Rd
Exeter EX4 4QB
Box Office: 01392 493493
www.exeternorthcott.co.uk

**Glasgow: Citizens Theatre**
119 Gorbals St
Glasgow G5 9DS
Box Office: 0141 429 0022
www.citz.co.uk

**Glasgow: Tramway**
25 Albert Drive
Glasgow G41 2PE
Tel: 08453303501
www.tramway.org

**Glasgow: Tron Theatre**
63 Trongate
Glasgow  G1 5HB
Box Office: 0141 552 4267
www.tron.co.uk

**Harrogate Theatre**
Oxford St
Harrogate HG1 1QF
Box Office: 01423 502116
www.harrogatetheatre.co.uk

**Headlong Theatre**
34-35 Berwick Street
London W1F 8RP
Tel: 020 7478 0270
www.headlongtheatre.co.uk

**Hornchurch: Queen's Theatre**
Billet Ln
Hornchurch RM11 1QT
Box Office: 01708 443333
www.queens-theatre.co.uk

**Huddersfield: Lawrence Batley Theatre**
Queens Square
Queens St
Huddersfield HD1 2SP
Box Office: 01484 430528
www.thelbt.org

**Hull Truck Theatre**
50 Ferensway
Hull, HU2 8LB
Box Office: 01482 323638
www.hulltruck.co.uk

**Ipswich: Sir John Mills Theatre**
Gatacre Rd
Ipswich IP1 2LQ
Box Office: 01473 211498
www.easternangles.co.uk

**Kendal: Brewery Arts Centre**
122A Highgate
Kendal LA9 4HE
Box Office: 01539 725133
www.breweryarts.co.uk

**Keswick: Theatre by the Lake**
Lakeside
Keswick CA12 5DJ
Box Office: 01768 774411
www.theatrebythelake.com

**Lancaster: Duke's Cinema & Theatre**
Moor Lane
Lancaster LA1 1QE
Box Office: 01524 598 500
www.dukes-lancaster.org

**Leeds: Grand Theatre**
46 New Briggate
Leeds LS1 6NZ
Box Office: 0844 848 2706
www.leedsgrandtheatre.com

**Leeds: West Yorkshire Playhouse**
Playhouse Sq
Quarry Hill
Leeds LS2 7UP
Box Office: 0113 213 7700
www.wyp.org.uk

**Leicester: Curve**
Rutland Street
Leicester LE1 1SB
Tel: 0116 2423595
www.curveonline.co.uk

**Lincoln: Theatre Royal**
Clasketgate
Lincoln LN2 1JJ
Box Office: 01522 519999
www.lincolntheatreroyal.com

**Liverpool: Empire**
Lime St
L1 1JE
Box Office: 0844 847 2525
www.liverpoolempire.org.uk

**Liverpool: Everyman Theatre**
5-9 Hope St
Liverpool L1 9BH
Box Office: 0151 709 4776
www.everymanplayhouse.com

**Liverpool: Playhouse**
Williamson Square
Liverpool L1 1EL
Box Office: 0151 709 4776
www.everymanplayhouse.com

**London: Almeida Theatre**
Almeida St
Islington
London N1 1TA
Box Office: 020 7359 4404
www.almeida.co.uk

**London: Barbican Centre**
Silk St
London EC2Y 8DS
Box Office: 020 7638 8891
www.barbican.org.uk

**London: Donmar Warehouse**
41 Earlham St
London WC2H 9LD
Box Office: 0844 871 7624
www.donmarwarehouse.com

**London: Hampstead Theatre**
Eton Ave
Swiss Cottage
London NW3 3EU
Box Office: 020 7722 9301
www.hampsteadtheatre.com

**London: Lyric Theatre**
King St
London W6 0QL
Box Office: 0871 2211 729
www.lyric.co.uk

**London: National Theatre**
South Bank
London SE1 9PX
Tel: 020 7452 3000 (Box Office)
www.nationaltheatre.org.uk

**London: New Wimbledon Theatre**
The Broadway
Wimbledon
London SW19 1QG
Box Office: 0844 871 7646
www.theambassadors.com/newwimbledon/

**London: Open Air Theatre**
Inner Circle
Regent's Park NW1 4NR
Box Office: 0844826 4242
www.openairtheatre.org

**London: Polka Theatre for Children**
240 The Broadway
Wimbledon
London SW19 1SB
Box Office: 020 8543 4888
www.polkatheatre.com

**London: Royal Court Theatre**
Sloane Sq
London SW1W 8AS
Tel: 020 7565 5050
Box Office: 020 7565 5000
www.royalcourttheatre.com

**London: Sadler's Wells Theatre**
Rosebery Av
London EC1R 4TN
Tel: 020 7863 8198
Box Office: 0844 412 4300
www.sadlerswells.com

**London: Shakespeare's Globe Theatre**
21 New Globe Walk
Bankside
London SE1 9DT
TBox office: 020 7401 9919
www.shakespeares-globe.org

**London: Theatre Royal Stratford East**
Gerry Raffles Sq
London E15 1BN
Tel: 020 8534 0310
www.stratfordeast.com

**London: Tricycle Theatre**
269 Kilburn High Rd
London NW6 7JR
Box Office: 020 7328 1000
www.tricycle.co.uk

**London: Unicorn Theatre for Children**
147 Tooley Street
More London
Southwark
London SE1 2HZ
Tel: 020 7645 0560
www.unicorntheatre.com

**London: Young Vic**
66 The Cut
London SE1 8LZ
Tel: 020 7922 2922
www.youngvic.org

**Manchester: Contact Theatre**
Oxford Rd
Manchester MI5 6JA
Box Office: 0161 274 0600
www.contact-theatre.org

**Manchester: Library Theatre**
Moved out of the Manchester Central
Library in July 2010 and will be performing
at alternative venues across the region until
moving into a new permanent home. Most
bookings should be done through the website.
For general enquiries: Tel: 0161 234 1913
www.librarytheatre.com

**Manchester: Opera House**
Quay Street
Manchester M3 3HP
Tel: 0844 847 2275
www.manchesteroperahouse.org.uk

**Manchester: Palace Theatre**
Oxford Street
Manchester  M1 6FT
Box Office: 0844 847 2275
www.manchesterpalace.org.uk

**Manchester: Royal Exchange Theatre Co**
St Ann's Sq
Manchester M2 7DH
Box Office: 0161 833 9833
www.royalexchange.co.uk

**Manchester: The Green Room**
54 Whitworth St West
Manchester M1 5WW
Box Office: 0161 615 0500
www.greenroomarts.org

**Milford Haven: Torch Theatre**
St Peter's Rd
Milford Haven SA73 2BU
Box Office: 01646 695267
www.torchtheatre.co.uk

**Musselburgh: Brunton Theatre**
Ladywell Way
Musselburgh EH21 6AA
Box Office: 0131 665 2240
www.bruntontheatre.co.uk

**Newbury: Watermill Theatre**
Bagnor
Newbury
Berks RG20 8AE
Box Office: 01635 46044
www.watermill.org.uk

**Newcastle under Lyme: New Vic Theatre**
Etruria Rd
Newcastle under Lyme ST5 0JG
Box Office: 01782 717962
www.newvictheatre.org.uk

**Newcastle upon Tyne: Live Theatre Company**
27 Broad Chare
Quayside
Newcastle upon Tyne NE1 3DQ
Box Office: 0191 232 1232
www.live.org.uk

**Newcastle upon Tyne: Northern Stage**
Barras Bridge
Newcastle upon Tyne NE1 7RH
Tel: 0191 230 5151
www.northernstage.co.uk

**Northampton Theatres Trust: Royal & Derngate Theatre**
Guildhall Rd
Northampton NN1 1DP
Box Office: 01604 624811
www.royalandderngate.co.uk

**Northern Broadsides**
Dean Clough
Halifax HX3 5AX
Tel: 01422 369704
www.northern-broadsides.co.uk

**Norwich Playhouse**
42 - 58 St. George's Street
Norwich NR3 1AB
Box office: 01603 598 598
www.norwichplayhouse.co.uk

**Norwich: Theatre Royal**
Theatre St
Norwich NR2 1RL
Box Office: 01603 630000
www.theatre-royal-norwich.co.uk

**Nottingham Playhouse**
Wellington Circus
Nottingham NG1 5AF
Box Office: 0115 941 9419
www.nottinghamplayhouse.co.uk

**Nottingham: Theatre Royal**
Theatre Square
Nottingham NG1 5ND
Box Office: 0115 989 5555
www.royalcentre-nottingham.co.uk

**Oldham Coliseum**
Fairbottom St
Oldham OL1 3SW
Box Office: 0161 624 2829
www.coliseum.org.uk

**Out of Joint**
7 Thane Works
London N7 7PH
Tel: 020 7609 0207
www.outofjoint.co.uk

**Oxford Playhouse**
Beaumont St
Oxford OX1 2LW
Box Office: 01865 305305
www.oxfordplayhouse.com

**Perth Theatre**
185 High St
Perth PH1 5UW
Tel: 01738 621 031
www.horsecross.co.uk

**Pilot Theatre**
c/o York Theatre Royal
St Leonard's Place
York YO1 7HD
Tel: 01904 635755
info@pilot-theatre.com
www.pilot-theatre.com

**Plymouth: Theatre Royal**
Royal Parade
Plymouth PL1 2TR
Box Office: 01752 230440
www.theatreroyal.com

**Portsmouth: New Theatre Royal**
Guildhall Walk
Portsmouth
Hampshire PO1 2DD
Box Office: 02392 649000
www.newtheatreroyal.com

**Royal Opera House**
Covent Garden
London WC2E 9DD
Tel: 020 7304 4000 (Box Office & Info)
www.roh.org.uk

**Salford: The Lowry**
Pier 8, Salford Quays
Manchester M50 3AZ
Tel: 0843 208 6000
www.thelowry.com

**Salisbury Playhouse**
Malthouse Lane
Salisbury SP2 7RA
Tel: 01722 320117
Box Office: 01722 320333
www.salisburyplayhouse.com

**Scarborough: Stephen Joseph Theatre**
Westborough
Scarborough YO11 1JW
Tel: 01723 370540
Box Office: 01723 370541
www.sjt.uk.com

**Shakespeare at the Tobacco Factory**
Raleigh Rd
Southville
Bristol BS3 1TF
Tel: 0117 963 3054
www.sattf.org.uk

**Shared Experience Theatre**
The Soho Laundry
9 Dufour's Place
London W1F 7SJ
Tel: 020 7587 1596
www.sharedexperience.org.uk/

**Sheffield: Crucible Theatre**
55 Norfolk St
Sheffield S1 1DA
Tel: 0114 249 5999
Box Office: 0114 249 6000
www.sheffieldtheatres.co.uk

**Sheffield: Lyceum Theatre**
55 Norfolk St
Sheffield S1 1DA
Tel: 0114 249 9922
Box Office: 0114 249 6000
www.sheffieldtheatres.co.uk

**Southampton: Nuffield Theatre**
University Rd
Southampton SO17 1TR
Tel: 023 80 315 500
Box Office: 023 80 671 771
www.nuffieldtheatre.co.uk

**Southend on Sea: Palace Theatre**
Cliffs Pavillion
Station Rd
Southend on Sea
Essex SS0 7RA
Box Office: 01702 351135
Admin: 01702 390657
www.thecliffspavilion.co.uk/

**Stoke-on-Trent: Regent Theatre**
Piccadilly
Cultural Quarter
Stoke-On-Trent ST1 1AP
Box Office: 0870 060 6649
www.ambassadortickets.com/Stoke-On-Trent

**Stratford-upon-Avon: Royal Shakespeare Theatre**
Waterside
Stratford-upon-Avon
Warwickshire CV37 6BB
Tel: 01789 403444
Box Office: 0844 800 1110
www.rsc.org.uk

**Stratford-Upon-Avon: Swan Theatre**
Waterside
Stratford-Upon-Avon
Warwickshire CV37 6BB
Box Office:0844 800 1110
www.rsc.org.uk

**Stratford-Upon-Avon: The Other Place**
Southern Lane
Stratford-Upon-Avon
Tel: 0844 800 1110

**TARA ARTS**
356 Garratt Lane
London SW18 4ES
Tel: 020 8333 4457
www.tara-arts.com

**Théâtre de Complicité**
14 Anglers Lane
London NW5 3DG
Tel: 020 7485 7700
www.complicite.org

**Tie Tours**
TIE Tours Actionwork
PO Box 433
Weston Super Mare
BS24 0WY
Tel: 01934 815163
www.tietours.com

**Wakefield: Theatre Royal & Opera House**
Drury Lane
Wakefield WF1 2TE
Box Office: 01924 211311
www.wakefieldtheatres.co.uk/

**Watford: Palace Theatre**
Clarendon Rd
Watford WD17 1JZ
Tel: 01923 235455
Info Line: 01923 225671
www.watfordtheatre.co.uk

**Worcester: Swan Theatre**
The Moors
Worcester WR1 3ED
Tel: 01905 726969
Box Office: 01905 611427
www.huntingdonhall.com

**York Theatre Royal**
St Leonards Place
York YO1 7HD
Tel: 01904 658162
Box Office:  01904 623568
www.theatre-royal-york.co.uk